LINDLEY J. STILES
Dean of the School of Education
University of Wisconsin
Advisory Editor to Dodd, Mead & Company

The Role of the School in American Society

The Role of the School
in American Society

ΛΛΛ

V. T. THAYER

ΛΛΛ

DODD, MEAD & COMPANY · 1960

New York · Toronto

EDITOR'S INTRODUCTION

/\\./\\./\\.\\

The role a nation assigns to its schools forecasts its future. An explosive awareness of this fact has promoted widespread interest in and controversy about education in the United States in recent years. Criticisms of schools have intensified as citizens, along with teachers, probe for agreements relative to the functions educational programs must serve, and seek to appraise how well our schools are fulfilling their responsibilities.

To bring historical perspective, facts, and refined educational theory to bear upon the definition of the task of our schools is the central objective of this book. Drawing on a depth and breadth of scholarship rarely matched in educational literature, the author skillfully analyzes the essential characteristics of the unique heritage that has nurtured the world's greatest system of public education yet known and identifies the critical issues that now threaten to destroy it. To help the student of education to think deeply and reflectively about the role of the school in American society, rather than to provide a blueprint for mastery, is the intent. The clarity with which basic educational values and principles are appraised make of this book a compass to help keep schools on course toward the objectives of a democratic nation.

The Role of the School in American Society is a challenging antidote for anyone who may have been led to believe that the study of the purposes and functions of schools is professionally unnecessary for the teacher and intellectually unstimulating to the good student. Its contents are so significant that they should be a part of the knowledge of every American—and especially of every teacher—who calls himself educated. The ideas and issues presented are such that no serious mind, however brilliant, will find them trivial or unexciting. The objectivity and honesty of the treatment, much as they may challenge the views of some individuals and groups, are like a breath of fresh air to professional literature. The style of writing, personal and thoughtful yet lucid and forceful, leads the reader logically and interestingly through arguments of great complexity. In short, here is a quality text for the teacher and student of education that compares with the best in other fields of study.

Dr. V. T. Thayer has incorporated in this work a lifetime of dedicated scholarship and highly successful experience in various types of educational positions. He is recognized internationally as an educator and author of highest distinction. The reader will readily sense that this book is written by a man of sterling character and kindly disposition who is highly sensitive to and respectful of the differences in educational ideas and goals that motivate his fellow citizens. Yet those who study this book will be thrilled by the courageous manner in which the author does not hesitate to join boldly in the most heated debates of the times, clearly revealing his personal commitments for the reader to contemplate. It should be clear, too, that this book comes from a man who is himself a sparkling example of the kind of creative, thinking citizen that the American public schools have produced and must continue to develop in ample quantity if self-government and free institutions are to survive.

LINDLEY J. STILES

PREFACE

/\/\/\

Public education in the United States confronts a situation both unique and contradictory. On the one hand, the traditional importance of education in the mind of the average citizen has been enhanced by recent evidence that democracy and totalitarianism are engaged in world-wide competition for the loyalties of men and that education plays an indispensable role in this competitive struggle. Since the launching of Sputnik I by the Russians, it has become ever more clear that ways and means must be found to channel young people talented in science, mathematics, and engineering into these fields. To the discerning, it is no less obvious that an education designed to perpetuate and develop the institutions of a free society cannot safely be limited to the training of specialists and technicians. Consequently, the need for expanded programs in the social sciences, the humanities, and the arts looms large, programs which will bring to the fore minds informed and disciplined in methods of thinking and ways of living that will not only safeguard but develop and enrich an open society. In short, the times emphasize a one-to-one relationship between a high level of education, both general and technical, and the survival of free nations.

Nevertheless, a strange lethargy seems to pervade American communities. Bond issues designed to offset building shortages and inadequate teaching facilities are defeated with increasing frequency. Overcrowded classrooms persist and farsighted planning to accommodate the expanding school enrollments of tomorrow enlist but indifferent public attention. Teachers' salaries, although improved slightly over several years back, are still conspicuously below wage and salary schedules in occupations less demanding in preparation and training, a situation which makes it difficult to man the schools with a quality of personnel competent to meet contemporary challenges to American education.

One explanation for this unique situation is a want of confidence in public education caused, in no small measure, by attacks upon the schools which have been characteristic of the past ten to fifteen years. During this period, the electorate have been told repeatedly that their schools fail to measure up to normal requirements. The able and the gifted children are crippled rather than encouraged in the full realization of their powers, and the handicapped and mediocre are taught neither to read nor to write with any degree of proficiency nor to perform the simplest operations in mathematics. To these indictments are commonly added the serious charge that neglect of character education and instruction in moral and spiritual values explains a rising tide of juvenile delinquency.

Indictments of the organization of the curriculum are equally severe. Efforts to meet the needs of a diversified student body, it is asserted, have resulted in a general lowering of standards, thus fostering a flabbiness of mind at precisely the time when our competitors, the Russians, are cultivating to the full the talents and the abilities of their young.

Nor is this situation bettered by a confusion of tongues characteristic of educational discussions. One group of educators envisages the speedy disintegration of American society unless the schools return to a type of education characteristic of yesterday. Still others, impressed by the influence of work upon character, ascribe many of our difficulties to an excess of zeal for universal and compulsory education. This, they believe, has been carried too far. Accordingly, they suggest that steps be taken to separate the sheep from the goats. Raise the standards for the academically competent, they urge, and shorten the period of compulsory schooling for the incompetent. Others, again, believe that school and home and community face today genuinely novel conditions— that we are living in one of those dramatic periods of human history in which men engage in the creation of new institutions and the formulation of new ideas and ideals of living relationships. Under these circumstances, the failure of old institutions to function vitally or of people to devise adequately substitutes for long-confirmed ways of thinking, feeling, and acting exact a heavy toll. But this in no way implies ultimate disaster. It constitutes, rather, a challenge for home and school and community agency to adopt an experimental attitude and to travel hopefully with a faith grounded in the conviction, as L. P. Jacks once emphasized, that "It is precisely when his circumstances are easiest that he [man] gives the poorest account of himself, and the best when he is fighting against odds. Never is he more at home in this universe than when he finds himself 'upon an engagement very difficult.' "

Different as these suggestions are (and we might have added to the list others equally at odds with each other), one common note may be detected in them. Schooling is important and decisive if the school will but define its boundaries, recognize and concentrate upon its legitimate functions, and slough off the irrelevant!

This shared faith in the importance of schooling would seem to justify an attempt to survey the task of public education in the light of changes that have taken place in American culture from the colonial period to the present and to consider the impact of these changes upon the school, changes in the economic and social status of young people, in the psychology of learning, and in the bearing of these many factors upon the theory and practice of education today.

The Role of the School in American Society consists of four parts. Part I draws attention to certain basic assumptions or formative ideas in American life and education of the past which still serve to guide all concerned with education on local, state, and national levels. Part II is devoted to an analysis of fundamental transformations in the status of children and adolescents in American society, together with their implications for the curriculum of the school. The concern here is to identify factors of significant change in the economic and social status of young people which should give character to subject matter and method, to the guidance functions of the school, and to relations between school and home and community. Part III attempts to provide further background, historical and psychological, with which to understand the development of the curriculum, methods of teaching, and the administrative structure of the school. Stages of development in

American culture are described, together with the influence of each stage upon conceptions of the nature of the individual and how he best learns, as well as the influence which these varying conceptions have exercised upon educational ideals and practices. Finally, in Part IV, consideration is given to a number of critical issues in public education of today. The effort in this section has been to describe briefly the origin and background of a critical issue, the circumstances and conditions that make it a crucial problem in education today, and to review suggested solutions. As in other sections of the book, the author attempts to do justice to all relevant points of view without necessarily disguising his own conclusions. To know where a writer stands, he believes, is the privilege of the mature reader.

The author gratefully acknowledges indebtedness to the many publishers who have granted permission to quote from publications cited in the text.

V. T. THAYER

CONTENTS

∿∿∿

PART IV / Critical Issues in Contemporary Education

The Role of the School in American Society

PART I

Formative Ideas in American

Education

/\.\/\.\/\.\/\.\

/\.\/.\/.\/.\

1

Faith in Education

A Common Faith

Following World War II Switzerland commissioned one of its distinguished educators, Hans Casparis, to visit the United States with instructions to study the significant characteristics of American education and to report his findings to his government. It was realized that prior to the advent of National Socialism, education in Switzerland had been influenced intimately by education in Germany, but now a new alignment of cultural forces was in process, and Switzerland, as many another country, was "looking toward a new, strong, creative relationship with the great western democracies, England and the United States."

Before returning to his country, Hans Casparis shared some of his observations with American readers in an article written for *School and Society* under the title, "A Swiss Educator Looks At American Education." One conclusion is of unique significance. Speaking of the apparent conflict in educational philosophy which divides the leaders of American education, Casparis remarks,

It is possible that for an American the controversies, for instance, between the philosophy of John Dewey and some Neo-Thomistic ideas of Robert M. Hutchins, are more obvious than the common ideas. For a European the special features and attitudes visible in *all* the theories of American education are much more striking. I have tried to extract these common and, I think, typical American features. In the first place, I found that the attitude here "from left to right" is decidedly *optimistic*—an extremely valuable basis for any education! There seems to exist a sort of silent agreement *that it is really possible* to build up a free and better society, and that education is one of the most effective means to achieve that end. Every educator seems to have a strong and unshaken faith that it is really and truly possible to educate "All American Youth" for freedom or for free citizenship in a free society, if it is done in the right spirit and the right way! In other words, there seems to exist the common belief that the goal can be reached, that man can be educated as a free and self-responsible individual in a free society, if one condition is fulfilled: that those responsible for this education have the right philosophy and know the right way or the right method. So it seems now to be the chief task for American education to find that right philosophy and to work out the right methods.

For most people in Europe . . . such a belief has long ago been smashed by the hard experiences they had to undergo, and the opposite idea gained ground, that man is by nature bad and corrupted, and that only force can keep him in order, or as the church preaches: he is a lost sinner altogether and only the grace of God through His Word can save him.[1]

One explanation for these contrasting attitudes doubtless follows from the mutually sustaining relationship that has obtained between popular psychology and material conditions in America. During the period of the origin and development of public education, life in the United States seemed to confirm the theory that all men are born essentially equal in their potentialities or, as that vigorous advocate of public schools, Horace Mann, was wont to insist, "there is by nature little or perhaps no distinction among men with respect to their original power of intellect. The seeds of knowledge, of refinement, and of literary excellence are implanted with a liberality, nearly or completely equal, in the mind of the ignorant peasant, and in the mind of the most profound philosopher."[2]

The School As an Open Frontier

Life on the ever expanding frontier, with its democratic faith in the potentialities of each individual, seemingly reinforced this

---

[1] See Hans Casparis, "A Swiss Educator Looks At American Schools," *School and Society*, May 17, 1947, pp. 362–364.

[2] Quoted in Merle Curti, *The Social Ideals of American Educators* (New York: Charles Scribner's Sons, 1935), p. 104.

assumption of original equality among men. The frontier invited
the oppressed and the underprivileged of the earth to seek anew
their fortunes in America. So alluring, indeed, was this invitation
that in the colonial period many an ambitious soul became a
bonded servant, subject to purchase and sale, in order to pay for
his passage from Europe to America. Others cheerfully welcomed
the hardships involved in clearing the forests and breaking virgin
soil in order to insure for themselves and their children a fresh
start in life. For a period, these opportunities derived principally
and directly from the open country, but, in the course of time,
the opportunities of an industrial economy proved equally attractive. With the exploitation of these later opportunities, however, both a general and technical education assumed ever more
importance.

The agricultural and industrial attractions of the frontier have
thus led Americans to ascribe to education, and, in particular, to
a system of tax-supported education on all levels—elementary,
secondary and higher—a status unique in history.

This is not to say that what constitutes an adequate education
has been at all times or in all places the same. What constitutes
functional literacy, for example, or what is essential for the average
individual to be competent in practical affairs has become ever
more demanding with developments in the American economy.
Once it involved little more than the ability to write one's name
or to read the simplest sentences. Later the mastery of the three
R's to a degree somewhat less than that now provided in the curriculum of the elementary school became a minimum requirement,
with the result that throughout the nineteenth century the term
"common school" was used to designate the elementary school. In
the early 1900's, however, the junior high school came into existence with a view to providing a "terminal education" for a rapidly
expanding school population. But after a relatively short period,
the need for further schooling was felt. Soon the upper years of the
secondary school were confronted with a similar obligation and,
today, it is widely recognized that graduation from the secondary
school constitutes an inadequate preparation for successful and
responsible participation in contemporary life. Indeed, with the
emergence of the junior college, terminal education has invaded
the college years.

Paralleling, or should we say, supporting these increasing demands for formal schooling has been a sustaining confidence in the magical powers of an education. Often this has been of a materialistic and narrowly practical character. "Do you want to join the ranks of the well-to-do?" a poor boy will be asked. "Then go to school!" The school was conceived of as a great democratic opportunity, an agency designed to enable those who wanted to better their lot in life to do so. Poor and rich alike might attend it and thus acquire the information and training indispensable for individual advancement.

Some see in this faith in education little more than an expression of the materialism which dominates American life. That there has been and still is a materialistic core to it is no doubt true. Horace Mann, for example, despite his idealism, was shrewd enough to know that his fellow citizens required hard-headed arguments if they were to agree to tax themselves on behalf of public schools. Consequently, he sought to demonstrate that ". . . education has a market value; that it is so far an article of merchandise, that it may be turned to pecuniary account; it may be minted, and will yield a larger amount of statuable coin than common bullion. . . . The aim of industry is served, and the wealth of the country is augmented, in proportion to the diffusion of knowledge." [3]

Witness, too, the publications of the Office of Education throughout the years designed to persuade youth to resist the attractive inducements of wages and salaries out of school. Recent evidence of the financial rewards that come with schooling appears in a document prepared for the Office of Education by Ernest V. Hollis and associates, entitled *Costs of Attending College*. Utilizing the results of a study by Paul C. Glick and Herman P. Miller of the Bureau of the Census, which estimates that the average male receives $133,000 during his economically productive years, it is shown that the income of the functionally illiterate is less than one-half this amount, in contrast with twice that amount earned by the man who has completed four years or more of college and university study. It is also estimated that the college graduate receives at least $100,000 more in the course of his working years than a man who has merely graduated from high school. [4]

---

[3] *Ibid.*, pp. 112–114.

[4] Bulletin 1957, no. 9. See also Paul C. Glick and Herman P. Miller, "Educational

We agree that these expressions of faith in education are materialistic. It is easy, however, to oversimplify one's judgments. Frequently, the work of an educated man provides a way of life comprising the enjoyments and refinements of living commonly denied to those who are condemned to "work with their hands." Moreover, this way of life might well include values nonmaterialistic as well as materialistic. It is not uncommon for the "cultured," or the fortunate possessor of conditions which make for ease and comfort, to condemn as evidence of "the materialistic spirit of the times" the strivings of a submerged group for similar refinements of living!

At all events, it is well to recognize that the schooling which an individual prizes initially for the purpose of bettering his status economically may have the added advantage of opening his eyes to values to which he was previously blind. We can thus draw the moral that one way to transform the material aspirations of an individual or a people into values of a higher order is to provide more education. In the case of the individual as well as a group, economic well-being constitutes a soil more favorable than poverty and undernourishment for the cultivation of the values of a liberal education.

Free Schools and the Conservation of Values

Thus far we have emphasized the individualistic expression of the American's faith in education. This is but half the story. Equally significant has been a vision of the social mission of the school.

The social conception of the functions of education in America dates from the origin of the first schools. In New England and the Middle Colonies, as we shall observe in more detail later, a primary purpose in establishing schools was to insure the perpetuation of the religious faith of the community without contamination. To be sure, what constituted religious truth varied as one moved from one colony to another. In New England, for example, to which the Puritan had journeyed, impelled by the conviction that "The God of Heaven had carried a nation into the wilderness upon the designs of a glorious transformation," [5] schools were an indispensable means for insuring undeviating allegiance to what Cotton Mather also described as "the pure and full dispensations of the Gospel."

Similar motives prompted the good people of the Middle Colonies to establish schools, but heterogeneity of religious faith rather than homogeneity prevailed. Each community in this checkered pattern was convinced of the validity of its own faith, and schools were recognized as essential in order to perpetuate truth in competition with error. Thus schooling, both in subject matter and method, served the commonly accepted purpose of education for conformity. So axiomatic was this conception of education, even with respect to higher education, that the authors of Statutes of the College of William and Mary were constrained to enjoin instructors to "take special care that if the author is never so well approved on other accounts, he [the Master] teach no such part of him to his scholars as insinuates against religion and morals." [6]

With the advent of manhood suffrage and the increasing participation of the common man in government, the attempt to use education as a means of forming the mind of the young assumed political importance. Members of the upper classes now envisaged the possibility of government by "the mob." As Catherine Beecher put it, the common people had become masters, and, consequently, ". . . the education of the common people . . . is the point around which the wisest heads, the warmest hearts, the most powerful energies should gather for conservation, for planning, for unity of action, and for persevering enterprise." [7]

As Richard D. Mosier amply illustrates in his careful study of the influence of the McGuffey readers, the compilers of these books turned to the Beechers along with many others for material with which to influence the minds of the young and thus "safeguard[ed] established institutions from the inroads of Jacksonian hordes" by

---

[5] Quoted in Herbert Schneider, *The Puritan Mind* (New York: Henry Holt & Co., Inc., 1930), p. 27.

[6] See Elmer Ellsworth Brown, *The Making of Our Middle Schools* (New York: Longmans, Green & Co., Inc., 1914), chap. VII, for an excellent account of education in colonial schools. See also Adolphe Meyer, *An Educational History of the American People* (New York: McGraw-Hill Book Co., 1957), Chap. 6.

[7] Quoted in Richard D. Mosier, *Making the American Mind* (New York: Kings Crown Press, 1947), p. 17.

instilling the proper political as well as social and moral concepts.[8]

There is a temptation to see, as some critics have done, in this deliberate and earnest effort to form the minds of the young the attempt of groups, once dominant, selfishly to perpetuate their ideals and ways of living in a shifting and changing situation. Although partially true, this explanation fails to do justice to the disinterested and generous aspirations of many a pioneer in early American education. Some of these men were ardently committed to change and saw in public education an instrument with which to insure for all the blessings commonly enjoyed only by the few. Certainly we should hesitate to describe the motivations of Horace Mann and Henry Barnard exclusively in terms of a class consciousness, even though their concepts of the good life may have been identical with the virtues and values of one class of society rather than another.[9] It is more accurate to credit them with an insight, rare in their day, into the relationship between free schools and a free society.

At the same time, profiting from the record, we can identify an excess of optimism in some of the arguments put forth in support of a system of tax-supported schools. Thus, we find Horace Mann looking to popular education as an automatic cure for the dangers that follow from an excess of wealth in one class and poverty in another. "Education," he asserts in his famous report of 1848 to the Massachusetts State Board of Education, "is the great equalizer of men, the balance wheel of the social machinery."

More sophisticated, perhaps, are the somewhat similar sentiments of James Bryant Conant, as expressed in 1952 in an address to school administrators: "If we so desire it, [secondary education] can be used to restore fluidity to our social and economic life each generation, and in so doing make available for the national welfare resources of potential talent now untapped." [10]

Not all individuals, however, are equally moved by broad, general, social objectives. They require more direct and immediate evidence of ways in which new proposals will better their lot. The advocates of free schools early in the last century were keenly aware of this fact. Accordingly, we find not only educators, such as

---

[8] *Ibid.*, chaps. I, IV.
[9] For an excellent presentation of these views, see Curti, *op. cit.*, chaps. III, IV.
[10] Reprinted in *Saturday Review*, May 3, 1952, pp. 11–24.

Horace Mann and Henry Barnard in the North, Caleb Cushing
in the South, and Calvin Stowe in the West, but liberal-minded
laymen, labor leaders and statesmen emphasizing the practical
importance of a free education in a free society. To stubborn ob-
jectors, similar to that irate Rhode Island farmer who threatened
to do bodily harm to Henry Barnard for "preaching such a horrible
heresy as the partial confiscation of one man's property to educate
another man's children," [11] the advocates of a tax-supported school
put this question: "Which do you prefer? To tax yourselves for
jails or for schools?"

Thaddeus Stevens employed this argument most effectively in
the Pennsylvania Legislature in 1834 when engaged in one of the
most dramatic and influential battles over the issue of free education. In an address later printed and distributed widely throughout the country, Stevens answered virtually all the common objections to a publicly supported education and demonstrated as
well the benefits that would flow from it.

To the argument that it is unjust, if not immoral, to tax people
to provide educational facilities from which they can observe no
direct or indirect return, Stevens replied that it is nevertheless
for their own benefit since it sustains government and the laws
which protect their lives and property. Furthermore, inquired
Stevens, why not urge the same objections to other taxes? "The
industrious, thrifty, rich farmer" pays taxes to support courts,
jails, sheriffs, and other officials whom he will probably never use,
"but loudly complains of that which goes to prevent his fellow-
being from becoming a criminal and to obviate the necessity of
these humiliating institutions." [12]

The virtues of an education for citizenship, as Thaddeus Stevens
and his associates envisaged it, were essentially political in character. It is understandable, therefore, why a predominantly rural
population accustomed to relatively simple institutions and face-
to-face relations with their public servants should remain skeptical
of the indispensable character of formal education. For many decades, in fact, the friends of tax-supported schools were confronted

[11] Edgar W. Knight, *Education in the United States* (Boston: Ginn & Company,
1934), p. 250.
[12] Thomas Frederick Woodley, *Thaddeus Stevens* (Harrisburg, Pa.: Telegraph
Press, 1934), pp. 153–167.

with arguments similar to those of a rural correspondent for a Raleigh newspaper who inquired whether it might not be of as much advantage to young people as well as to the state "if they should pass their days in the cotton patch, or at the plow, or in the cornfield, instead of being mewed up in a schoolhouse where they are earning nothing." [13]

In the rapidly growing cities of the country the importance of schooling was more obvious. Here the children of immigrants from abroad, together with the children of families accustomed only to rural living, were growing up under slum conditions. These conditions profoundly disturbed many who were accustomed to thinking of America as a land of open opportunities and who were also resolved to keep it so. To these individuals—representatives of labor, humanitarians, statesmen, educators—we are indebted for the concept of the school as an agency designed to serve the children of all classes in much the same way as the open country with its free land had long served adults by providing an opportunity to better their status in life. Out of these efforts came eventually the decision of all states in the Union to provide schooling free to all able and willing to profit therefrom.

Nor did schools fail in this objective. They were so conspicuously successful that with steady progress in industrialization and the gradual transformation of a predominantly rural and agricultural economy into an urban and industrial economy, a schooling that was once optional for the young became compulsory. Massachusetts was the first state to set this example with the passage of a compulsory school attendance law in 1852. Other states followed with varying degrees of rapidity. Not until 1918 was the circle complete when Mississippi, as the last of the southern states, finally adopted its compulsory school attendance law. [14]

Many of the conditions which seemed to dictate free education

---

[13] Knight, *op. cit.,* p. 244.

[14] It is one thing to pass a law and altogether another to provide adequately for its enforcement. In a number of instances states made no provision for the enforcement of these acts. Even today considerable variation exists as to the years covered by compulsory acts and the means of enforcement. In Virginia, for example, the first act was passed in 1908. However, as late as 1944 local authorities were permitted to ignore the law if "buildings were inadequate." Opposition to the decisions of the United States Supreme Court on segregation in education has further weakened efforts at enforcement. Thus, by act of the Virginia Legislature in April, 1959, the compulsory school attendance act of that state becomes effective only when reinforced by local legislation.

and, later, compulsory school attendance likewise suggested an ever enlarging area of responsibility for the school. For both the children of the foreign-born and the children of underprivileged rural families, the school has functioned as a "melting pot" in the sense that it has striven to instill in the young the ideas and the ideals, the specific habits, and the dispositions of ways of life unlike their original backgrounds. Indeed, not infrequently, the process of assimilation has been carried so far that the school has been charged with creating unfortunate gaps between the generations, with the further result that the potential contributions of peoples from widely different cultures have been lost to American life.

Be this as it may, economic, social, and political life since the day of Thaddeus Stevens has complicated and extended the services of the school far beyond what Stevens and his fellow pioneers envisaged. Although the information that Stevens considered basic for the citizen is still relevant, it is too exclusively political to satisfy the needs of present-day citizenship. Accordingly, within the area of citizenship education "knowledge about" the political structure and activities of government is no longer sufficient. To this has been added "community civics" and a more immediate and functional introduction to the institutions and agencies— local, state, national, and even international—that are today meeting the many-sided and diverse needs of a people, a people which, for better or worse, seem destined to live in a sensitively organized and closely interknit world.

So, too, in areas other than citizenship education, the responsibilities of the school with respect to subject matter and methods of instruction have undergone change in response to transformations in American life.

Thus has the American's faith in education both persisted and expanded throughout the years. Out of the past, however, and the uses to which this faith has been put, have come problems. Principles and procedures which in a simple and relatively homogeneous community seemed self-evident become less so, even questionable, in a complex and heterogeneous society. Take, by way of illustration, the concept of teaching as synonymous with the instilling of approved ideas in the minds of the young. This was accepted as the legitimate function of the school during the colonial period as well as later, when, with the advent of heavy immigration, the school was conceived as a "melting pot," in which the children of the foreign-born were transformed into good Americans.

This concept of education, however, is difficult to apply once communities become genuinely heterogeneous in politics, in religion, and in social and cultural background.

Out of the practical necessity of maintaining peace and furthering understanding within diversity in American life, there has emerged the concept of freedom of thought and expression and the discipline of free inquiry as an essential value in American society. This second tradition is the younger, although older by far than the public school, and is grounded in principles sanctified by the federal Constitution.

Thus it is that two traditions in education are in conflict, each contending for a central position in the school: one a tradition of conformity and orthodoxy, the other a tradition of free inquiry, each with its appropriate discipline of thought. One of the problems in present-day education is to determine the relations that should obtain between these two traditions and the educational procedures that derive from each.

Consistent with the first tradition is the tendency of earnest individuals and groups to use the schools as an instrument with which to implant in the minds of the young the information and the convictions which they believe all-important.

The second tradition, on the other hand, has the problem of rendering more explicit than it has done thus far the relation of the discipline of free inquiry to the entire program of the school and to areas of knowledge not visibly subject to change as well as to areas still uncertain and controversial.

The adherents of both traditions, however, are as one in their faith in education. To this faith, in large measure, may we ascribe the phenomenal growth and development of the public school system of the United States.

Suggested Reading

Casparis, Hans, "A Swiss Educator Looks At American Education," *School and Society*, May, 1947, pp. 362–364.

Commager, Henry Steele, *The American Mind* (New Haven: Yale University Press, 1952), chap. I.

Cremin, Lawrence A., *The American Common School* (New York: Bureau of Publications, Teachers College, Columbia University, 1951), part II.

Curti, Merle, *The Social Ideals of American Educators* (New York: Charles Scribner's Sons, 1935), chaps. II–IV.

Thayer, V. T., *The Attack Upon the American Secular School* (Boston: Beacon Press, Inc., 1952), chap. I.

/\\/\\/\\/\\

CHAPTER

2

Acceptance of Change

Change Optimistically Viewed

"No other people," writes Henry Steele Commager, "ever demanded so much of education as have the American people. None other was served so well by its schools and education." [1]

The American school, Commager continues, has discharged three important tasks. It has provided "an enlightened citizenry in order that self-government might work," it has created "unity out of diversity, nationalism out of particularism," and it has Americanized millions of newcomers. "Economic and social distinctions and privileges, severe enough to corrode democracy itself, had to be fought. To our schools went the momentous responsibility of inspiring a people to pledge and hold allegiance to the principles of democracy, nationalism, Americanism, egalitarianism."

These achievements are the more remarkable when we consider that they run counter to the original intentions of the fathers of American education. Had John Cotton and his New England associates foreseen that the schools they were so eager to establish would evolve into the instruments of "democracy" and "egalitarianism," they would indeed have concluded that the ultimate victory was Satan's. Schools, as they envisaged them, were to confirm known truths in the minds of the young and to perpetuate the status quo.

---

[1] "Our Schools Have Kept Us Free," *N.E.A. Journal,* January, 1951, pp. 18–19.

Two hundred years later a new and different spirit had come to permeate the land. In the process of pushing back the frontier and developing what seemed to be the inexhaustible resources of a new continent, a concept of man and his possibilities as extravagantly optimistic as John Cotton's was pessimistic had come to pervade the consciousness of people. As a French observer, André Maurois, once remarked, the American is an optimist "because he lives in a country that has never betrayed him and he knows that a strong daring man may always succeed a little farther on."

Two basic assumptions in American education thus have reinforced each other: the faith in education with which we have dealt in Chapter 1 and the faith in what tomorrow holds forth. These two assumptions are related to each other as cause and effect.

An interesting affirmation of the American's faith in the future is found in James Bryant Conant's *Education in a Divided World*.[2] Conant is writing with specific reference to the consequences for American life of a long, drawn-out period of competition with Russia. He envisages the possibility that this may continue for fifty years or more with serious strains upon the very institutions and freedoms which Americans are seeking to defend, since wars, be they hot or cold, are conducted in an atmosphere unfavorable to the ways of democracy.

Of the conditions essential for survival in this struggle with Russia, Conant considers two as peculiarly relevant to education: equality of opportunity and social mobility.

The educational implications of these two objectives are far reaching. They explain, for example, the concern of Conant, when President of Harvard University, to attract by means of scholarships young people of ability from all sections of the country. It is now suggested that federal and state governments make available to a much larger group what Harvard and other colleges and universities provide on a limited scale. Thus our schools may realize what Jefferson hoped for in his day: that the school would enable the state to avail itself "of those talents which nature has sown as liberally among the poor as the rich, but which perish without use, if not sought for and cultivated."

The attempt to maintain an open road for talent likewise ex-

---

[2] Cambridge: Harvard University Press, 1949.

plains the concern of many that public funds in support of education be distributed within each state in a manner designed to
offset inequalities among communities; and it bears directly as
well upon the problem of federal aid to education within the
states.

Nor is the curriculum provided by the school unrelated to
Conant's thesis. For example, the diversified curriculum characteristic of our best schools and colleges has resulted, in large
measure, from a growing recognition of differences in ability and
talent within student bodies, differences that require recognition
and cultivation if our educational institutions are to take seriously
the fact that the abilities which characterize the gifted student are
plural, not singular. That is to say, just as leadership in the complex society of today is of many kinds and involves the use of different talents and abilities—some verbal, some manual, some
executive and practical, some intellectual, some theoretical and
abstract—so the gifted in school, the future leaders of American
society, are of many types of mind and thrive on different educational diets.

But Some Fear Change

All of this assumes, of course, that the dominant attitude of the
American is friendly toward change. Is it not equally true, however, that many fear change? Is this fear not reflected in their
attitudes toward the schools, attitudes which likewise bear directly upon the curriculum and methods of instruction? Indeed,
is not this fear of change one explanation for contemporary "attacks" upon the public schools?

This is correct. Two contradictory attitudes toward change are
today operating within American life, each of direct moment to
education: the one friendly, the other fearful.

Acceptance of change, as we have thus far considered it, applies quite largely to the traditional status of the individual and
to transformations that are nevertheless within the established
structure of American society. Change so conceived has served individuals well, on the whole, and is therefore welcome. Nor is it
threatened too conspicuously by Conant's two principles, so long
as they bear upon individuals alone. Many a southerner, for ex-

ample, will gladly assist an individual Negro of talent, a potential George Washington Carver, or a Marian Anderson, to develop his or her abilities and to rise in the social scale but will oppose vigorously "the mixing of the races" in the schools or other measures designed to promote "equality of opportunity" and thus transform the "southern way of life."

Fear of change is not confined to the South or to new patterns of relationships between races and classes which seem to be emerging. It has permeated all sections of the country and all elements of the population sufficiently to cause some authorities to consider "loss of nerve" and a sense of insecurity characteristic of contemporary America. Others, less pessimistic, seek to explain it as a temporary phenomenon, serious to be sure, resulting from World War II from which we are slow to recover.

Few wars, indeed, have been more destructive of physical property or of long-established relations among people. Consider, for example, the effects—economic, social, and psychological—of the uprooting of whole populations and the world-wide dispersal of homeless individuals, many of whom have been handicapped in their new adjustments by the very skills and habits which promised them security and comfort in their original environments. Or the failure of the nations to re-establish normal relations, economic, political, or cultural, because of the fact that with the cessation of hostilities there has been no peace, merely the substitution of a cold war for a hot war.

The conclusion of World War II also found American schools in serious difficulty with respect both to their physical plants and their educational services. The curtailment of building programs during the war necessitated a concentration upon physical needs, once hostilities ceased, often to the sacrifice of other needs. This backlog of needs was accentuated by rapid increases in enrollment, resulting from a rapid rise in the birth rate, which even today gives little evidence of leveling off. Teachers who had left the schools in large numbers during the war failed to return, in part, because of unattractive salaries in education as compared with salaries in business and industry and, in part, because the profession of teaching lacked for them its former appeal.[3]

---

[3] Nor are the prospects for bettering this situation encouraging. Writing in the *Atlantic Monthly* for September, 1956, Oscar Handlin, Professor of History at

To this difficulty, which time does all too little to remedy, has been added the fear of the novel that came from the attempts of Communists to bore within the institutions of democracy. The layman, frightened by the disclosures of investigating committees of Congress as well as by publications such as those of Allan Zoll's National Council for American Education and *The Educational Reviewer,* a publication which presumed to pass upon textbooks used in schools, was only too ready to identify the school's efforts to foster the "inquiring mind" with a subversive spirit, and teachers who failed to inculcate in their students an uncritical acceptance of the status quo were identified with the enemies of democracy. In numerous instances the serious and patriotic efforts of school staffs to reorganize the school curriculum so that children might study their communities at first hand, the diseased spots as well as the healthy, or examine realistically the growing pains of the world in which they live have led to the charge that the schools are fostering a dangerous "collectivism."

Some indication of the effects upon instruction of this fear of change became evident in the early 1950's from surveys conducted for *The New York Times* by Benjamin Fine. According to Fine, pressures toward conformity had transformed the spirit of the college campus, hampering free and objective inquiry within the classroom and narrowing the choice for research and investigation by students who were writing theses and dissertations.[4]

Similar influences were operating on the elementary and secondary school levels, according to the 1951 report of the Committee on Tenure and Academic Freedom of the National Education Association.

Outside the schools there is an obvious relaxation of tension in the public mind which suggests that the hysteria of the early 1950's was indeed temporary, and a resurgence of freedom of thought is now evident. Within the schools, however, there is still less disposition to develop through practice the habits of mind,

---

Harvard University, estimated that to prepare the number of new teachers needed for school and college in the next few years would require the enlistment of about half the total recipients of bachelor degrees.

[4] Reports by Benjamin Fine which are helpful in this connection are found in *The New York Times* for February 25, 1951, May 23, 1952, and June 29, 1952. See also the chapter entitled "Charges of Freedom Curbs Rising" in Ernest Melby and Morton Pruner, *Freedom and Public Education* (New York: Frederick A. Praeger, Inc., 1953), pp. 98–103.

which, in Tennyson's words, are prone to follow "knowledge as a sinking star beyond the utmost bounds of human thought." Nor has there been any conspicuous evidence as yet of the repeal of the restrictive acts of boards of education and state legislatures bearing upon the selection of textbooks and other instructional materials, acts which, so long as they remain unrescinded or unmodified, will continue to hamper the legitimate functions of the teacher. Nor is the continued shortage of competent teachers likely to encourage the average superintendent, principal, or supervisor to strike out boldly from conventional shores.

Despite these evidences of "loss of nerve," it would be unwise to conclude that Americans, as a whole, have lost confidence in the future or abandoned the hope that their schools will equip the young "to grasp the winds of change in their fists." By and large, also, they remain friendly to equality of opportunity and social mobility to what Conant terms "low visibility of class lines."

Effects of Transition from a Stable to a Changing Society

This is not to say that acceptance of change in its educational applications constitutes an unmixed blessing. Social mobility, or the opportunity for individuals to move freely up and down the ladder of social recognition, can create pains of adjustment. Children, under these conditions, often find it difficult to maintain free and easy relations with their parents and friends who fail to keep pace with them; whereas those who are left behind tend frequently to nurse feelings of hurt and inferiority. Moreover, when change involves, as it does, the discovery of new knowledge and the attendant necessity of a revision of accepted facts, even a revision of the codes of yesterday, a transformation in age-long attitudes in education becomes imperative. The traditional confidence in the past as the custodian of the truth gives way to dependence upon and sometimes, even, an uncritical faith in the future.

Let us consider some of the consequences for education that follow upon an education keyed to a changing society in contrast with one that is static or relatively stable.

In the latter, what is important to transmit from generation to generation is easily determined by analogy. Children and youth are raised without question in the image of the past, and parents and teachers may draw with confidence and assurance upon their own experiences or the recipes of earlier generations in selecting the materials and procedures to follow in home and school.

Not so when change calls the tune. Flexibility now becomes the price of a tolerable state of mind together with a willingness to accept "facts" as valid for one day only, or to be used with caution tomorrow. Emphasis shifts from content to process, and the accepted conditions of survival shift from dependence upon the tried and true to an experimental attitude and a willingness to operate on tentative conclusions.

The consequences of this situation can be both amusing and tragic.

Early in the century, for example, conscientious parents began to realize that science and technology were effecting revolutionary transformations in traditional relationships between members of the family. Conventional methods of raising children no longer yielded satisfactory results. Accordingly, progressively minded parents turned to science and "controlled" experiments in child care for guidance, and "child study" assumed prominence. Since science and the scientific attitude were revolutionizing business and industry through a meticulous control over the minutiae of physical operations, and "scientific management" seemed to bring equally effective results when applied to the human factor, it was assumed that only good would flow from the application of similar procedures to home and family life. Accordingly, home economics began to concentrate upon the scientific control of operations within the home, not merely in cooking and sewing and budget making but also in child care. Mothers were urged to curb their normal instincts and to bend their practices into conformity with the conclusions derived from the scientific handling of children.

A pioneer in this field was John Watson. Armed with the results of careful experiments on infants "in the Maternity Ward of Johns Hopkins Hospital, the Harriet Lane Home for Crippled Children, at the Heckscher Foundation, and in many private homes," Watson published a volume entitled *Psychological Care of Infant and Child.*[5] It was his hope that this book would exercise an influence upon the psychological care of children similar to the influence exerted by one of the best sellers of the time, Holt's *The Care and Feeding of Children,* upon the physical care of children.

Watson was impressed with the unfortunate effects of excessive, even selfish, expressions of mother love and the positive benefits that seemed to emerge from a consistent application of a calm, objective, and unemotional cultivation of desirable habits. Take by way of illustration, a mother's response to her child's crying. A quick and warm response may be comforting to her, but what of its potential consequences for the child? "Mothers," he warns, "just don't know, when they kiss their children and pick them up and rock them, caress them and jiggle them upon their knee, that they are slowly building up a human being totally unable to cope with the world it must later live in." [6]

So impressed was Watson with the difficulty of controlling parent behavior that he exclaimed, "I sometimes wish that we could live in a community of homes where each home is supplied with a well-trained nurse so that we could have babies fed and bathed each week by a different nurse." [7]

This was 1928. What of today?

To the generation of parents raised under the influence of these doctrines the specialist is now preaching the opposite doctrine: the importance of fostering in children a sense of inner security and a conviction that they are loved and accepted.

Consider, for example, the advice of one of the leading pediatricians of today, one who has added to his medical training and years of practical experience the special insights of a psychiatrist. Speaking to the mother about her attitude toward her baby, he states:

Don't be afraid of him. You'd think from what some people say about babies demanding attention that they come into the world determined to get their parents under their thumb by hook or crook.

---

[5] New York: W. W. Norton & Company, Inc., 1928.
[6] *Ibid.,* p. 44.
[7] *Ibid.,* p. 83.

This isn't true. Your baby is born to be a reasonable, friendly human being.

Don't be afraid to feed him when you think he's really hungry. If you are mistaken, he'll merely refuse to take much.

Don't be afraid to love him and enjoy him. Every baby needs to be smiled at, talked to, played with, fondled—gently and lovingly—just as much as he needs vitamins and calories. That's what will make him a person who loves people and enjoys life. The baby who doesn't get any loving will grow up cold and unresponsive.[8]

Research since Watson's experiments likewise tends to demonstrate the ill effects upon a child of the objective and impersonal treatment which seemed to him ideal. Lawson G. Lowrey concludes, for instance, from his study of the effects of institutional care in infancy that infants so dealt with undergo an isolation type of experience which seriously retards social and emotional development and renders it difficult for them later to enter into free and cooperative relations with their fellows.[9]

When experts reverse each other so drastically in the short space of a few years, is it surprising that the devoted mother, who leans heavily upon them for advice, feels helpless without the most recent authority at her elbow or his latest report on her library table? Only thus can she be assured that her handling of the child is nourishing the inner core of his being rather than confirming some abnormal fixation which may bob up like a jack-in-the-box to wreck his career at a critical moment in later life.

Such is the price parents must pay when finality moves from yesterday into tomorrow!

Educational Theory, Too, Can Be Fickle!

Contradiction and confusion, in a changing society, are in no way confined to education in the home. School practices in the past forty or fifty years have been subject to similar shifts in the winds of doctrine. "Scientific" psychology profoundly influenced classroom teaching and school organization during the first third of

---

[8] Benjamin Spock, *Baby and Child Care* (New York: Pocket Books, Inc., 1959), pp. 42–43.

[9] "Personality Distortion and Early Institutional Care," *American Journal of Orthopsychiatry*, vol. 10, pp. 576–585.

the century. Job analysis and scientific management, as applied
to industry, served as models for schools to follow in determining
the curriculum and methods of teaching. All learning is habit
formation, it was concluded, a mere matter of cementing connections between situations and responses (S → R bonds). This
became a psychological dogma which earnest teachers sought to
translate into the particulars of subject matter and the details of
method in the instruction of their pupils.

With disillusionment in the twenties and the depression in the
thirties, a more broadly sympathetic understanding of childhood
and youth found its way into the schools. Clinical studies and
research into personality development, influenced in large measure by the Europeans, Freud, Jung, and Adler, and their American disciples, began to transform traditional conceptions of discipline and methods of teaching as well as the purposes and the
functions of subject matter. "Child-centered" schools sprang up
in great numbers to shock conventional educators out of their
complacency, and, often, unfortunately, to encourage a skewed
emphasis upon the individuality of the child so extreme that it
left many incapable of living sympathetically and responsibly
with their fellows.

These limitations were quickly sensed, however, since they
were basically out of key with a closely knit and sensitively interrelated society and an emphasis upon the essentially social nature
of learning which followed upon a growing consciousness of interdependence. Respect for the integrity and the uniqueness of
child nature remained, but attention came to center more upon
"developmental tasks" (social as well as individual and personal)
than upon interests in the raw. Thereupon, education on both
the elementary and secondary levels set about the task of reorganizing the curriculum of the school with an eye to the factors
of *interplay* between the child and *his* community.

These new trends were scarcely at the point of yielding educational fruit when "the lights of the world went out," and mankind plunged itself into World War II, a war which concluded
with little evidence of a lasting peace, merely a "divided world."
War and its aftermath, as we have seen, generated a spirit quite
different from that which seemed on the point of emerging from
the depression of the 1930's. Whether a tender and understanding

concern for the inner sensibilities of childhood and youth can survive the corroding influences of a "cold war," in which both the atmosphere of home and school are charged with daily speculations regarding the probable uses and effects of weapons of indescribable cruelty, is a grave question. The ever present possibility of war tomorrow in itself tends to create an attitude of mind and spirit unfriendly to the development of a warm and generous nature.

Growing Pains in Parent-Child Relationships

A further contrast between education in a static and a changing society relates to the respective roles of young and old. In a stable society, the old tend to be wise and the fruits of their experience tend to dominate the education of the young. In a changing society, these roles are often reversed.

The transition from old ways to new brings, often, acute growing pains to old as well as to young, since it seems impossible for the generations to keep in step.

Nor are the reasons difficult to understand. The modern community is a heterogeneous not a homogeneous community. It is composed of families of different national, racial, and cultural backgrounds and the diversity in family standards and customs that go with plural origins. Children from these families live on the same street, attend the same school, and mingle in the same recreational group. Intimate associations encourage a comparison of homes and standards, usually to the disadvantage of the home to which each young person belongs!

Differences in family background constitute but one of many factors that seem bent upon changing the traditional patterns of family living and the long-accepted roles of its members. To these factors we shall return in a later chapter. The point of these preliminary observations is to draw attention to the fact that parents are finding it increasingly difficult to raise children with the former confidence and assurance of parents, and the young in turn are often confused and bewildered by factors of change, at a time when each is prone to picture for himself the kind of person he most wishes to become. Both young and old thus hunger for the guidance and the assistance that a good school can give. This constitutes a challenge for education, a challenge which forward-looking institutions are attempting to meet with increasing frequency.

We should observe, however, that in assuming the task of a professional guide in an era of contradiction and confusion, the school helps to shape the future. No longer is it restricted to the teaching of salted-down truths or to the inculcation of habits specified in advance. It now ventures to break new soil and to assume the role of an agency of the community charged with the responsibility of preparing young people to live significantly with their fellows in a changing society.

Conflicting Concepts of Law and Morality

One final item of contrast between education in a changing and heterogeneous society, on the one hand, and a relatively stable and homogeneous society, on the other, merits attention. When people live together over long periods of time, and under conditions essentially similar, their accepted ways of earning a living, their political forms of government, and the relations among the classes which compose their society tend to assume a fixed and eternal character. Moreover, the origins of these institutions date often from beyond the memory of man and seem, accordingly, to be grounded in the structure of the universe rather than in the obvious needs of people. Indeed, insofar as time succeeds in exercising an influence upon them it seems often to confirm their benefits for the few rather than to bring them into line with the needs of the many. Their theoretical justification is often found, therefore, not in the nature of man and his relationships but in the laws of nature.[10] Thus the office of king came to be grounded in a divine right to rule and the nature of the peasant or the tradesman to be qualitatively lower than that of the nobleman. The revolutionary who ventured to challenge or to destroy these arrangements was thought to offend against God as well as man.

Under a society of this character, the task of the school is clear and circumscribed. It is to instill in the young a loyalty to convictions not subject to question and to principles that serve as

---

[10] See, in this connection, John Dewey, *Freedom and Culture* (New York: G. P. Putnam's Sons, 1939), chap. V.

the major premises from which the student can infer the specific answers or solutions to problems as they arise in his daily experience.

The American continent was settled by people who accepted this external conception of government and law and the existence of rigid distinctions among social classes. But the American climate was unfavorable to its perpetuation. For generations, Americans enjoyed firsthand evidence of their ability to transform their physical environment and to create organized communities in localities where none had previously existed. They pushed back the forest, literally made the desert to blossom as the rose, and developed marts of trade and commerce and cultural centers where no civilized man had trod before. All this was done within the memory of living men. Under these circumstances, class distinctions were forced to give way before a new ideal, that of social mobility and the potential equality of man—an ideal that seemed to find repeated verification as individuals, through the exercise of their own initiative, raised themselves from the position of the humblest to the highest in the land. Moreover, in the process of transforming a continent, they were forced to create new institutions and to modify these institutions as occasion necessitated, to write their own laws, and to insure their enforcement. From this experience, it was easy to conclude that institutions—political, social, economic—are born of men and are designed to meet the needs of men.

This revolution in thought was, of course, no straight-line development. Nor has there been a clear-eyed and conscious replacement of one concept of man and nature by another. Rather, we find operating in the thought and the practice of the average person two contradictory concepts of government, of law, and of institutions in general.

No one has pointed this out more clearly than Boyd H. Bode.[11] Bode shows, for example, that the founding fathers, in adopting the Constitution, had in mind both restricting the powers of the new government, on Jefferson's theory, born of hard experience with arbitrary rulers, that the best government is one which

---

[11] Chapter on "Reconstruction in Education" in *Modern Education and Human Values*, Pitcairn-Crabbe Foundation Lecture Series, vol. I (Pittsburgh: University of Pittsburgh Press, 1947).

governs least, and creating an instrument which would, as the Preamble to the Constitution states, "establish justice, insure domestic tranquility, provide for the common defense, promote the general welfare, and secure the blessings of liberty to ourselves and our posterity." The second purpose, states Bode, "was clearly staking out considerable new ground and not just paring down the operations of government." Continuing, Bode remarks:

According to the Declaration of Independence the new government was to be founded on the *self-evident truths* that all men are created equal and that they are endowed by the Creator with certain inalienable rights, such as the right to life, liberty, and the pursuit of happiness. In other words, the purpose of government was to seek conformity to the will of God. The Declaration also states, however, that governments derive their just powers from the consent of the governed, which seems to say that government is only an instrumentality for securing what the people want, and that the test of its worth is conformity to the will of the people.[12]

The criteria of social well-being and of obedience to principles that derive their authority from improved relations among people have transformed the concept of law and rendered more flexible the judgments of the courts. No longer are decisions based solely on precedents and legal principles which have little reference in their application to unique situations, or to the peculiarities of the context in which they operate. As the late Chief Justice Vinson of the United States remarked in the case of Eugene Dennis and his fellow Communists, "Nothing is more certain in modern society than the principle that there are no absolutes, that a name, a phrase, a standard has meaning only when associated with the considerations which gave birth to the nomenclature."

When Abraham Lincoln spoke at Gettysburg of "a government of the people, by the people, and for the people," he was not so much stating an ideal as he was summarizing the results of two hundred years of political experience on this continent. Law is no longer an injunction or a principle originating in a manner foreign or external to the interests of those who must obey, a Procrustean bed to which they must conform. It is rather analo-

---

[12] *Ibid.*, p. 5.

gous to the rules of a game which the players have agreed to observe in order that they may get the most out of the game. It is "an instrument of social policy" dependent for its origin as well as for its validity upon the consent of the governed. Legal justice, in ideal at least, becomes one with social justice, and, as Justice Brandeis once remarked, "the dry bones of legislation" can no longer serve to screen the courts from the political, economic, and social realities of the real world." [13]

The step leading from a redefinition of law in civil society to a revision of the concept of law in the moral field is a short and inevitable one. Here, too, the principle of "by their fruits ye shall know them" has gained increasing recognition in a society marked by religious diversity. The general pattern of American communities in the beginning was religious, and the assumption that individual and social morality are grounded alike in religous orthodoxy was well-nigh universal. But life on the changing frontier, where men and women of many religious backgrounds and affiliations came to share a common lot, together with the practical necessities of providing a common education in mixed communities, tended to undermine an extreme interpretation of this formula. In communities where no one religious sect was in a position to enforce its dicta there grew up a secular morality or a morality of consensus, one that concerned itself with channeling and harmonizing the interests of the inhabitants because of the obvious necessity of regulating intercourse in all of the essential relationships of living.

Similarly, in education the evolution of the nonsectarian school led to the stressing of moral principles which the religious groups held in common. This soon rendered it difficult to convince the young that the virtues of everyday living derived solely from items of creed which marked a man off from his neighbor's faith rather than from those which were accepted in common. Ultimately, this ever widening concept gave birth to the secular state and the secular school.

Needless to say, these developments have complicated the task of education in school. The dualism which Bode tells us characterized the thinking of the founding fathers continues to exist

---

[13] Alpheus Thomas Mason, *Brandeis, A Free Man's Life* (New York: The Viking Press, Inc., 1946), p. 250.

in the minds of many today. In certain areas of living, people are experimental and pragmatic. In others, they remain loyal to authoritarianism. Nor are the experimentalists free of difficulty. When "right" human relations—be they in politics, economics, or in person-to-person relations—are determined with an eye to consequences in the future, as well as to the past, the subject matter as well as the procedures in education are required to undergo re-examination. Emphasis shifts from the acquisition of knowledge and truths firmly rooted to a training in methods of thinking and ways of living that foster the ability to cope with, if not to control, events unseen as well as the tangibles at hand. Principles, in the form of funded experiences, and expressions of wisdom gleaned from the past remain of value and cannot safely be ignored, but novel data and the import of new situations likewise intrude upon the scene and demand consideration, perhaps, even, the replacing of old truths with generalizations more in harmony with the times.

But when should one hold fast to the old and when should one welcome the new? In what areas should the school encourage the experimental method and in which, if at all, should it follow tradition? How should it deal with factors of change when the community is fearful of change or is not of one mind?

These are questions with which we must deal in chapters to come.

Suggested Reading

Bode, Boyd H., "Reconstruction in Education," chap. I in *Modern Education and Human Values*, Pitcairn-Crabbe Foundation Lecture Series, vol. I (Pittsburgh: University of Pittsburgh Press, 1947).

Commager, Henry Steele, "Our Schools Have Kept Us Free," *N.E.A. Journal*, January, 1951, pp. 18–19.

Conant, James Bryant, *Education in a Divided World* (Cambridge: Harvard University Press, 1949), chaps. I–IV.

Edman, Irwin, *John Dewey, His Contribution to the American Tradition* (New York: Bobbs-Merrill Company, Inc., 1955), chap. VI.

Thayer, V. T., *Public Education and Its Critics* (New York: The Macmillan Co., 1954), chap. I.

CHAPTER

3

The School As a Supplementary
Institution

Education and the "Permanent Studies"

Two attitudes toward change, as shown in Chapter 2, are influencing education today: the one hopeful and optimistic, the other timid and fearful. We should not conclude, however, that all who oppose the keying of instruction in the schools to the concept of change do so in response to the threatening aspects of modern life. There is still a third group of laymen and educators who consider the contemporary emphasis upon change to be a serious error. What appears as change, this group insists, is no more than the variations of a constant, not unlike the surface currents on a lake, caused by a passing breeze. Similarly with the novel in human society. Upon inspection and reflection, the novel idea reveals itself as little more than the individual expression of an unchanging principle or law. Accordingly, to tamper with the true and tried content of the curriculum, or to change its emphasis in response to what seem to be fundamental transformations in contemporary society, is to do violence to a valid education.

A vigorous justification of this point of view, together with an attack upon what he considers to be the fallacies of "progressive education," is found in the writings of Robert M. Hutchins and his fellow advocates of a curiculum grounded in the "permanent studies." Thus, we find Hutchins insisting that the major purpose of education is to "draw out the elements of our common human nature." Since these elements are the same in any time or place, "The notion of educating a man to live in any particular time or place, to adjust him to any particular environment, is therefore foreign to a true conception of education." [1]

Hutchins' basic thesis has received support in recent years from an influential group of writers such as Walter Lippmann, Bernard Iddings Bell, Louis Bromfield, Dorothy Thompson, and others.[2] For example, Dorothy Thompson, in a series of articles written for *Ladies Home Journal,* questions the wisdom of equipping young people to cope with change by means of instruction in contemporary materials and the use of contemporary problems. It would seem to be far better to insulate the young from the tensions of the present and to introduce them instead to the tried and true materials of the traditional curriculum. Miss Thompson illustrates the superiority of the training provided by the high school of her day over that of the present by calling attention to the "avoidance" in the former "of the transient and the currently controversial."

A further virtue in the old education, as Miss Thompson views it, was its refusal to adapt instruction to individual differences. These were safely ignored, since the training afforded the student enabled him to "turn his training to his particular bent" by virtue of the fact that "the same training would serve anyone of any bent." [3]

There is little question but that this type of education has the virtue of simplicity. Were it adhered to, no inquiry into the relations of the school to the community or the contemporary social order would be necessary. Courses of study and methods of instruction would vary only superficially with time and cir-

---

[1] Robert M. Hutchins, *The Higher Learning in America* (New Haven: Yale University Press, 1936), p. 66. See also Hutchins, *Education for Freedom* (Baton Rouge: Louisiana State University Press, 1943) and his *The Conflict in Education* (New York: Harper & Brothers, 1953).

[2] See Walter Lippmann's *The Public Philosophy* (Boston: Little, Brown & Co., 1955), chap. VII; Bernard Iddings Bell, "Know How vs. Know Why," *Life,* October 16, 1950; Louis Bromfield, "The Shame of Our Colleges," *Esquire,* March, 1953; and Dorothy Thompson, "Do Our Schools Need an S.O.S.?" *Ladies Home Journal,* February, 1953.

[3] *Ladies Home Journal, op. cit.,* p. 60.

cumstance. Nor would there be evidence of any fundamental interplay between educational institutions and the society they serve. Despite the significant transformations in living that follow upon the transition from an agricultural to an industrial economy, from predominantly rural to urban ways of living, from an insulated national existence to life in a closely interknit world, or from subservience to an autocratic ruler to a complicated relationship between individuals and groups common to the freer air of a modern democracy, the schoolmaster might go about his work undisturbed, eliciting from successive generations of pupils consistent expressions of their "common human nature" by means of the unchanging content of the trivium and quadrivium.

Whatever we may conclude with respect to the concepts of human nature and society underlying Hutchins' philosophy of education, the history of curricula, as these have operated in schools in this country and abroad, would indicate that education in fact has not been everywhere the same. There has also been considerable variation in the actual content of the seven liberal arts—the trivium and the quadrivium—which, we are told, constitute today as yesterday the sole valid instruments of a liberal education. A careful inspection of these arts as taught throughout the years reveals clearly that factors other than unchanging criteria have given them whatever validity they possess. An inspection of the curricula of schools and colleges indicates not only constant change in subjects taught but transformations in the content of the "permanent studies," changes in response to what the times have brought forth, not only with respect to changing circumstances but in human values and aspirations as well. There is little resemblance, for example, between the concept of human nature and its destiny which the colonial school sought to convey and that promoted by the school of today. In purpose and life goals as well as in subject matter taught, in methods of instruction, and in administration of the school, profound transformations have taken place.

In one respect, however, education in this country is the same today as yesterday. Throughout their history, as we indicated in Chapter 1, Americans have attributed well-nigh magical qualities to the influence of the school. It was this influence which Governor Berkeley of Virginia feared when he thanked God that there

were no free schools or printing presses in his colony, just as this
magical influence was welcomed by the Puritans of New England,
who envisaged the establishment of schools, primary through
college, as the indispensable means for realizing what Cotton
Mather termed "the designs of a glorious transformation," the
establishment and the perpetuation of the Holy Commonwealth
on this continent.

Faith in education, together with a conscious recognition of
change, has led to a third formative principle, or concept: that of
the school as a supplementary institution.

The Curriculum Responds to the Times

Take first the colonial school. This began with an exclusive emphasis upon academic education. In this respect it bore witness
to its European origin and the persistence of European influences
upon the intellectual life of the colonies; but it was by no means
a passive imitator. In New England, which is frequently spoken
of as the cradle of public education, its founders saw in the school
one means of rendering children immune to the wiles of that "old
deluder Satan." This required instruction in the written word;
and so determined was the New Englander on this point that
within a few short years of his landing on New England's shores,
he had established a complete system of education, extending
from the primary school through college.

The curriculum, however, was narrow, centering primarily
upon literary materials (if we may apply the term literary to the
catechetical contents of the *New England Primer* and the *Horn-
book*, as well as to the classical materials used in secondary school
and college) and only incidentally upon mathematics. Science was
non-existent. Since life in home and community was comparatively rich in practical experiences essential for the preparation of
the young for adult life, it was access to books and the values
which books alone might develop that seemed to require the
establishing of schools.

These values loomed large in the Puritan mind. Both the
Puritan and his neighbor, the Pilgrim, or Separatist, had left their
homes because of religious conviction. The truth, of which they
believed they were in possession, derived from the Bible and

from learned commentaries upon its meaning. The substance of this truth they wished the school to convey to the young: the elementary school to the mass, the secondary school and college to the future leaders of church and state.

As schools followed the pioneers into the virgin territory of the West, they continued to afford virtually the only opportunity young people had of acquiring the rudiments of an academic education. Consequently, the three R's loomed large. Public libraries were, of course, nonexistent, and the scarcity, if not total absence, of books in the home was a common phenomenon. With the appearance of the academy as a successful competitor of the colonial grammar school, the curriculum was enlarged to include practical subjects relevant to the needs of young people in a rapidly expanding commercial and industrial economy.

Nor was there a significant change of emphasis as the academy gave way to the public high school. What the schools continued to provide, by and large, was an ever richer and fuller curriculum in the elementary school and an expanding curriculum on the secondary and college levels to which was added for special groups the specific skills and techniques of a vocation.

What of today?

Books and academic education are still indispensable and properly occupy a central place in the school. Indeed, we might say that books and the abstract education they symbolize are more important today than yesterday. We have become a verbal civilization and are heavily dependent upon the ability to communicate with people beyond the range of our immediate senses. This carries with it the necessity of familiarity with and ease in the use of abstract symbols. But, at the same time, the out-of-school conditions which once gave import and meaning to abstractions, such as number concepts and economic and social principles, are lacking to the extent that was once true. Consequently, alert teachers seek to bring into the classrooms of both the elementary and secondary schools experiences that will infuse abstract symbols and principles with the breath of life. Children from urban homes are thus encouraged to manipulate objects in order to develop concepts of number that come naturally to the rural child who gathers the eggs daily and reports the number to his elders. So, too, with other concepts conveyed by the printed word. By means of excursions and out-of-school projects, the use of the arts and crafts, and an early introduction to the science laboratory, the modern school strives to infuse good red blood into class-room experiences which without this enrichment would take on a pale and hollow look.

Many critics of modern procedures in the schools do not appreciate this need to provide fertile soil in which abstractions can germinate and grow. They fail to sense the full implications of the fact that children of today, in contrast with the children of yesterday, begin their schooling at a younger age than formerly and are thus introduced early to verbal materials and abstract concepts once reserved for a later age but, at the same time, modern children are increasingly denied the living experiences out of school which once gave substance and meaning to these concepts.

Nor is the attempt to fuel the imagination and intell'gence appropriate only on the elementary level. Secondary school and college are likewise finding it essential to give reality to the concepts and principles basic to subjects such as economics, political science, and sociology. We live today in a world of chain reactions. Increasingly, the well-being and perhaps even the lives of people are intimately affected by events occurring far away. What we decide to do or not to do in one locality may spell life or death for individuals in another with whom we have no firsthand acquaintance. Young people have to learn, as many of their elders have not yet learned, that principles—economic, political, social —are descriptions of living relationships among people, not mere abstract formulations. A strike or a lockout, for example, is more than a local economic phenomenon, or an instrument of limited effect used by one party in a labor dispute in order to fix wages or to acquire profits. It is as well an act of far-reaching import for the lives of people no less intimately affected because of their exclusion from the conscious awareness of the immediate contestants.

Not until young people have learned to translate concepts and principles into living relationships and to sense them as descriptions of transactions among men caught up in the complicated web of modern life has the school discharged its educational responsibility. But to achieve this objective, more than the written word is required. Firsthand observation, excursion, radio and television, the visual and dramatic arts, and, on occasion, the work project must supplement the written word so that the one may reinforce the other.

Emphasis upon the nonverbal experiences need not be distractions from or weak substitutes for an academic education. Rather, they are, at their best, the means and conditions of giving vitality to it. Much the same may be said of many, although not all, of the additions to the curriculum of the school which have been subject to criticism and ridicule. These indictments are valid only when the subject or the course in question is shown to be a substitute for an academic concern of importance. A school that provides a course in "driver education," for example, in place of a course in science or mathematics has lost its sense of revelance. But what is more appropriate than for a community to charge the school, an agency established to meet the needs of youth, with the responsibility for instructing youth in the habits and skills of safe driving?

From Specific to General Vocational Education

The contrast between education for vocation today and yesterday illustrates further the supplementary function of the school. Under the relatively simple conditions of the colonial period and the frontier, the vocational responsibilities of the school were easily discharged. Once mastered, the three R's constituted a sufficient equipment for economic life. The specific skills and processes employed in carrying on a trade after the academic foundations were laid were commonly acquired through an apprenticeship with a master craftsman, and the essential preparation for a profession, such as the law or medicine, was obtained from direct association with a practicing attorney or physician.

This is not the method of acquiring skills in the intricate, complex, and rapidly changing economic society of today. Without guidance there is no way in which young people can know about, let alone perform, the operations required in a modern industrial plant. Some preliminary introduction and training therefore become essential. On the other hand, specialization and the rapid spelling out of new functions and processes require a sensitive adaptation and readaptation to the vocation, including, on occasion, the ability to scrap one skill and to acquire quickly a new one. This calls for a vocational education that cuts through numerous specialized performances and introduces the student to "families" of occupations and to the basic principles of science which are easily translated into practical skills. Moreover, as we shall stress later, the comparatively simple operations called for in many occupations suggest that character traits may be as important as specific skills in the initial preparation of a good worker. If so, a general education which centers upon desirable qualities of personality becomes of immediate concern in vocational education. What this suggests for the school is strikingly different from the original functions of the "common branches" of the school or the early limited attempts to equip young people in school with the specific skills employed on the job. To these are now added a concern for the social functions of a profession or a vocation as well as its exclusively technical requirements.

A Broadened Responsibility for Citizenship Education

Education for citizenship has a similar tale to tell. For a period this was identical with religious instruction. Since no line divided church and state, it was natural for church authorities to translate religious teachings into their implications for public and private conduct. In New England, for example, the clergy more or less proclaimed the law, moral and religious, and the magistrates saw to its enforcement, whereas the schoolmaster instructed his pupils in the virtues of obedience. The Blue Laws of Connecticut, and similar legislation in other colonies, testify to the dominance of religious ideas in regulating the transactions of men in all areas of living. Gradually, as people became more tolerant in religion and the citizen acquired the right to worship according to the dictates of his own conscience, moral conduct and religious behavior ceased to be identical, and citizenship, as one phase of a secular morality, undertook to stand on its own feet.

With manhood suffrage citizenship education became increasingly secular. Its emphasis centered chiefly upon political office and the information and knowledge adults might require as voters to win political preferment for themselves. Accent upon the political in civic education continued well into the period following the Civil War, indeed, until industrial development and the growth of cities with their magnetic attraction for people unaccustomed to urban living promoted, of necessity, a broader preparation of young people for associated living. Contrast, in this connection, Reverend James E. Lapham's description of Townsend's *Analysis of Civil Government,* a secondary school textbook published in 1868, with the table of contents in a modern text.

"He has drawn the materials for his work from original sources and from commentaries and from classic excellence. We see traces of interminable rumblings of *The Madison Papers, The Federalist, Elliott's Debates,* Story and Rawle on the Constitution, Kent and Blackstone's *Commentaries,* as well as the most patient gleanings from official statistical and chronological tables." [4]

The steady drift of a people, once predominantly rural, to the city, the growth of cities, and the multiplication of the services communities now render their inhabitants; the struggle for greater integrity and efficiency in civil government; the entrance of women and children into industry, with the resulting necessity of correcting attendant abuses and rendering protection to them; the rise of labor organizations and the growth of corporations—to mention but a few developments within the last century—make obvious the need for a many-sided orientation of the young to economic, social, and civic institutions over and above the political introduction of the budding citizen to the responsibilities of a democratic citizenship, local, state, national, and international.

Obviously, this orientation requires more than a course in "civics," or, to adopt a more recent term, the "social studies," important as "knowledge about" political government and politics assuredly is. Certainly the intelligent citizen requires professional assistance in order to acquaint himself with the institutions and resources of the local community which serve his daily needs and stand ready to assist him in an emergency. Similarly, on the state, national, and international levels, information is indispensable.

---

[4] Quoted in J. E. Stout, *The Development of High School in the North Central States from 1860 to 1918,* Supplementary Educational Monographs, no. 3, University of Chicago, p. 182.

But today it is essential to have more than "knowledge about" these matters, in the sense of an exclusively intellectual preparation for citizenship. Young people require assistance in learning how to understand and to get along with people, how to respond sensitively to and live creatively with their fellows. They need to acquire through practice in relatively simple situations the qualities and the insights they must later apply in the solution of complex problems. Moreover, democracy has become a way of life in which the rules and the regulations that govern conduct emerge out of the thinking of the governed and derive their validity from the consent of the latter. This presupposes an association of healthy personalities. Consequently, education for citizenship both begins and ends with attention to sound emotional and social attitudes. Accordingly, we find the school slowly reorganizing its work in the classroom, its administrative structure, and its relations with institutions and agencies outside the school in the light of a fuller and richer concept of what constitutes education for healthy citizenship.

Moral and Spiritual Values in a Changing Culture

Contemporary emphasis upon the school's responsibility for education in moral and spiritual values will serve as a final illustration of the school as a supplementary institution.

This had its origin in an exclusively religious orientation. The religious motive loomed large in the early settlements of this country. People had migrated from Europe in order to develop in the new world a way of life in harmony with what they conceived to be religious truth. Once here, they established schools both to safeguard the young from ignorance of the Scriptures and to train the future leaders in church and state, that is, the ministers who would interpret the law and the magistrates who would see to its administration.

The desire for freedom of religion, so dominant a motive in the early colonial period, differed nevertheless from our present conception of religious liberty. The religious freedom so essential for the conscience of one was denied to others. Accordingly, Massachusetts drove the dissenters, Anne Hutchinson and Roger

Williams, into the wilderness and warned all religious "heretics" on pain of death not to pollute her soil. Virginia was equally intolerant of Congregationalists. In each instance, intolerance was grounded upon the assumption that religious orthodoxy is essential to individual morality and civic well-being.

The inhabitants of the Middle Colonies were the first to weaken, if not to undermine, this assumption. Here people of diverse religious affiliation dwelt side by side. Quakers and Mennonites, Lutherans and Baptists, Methodists and Presbyterians, together with a scattering of Catholics and Jews, gradually evolved a community of interests. They raised their crops, exchanged their wares, practiced their professions, determined the laws to govern them, and united for defense. In short, they evolved common ways of life that were more firmly rooted in interlocking interests than in their separate theologies.

For a time, each religious sect assumed the responsibility of educating its own children, but in a mixed population where numbers were small this was no easy undertaking. Ultimately, there developed the nonsectarian school, a device first employed by the Quakers but soon adopted by others. This was a school in which religious instruction centered upon items common to several denominations rather than upon credal differences. It proved to be admirably adapted to the needs of a growing country and a population heterogeneous in religion.

Nonsectarian instruction continued to rest, nevertheless, on the assumption of a one-to-one relationship between morality and religious orthodoxy. It merely broadened the religious base from which morality seemed to flow. To a Protestant child attending a school with children of varying sects who was thus instructed in religious tenets common to all, it soon became obvious that the virtues of honesty, truthfulness, dependability, and the like bore no exclusive relation to the doctrines which divided Protestants even though he continued to believe, as he was taught, that he must be on his guard when dealing with Catholics, or Jews, or atheists. Not until Catholics and Jews gained admission to the schools in considerable numbers was it possible to broaden still further the basis of a common morality. Finally, with the passage of laws forbidding all instruction of a sectarian character in public schools the secular school was born.

The exclusion of sectarian instruction from public education was in no way unfriendly to religion. On the contrary, as the Superintendent of Schools in New York State wrote in 1853, it seemed the only way to avoid either an official religion or a multiple establishment in religion.

To form for the schools a course of instruction . . . which could bear the name of a religious one, and which would meet the views of all, was manifestly impossible. To give to every sect a pro rata share of the school moneys to enable it to support its own schools and teach its own system of religious faith in them, would be . . . to divide the children . . . into a dozen or more schools. . . . In view of the above facts, the position was early, distinctly, and almost universally taken by our statesmen, legislators, and prominent friends of education— men of the warmest religious zeal and belonging to every sect—that religious education must be banished from the common schools and consigned to the family and church. . . . Accordingly, the instruction in our schools has been limited to that ordinarily included under the head of intellectual culture, and the propagation of those principles of morality in which all sects, and good men belonging to no sect, can equally agree. . . .[5]

Moral education which centers upon "the propagation of those principles of morality in which all sects, and good men belonging to no sect, can equally agree" is vital, as verbal instruction, only so long as the principles taught reflect or summarize the obvious facts of common experience. The moral maxims in *Poor Richard's Almanac,* for example, embodied in apt phrase the wisdom of this common experience, and from this fact came their influence. Thus, "The sleeping fox catches no poultry. Up Up," "Early to bed and early to rise makes a man healthy, wealthy, and wise," "Keep thy shop and thy shop will keep thee," reflect the experience of generations of a frugal and industrious people under simple and relatively stable conditions of living. When taught in school, they enabled children to verbalize in a happy phrase the pressures and influences of home and community consistently playing upon them. Precept and example worked hand in hand. But, like the Biblical warning that "Whatsoever a man soweth

[5] Quoted in R. Freeman Butts, *The American Tradition in Religion and Education* (Boston: Beacon Press, Inc., 1950), p. 136.

that shall he also reap," these wise sayings were keyed essentially to and their effectiveness was dependent upon a consistent relationship between verbal statement and daily event.

Change the cultural setting, and these words lose their convincing quality. Two families, for example, live side by side on the same street in a suburban community. The one wishes its children to retire at night at what it considers to be a reasonable hour. The other is lax in its regulations. Should the mother of the first seek to bolster her position by quoting from Poor Richard, "Early to bed and early to rise, makes a man healthy, wealthy, and wise," she is likely to receive the reply: "But Mother! the children next door don't have to go to bed as early as we, they are healthy; and they have more money than do we!"

Once life outside the school began to deprive children and adolescents of firsthand experiences in coping with the serious problems of living and life in the city transformed family relationships that were peculiar to the country, moral maxims and verbal instruction appropriate to a simpler order weakened in influence, and education in moral and spiritual values was forced to enlist new allies.

Increasingly these allies have been found in new forms of educational experience in the classroom and in projects that once more grip young people vitally or relate them intimately to institutions and agencies in their community, experiences which, in William H. Kilpatrick's happy phrase, enable them to learn what they live and to live what they learn.

The times have also changed in other respects since the colonial period. Moral instruction by means of sectarian religious material, within the school, no longer insures the spirit of brotherly love. Nor are religious tenets recognized as the exclusive source of the moral values common to all members of the community. Equally inadequate is an education that depends chiefly upon verbal materials, the roots of which do not permeate deep into the soil of daily experience. New wine thus flows into old bottles, but the old bottles remain, in the sense that the school still functions as an institution dedicated to the task of bringing to flower in the lives of the young the values cherished in common by the community.

Differences Between Communities Are Significant

It is not suggested that the adaptation of the school to changes in the social order is a straight-line development. Education in the United States remains largely a local enterprise. This is both an asset and a liability to educational progress, since it subjects education to the dominant convictions governing the community upon which it is dependent for its support. A progressive and experimentally minded community will profit from this autonomy, whereas the same freedom enables the backward community to impose atavistic concepts and ways of living upon its children.

Nor are the needs of all communities identical. Needs in a rural and agricultural community differ in essential respects from those of an urban and a metropolitan center. Similarly, the demands upon a school in a prosperous northern state may have little resemblance to those in a southern state where erosion of the soil and cultural undernourishments sap the vitality of its inhabitants.

Differences in educational practice also reflect differences in educational theory, conflicting notions of child nature and of ways in which children learn best. Identical conditions may thus produce practices at variance with each other. One urban school, impressed by the limited opportunities of its children to engage in activities out of school and to reinforce their schoolwork, will undertake to provide a groundwork for abstractions in firsthand, concrete, active experiences. This was, indeed, one of the objectives of the "activity curriculum" which assumed prominence some years ago. A second, identifying schooling with the training of the mind and intellectual functioning with the facile manipulation of verbal symbols, will condemn the first as an example of "soft pedagogy" and resolve to "leave experience to other institutions and influences and [to] emphasize in education the contribution that it is supremely fitted to make, the intellectual training of the mind." [6]

The philosophies and psychologies of learning which find expression in our schools are thus as relevant to our study as are the

---

[6] Hutchins, *The Higher Learning in America, op. cit.*, p. 69.

more obvious consequences of change. Theories of education, as the methods of instruction they father, are expressions of the culture and can be dated. Not infrequently they are atavistic and tend to retard progress. At times, they are used by counterrevolutionists to "reform" education and to restore to it the "fundamentals." Again they represent earnest efforts to utilize the most recent findings of the science of education and studies of personality in a manner most appropriate to the hour.

That is to say, there is no one fixed and final or commonly agreed upon relationship between educational practice and the needs of young people and their community which a wise and competent student of education can define. But this in no way refutes the general principle that the school is a supplementary institution, an agency established and maintained by a community in order to afford to its young, through collective effort, what its members value for them but are unable to provide individually; an institution which, by its very nature, must change as hopes and aspirations for the young assume ever new forms.

Suggested Reading

Association for Supervision and Curriculum Development, *Forces Affecting American Education* (Washington: National Education Association, 1953), chaps. I–III.

Hutchins, Robert M., *The Conflict in Education* (New York: Harper & Brothers, 1953), chaps. I–III.

Kandel, I. L., *The New Era in Education* (Boston: Houghton Mifflin Co., 1955), chap. 3.

Meyer, Agnes, *Education for a New Morality* (Kappa Delta Pi Lecture) (New York: The Macmillan Co., 1957).

Rugg, Harold, *Foundations for American Education* (Yonkers, N.Y.: World Book Company, 1947), chaps. I–II.

Thayer, V. T., *The Attack Upon the American Secular School* (Boston: Beacon Press, Inc., 1952), chap. XI.

/\.\/.\/.\.\

4

Local Autonomy in Education

The Citizen and His School

One morning at breakfast Johnny Miller became involved in an argument with his father over the question of municipal ownership of the local street railway system. To the father, the head of the largest plumbing supply firm in town, this was clear evidence that his son had become infected with views of a "creeping socialism." Imagine his alarm, therefore, in learning that the boy's teacher was considering in class the issue of public vs. private ownership of public utilities and had organized the class into two sections, one to gather all possible data and arguments favorable to public ownership and the other in opposition; and his son was chairman of the group giving support to the affirmative! As the father saw it, there was but one thing to do: to snuff out heresy as quickly as possible.

Accordingly, Mr. Miller decided to stop at the school and speak to either the principal or the boy's teacher on his way downtown to his office. Upon arriving at the school, he observed the teacher in earnest conversation with a group of students. Rather than arouse the curiosity of the young people, or create a scene in their presence, he resolved to speak immediately to the principal. This he did, only to be informed calmly, but firmly, that the topic under consideration by the class was an inherent part of the course of study in the field of the social studies, and as long as the teacher handled the topic objectively and with an eye to furthering an understanding of all points of view, the father should welcome the inclusion of the topic rather than its exclusion. However, if Mr. Miller were still unsatisfied, he was free to appeal to the superintendent and/or the board of education.

"So this is the way I must cope with subversion in the schools," muttered Mr. Miller to himself. "Well, where duty points, I shall go." The result was that he shortly found himself at the head of a body of like-minded citizens who were determined to discipline the teacher and the principal through the board of education. In addition, to avoid similar difficulties in the future, they wished to survey courses of study, textbooks, and supplementary teaching materials in the schools with a view to weeding out anything conducive to the introduction of un-American ideas in the minds of their youth. Moreover, in the event the board of education should refuse to grant these demands, they were resolved to take their case to the people and thus insure the election of proper members to the incoming board of education.

Mr. Miller, in the above illustration, is a fictional character, but the incident described has been duplicated on numerous occasions in communities of the United States, for one of the unique features of education in this country is a high degree of community autonomy. In the vast majority of instances the school board is elected directly by the people of the school district. This board selects the administrative and instructional staff; prepares the budget; writes the rules and regulations governing the functions and the behavior of the administrative staff, the teachers, and students; approves the curriculum; and, in many other respects, acts as the governing body of the schools.

So conspicuously, indeed, is the average board of education in charge of the public schools that Mr. Miller and his associates have little cause to consider, as we shall do in a moment, that these functions are delegated functions and are subject to the will of the state. They conceive of their schools, as does the average American, as directly expressive of the will of the people of each locality.

How do we explain the fact that school systems which are both created by the state and subject to its control and regulation are, nevertheless, thought of as essentially local in authority and responsibility?

The Child Is Father of the Man!

The answer is found, in part, in the American tradition of local self-government, a tradition which derives from the peculiarities of settlement in the colonial period and which was reaffirmed by each generation thereafter as individuals and groups, in the course of the conquest of the continent, constantly penetrated into new areas and established new communities in advance of a central government. In part, also, the explanation lies in the manner in which the state related itself to education in the early stages of development. Were we to consider the relation of local schools to the state as analogous to that of child and parent, we should have to say that the child is father of the parent!

In early New England, for example, a number of communities in their town meetings established schools in advance of legislation by the General Court requiring all towns to do so.[1] Moreover, with the advent of general legislation in 1642 and 1647, the responsibility for enforcement was lodged directly in the hands of the "chosen men appointed to manage the prudential affairs" of the town, rather than in state officials. In the course of time, as towns came to grant to outlying districts the privilege of establishing and maintaining their own schools, local self-determination in the conduct of education became firmly grounded in practice and theory. Not for a century and a half following the mandatory act of 1647 was a state agency of education established in Massachusetts.

In the Middle Colonies, as in New England, a motivating factor in the establishment of schools was the religious concern that young people grow up possessed of the faith of their fathers. But, here, diversity rather than uniformity of religious conviction prevailed. As Edwards and Richey point out, in no other section were Protestants more divided in their concepts of the relation of God to man, nor in any other section was the population more heterogeneous in social origins and in social outlooks. To these colonies came representatives from all northern Europe, and "the only non-English people to found colonies within the limits of the original thirteen established them in this middle region."[2]

---

[1] For example, Boston in 1635 and Ipswich and Salem in 1641.
[2] Newton Edwards and Herman G. Richey, *The School in the American Social Order* (Boston: Houghton Mifflin Co., 1947), p. 128.

Under these circumstances, the state soon found it inexpedient to enforce religious orthodoxy through education and willingly left the responsibility for schooling in the hands of family, church, and other religious and philanthropic organizations. The sole exception, but one pregnant with later possibilities, was state provision for the education of the poor as charity pupils.

Much the same was true in the South. Here no school system as such existed prior to the Revolution or, indeed, for some time later. Despite the influence of Thomas Jefferson and others of broad vision, there was little public sentiment with which to give substance to the concept of general education either as a public obligation or as a public asset, least of all to bring about the "taxation of one man's property for the education of another man's child." Nevertheless, here, as in the North, there were scattered seeds of a future public school system in the form of public provision for the education of the "children of barbarians" and of the poor.[3] Here, too, were to be found transient and isolated schools sustained by private initiative and serving private interests.

On the whole, then, as we have said, individual and local efforts tended to antedate state efforts in the establishment of schools, although, in the course of time, it became necessary for the state to intervene in order to require lagging communities to follow in the footsteps of more progressive communities. The states either enacted mandatory legislation, similar to that enacted in Massachusetts in 1647, requiring the towns to make provisions for the education of all children in the rudiments of knowledge or else they established, as did Pennsylvania in its constitution of 1790, the less ambitious but nevertheless pioneering requirement that "the legislature shall, as soon as conveniently may be, provide for the establishment of schools throughout the state in such a manner that the poor may be taught gratis." But legislation that was mandatory in form was in fact only hortatory and dependent

---

[3] Ten years after the settlement at Jamestown (1617) King James I wrote a letter to the bishops of the English churches ordering them to instruct the bishops in Virginia "to give orders to ministers and other zealous men of their Dioceses" to encourage contributions in support of churches and schools for the education of the children of "barbarians." Two years later, some 1500 pounds had been raised for this purpose, as well as for "a seminary for the breeding of good ministers." These efforts marked the beginnings of the College of William and Mary, the actual opening of which as a college was delayed until 1710 because of wars and hardships and official apathy.

for its enforcement upon the enlightened will and determination of the people of each community. Moreover, the details of administration, such as the selection of teachers, the determination of subjects to be taught, and other items affecting the operation and administration of the schools, were locally determined and lacked both central determination and central supervision. The result, of course, was that wide differences in the amount and the quality of education provided by communities characterized schools well into the nineteenth century. For example, when Massachusetts, in 1837, established its State Board of Education and selected Horace Mann as its secretary, the "gnarls of a century's growth" had to be smoothed out. Private schools viewed the development of public education with jealous eyes and placed obstacles in the way of its progress. Churches, fearing the encroachments of nonsectarian education, were likewise commonly opposed. Teachers were ill-prepared and both professional education and professional standards waited upon future efforts. "Moreover, school architecture had to be studied, school funds must be found, regularly provided and husbanded and legislators instructed. All this Mr. Mann did and more." [4]

Conditions elsewhere in New England in the early nineteenth century were no better than in Massachusetts. In Connecticut, for example, according to the report of Henry Barnard in 1839 to the State Board of Commissioners, expenditures upon the education of 12,000 pupils in private schools were as large as those upon 40,000 in public schools. Children in primary grades were neglected in both. There was virtually no gradation of schools. Public funds for education were often misappropriated, and although in the cities and populous districts of the state provision for education was as good as elsewhere in New England, there were wide differences in the quality of education provided. [5]

Developments in the Middle Colonies and the South

Outside "enlightened" New England, conditions were even worse. But, as in Massachusetts and Connecticut, ardent advocates of

---

[4] Richard G. Boone, *Education in the United States* (New York: D. Appleton and Co., 1909), p. 104.

[5] *Ibid.*, p. 105.

reform were also succeeding in arousing the public mind and convincing state legislatures of the necessity of state provision for education and the exercise of state authority and control over education.

Active efforts at state provision for education date roughly from the period following the Revolution. Most frequently mentioned in this connection is Jefferson's plan for the universal establishment of common schools in Virginia. An act embodying his ideas was introduced in the Virginia legislature in 1779 but failed of passage.[6] Not until 1796 was legislative provision made in Virginia for a comprehensive system of elementary schools, and not until 1810, with the establishment of a literary fund, was assistance from the state extended to counties in support of public education. The influence of Jefferson's ideas, however, was not limited to Virginia. Nor was his voice as one in the wilderness. In 1786 Benjamin Rush in Philadelphia produced a plan for the education on a national scale of all American youth, including both sexes, a plan specifically designed to emphasize the principles of democracy and to insure an understanding of the machinery of government with which to maintain the institutions of democracy.[7] Others, similarly inspired, produced equally interesting plans with a view to the promotion of national progress and national unity. Active in this connection were the members of the American Philosophical Society, an organization founded by Benjamin Franklin and others and to which belonged many of the leading minds of America.

Following the adoption of the federal Constitution in 1789 and the approval of the Tenth Amendment to the Constitution in 1791 with its provision that "The powers not delegated to the United States by the Constitution, nor prohibited by it to the States, are reserved to the States respectively, or to the people," comprehensive schemes for the education of the young were of necessity confined to state boundaries. Within the states, however,

[6] This plan was designed, in Jefferson's words, "to avail the state of those talents which nature has sown as liberally among the poor as the rich, but which perish without use, if not sought for and cultivated." It was, therefore, selective in character. Schools for the teaching of reading, writing, and arithmetic to children without cost were to be established in districts of convenient size, from which the competent might go on to middle schools, also without cost, and, again, from these, all who demonstrated their ability to do so, might go on to college.

[7] For an excellent discussion of these plans, see Oscar Allan Hansen, *Liberalism and American Education* (New York: The Macmillan Co., 1926), pp. 48–63.

a number of practical as well as theoretical considerations favored the gradual development of state systems of education.

Factors Stimulating State Responsibility for Education

First was the obvious need that funds which the states set aside to assist communities in the discharge of their educational responsibilities be wisely administered.

In a number of states a "literary fund" was established with which to encourage education in the subdivisions of the state—counties in the South, towns or districts in the North. Intended as these funds were, in the first instance, to assist communities in the education of the poor, they provided, nevertheless, a nucleus for wider employment later.

The sources of these funds were varied: income from lotteries, liquor licenses, marriage licenses, and, as in Virginia, in accordance with an act of 1810, the income from all escheats, confiscations, penalties, and forfeitures, together with all rights in personal property found derelict. Substantial additions to state funds were made in 1837 by a grant of $28,000,000 from the federal government under the Surplus Revenue Act and in 1841 and 1850, respectively, by the Federal Internal Improvement Act and the Swamp Land Grant Act. In the West, public lands constituted a boon for the cause of education. As early as 1785, the Continental Congress, in adopting the Northwest Ordinance, provided for the setting aside of the sixteenth section of each township for the maintenance of schools. This served as a suggestive precedent for later action by both state and federal governments. Thus, when Connecticut, in 1786, agreed to cede to the United States her claims to lands in what is now northeastern Ohio, it was stipulated that a portion of this area, called the "Western Reserve," be used in support of education. Eventually this yielded the sum of $1,000,000 which was turned into a school fund. Similar restrictions were placed upon the sale of land granted to the states by the United States government, with stimulating effects upon the development of public education, despite the unfortunate circumstances of theft and waste and unwise practices which often accompanied the disposal of public land and its resources.

In both the West and the East, the emergence of state funds in support of education led to the creation of committees and boards of control charged with the responsibility, in the first instance, of distributing the income of these funds equitably and, later, of stimulating local initiative on a matching basis not unlike the various forms of state aid employed at present.

By the middle of the nineteenth century, every state in the Union had established a school fund and every state, with the exception of Arkansas, had, as a further step, enacted legislation authorizing localities to impose taxes in support of education. This legislation stemmed from the realization that resources more substantial than the income from state school funds were essential to meet new demands of the people for education.

These demands were for nothing less than schools to be maintained at public expense and open and free to all children, without the taint of charity.

As we have seen, the origins of this demand were plural. In New England it derived in large measure from the religious concern of the early New Englander that each child be provided with the means of determining his own salvation. In other colonies these seeds were found rather in their faltering provision for the education of the "poor." By the first quarter of the nineteenth century, however, the commercial and industrial development of the country gave birth to forces other than those religious and humanitarian in favor of a free education. These forces derived from an alliance of groups strikingly different in complexion and motivation but, nevertheless, united in support of schools.

One was the growing importance of labor. Although weak according to present standards, labor, by the second quarter of the nineteenth century, had become outspoken in its demands for an education which would enable young people to better themselves economically and to share more abundantly in the advantages of a general education. Labor was also becoming aware of its growing political power through united action. "Let us unite at the polls and give our vote to no candidate," declared the constitution of the Association of Working Men of New Castle, Delaware, in 1830, "who is not pledged to support a national system of education to be paid for out of public funds." And as early as 1820, the workingmen of Philadelphia requested

of each candidate for the state legislature that he state his attitude toward an equal and general system of education for the
state.[8]

The early effects of industrialization and urbanization upon
children as well as adults were not altogether friendly to the
American ideal of an open road to opportunity. One authority
states that two-fifths of all laborers in factories in 1832 were
children, few of whom had an opportunity to learn to read and
to write.[9] The historian, Carl Russell Fish, informs us that "As
late as 1840 only one-half of the children of New England were
given a free education, one-seventh of those of the Middle States,
and one-sixth of the West." [10] As Edwards and Richey point out,
the mills and factories were attracting children as well as adults
from the farm. These factories and the cities which grew up about
them were increasing more rapidly than the social insight required to solve the problems generated by their development.
"Illiterate and unruly children roamed the streets uncared for
and considered only as potential workers in factories which took
them at a tender age." The mother as well as the father of the
family was employed, but the wages of the entire family provided
only a bare subsistence.[11]

Fortunately, to many Americans, these conditions came as a
shock. Nor was the emerging common man disposed to accept
them as necessary and inevitable. Labor, as we have said, proceeded to organize in order to better its condition and to demand
schools free from the taint of charity or dependence upon philan-
thropy. Individuals from all classes (members of the rapidly increasing middle class, who saw in education an indispensable
means for the advancement of their children, humanitarians, political leaders, educators in all sections of the country, and forward-
looking businessmen, from whose resources the increased revenues
for public education would have to be drawn) united with labor
in demanding the establishment of a tax-supported public school
system.

---

[8] William E. Drake, *The American School in Transition* (Englewood Cliffs, N.J.:
Prentice-Hall, Inc., 1955), pp. 205–218, gives an excellent summary of these developments.

[9] *Ibid.*, p. 209.

[10] Quoted in Charles and Mary Beard, *The American Spirit* (New York: The
Macmillan Co., 1942), pp. 251–252.

[11] Edwards and Richey, *op. cit.*, p. 328.

As we have also seen in Chapter 1, Horace Mann and others sought to convince the business community of the market value of education. Merle Curti, however, has shown that motives of fear as well prompted many to support a broadening of the base of education. "Anxious to wring support for public schools from propertied interests, then opposed to taxation for such a purpose," writes Curti, "educational spokesmen warned them of the dangers to property rights from universal suffrage, Jacksonian democracy, and even, possibly, revolution—any of which might result if the masses were left undisciplined by education." [12]

Equally urgent words of warning and admonition came from intellectuals and statesmen of the caliber of Edward Everett, who saw dangers to the status quo from the use of the ballot by frontier folk as well as by labor. Thus, in addressing a group of Boston capitalists in 1833, Everett used the following argument in support of contributions to education in the far-off state of Ohio: "We can, from our surplus, contribute toward the establishment and endowment of the seminaries where the mind of the West shall be trained and enlightened," . . . in order "to give security to our property, by diffusing the means of light and truth throughout the region where so much of the power to preserve or to shake it resides." [13]

Eventually, united effort brought about the establishment of free schools in a manner characteristically American, that is, by means of state authorization for individual communities to levy taxes upon the local population in support of public schools. Typical of these acts was the passage of a law in Missouri in 1824 which permitted school districts to levy taxes in support of schools, provided two-thirds of the voters approved so doing. Only after experimentation with local autonomy in taxation did it become common practice for the states to enact laws which made it mandatory for communities to levy taxes on behalf of their schools. So acceptable, however, had the principle become by the third quarter of the nineteenth century that every state admitted to the Union since 1876 has been required by Congressional resolution to provide in its constitution "for the establishment

---

[12] Merle Curti, *The Social Ideas of American Educators* (New York: Charles Scribner's Sons, 1935), p. 81.

[13] Edward Everett, *Importance of Practical Education and Useful Knowledge* (New York: Harper & Brothers, 1856), pp. 169–170.

and maintenance of a system of public schools which shall be open to all children of the State and free from sectarian control. . . ." [14]

The final step in the assumption of state responsibility for the education of all children came with the passage of compulsory school attendance laws. In this, as in earlier developments in education, Massachusetts led the way in 1852. New York followed in 1853. By 1895, according to the report of the United States Commissioner of Education, W. T. Harris, 28 states and the District of Columbia had passed compulsory school attendance laws.[15] Not until 1918, however, was the circle complete.

Provision for free and universal education within a state requires more in the way of financial assistance than irregular appropriations from school funds derived from miscellaneous sources. It requires legislation designed to yield revenues upon which local school boards can depend both in the process of constructing their annual budgets and in laying plans for the future. It also requires, as we have seen, the creation of boards of control to insure the proper distribution and use of these funds. It was not long, however, before even this proved insufficient. As school attendance grew in volume and, eventually, became mandatory for all children within a given age bracket, leadership and encouragement on the part of the state became ever more imperative. It is not surprising, therefore, to find each of the states eventually rounding out its provision for education by the establishment of some form of supervision and control over the operations of educational programs within the various school communities of the state.

Local Autonomy with the Consent of the State

From this brief survey of the evolution of public education in the United States, it should be clear that a unique relationship between locality and state has existed from the beginning. Gen-

---

[14] See in this connection, footnote 9 in Justice Frankfurter's concurring opinion in *McCollum* v. *Board of Education*, 333 U.S. 203 (1948).

[15] See J. L. Blair Buck, *The Development of Public Schools in Virginia* (Richmond: State Board of Virginia, 1952), p. 117. It is well to bear in mind, however, that for a time, in a number of states, no machinery was provided for the enforcement of compulsory school attendance laws. Even today enforcement is far from uniform.

erally speaking, one or more localities have pioneered in meeting the needs of the community, needs, however, in no way peculiar to one place or to one people. These efforts have stimulated other communities to follow the example of the pioneers, and, eventually, the state has entered the picture to render general or binding upon all what were for a time the innovations of the few.

Observe, however, that ultimate authority to stimulate or to retard experimentation resides in the state, and in the exercise of their educational functions, local school officials act as agents of the state. Although significant variations exist among the states with respect to the structural or organizational pattern of education, the general outlines are strikingly similar. In each instance, the constitution, as an expression of the will of the people, instructs the legislature to provide for the establishment of free schools. In most states, the legislatures have set up state boards of education, charged with specific functions, and, at the same time, have assigned other functions to local boards (city, county, town, or district, as the case may be). Within these respective areas, each acts as a direct representative of the state. As Mort and Ross emphasize in their *Principles of School Administration,* the state legislature may be viewed as a state board of education and the state department of education as its executive agent, with power to act in strictly defined areas. In other areas, local districts are authorized to act. "Neither is justified under this theory in encroaching upon the powers of the other. Both are state agents. With respect to these powers they are coordinate." [16]

Considerable variation exists within the states with respect both to the powers and responsibilities of state boards and to the relations of local communities to the state. These range from extreme home rule, as in New Jersey and Rhode Island, to a high degree of centrally controlled education in others.

The degree of responsibility lodged in state boards of education also varies from state to state. In a majority of states, state boards exercise considerable control over elementary and secondary education, whereas in others this authority is more restricted.[17] Methods for the selection of state boards and their

---

[16] New York: McGraw-Hill Book Co., 1957, p. 269.

[17] See Lee M. Thurston and William H. Roe, *State School Administration* (New York: Harper & Brothers, 1957), for a discussion of different types of state boards of education.

officers also vary. For example, in a few states, the members of state boards are elected directly by the people. In others they are appointed by the governor or the legislature. Likewise with the chief executive officer of the state board (commonly called the commissioner or superintendent of public instruction). In some states this officer is elected directly by the people. A second method is appointment by the governor; a third method, which is considered preferable, is appointment by the state board of education.

But to return to the major theme of this chapter, however varied may be the structural and organizational pattern among the states or the assignment of powers and responsibilities to local school authorities, on the one hand, and to state officers, on the other, education in each instance is a state function and is thus subject to the control and direction of the state, as expressed through the legislature.[18] For example, it is the legislature which decides whether or not school boards are to be elected or appointed or whether the locality may decide this question by referendum. Unless otherwise provided in the constitution, the legislature also determines the functions which the state board of education and local school boards, respectively, shall exercise with respect to items such as the selection and retention of teachers, salary schedules, content of the curriculum, choice of textbooks, construction of buildings, and the like.

Interesting confirmation of the potential domination of the state over the locality in educational matters has been afforded recently by the attempts of southern states to resist the decisions of the United States Supreme Court on segregation in education. Many of these attempts remove virtually all authority from local school boards to determine policies for the admission of pupils. When Arlington County, Virginia, for example, announced its plans for complying with the decision of the United States Supreme Court, an indignant state legislature deprived it of the privilege of electing its school board and lodged this authority in the county board. Moreover, to discourage any school system in the state from admitting a Negro student into a white school, the legislature adopted an act which transferred final authority for

---

[18] In some instances state constitutions place limitations upon the powers of the legislature in certain areas.

the placement of pupils from the locality to a state commission. A Virginia act provided further that any public school in the state which "mixed the races," even on court decree, should be deprived of its share of state funds. Acts of similar intent have been passed by other southern states. On the other hand, in the North, acts of quite a different character have found their way onto the statute books. Illinois, for example, prohibits the distribution of state funds to any school district which maintains segregated schools and requires school officials to certify that their schools are nonsegregated as a condition for receiving their share of state appropriations.[19]

Fear of "subversion" in education has also induced state legislatures in recent years to intervene directly in the educational concerns of local communities through the enactment of laws respecting the selection of textbooks and library materials, the imposition of loyalty oaths for teachers as a condition of employment, and the creation of investigating committees charged with the responsibility of identifying un-American activities on the part of teachers and un-American ideas in textbooks and other instructional materials. Mandatory legislation with reference to what schools should or should not teach in the way of specific ideas—ranging from the effects of alcohol and tobacco upon the human system to concepts such as the validity or lack of validity of the concept of evolution—are familiar illustrations, not only of the authority which resides in state legislatures but of a willingness to exercise this authority. Apparently, the only limits upon actions of this character are those imposed by constitutions, state or federal, as determined by the courts.

To those who prize local initiative in education, the increasing cost of education and the apparent inability of local school units to bear the full cost of conducting their schools constitute a threat to local autonomy. The proportion of the cost of education borne by local school systems, in comparison with that assumed by the state, varies widely, both within a state and among the states. In many states, local school units are contributing a constantly shrinking share of the cost of maintaining and conducting their schools. For example, in Tennessee in 1957 the state pro-

---

[19] See William R. Ming, Jr., "The Elimination of Segregation in the Public Schools of the North and West," *Journal of Negro Education*, Summer, 1952, p. 267.

vided funds equal to 80 per cent of the annual school budget in
one county whereas in the city of Nashville the state contribution
was less than 50 per cent of the annual school budget. Often these
discrepancies testify to paralysis of will or an unfortunate disposition on the part of one locality to draw upon the funds available from the state rather than to impose local taxes. In other instances, they testify to the difference between wealth and poverty.
In each instance, however, the trend toward increased financial
support on the part of the state can be serious in its effects upon
local initiative.

The common assumption that he who pays the piper will eventually call the tune also explains the opposition of many to the
extension of federal aid to education.

As we have seen, the federal Constitution contains no specific
provision for the support of education. Under the Tenth Amendment this remains one of the powers reserved to the states. Consequently, with the exception of educational activities which
clearly serve the national interest (such as military training and a
generous list of activities subsumed under the title of "emergency
training," together with various types of departmental programs
of education, all financed and administered directly by the federal
government), the national government has been content to assist
education in the states rather than to give body to the dream of
Benjamin Rush of a national system of education.

This assistance has been both substantial and varied in character, as, for example, grants of public lands to the states upon
their admission to the Union, outright appropriations in support
of general education, the distribution of surplus revenue, grants-
in-aid to special types of education, etc.[20]

With the exception of grants for vocational education and the
emergency legislation of the 1930's setting up the National Youth
Administration and the Civilian Conservation Corps, the federal
government has refrained to a remarkable degree from exercising
control over the educational activities it has fostered and assisted.
On the whole, federal support of education in the states has ad-

---

[20] For an excellent review of federal assistance to education, as well as educational
programs conducted by the federal government, see Chris A. De Young's *Introduction to American Education,* rev. ed. (New York: McGraw-Hill Book Co., 1955),
chap. I.

hered to a statement of policy put forth by the Educational Policies Commission in 1941 on *The Civilian Conservation Corps, the National Youth Administration and the Public Schools:* "We conclude, therefore, that the federal government is responsible for promoting and safeguarding the national welfare through education, and that its proper functions are to provide leadership and financial aid. These functions are not only proper; they are essential. Increasingly the educational problems which confront the American people require federal aid for their best solution."

The phrase, federal leadership and financial aid, but *without control,* expresses the prevailing judgment of educators and legislators today as to the desirable relation of the federal government to public education. It is this policy which defines the activities of the United States Office of Education within the recently established Department of Health, Education, and Welfare.

Nevertheless, there are certain conditions, more or less peculiar to the present, which seemingly dictate some form of direct federal intervention in education as conducted by the states.

One relates to the needs of defense. So important is education today in providing an adequate personnel for the defense of the United States, not merely in the Defense Department itself, or the conventional services—military, naval, air, etc.—but also within the civilian population, that the national government cannot afford to remain indifferent to the nature of the education provided on all levels within the states. It was recognition of this intimate relationship between education and the well-being of the nation that prompted the national government in the 1930's to assist education directly through special instruments such as the National Youth Administration and the Civilian Conservation Corps, and, more recently, to provide scholarships for individuals within the fields of science and foreign language as well as grants to institutions within the states for purposes of instruction and research.

Decisions of the United States Supreme Court in recent years have also drawn attention to a number of areas in which national principles take precedence over both state and local self-determination in education. These principles have to do with civil rights, as defined in the Constitution of the United States. For example, the First Amendment of the Constitution, as interpreted by the

Supreme Court, prohibits public schools from engaging in religious instruction of a sectarian character. Similarly, according to the decisions of the Supreme Court in May, 1954, and May, 1955, on segregation in education, no school can lawfully exclude a child from attendance upon that school on grounds of race. Moreover, to enforce this decree, the lower courts are specifically instructed, when cases of violation are brought to their attention, "to take such proceedings and enter such orders and decrees consistent with this opinion as are necessary and proper to admit to public schools on a racially non-discriminatory basis with all deliberate speed the parties to these cases."

We conclude that it is inaccurate to speak of local autonomy in education in the United States as a legal fact. Neither as a matter of practice nor of law is it an accurate description of education as it actually operates. We can say, however, that both in practice and law, school communities in the United States are encouraged to exercise a high degree of local self-determination and to adapt their educational programs to the needs and peculiarities of their own communities. In some 80 per cent of the school districts of the United States, the people elect by direct vote the members of their boards of education. Although these boards are commonly required to meet standards set by state authorities, such as minimum qualifications of teachers, minimum salaries, and the teaching of specific subjects, they are, nevertheless, encouraged by the state to better these minimum requirements, with the result that the quality and character of education provided by the wisest and best communities continue to serve as beacon lights for others to follow; and no community, as a result of control by a central bureaucracy, is condemned to a state of mediocrity. Perhaps we should add, as a generalization, that state departments of education, by and large, prefer to exercise their powers of supervision and direction in areas where they are supreme, with an eye to the stimulation of self-direction on the part of localities rather than to passive compliance.

Suggested Reading

Cremin, Lawrence A., *The American Common School* (New York: Bureau of Publications, Teachers College, Columbia University,

1951), parts II and III.

De Young, Chris A., *Introduction to American Education* (New York: McGraw-Hill Book Co., 1955), chaps. I–IV.

Drake, William E., *The American School in Transition* (Englewood Cliffs, N.J.: Prentice-Hall, Inc., 1955), chaps. VI, VII.

Edwards, Newton, and Herman G. Richey, *The School in the American Social Order* (Boston: Houghton Mifflin Co., 1947), chap. 9.

Hansen, Kenneth H., *Public Education in American Society* (Englewood Cliffs, N.J.: Prentice-Hall, Inc., 1956), chap. II.

Mort, Paul R., and David H. Ross, *Principles of School Administration* (New York: McGraw-Hill Book Co., 1957), chap. 16.

CHAPTER

5

Equality of Educational Opportunity

Equality As a Philosophical Concept

The faith of the fathers in the potentialities of each individual, referred to in Chapter 1 impelled them to provide, insofar as possible, equal opportunities for all young people through education. This is, of course, an applcation, under American conditions, of the democratic concept of equality, which originated in Europe, but has assumed a unique form of expression on American soil. As Irwin Edman wrote in his *Fountainheads of Freedom,*

> It is not enough to point out that liberty and equality were themes as old as the Greeks, or in their peculiarly constitutional form as old as John Locke. America was a new continent and like other ideas and institutions that had a European heritage, the ideas of liberty and equality had a career in America that was necessarily different from what it would have been in Europe. Circumstances alter not only cases but principles also. Because it was a new world, free or relatively free from many of the established encrustations of the old, the democratic idea in America was to take its own form, and in almost a chemical sense, a purer form.[1]

Perhaps the most familiar affirmation of the ideal of equality for Americans occurs in the Declaration of Independence with its

---

[1] Irwin Edman, *Fountainheads of Freedom* (New York: Reynal & Hitchcock, 1941), p. 133. Now published by Harcourt, Brace & Co.

assertion: "We hold these truths to be self-evident: that all men are created equal; that they are endowed by their Creator with certain inalienable rights; that among these, are life, liberty, and the pursuit of happiness; that to secure these rights governments are instituted among men, deriving their just powers from the governed. . . ."

Two basic assumptions are involved in this Declaration: (1) the psychological assumption that all men are born essentially equal in their potentialities and (2) the political assumption that a primary function of government is to insure to individuals an opportunity to realize the rights of life, liberty, and the pursuit of happiness, with which they are endowed.

The psychological principle derives in large measure from the philosophy of John Locke, an intellectual godfather of the leaders of the American revolution. According to Locke, men bring little into this world by way of inheritance. Contrary to the assumptions of the rationalists and hereditarians of his time, he denied the existence of innate ideas (a native tendency to accept and apply specific logical and moral principles). Rather are men born with minds analogous to a white sheet of paper upon which experience writes all of the originals of knowledge. Thus, what an individual is at a given moment represents the outcome of the experiences which he has had and the use he has made of them.

"As it is in the body," writes Locke in *The Conduct of the Understanding,* "so it is in the mind: practice makes it what it is; and most even of those excellencies which are looked on as natural endowments, will be found, when examined into more narrowly, to be the product of exercise and to be raised to that pitch only by repeated action." [2]

Locke did not deny altogether that natural disposition may "give the first rise" to rare ability, but he insisted "that [it] never carries a man far without use and exercise, and it is practice alone that brings the powers of the mind, as well as those of the body, to perfection."

As so frequently happens, however, the disciples of the master very shortly outdid Locke in their assertions of innate equality. In France, for example, Helvetius, in the eighteenth century,

---

[2] See Bohn's Standard Library, *The Philosophical Works of John Locke* (London: George Bell and Sons, 1902), vol. I, sec. 14, p. 35.

expounded the doctrine that all intellects in their original state are equal and the differences which do in fact distinguish men result from their education.

In America, as well as in Europe, the concept of innate equality fell upon fertile soil and soon brought forth revolutionary fruits. For here, the constantly expanding frontier seemed to confirm with each generation the principle that men are to be judged in terms of what they are, by what they demonstrate themselves to be, rather than by the accidents of birth and inheritance.

It was for this reason that the committee which the Continental Congress charged with the responsibility of preparing the Declaration of Independence—Thomas Jefferson, Benjamin Franklin, John Adams, Robert Livingston, and Robert Sherman—knew full well it was appealing to commonly held sentiments when it put forth the twofold doctrine that all men are created equal and that one important function of government is to secure for them the enjoyment of the rights which derive from equality. Nor is it strange that throughout our history, reformers have consistently appealed to government to provide the conditions that make for equality.

Plural Sources of the Doctrine of Equality

It would be a mistake, however, to assume that the principle of equality, as Americans have both conceived it and applied it, is grounded exclusively in John Locke's theory of the mind as analogous at birth to a white sheet of paper upon which experience is to write. Equally potent has been precisely the opposite assumption, namely, that men are originally endowed by their Creator with an infinite worthiness. Emerson gives expression to this view in his well-known definition of reform in his essay on *Man the Reformer.* "The power, which is at once spring and regulator in all efforts at reform," he writes, "is the conviction that there is an infinite worthiness in man which will appear at the call of worth, and that all particular reforms are the removing of some impediment." [3]

But how should we conceive of this infinite worthiness? As

[3] *The Prose Works of Ralph Waldo Emerson* (Boston: Fields, Osgood and Company, 1870), vol. I, p. 135.

essentially alike in all to be developed through essentially similar means or as a uniqueness or distinctiveness calling for infinitely varied instrumentalities of development?

The answer which Emerson gave was clear. "To thyself be true"; and being true meant having the courage to develop one's individuality and to follow one's own reason, irrespective of whether or not the world was in agreement. Freedom, he wrote in his journal in 1834, is rooted in the sacred truth that "every man hath in him the divine reason," and, although few have lived according to its dictates, all "are created capable of so doing. That is the equality and the only equality of all men." With respect to the state, its only interest "is persons; . . . the highest end of government is the culture of men." [4]

What this might imply in the way of the education of a young person is suggested in Emerson's poem on *Culture.*

> Can rulers or tutors educate
> The semigod whom we await?
> He must be musical,
> Tremulous, impressional
> Alive to gentle influence
> Of landscape and of sky,
> And tender to the spirit-touch
> Of man's or maiden's eye:
> But, to his native centre fast,
> Shall into Future fuse the Past,
> And the world's flowing fates in his own mould recast.[5]

This, however, was too strong a medicine for the educators of the period, even for those who, in their own minds, were dedicated to the task of eliciting the worth which they posited within the soul of each child.

For example, Froebel, the founder of the kindergarten, and his American followers likewise saw in each child a replica of the Infinite Spirit, a divine spark which defined his original nature. This elicited their reverence and respect and dictated to them the methods they should employ in order to transform the spark into

---

[4] See Edman, *op. cit.,* p. 147.

[5] *The Complete Poetical Works of Ralph Waldo Emerson* (Boston: Houghton Mifflin Co, 1910), p. 273.

a steady flame. Or, to change the analogy, just as the successful gardener adapts soil and moisture and light to the nature of the plant, so the educator and the parent were to take as their cue the nature of the child and the laws of his development. Materials and methods thus became instrumental to the major purposes of education, the spiritual growth of the child.

Following the lead of the child, however, was in no way identical with a hands-off policy. On the contrary, it imposed a heavy obligation upon child and adult alike, since both were required to regulate their activities so as to bring to fruition the full promise of child nature. Discipline, materials of instruction, methods of teaching, all the instrumentalities of education, were thus subordinated to the supreme end of education, the spiritual development of the individual.

Inspiring as this program was in its beginnings, it suffered eventually from its assumption that the spiritual potentialities within the child are reflections of a spiritual unity. The curriculum it developed soon became rigid and formal, leaving little room for individual differences. Thus, although the movement drew attention to childhood as a distinctive stage of development, with its own criteria for education, in contrast with the earlier tendency to consider children merely as adults in miniature, it did little to transform the conventional notion that schooling should properly be identical for all.

Not until the end of the nineteenth century do we find educators giving serious consideration to the significance of uniqueness of personality, or, to use the jargon of the educator, individual differences.

One of the first of these was Felix Adler, a pioneer in the establishment of the kindergarten in the United States and the founder of a school in New York, in 1878, dedicated to what he termed the "creative principle" in education.

Adler, too, grounded his educational philosophy in the metaphysical assumption of an original uniqueness in people. Just as in the empirical world each individual is demonstrably different in essential respects from his fellows, so he is also unique as a member of a spiritual universe, of which the empirical is merely a reflection. Moreover, to Adler, healthy development, individual and social, consists in each one fostering this uniqueness through mutually stimulating and creative relations with others. He enjoined his fellows to act in such a manner as to further the distinctive expression of others and thereby further their own distinctive expression.

This conception obligates the educator to search for the unique potentiality within each individual, to observe the inner life of the child as well as his outer behavior. Moreover, all acts of discipline, as all educational materials and methods, are evaluated in terms of their effects upon personality. It dictates a subordination of the professional activity of the teacher and the functions of parenthood to an overarching ideal at once individual and social, an ideal of equality predicated upon widening the opportunities for the expression and development of differences as well as identities.

Needless to say, this conception of equality which is grounded in an assumption of primary differences among people is fraught with significance in a society that is essentially characterized by heterogeneity rather than homogeneity.

It appears that the principle of equality in education, as in other relationships of life, has served as a guiding light for reformers who have nevertheless grounded their convictions in quite different metaphysical, even theological, premises. Nor would our description be complete without calling attention to the fact that still others, who accept and live by the principle of equality, see no impelling reason for grounding it either in philosophy or religion. For example, Sidney Hook, writing as a pragmatist, contends that democracy, together with its concept of equality, can be demonstrated as superior to other forms of government by pointing to its results, to the qualities of relationships which it yields in contrast with the qualities fostered by a nondemocratic society. By and large and in the long run, Hook would hold, there is no more convincing criterion than, "By their fruits ye shall know them."

What are these fruits?

In contrast with inequality, the application of the principle of equality yields "a maximum of creative voluntary effort from all members of a community . . . and a maximum of intelligent loyalty." It furthers an enlargement of "the scope of our experience by enabling us to acquire insight into the needs, drives, and aspirations of others. . . . In aiding the growth of others, we aid our own growth." It makes for "less cruelty of man toward man especially where cruelty is the result of blindness to, or ignorance of, other needs." It encourages "the widest forms of mutual consultation and communication" in resolving conflicts and interests.[6]

Without attempting to mediate among these different methods of validating or justifying the principle of equality (whether in terms of the consequences of its application in a democratic society or by means of metaphysical and theological presuppositions respecting the original nature of man), it is evident that the concept of equality is both flexible and plural in its applications. In one set of circumstances, it implies identical treatment for all. In another, it implies not only the right to be different but conscious provision for the exercise of this right. "It is not," to quote Hook once more, "a policy of restricting the freedom of being different or becoming different." Rather is it, "a policy of *encouraging* the freedom to be different, restricting only that exercise of freedom which converts talents or possessions into a monopoly that frustrates the emergence of other free personalities."

Finally, equality implies a fundamental respect for personality and a realization of the fact that since personality is a growing and ever changing pattern, one must be ever on the alert in a changing society to insure conditions that are favorable to the growth of personal integrity.

So much for the assumption "that all men are created equal" as applied to education. What this has led to in actual practice, we shall observe in a moment. But first, let us recall the second basic affirmation in the Declaration of Independence: the assertion that "governments are instituted among men" to insure the realization of rights which derive from equality.

This would seem to assign to government a never ending task of adjustment and readjustment in a society characterized by change. From a review of American education, we may conclude that there has been steady progress in the direction of equalizing the opportunities of education, although much remains to be done before the goal is reached.

---

[6] See "The Philosophical Presuppositions of Democracy," *Ethics*, April, 1942, pp. 275–296.

The Road to Equality Hath No Ending

Efforts at equalizing educational opportunity have consistently encountered prior assumptions of inequality as natural and normal, assumptions that time and circumstance have firmly established in the warp and woof of daily practice. Distinctions of class, for example, received conspicuous attention in our early schools, from infant school through college. Thus, when John Adams was a student at Harvard, classes were graded according to the social standing of the student's family rather than academic ability. Consequently, if one were the son of a governor, or a judge, or a prominent minister, he was ranked first and assigned the best room in the hall, the upper seat at the table, the first place in academic processions, and the privilege of helping himself first at the commons.[7] Need we add, as well, the attention of the professor?

Tuition charges for education necessarily constituted a barrier which children of the poor could not surmount. With the institution of scholarship grants and the establishment of charity schools for young people willing to be labeled objects of charity, the doors of opportunity were opened slightly. Not until the advent of free schools, which all might attend as a matter of right, do we observe the principle of equality bringing about significant change. Nor was it a matter of accident that the movement on behalf of free schools gained little momentum until the period of Jacksonian democracy with its "leveling tendencies." Finally, with the passage of compulsory school attendance laws, the benefits of an education were extended to all children, even in opposition, if need be, to parental will.

With each step in this development, the adoption of one measure designed to enlarge educational opportunity has revealed the necessity of still further change in order to insure its fuller realization. Thus to free instruction, we find added, in the course of time, free textbooks, free materials of instruction, free lunches, free transportation, etc., all designed to offset limitations beyond the control of the recipient. Similarly, as we move up the educational ladder into college and graduate school, we encounter plans and programs designed to keep open the road to advancement for all

---

[7] Catherine Drinker Bowen, *John Adams and the American Revolution* (Boston: Little, Brown & Co., 1950), p. 78.

who demonstrate not only the ability and willingness to progress but for all those whose talents are recognized as potential contributions to society. Indeed, a growing recognition today of an impending shortage of personnel and an increasing inability to man the strategic positions in our society—the classrooms of our schools, scientific research, positions in business and the professions which call for a high degree of technical proficiency—have introduced a note of urgency in plans for widening still further opportunities in education.

These steps, however, may be classified as primarily administrative in character. The gradual enrichment and diversification of the curriculum in school and college with an eye to serving a student body ever more diversified in composition are, of course, efforts in the same direction. Up to the present, a major emphasis in curriculum development, as in other provisions for differences in ability and interest, has been largely that of ministering to the underprivileged—the underprivileged economically and the underprivileged in terms of academic neglect. This has been true to such an extent that critics of American education often charge that our schools have become keyed to the mediocre and thus deny to the able their educational birthright.

Must Provision for Equality Sacrifice Talent?

An increasing number of American educators, as well as the lay public, are prone to agree with this conclusion, if we may judge from recent lay and professional writing. We may expect this criticism to increase in volume as the need for talent becomes more acute.

One of the most able of these critics is I. L. Kandel, Professor Emeritus of Education, Teachers College, Columbia University. Kandel believes that educators, in their eagerness to provide equality of opportunity for all American youth, have made the fatal error of identifying equality of opportunity with identity of education. Consequently, the problem now is how to avoid the cult of mediocrity, or a "colorless mean," as the Harvard Report on *General Education in a Free Society* of a few years ago describes it.[8]

According to Kandel, a number of factors have contributed to

---

[8] For Kandel's criticism, see "Some Unsolved Issues in American Education," *The Educational Forum*, March, 1956, pp. 269–278.

this unfortunate interpretation of equality. One is the notion that "it is undemocratic to attempt to distinguish between pupils of different abilities, as though intellectual ability can be defined in the same terms as political equality." Another is the transformation of an administrative device, the device of educational equivalents, into a policy of "educational egalitarianism."

The Committee of Ten in 1895 and the Committee on College Entrance Requirements in 1899 adopted the principle of educational equivalents among those subjects recognized as legitimate for admission to college. According to this principle or formula, two subjects, let us say mathematics and Latin, which a student pursues for the same length of time and in class periods of equal length are to be accepted by admission officers of college as of equal value. Originally, this equating of values for accounting purposes was extended only to a limited number of subjects, and insofar as colleges and universities of today still use this formula, it applies only to a restricted number of subjects. With the expansion of our educational system, however, educators soon came to apply the formula without restriction for graduation from secondary schools. "Equality of educational opportunity could now be assured by the acceptance of the notion of the equality of all subjects that any group of students might think that they wanted."

This procedure received reinforcement, Kandel continues, by a similar misinterpretation of the results of experiments on "transfer of training." These experiments indicated "that transfer of training, so long used as an argument for retaining the traditional subjects, did not take place automatically but that it did take place if there were present certain identities between two subjects or situations." Ignoring this important qualification, educators have assumed that the doctrine of formal discipline is exploded and have proceeded to organize curricula on the theory that "all subjects—old and new or to be added as students wanted them—were of equal educational value."

Finally, the adoption of the concept of functional values has completed this tragedy of errors. According to this notion, "it doesn't matter what a pupil studies, so long as he likes it."

As a result of these trends, some 300 different courses are now offered in the high schools of the country and there has been an unfortunate "shift of emphasis from the traditional studies to more practical and functional subjects without any justification in terms of educational values."

In thus democratizing the curriculum, continues Kandel, our schools have not only deprived gifted students of a type of education appropriate to their abilities, but they have failed to meet the grave shortage of personnel now evident in the fields of science and mathematics.

Kandel, in common with some other critics of the curriculum of secondary schools of today, believes that we shall continue to waste talent unless or until the schools return to the "traditional subjects." Others, equally impressed with the failure of our schools to meet contemporary demands, not merely for engineers and scientists, but in the humanities and social sciences as well, doubt that this spells a return to a curriculum essentially common to all. They also sense a grave danger in the tendency to identify the gifted student with one type of mind, the academically gifted. If we assume that the gifted students of today are to be the leaders in the increasingly complex society of tomorrow, it is highly important for us to recognize that leadership will demand plural abilities and that it is highly diversified, not singular or uniform in character. Consequently, it calls for an education and a training of many types of minds in many different fields. Moreover, it is hazardous to assume, without careful prior investigation, that subjects of study which served the "gifted" in the simpler and less complex society of yesterday remain an infallible preparation appropriate for the education of the gifted of today.

These skeptics also question the wisdom of a return to the doctrine of formal discipline which underlies the faith of Kandel and his fellow critics in the supremacy of the traditional subjects as well as their out-of-hand rejection of the concept of functional values. We shall return to the doctrine of formal discipline in a later chapter because of the central position it continues to occupy in the minds of an influential school of contemporary educators. It is appropriate, however, to point out here that the evidence of transfer to which Kandel points in the quotation above justifies neither the conclusion he deplores nor his own disdain of functional education. That is to say, the fact that experiments early in the century demonstrated that transfer of training "did not take place automatically but that it did take place if there were present certain identities between two subjects or situations" tells us very little about the facts of transfer, until we know what creates the identities. The obvious fact that an experience which contains the identities essential for transfer of training for one individual will lack these identities for another suggests that what are termed identities are not self-contained and self-sufficient items of existence but are rather qualities of relationship. If so, the identification of the student with the subject studied, or his lack of identification with it, may be the all-important factor in determining whether or not learning will take place! This, of course, does not justify the conclusion that all subjects are of equal value provided only that a student likes them equally well. But neither does it warrant a return to the one-track curriculum of traditional education.

These reservations with respect to the criticism which Kandel and others have leveled at the curriculum of the schools should not, however, blind us to what is valid in their indictment. They are doubtless correct in the charge that in our efforts to provide an education for all American youth, that is to bring into the school and to retain in the school the underprivileged and the handicapped, we have failed to develop a curriculum keyed not only to our ablest minds, howsoever we may conceive of "able," but relevant as well to rapid transformations in the society in which these young people must shortly work out their destinies.

Educators are now beginning to question, for example, whether either the curriculum of the typical elementary school or that of the typical secondary school provides our young people with an adequate preparation for successful participation in the technological society of today. Competition with Russia, for example, is becoming ever more keen in spheres of activity where scientific training is one of the factors determining success or failure. Nevertheless, there is increasing evidence that both in numbers and in scientific preparation the youth of Russia have the lead over American youth. According to a report issued by the Office of Education in November, 1957, on *Education in the U.S.S.R.*, Russian children receive more hours of formal instruction in their ten years of elementary and secondary school attendance than American children receive in twelve years. Moreover, all Russian pupils begin the study of basic sciences and of foreign languages in elementary school and continue through high school.

Competition on the international front of a character relatively novel for the American people is by no means the only reason why educators should question the appropriateness of the conventional curriculum. The implications of change in our domestic economy are equally demanding. As Sumner H. Slichter, the economist, has pointed out, impressive changes have taken place in American economic and social life in recent years "that have escaped general attention because they have been occurring so gradually." He refers particularly to the increase in middle-class occupations. "In 1910 the workers in these occupations constituted 39.6 per cent of employed persons; in April, 1956, they formed 45.8 per cent— in spite of a big drop in the number of self-employed farmers from 17.3 per cent of employed persons in 1910 to 6.1 per cent in April, 1956." [9] Significant for education, in this connection, is the increase in occupations that are related to science and mathematics. In 1900, for example, there was no cost accounting in American business. Consequently, there were but 250 C.P.A.'s in the entire country. By 1956, there were 40,000. Engineers increased from 41,000 in 1900 to 850,000 in 1956. The emergence of what Slichter terms an "industry of discovery" is even more conspicuous. Industrial research now employs over 200,000 research scientists and technologists, a number that is increasing "just as rapidly as the colleges and universities can turn out trained men."

By an "industry of discovery," Slichter means research devoted particularly to the discovery of new products and new areas of investment and expansion in industry. According to Slichter, this is one of the most rapidly growing industries in the country. In 1930, he states, industry spent $116 million on research and development, in 1940, $235 million, and in 1953 about $1.5 billion. "Outlays on research and development," he adds, "would grow even faster were they not limited by the shortage of engineers and scientists." [10]

Automation in industry is a further factor of significance for education, since it is bringing about the elimination of unskilled labor. Thus the number of common laborers dropped from 8.9 million in 1910 to 5.9 million in 1956, and from one-fourth of all employed persons to one-eleventh. [11]

[9] Sumner H. Slichter, "The Growth of Moderation," *Atlantic Monthly,* October, 1956, p. 61.

[10] Sumner H. Slichter, "The Passing of Keynesian Economics," *Atlantic Monthly,* November, 1957, pp. 141–146.

[11] Slichter, "The Growth of Moderation," *op. cit.,* p. 62.

It appears, then, that developments at home as well as abroad render imperative a reappraisal of a number of features of American education if the schools are to insure the advantages to American youth of equal opportunities in education.

Obstacles to Realizing Equality

Kandel's criticism of the curriculum of the secondary school omits the failure of schools to motivate and stimulate a sizable proportion of gifted graduates to continue with their education.

From extensive studies which he and others have conducted on motivation, Robert J. Havighurst concludes "that of the superior fifth of our youth 40 per cent are not sufficiently motivated to go beyond high school, 20 per cent would go if they had financial assistance, and 40 per cent go under present conditions." [12] That is to say, some 60 per cent of our gifted youth, at present, do not go on to receive higher education. Of this group two-thirds fail to go on because they lack motivation and one-third because they lack financial resources! If this be true, and it seems to be substantiated by studies conducted by other investigators, the American secondary school is indeed challenged to examine the quality of its educational program.

It is not entirely fair, however, to charge the schools with sole responsibility for lack of motivation. Factors of socioeconomic status also exercise a decisive influence in a young person's decision to continue or not to continue with his education. For example, Warner, Havighurst, and Loeb [13] suggest that the differentiated curriculum of the secondary school serves often as an index of the socioeconomic status of students within the school community, students of upper socioeconomic status tending to gravitate toward the college preparatory courses and students of lower status toward curricula of a more immediate vocational application. [14]

These findings suggest that socioeconomic status is a determining factor in deciding whether or not young people are to enjoy equal educational opportunities, a factor which the school is none

[12] In Byron S. Hollinshead, *Who Should Go to College?* (New York: Columbia University Press, 1952), p. 162.

[13] W. Lloyd Warner, Robert J. Havighurst, and Martin B. Loeb, *Who Shall Be Educated?* (New York: Harper & Brothers, 1944), pp. 60–61.

[14] *Ibid.*, p. 61.

too successful in counteracting.

Other factors which are outside the direct influence of the school but which bear, nevertheless, upon educational opportunity merit at least brief mention.

Geographical Location Often Handicaps

It is an obvious fact that children born and raised in a "poor" section of the country do not receive educational advantages equal to those afforded children more favorably placed. Indeed, nature seems to have decreed that where economic circumstances are at their worst, children and youth are most plentiful.

For example, if we list the upper quarter of the states of the Union and the District of Columbia on the basis of the least number of children five to seventeen years of age per 1000 of the adult population, aged twenty-one to sixty-four, and, again, the upper quarter of the states on the basis of the estimated income payments per child of school age, we find the groupings include the same states, with the exception of the absence of Ohio and Mary-

TABLE 1

School-Age Children per 1000 Adults Aged 21–64, 1957	Income Payments per Child of School Age (5–17), 1957
303 District of Columbia	$14,308 District of Columbia
367 New York	12,858 Connecticut
384 New Jersey	12,245 Delaware
390 Massachusetts	12,167 New York
397 Rhode Island	11,644 New Jersey
397 Connecticut	11,362 California
406 Illinois	11,084 Massachusetts
409 Pennsylvania	11,034 Illinois
420 Missouri	10,966 Nevada
422 California	9,700 Ohio
426 Delaware	9,502 Pennsylvania
428 Nevada	9,423 Rhode Island
434 Florida	9,073 Maryland

(NOTE: Information is not currently available with regard to income payments per child of school age in Alaska and Hawaii, but the 1957 figures for the number of school-age children per 1,000 adults aged 21–64 are as follows: Hawaii, 869; Alaska, 592.)

SOURCE: *Ranking of the States*, Research Report 1959-R4 (Washington, D.C.: Research Division, National Education Association, April, 1959) pp. 13, 31.

land in the first and of Missouri in the second.

Again, a comparison of the states in the upper quarter, when grouped according to the largest number of children per 1000 of the total population and the lowest income payments per child, yields the following:

TABLE 2

School-Age Children per 1000 Adults Aged 21–64, 1957	Income Payments per Child of School Age (5–17), 1957
656 New Mexico	$3,420 Mississippi
635 South Carolina	4,088 South Carolina
618 Mississippi	4,275 Arkansas
591 Utah	4,800 Alabama
572 Arkansas	4,937 North Carolina
569 Alabama	5,202 Kentucky
562 Georgia	5,332 Georgia
562 Idaho	5,420 Tennessee
559 Louisiana	5,467 North Dakota
557 Arizona	5,805 West Virginia
549 North Carolina	5,851 Louisiana
546 Kentucky	6,004 New Mexico
539 West Virginia	6,029 Idaho

SOURCE: *Ranking of the States,* Research Report 1959-R4 (Washington, D.C.: Research Division, National Education Association, April, 1959) pp. 13, 31.

Here again the two columns are identical except that Arizona and Utah are in the first but not in the second and North Dakota and Tennessee are in the second but not in the first. Were we to group the states of the Union in accordance with their educational expenditures per pupil, we should find, with few exceptions, that the states with the least number of children of school age rank highest in outlay per pupil, and those with the largest number rank lowest.[15]

Perhaps there was a time when the consequences of local and state differences in educational opportunity were chiefly of local and state import. Not so today. Mobility has become more and more characteristic of our people. According to the census,

---

[15] *Ranking of the States,* Research Report 1959-R4 (Washington, D.C.: National Education Association, April, 1959).

8,000,000 children changed residence in the year 1948–1949. Although about two-thirds of these changes occurred within the same county, the number crossing state lines and moving from one section of the country to another is sufficiently large to indicate that what one section of the country sows in the way of the education and the training of its young another commonly reaps. Improved means of transportation and communication are rapidly creating conditions which cause many to believe that the nation as a whole should attempt to equalize educational opportunities for youth on much the same grounds that individual states have attempted to equalize these opportunities within their borders.

Unfortunately, not even the latter holds without exception.

Limitations of Family Income

Family income is a second factor of significance in determining educational opportunity.

Hearings before the Eighty-fifth Congress on a proposed Federal Scholarship and Loan Program did much to acquaint the American public with the extent to which young people of ability are today denied the opportunity to continue with their education upon graduation from high school.[16] For example, to take but one illustration submitted by Commissioner Derthick from a study conducted in 1955, it was concluded that higher education is losing each year between 60,000 and 100,000 highly able secondary school graduates who fail to attend college for financial reasons.[17]

To the extent that there exists a correlation between family income and the educational status of parents, we should expect a

---

[16] A comprehensive summary of studies in this area was presented to the Committee on Education and Labor of the House of Representatives by Lawrence G. Derthick, Commissioner of Education, on February 19, 1958. See *Hearings Before a Sub-Committee of the Committee on Education and Labor on H.R. 10,381, H.R. 10,278 (and Similar Bills) Relating to Educational Programs*, Eighty-Fifth Congress, Second Session (Washington, D.C.: Government Printing Office, 1958), part 2, pp. 808–810.

[17] This study was conducted by Charles C. Cole, assistant dean of Columbia College, Columbia University, and was published in 1956 by the College Entrance Examination Board under the title "Encouraging Scientific Talent: A Study of America's Able Students Who Are Lost to College and Ways of Attracting Them to College and Science Careers."

similar relationship to exist between family income and inducements within the family which play upon the young to advance themselves educationally. Havighurst and Rodgers, for example, inform us that practically all of the superior youth who do not continue with their education beyond high school are children of parents with less than a high school education, that is, children from families which are not accustomed to postponing the earning of money or marriage in favor of a long and costly period of education. They "do not regard college for their children as really within the reach of their aspirations or their financial means." [18]

The Curriculum May Not Serve All Equally

Investigations of the extent to which the school curriculum serves the needs of its pupils likewise suggest that our educational institutions have not succeeded in adapting their work to the needs of all their wards. Thus, in a study of Elmtown, a typical midwestern city, Hollingshead found that the high school provided twenty-three different types of extracurricular activities open to general pupil participation. Despite these seemingly rich opportunities for the expression of interests, one student out of twenty-three failed to participate. It was observed, moreover, that the percentage of participation was "associated very strongly with class position." Interviews with students established clearly a consciousness of a class system within the school and the self-elimination of the lower-class students from social activities because, as one girl remarked, "Well, why go? We're made to feel out of place and that's the way it is." [19]

Social class also affected academic recognition. A comparison of grades assigned to students with intelligent ratings (as determined by the Otis Group Intelligence Test, Advanced Examination: Form A) revealed that membership in a social class was more potent than intelligence in determining the awarding of grades and the assignment of failures.[20]

---

[18] Hollinshead, *op. cit.*, pp. 162 ff.

[19] A. B. Hollingshead, *Elmtown's Youth* (New York: John Wiley & Sons, Inc., 1949). The study is summarized in B. Othanel Smith, William O. Stanley, Kenneth D. Benne, and Archibald W. Anderson, *Readings in the Social Aspects of Education* (Danville, Illinois: Interstate Printers and Publishers, Inc., 1951). Page references in the following footnotes are to the latter.

[20] *Ibid.*, p. 110.

When the Elmtown students were grouped according to intelligence ratings, it was found that they averaged considerably higher than the general population. For example, out of 507 adolescents examined, only 20, or about 4 per cent, were in the 70–90 I.Q. range, in contrast with a country-wide average of 23. Nevertheless, "In so far as Class V was involved" (that is, the lowest socioeconomic group), "only 11 per cent of the adolescents for whom we had scores had an I.Q. below 90, but 89 per cent of those who completed a semester or more of high school failed at least one course." [21]

Elmtown cannot be said to represent all schools, and one should be careful not to generalize too readily from the conclusions of one sociological study. Indeed, there is reason to believe that in many communities class lines are far less rigid than in Elmtown and schools are more democratically disposed to serve all youth. Granting this, it remains a disturbing fact that an impressive number of studies have established a growing consciousness of class distinctions within American communities and of class favoritism sufficiently potent to find expression in the work of the school.

Race, Too, Is a Handicap

Perhaps the most stubborn factor contributing to inequality in education is that of race. Children born of one race are by that fact denied from birth opportunities which invite the young of more fortunate background. Moreover, since these differences are more analogous to differences of caste than of class, their effects are the most difficult to overcome. A conspicuous illustration of this fact is, of course, the resistance not only in the South but in other sections of the country as well to the injunctions of the United States Supreme Court with respect to segregation in education.

It should not be forgotten, however, that the Negro is not the sole victim of segregation. Similar obstacles confront the Indian and the Mexican in the Southwest. In milder form, other racial and national groups are subject to discrimination in various sections of the country, groups such as the Jew, the Italian, the

---

[21] *Ibid.,* p. 113.

Chinese, the Japanese, etc. When discrimination results in blocking opportunities to enter college or professional school, as it often does, or closing certain vocations to members of minority groups, its effects upon the personalities of young people early in their careers can be serious.

Teachers Have Their Limitations

Not all discrimination is conscious. There is evidence to suggest that teachers often find it easier to work with children of the middle and upper classes than with those from the lower class. Methods of discipline, ways of dealing with children in school, the faith and the confidence in the individual which teachers express in their person-to-person relationships, "actions that speak louder than words," are not altogether free from cultural backgrounds and the class distinctions to which these testify.

This is but another way of saying that teachers are predominantly of middle-class origin and are emotionally identified with the values and customs and the morals and manners of the upper and middle-class segments of society. As a result, they find it difficult to deal objectively and unemotionally with the child or adolescent behavior that runs counter to their accustomed and cherished ways. It is not always easy, in short, to temper the wind to the shorn lamb.[22]

Obviously, the difficulties teachers encounter in their training continue to operate later in the practice of their profession. Differences in manners and customs, habits of cleanliness, methods of speaking to and addressing one another, and characteristics of a member of an "out-group" are often as emotionally disturbing as are the more serious violations of moral standards by a likable and "personable" member of an "in-group." Consequently, where experience and training have not conditioned a middle-class teacher to the normal behavior of the lower-class child, in a community where class lines are fairly rigidly defined, the latter is usually at a disadvantage, even though the teacher be unconscious of either prejudice or willful discrimination.

---

[22] For an excellent discussion of the American teacher in this connection, see Lindley J. Stiles (ed.), *The Teacher's Role in American Society* (New York: Harper & Brothers, 1957), chaps. 1–5.

Teachers are not alone in their failure to understand. There is some evidence to suggest that the "objective instruments" of the educational scientists are not altogether free of class influence. As Allison Davis has pointed out:

> Recent research indicates that many slum children who do poorly in school and on present intelligence tests have higher real (or native) intelligence than many individuals whose home training enables them to do well on school-types of learning. Thus to measure real intelligence we need tests which will not be based primarily upon school-training and school problems.
>
> The previous test-makers have felt that the quickest way to predict a person's chances for success in school or college was to test him with school-type problems—not with exactly the same problems which he had studied in school, but with problems very similar to school problems, and whose solution was greatly aided by school training. The result has been to make the tests useless for measuring real intelligence in the lower socio-economic groups. "Identical" twins have exactly the same hereditary (innate) intelligence. Yet on the present tests, as Professors Newman, Freeman, and Holzinger found at the University of Chicago some years ago, identical twins show a marked difference in their "I.Q.'s" whenever one twin has been reared in a well-to-do home, and his identical twin has been reared in a working family. . . . Thus the best scientific test has made it clear that the differences in schooling and social environment between the middle and lower socio-economic groups account for the difference between their average "I.Q.'s" on the present tests.[23]

Davis shows further that when "cultural bias" is removed from the test questions, a "startling increase in the intelligence-rating of the lower socio-economic group resulted." These conclusions are of great significance when we recall the reliance widely given to the prognostic value of intelligence tests and the not uncommon inference that a close correlation exists between intelligence and economic and social status.

These sober afterthoughts with respect to the value and the use of intelligence tests in education throw light upon the lack of appeal in the conventional curriculum for many young people in the lower economic and social levels of society. We are becoming increasingly sensitive to the fact that much of the subject matter and content of the curriculum is foreign to the experience of

---

[23] "Education for the Conservation of the Human Resources of the United States," *Progressive Education,* May, 1950, pp. 221–226.

the lower-class children and they require a reinterpretation, if not a reorganization, in order to yield the richest educational fruit.

It seems fair to conclude that both in concept and in applica- tion much remains to be done if Americans are to assure all their youth a full realization of the blessings of "life, liberty and the pursuit of happiness" insofar as these are attainable through edu- cation.[24]

Suggested Reading

American Association of School Administrators, *The High School in a Changing World* (Washington, D.C.: The National Education As- sociation, 1958).

Butts, R. Freeman and Lawrence A. Cremin, *A History of Education in American Culture* (New York: Henry Holt & Co., 1953), chap. 7.

Conant, James B., *The American High School Today* (New York: McGraw-Hill Book Co., 1959), Section I.

Cook, Lloyd Allan and Elaine Forsyth Cook, *A Sociological Approach to Education* (New York: McGraw-Hill Book Co., 1950), chap. 11.

Edman, Irwin, *Fountainheads of Freedom* (New York: Reynal and Hitchcock, 1941), chap. VI.

Hechinger, Fred M. *The Big Red Schoolhouse* (Garden City, N.Y.: Doubleday Book Co., Inc., 1959), chap. 6.

Hollinshead, Byron S. *Who Should Go to College?* (New York: Colum- bia University Press, 1952), chap. VI

Hook, Sidney, "The Philosophical Presuppositions of Democracy," *Ethics*, April, 1942, pp. 275–296.

Stiles, Lindley J. (ed.), *The Teacher's Role in American Society* (New York: Harper & Brothers, 1957), chaps. 1–5.

Warner, W. Lloyd, *American Life: Dream and Reality* (Chicago: Uni- versity of Chicago Press, 1953), chaps. II, IV, VIII.

---

[24] To the factors mentioned above that make for inequality in education, we should add the disadvantages which presently follow upon the shortage of ade- quately trained teachers. Ironically, this accentuates the disadvantages which al- ready beset underprivileged communities and small school systems; since higher salaries and more favorable working conditions elsewhere tend to siphon off the more competent teachers. In his recent volume on *The Big Red Schoolhouse* (p. 137), Fred M. Hechinger estimates that of all high school graduates today, over 100,000 annually have had no opportunity to study either physics or chemistry, simply because they attended schools in which these subjects are not offered. There is probably no way of estimating the number of young people who are at present receiving inferior instruction in these subjects, and others as well, by virtue of the fact that their teachers are themselves the victims of inadequate, and, all too often, no prior preparation for the responsibilities they are asked to assume.

PART II

Changes in the Economic

and Social Status of Youth

/\\./\\./\\.\\

/\/\.\/\.\/\.\/\

6

Youth and the World's Work

The Changing Status of Youth

The twentieth century has thus far dealt none too kindly with American youth. Growing into man's estate has involved coping with both difficult and contradictory circumstances. The second decade exposed them to the influences of World War I. Then followed the ups and downs of the 1920's, with their illusions of prosperity and their cynical reaction to the naive idealism of a war that had been fought with the intention of making the world safe for democracy, but which seemed, instead, to have prepared the ground for the seeds of Fascism and Communism. On the heels of the 1920's came the depression of the 1930's, which experts interpreted as marking a permanent leveling off of the productive capacities of the nation and a narrowing of opportunities for the economic future of the young. In this decade the graduates of colleges and technical institutions commonly referred to themselves as members of a lost generation, since their skills and professional competence seemed destined to lie fallow. Indeed, did not the studies of the American Youth Commission provide convincing evidence of the steady exclusion of young people under twenty from occupations other than those of a blind alley character? And were not educators enjoined, in consequence, to provide substitutes for the one-time economic participation of children and youth in the world's work, lest the United States follow in the footsteps of Germany and reap the fruits of frustration and despair that were rapidly mounting in the hearts and minds of an educated and professionally trained but unemployed generation?

World War II transformed all this. Young men and women once more became indispensable. Schools and colleges were rapidly deserted for service in the armed forces or work in defense plants. The deferred values of the classroom were unable to compete with the appeals to patriotism or the lure of high wages in mines, factories, and industrial plants and work on the farm.

The capitulation of Germany and Japan in the mid-1940's seemed, for a time, to have ushered in a new era, uncertain and undefined in its implications for youth, a state of mind, unfortunately, confirmed by the cold war that quickly followed. Discussions of war and the rumors of war, air raid and atomic bomb drills, the ever present possibility that education in school and college might be interrupted by the draft or that marriage and family life might be postponed indefinitely unless entered into hastily, doubt respecting the stability of economic conditions and what this might portend for those eager to enter upon a career all remain to perpetuate tension and strain and to disturb what should be a calm and secure passage from childhood into adolescence and from adolescence into adulthood.

We are living in a period when influences of deep import for education are difficult to foresee or to control when foreseen. Nevertheless there are a number of trends in American life that have been operating with a fair degree of consistency for some decades and which carry their moral for education in school and college.

Old Age Competes with Youth

First is the changing ratio of young to old.

In 1850 the population under eighteen years of age was approximately equal to that between the years of twenty and sixty-nine. That is, for each 1000 adults between the ages of twenty and sixty-nine, there were 1000 young people under eighteen. By 1950, despite the rise in the birth rate in the 1940's, the percentage of children under twenty stood at no more than 35.8 per cent of the total population.[1]

---

[1] The statistical data presented in this chapter are drawn primarily from the following: *Recent Social Trends in the United States* (New York: McGraw-Hill Book

One of the surprises in the 1950's has been the continued rise in the birth rate, which authorities assumed would fall off with the conclusion of World War II and the cessation of hostilities in Korea. This, however, has not occurred. In 1956, for example, the per cent of change over 1955 was +3.2 per cent. Consequently, it is hazardous to predict the future with too great assurance. Equally impressive, however, is the apparent tendency for older people to become an increasing proportion of the population. Thus, advances made in the prolongation of life in recent years prevented the 13 per cent increase in the child population in the decade 1940–1950 from exceeding the increase in the adult population of 14 per cent.[2]

Of particular significance in this connection is the size of the group sixty-five years of age and above in proportion to that of others. This shows more than a tenfold increase between 1850 and 1930 compared with a fivefold increase in the population as a whole, and a fourfold increase since 1890. According to the monthly statistical bulletin of the Health Information Foundation of June, 1956, the population sixty-five and above increased from about 3 million in 1900 to more than 14 million in 1956. It is anticipated that by 1975 there will be 21 million Americans of sixty-five years and older.[3]

These data indicate that we are rapidly becoming a middle-aged and old population, in striking contrast with the situation that obtained when Americans laid the foundations of their government with its friendly and optimistic attitude toward the future. For example, in 1790 there were 1000 children for every 780 adults; whereas, according to present estimates, by 1970 the number of people between the ages of twenty and sixty-four will constitute 63 per cent of the population. (Should the present

---

Co., 1933); *The Effect of Population Changes on American Education* (Washington, D.C.: Educational Policies Commission, National Education Association, 1938); *Schools and the 1950 Census* (Washington, D.C.: National Education Association, 1951), Research Bulletin, vol. XXIX, no. 4; *The Postwar Struggle to Provide Competent Teachers* (Washington, D.C.: National Education Association, October, 1957), Research Bulletin, vol. XXXV, no. 3; and a paper presented at the Mid-century White House Conference on Children and Youth by Paul C. Glick, Chief, Social Statistics Section, Population and Housing Division, Bureau of the Census, entitled, "Population Changes: Their Effect on Children and Youth," December, 1950.

[2] See *The Postwar Struggle to Provide Competent Teachers, op. cit.,* p. 106, and *Schools and the 1950 Census, op. cit.,* p. 145.

[3] Summarized in *The New York Times,* June 24, 1956.

fertility rates continue until 1975, however, this may be reduced to about 52 per cent.)

As we have indicated, the fairly consistent rise in the fertility rate since 1940 weakens the reliability of prediction with respect to the future. On the long view, however, the increase in the proportion of old and middle-aged in our population is marked by a fairly consistent shrinkage in the proportion of the young. Consider, for example, the consistency with which the median age has risen. In 1850, this was 18.8 years; in 1930, 26.4; in 1950, 30.1.[4]

Influences Upon the Climate of Opinion

What implications have these data for education?

For one thing, they bear directly upon the extent to which our people are ready and willing, as well as able, to finance public education. Schools are rapidly encountering a rival in old age pensions and other necessary provisions for the security and the welfare of the population sixty years and above. As the number in this age group increases in proportion to that of the population as a whole, so will the problem of an equitable distribution of public funds in support of young and old become more acute. Already, in some states, commitments to the aged have led to the curtailment of appropriations for education and other social services. To meet the legitimate needs of young and old alike, in addition to the requirements of defense for an indefinite future, calls for a quality of statesmanship and foresight evidenced only too infrequently in the days of comparative abundance.

Equally significant is the intellectual and moral climate in which education is to carry on. Traditionally, as we have seen, Americans have welcomed change. Their attitude toward the future has been youthful, as well it might be in a predominantly young population. And at the time of the adoption of the Constitution with its Bill of Rights, the population was young in contrast with the situation of today. A middle-aged and old population is less disposed to venture far from the shore unless the wind is promising and the waters calm. Today, unfortunately, the winds of dangerous doctrines are sweeping rapidly over large sec-

---

[4] *Schools and the 1950 Census, op. cit.,* p. 145.

tions of the globe, threatening to weaken, if not to destroy, the traditional framework of our society. Take these two facts alone —competition between the ideologies of a free society and collectivism and the increasing dominance of the old in the population—and we can understand the concern with which many are scrutinizing the ideas which educators may be "planting" in the minds of the young. Wild oats in the form of ideas are viewed with alarm.

Moreover, the decreasing proportion of the young and the competition this engenders between old and young for status in social and economic areas give rise to a contradictory attitude on the part of the former toward the latter. The individual parent or guardian tends to manifest a sensitive concern for the well-being of his own children and their associates. That is to say, as children decrease in numbers provision for their healthy growth and development, physical and mental, receives increasing emphasis. Children are thus accorded a unique place and are dealt with in a manner strikingly different from the days in which they were thought to be possessed of an evil nature that required purging. On the other hand, young people *in general* constitute a "youth problem," an element in the community to be viewed with apprehension, if not fear. This, too, is one reason for a popular concern regarding the nature of the instruction received in school and college, just as it is an explanation, in part, for the support given to groups bent upon convincing the public that "progressive education increases delinquency" or that our schools are being used to undermine "free enterprise" at a time when they should be used, as one critic insists, to instill "traditions which are not subject to re-examination."

It should be pointed out, before concluding this section, that the ratio of young to old is not uniform throughout the country. Indeed, the percentage of young people of school age is highest where the financial resources of the state and community are lowest. For example, "24 per cent of minor children live in the densely populated Northeastern states, 29 per cent in the industrial and agricultural Middle West, 35 per cent in the South— with its declining dependence on agriculture, and 13 per cent in the fast-growing West." [5]

---

[5] Glick, *op. cit.*

These facts, taken with the facts of mobility of population, bear directly upon the problem of financing education in such a way that children will not suffer unduly from place of birth and residence, or from the fact that standards in one section of the country are weakened by the inability of another to provide the essentials of an education.

Consider, for example, the implications of the fact that the diffusion of nonwhites from the South to other sections of the country between 1940 and 1950 was so great that there were 50 per cent more nonwhites in the North and the West in 1950 than in 1940.

Nor is this exodus confined to nonwhites, who may be seeking more favorable conditions of living for themselves and their children. It applies as well to white youth who are migrating from the rural sections of the South to urban centers in the North in numbers so large as to render acute the economic difficulties of the section from which they come and to generate severe problems of adjustment in the communities in which they are seeking to establish a foothold.

Youth's Diminishing Economic Role

A second trend has to do with youth's diminishing economic role in contemporary society.

As we have seen, the proportion of the population below the age of twenty has steadily shrunk since the founding of the Republic. Paralleling this trend has been a transformation in our conceptions of the nature of children and adolescents. Children were once viewed as little adults. Observe, for example, the pictures of colonial children. As S. C. Parker points out, children are represented "by apparent maturity in dress, expression, and gesture. Either children were so trained and dressed that they actually did appear like miniature adults, or the artist's conception of the child as an adult prevented him from seeing the real child." [6] Alice M. Earle writes of Dolly Payne, later the wife of James Madison, that "she wore long gloves, a linen mask, and had a sun

---

[6] S. C. Parker, *The History of Modern Elementary Education* (Boston: Ginn & Company, 1912), pp. 171–172.

bonnet sewed on her head every morning by her devoted mother."
And she also states that sometimes little girls five years old were
bound up in stays "made of heavy strips of board and steel,
tightly wrought with heavy buckram or canvas into an iron frame
like an instrument of torture." Nor did boys fare much better.
"Little boys five to seven years of age had their heads shaved and
wore wigs." [7]

Compare these practices with the ease and freedom and comfort assured both girls and boys today, as they romp about in
warm weather in little more than loin cloth! Or the thought and
attention now given to children's needs, physical, intellectual, and
social, at different stages of their development.

S. C. Parker and Alice M. Earle were describing the status of
children in the upper classes. Children of laborers were likewise
conceived of as adults in miniature and were assigned hard tasks
with long hours. Nor was schooling an exception. Edgar W.
Knight reminds us that the school day, in the colonial period, was
unusually long. In some communities it was from seven o'clock
in the morning until five in the afternoon in the spring and summer and from eight to four from August to December. In New
Haven, in 1684, the school was in session nine hours each day
for six days each week in the summer, but for a somewhat shorter
period in the winter.

Nor were the hours of intermission uniformly available for
recreation. In New England, especially on Mondays, the middle
of the day was often used to examine children on the contents of
the sermon heard on Sunday and "to enable the master to take
notice of any mischief which the children may have been guilty
of on the Sabbath." [8]

As the economic value of children has decreased, their intrinsic
value seems to have increased. No longer are they conceived of as
little adults. On the contrary, childhood and adolescence are
commonly recognized as unique periods of development, each
with its distinctive characteristics and needs, which are to be
observed and ministered to properly if a healthy personality is to
ensue.

Here, again, a few statistics will help us to appreciate changes

---

[7] Alice M. Earle, *Child Life in Colonial Days* (New York: The Macmillan Company).
[8] *Education in the United States* (Boston: Ginn & Company, 1929), pp. 123–124.

that have taken place in the status of young people in American society and the implications of these changes for education.

Between 1890 and 1940 the total number of people in the labor market increased 127 per cent, but of those under twenty years of age the increase amounted to only 16 per cent of boys between the ages of fourteen and nineteen. At the beginning of the century, 60 per cent of the boys between the ages of fourteen and nineteen were employed, by 1930 the percentage had shrunk to 40 per cent and by 1950 to approximately 35 per cent.

The decade 1940 to 1950 altered somewhat the employment picture for young people. The demands of the war effort led to an exodus from school of large numbers above the age of fourteen and stimulated the part-time employment of many who continued in school. Consequently, the employment ratio for boys between the ages of fourteen and nineteen rose once again, reaching 42.6 per cent in 1946, only to recede again in 1950.

According to the census of 1950, 9 million or 60 per cent of 15 million youth between the ages of fourteen and twenty were in school. About 2½ million youth between fourteen and twenty years of age were neither attending school nor enrolled in the labor force, which left about 3½ million in the labor force. Again, only 1 in 25 children in the fourteen- to fifteen-year-old group in 1950 had left school to secure employment, although many in school held part-time jobs. In the eighteen- to nineteen-year-old bracket, one-fourth were still in school, one-half were out of school and employed, and the remaining one-fourth were neither in school nor employed.[9]

The decade 1940–1950, as we have seen, afforded a striking contrast to the depression years of 1930–1940. Despite this fact, the long-time trend in economic life points to the progressive exclusion of young people under twenty from participation in gainful occupations. Thus, "for boys ten to fifteen, the per cent employed fell from 26 per cent in 1890 to a little more than 6 per cent in 1930; for girls of the same ages, from 10 per cent to 3 per cent in the same period."[10] Nor do employment conditions

---

[9] Glick, *op. cit.*

[10] Since 1930 the census has not included statistics bearing on the employment of children below twelve. However, in 1950, an effort was made to secure data on the employment of children between the ages of ten through thirteen for the Bureau of Labor Standards of the U.S. Department of Labor. The results of this study are

for individuals under twenty give assurance of permanency or regularity. "Even in good times," states the Working Committee on Statistics for the Midcentury Conference on Children and Youth, "unemployment among youth is higher than among adults. . . . In bad times young people are at even greater disadvantage. Like other 'marginal' workers, youth are among the last to be hired and the first to be fired."

It is this uncertainty of continued employment, together with the steady rise in the standards of education and skill imposed by business and industry, which prompts labor leaders and government officials to urge young people to continue in school at least until graduation from high school, if they want to hold anything more than a blind alley job.[11]

American youth have pretty well anticipated this advice as is evidenced by the fact that in contrast with the early years of the century, when 60 per cent of all boys between the ages of fourteen and nineteen were employed, today, according to the census of 1950, some 60 per cent of all youth between these ages were in attendance at school or college.

The Shifting Occupational Pattern

One more factor of importance that merits our attention before we seek to draw an educational moral from the data presented is

---

incorporated in a circular issued by the Bureau of Labor Standards, dated January 24, 1951. The following quote is from this circular:

"In October, when boys and girls under fourteen years of age are expected to be in school, 86,000 of these working children ten through thirteen years of age were not enrolled in school. The children out of school were chiefly those in agricultural work (82,000 out of 86,000). Practically all of the children who were out of school and working for pay were employed in agriculture (40,000 out of 42,000).

"The 82,000 young children ten through thirteen years of age engaged in farm work in October who were not enrolled in school were obviously only a part of the total number out of school for the harvest season. It is noted that 178,000 of the young children of these ages working in agriculture worked 35 or more hours a week in that month."

[11] For example, in connection with a national back-to-school campaign in 1957, James P. Mitchell, Secretary of Labor, pointed out that of 71 occupations with shortages of personnel, the minimum educational requirements for all were high school graduation. On the same occasion, George Meany, President of the A.F. of L. and the C.I.O., was quoted as saying, "My advice to American youth is to stay in high school and graduate. The youngster without a high school diploma will find the doors of opportunity closed to him in tomorrow's world of automation and nuclear power." (*The New York Times*, September 8, 1957.)

the shifting occupational pattern and the consequences that follow upon the transition from predominantly agricultural and rural conditions of living to an industrial and urban civilization.

Of the gainfully employed in 1870, 52.8 per cent were farmers. By 1930, this had shrunk to 21.3 per cent. In 1950, only one out of eight of the nation's workmen was an agricultural worker. Moreover, between 1940 and 1950 agricultural workers decreased in number from 8,372,000 to 7,138,000, which suggests that this trend may not as yet have run its course.[12] At present, manufacturing attracts the largest number of workers, with nearly twice the number at present engaged in agriculture, and comprises one-fourth of the entire labor force.[13] Service industries constitute the second largest group, with over 12 million workers. The wholesale and retail trade ranks third, with over 10 million employed.[14]

These occupational shifts bear directly upon opportunities for youth. The transition from agriculture to other types of work carries with it fundamental changes in living conditions. Today, a majority of young people live in urban areas; only 19 per cent live on farms and 23 per cent in rural nonfarm areas (communities of less than 2500 inhabitants). As Paul C. Glick remarks, "The up-shot of these trends is that the lives of an increasing proportion of the children in the country are coming under the influences of the city, with its greater opportunities for stimulation and personal development, as well as a wider range of services for children, but also with its emphasis on a different value system than that prevailing in most of the smaller communities."

Schooling Replaces Work

From the date reviewed, it seems clear that the status of youth in our society has undergone revolutionary changes in the past fifty years. On the one hand, the proportion of young people living under rural conditions and engaged in rural occupations has steadily decreased. On the other hand, in urban areas, where

---

[12] *The Schools and the 1950 Census, op. cit.,* p. 159. According to Sumner H. Slichter, self-employed farmers comprised but 6.1 per cent of all employed persons in April, 1956. (*Atlantic Monthly,* October, 1958, p. 61).

[13] *The Schools and the 1950 Census, op. cit.,* p. 159.

[14] *Ibid.,* p. 159.

employment opportunities were once abundant for young people, employment conditions are relatively unstable and there is a general trend toward the exclusion of young people under twenty from desirable and responsible economic opportunities. More and more, the world's work is being monopolized by age groups above twenty.

To be sure, the data reviewed are country-wide. Both regions and localities within regions vary considerably, as Table 3 indicates, but even in predominantly rural areas the trends reviewed seem to support the inference that the future does not hold either enduring or attractive employment opportunities for the majority of young people under twenty.

TABLE 3

*Per Cent of Increase or Decrease in Urban
and Rural Population, 1940 to 1950*

| Region | Per Cent of Change, 1940 to 1950 [a] | | |
| | Urban Population | Rural Population | Total Population |
1	*2*	*3*	*4*
Northeast	6.8%	17.1%	9.7%
North Central	14.6	4.0	10.8
South	34.8	−0.2	13.3
West	41.2	37.9	40.9
Entire U.S.	18.7%	7.4%	14.5%

[a] Calculated on the basis of a uniform method of classification of communities in 1940 and 1950.

SOURCE: *The Schools and the 1950 Census* (Washington, D.C.: National Education Association, 1951), Research Bulletin, vol. XXIX, no. 4, p. 148.

An obvious reply to this conclusion might seem to be, "Fine! Is not schooling preferable to work at this age? Does not the progressive 'exclusion' of young people from economic life testify to the effectiveness of our compulsory education laws and child labor legislation? And do we not find in these same data an explanation for the increase in school enrollments during the period under review?"

To be sure, the gradual exclusion of children and adolescents from economic operations has proceeded hand in hand with compulsory education laws and the consistent rise in the age of compulsory school attendance. Indeed, one has been the cause as well as the effect of the other. But neither compulsory school attendance laws nor labor legislation affect all within the age group below twenty. Few states, for example, require school attendance above the age of seventeen. From a survey conducted by the Office of Education in 1950 it appears that the amount of schooling that states require of children differ by as much as 50 per cent. Seven require eight years, thirty-three require nine years, four require ten years, three place the requirement at eleven years, and one at twelve. Fifteen states insist upon the completion of high school as a condition of exemption from school attendance in order to go to work, but in twenty-one states only the completion of elementary schooling is insisted upon. In some states children of twelve and thirteen years can secure working permits upon meeting a literacy requirement, although most states have established fourteen as the earliest age at which to secure a permit to work. Others insist on high school graduation as a prior condition for the securing of a permit to go to work.[15] When we consider that 30 per cent of all youth between the ages of sixteen to seventeen, and three-fourths of those between eighteen and nineteen, are neither in school nor in all cases employed, it is obvious that the situation is not altogether a healthy one.[16]

What is society's obligation to its young? What do its interests dictate with respect to young people who have ended their schooling but remain unemployed? If schooling is the sole alternative to unemployment or a blind alley job (other than military service) for an increasing number of youth above the age of seventeen, what should be the nature of this experience? Or, if formal education is not to be their lot, what should be substituted?

An adequate answer to these questions would seem to be imperative for a nation that obviously must husband its resources of personnel to compete successfully in a cold war in which it is heavily outnumbered.

---

[15] Reported in *The New York Times,* December 31, 1950.

[16] It should also be borne in mind that in the United States about 4 million children between the ages of five and seventeen are not enrolled in school. See *The Facts on Federal Aid* (Washington, D.C.: National Education Association, September, 1950), p. 21.

The Need for Orientation to Economic Life

One suggestion is to bring the work of the school much closer to the world of adults than has been true of education in the past. On both elementary and secondary levels, as well as college, education should strive to provide orientation to economic life. Perhaps the term orientation is too weak, if more than knowledge about economic activity is meant. Information is important, but it is not enough inasmuch as what is needed is an understanding which will breed character and fibre.

We have seen that the urban population of the nation is increasing at the expense of the rural population. For the educator this signifies more than the mere fact that city dwellers outnumber people who live on farms. Urbanization testifies to the influence of science and technology upon ways of living on the farm as well as in the city. Machinery has transformed farm work as well as operations in the factory. Consequently, children no longer play the role on the farm they once did, nor are they, as a result, the economic assets they once were. Under the old order, the child might learn from firsthand experience and observation at home and in the community both the nature and the significance of economic processes. The crops which he helped to plant and tend, and eventually to harvest and market, were charged with a fullness of meaning and significance for living that transcended the profit motive. Economic operations overflowed their expression in abstract economic formulae, and economic principles, within the compass of the child's experience, were identical with concrete and living relationships of people.

No one has pictured better the effects upon children of the change from rural to urban living than has Joseph K. Hart in his *A Social Interpretation of Education.*

City children, as a rule, have plenty of the mere froth of feeling and emotion. They lack depth of feeling and emotion, just as they lack depth of knowledge, and for exactly the same reason. Their whole experience lacks essential elements. They lack, especially, what was left behind when the district school was brought to the city. They lack real chances to *make* and to *handle,* to *observe* and *manipulate,* to *care for* and *feel responsibility for;* they lack intimate contact with nature in all its infinite variety; they lack rootage in natural experience and activities like the work of the household and the farm; they lack participation in the life of the larger neighborhood with its interest in them, its criticism and its supports. These, not the things learned in the schoolroom, are the fundamental things in education.[17]

Hart might have mentioned a further significant difference between the education that life out of school once afforded children and youth but now denies to many rural as well as city children. Today there is a large and rapidly increasing proportion of young people who no longer receive their preparation for life work in direct association with their parents, relatives, and friends.

This has an obvious bearing upon the formulation of ideals, standards, and codes.

Consider, for example, the influence upon a young person's ideal of good workmanship when he worked with his father on the farm or in the shop or the local mill and acquired directly from his parent not only the skill of the specific operation but the style which gave quality to the skill and won the approbation of the neighbors. Or consider the stimulus to improve that came with his gradual promotion, on the basis of performance, from a boy's to a man's work. Once we recognize that the specifics of morality and character grow best out of membership in face-to-face relationships, out of shared experiences with others, that they are as much caught as they are taught, we can appreciate the potency of the intimate associations in the small community of yesterday in contrast with the more superficial and impersonal contacts afforded children and youth today.

This denial of opportunities to participate with one's intimates in the serious concerns of life bears directly upon the attitudes toward work and toward people which many young people are encouraged to develop today. It is one thing, for example, to absorb ideals and standards from one's elders and quite a different matter to work under circumstances in which personal identity is lost. What a contrast between the picture a young person tends to develop of himself as a worker under the more simple conditions

---

[17] *A Social Interpretation of Education* (New York: Henry Holt & Co., Inc., 1929), p. 232.

in which men prided themselves upon the quality and the quantity of work each might do and the picture drawn from association with strangers on a job for an employer known only through a foreman, and in the performance of work in which each one's stint is but a fraction of the complicated whole!

A New Emphasis Upon Qualities of Personality

Writing in *School and Society*,[18] Dwayne Orton, Director of Education for the International Business Machine Corporation, emphasizes that the evidence from exhaustive studies "calls for more attention to the development of psychological skills, such as resourcefulness, cooperativeness, adjustibility, responsibility and reliability" in vocational education. Orton also emphasizes that it is in the area of the semiprofessions particularly that a premium is placed upon the use of psychological skills; but it is here also that studies reveal the need for training in those qualities of personality which play an important role in the service occupations. Finally, he states, the development of democracy in industry enhances the importance of the worker's understanding of the social values of his occupation. "No longer can one's eight-hour shift be considered apart from the complex social order of the local community—yea, of the world community. The citizen does not 'go to work.' He is 'the citizen at work.'"

It seems to follow that the opportunities for developing character through firsthand experience with work and from intimate association with an admired adult in childhood and youth are on the decrease, whereas the importance of qualities of character for success, in proportion to other abilities, is on the increase!

What is important, regardless of the nature of job opportunities open to youth at a given period or in a section of the country, is the fact that advancement for the individual in the vocational field, broadly conceived, turns more and more upon qualities of character, a capacity for creative relations with people, general intelligence, and education, and less exclusively than was once the case upon prior training of a technical character.

Obviously, this does not mean that the latter are unimportant. Intelligence and skill are indispensable conditions of success in

---

[18] December 11, 1948, p. 403.

highly important areas of living, and modern industrial society would suffer acutely were it to fail in maintaining an open road for highly specialized ability dependent upon a rare order of intelligence. The moral is rather that (1) education on all levels should concern itself with social and emotional aspects of development as well as the "intellect," with conditions that make for health of personality rather than exclusive emphasis upon the "training of the mind" in lonely isolation and (2) attention must be given to bridging the traditional gap between general and vocational education on the level of the secondary school and junior college.

Youth's Changing Role in Home and Community

Parallel with the exclusion of young people from responsible participation in economic activities has been a corresponding elimination from responsibilities in home and community which once fostered social maturity. Obviously, the one-time participation of children and adolescents in the concerns of adults in store and shop and on the farm contributed to their social development as well as to their economic education. Indeed, it is difficult to overemphasize the importance in the life of a young person of adult recognition of his present contribution to the group and of the tasks of even greater significance which he may undertake tomorrow. In the rural home there was often a gradation of jobs, beginning with the simple chores for the young child and continuing through a series of promotions, on the basis of merit, to the full-fledged work of man or woman. With what pride, for example, did the small boy on the farm move from assignments in and about the house to the man's work in the barn! Or from the minor jobs in the garden and the fields to the skilled work of a grown man, such as guiding the plow or building a haystack that would withstand wind and rain and snow! Work, in other words, was suffused with social significance, and as such it was an indispensable means of furthering the social and moral development of the young.

Opportunities for children and youth to play a corresponding role in home and community are today on the decrease, since many of the services and functions which were once personal and individual have become institutionalized and are clothed with a public or semipublic garb.

For example, contrast the role of a young person today with what it was yesterday when sickness afflicts the family next door. This once confronted the neighboring boy or girl with an opportunity to assume the functions of an adult. The adolescent girl was sent into the afflicted home to do the housework or to tend the children, perhaps to help in nursing the sick. The boy assumed temporarily the responsibility for the chores or the work out-of-doors. Today, the seriously ill more or less automatically are sent to a hospital and group insurance or a social agency is relied upon to help the family meet the incidents of illness. And, of course, the obvious need of avoiding contagion necessitates keeping the young uncontaminated by contact with the unfortunate family!

The commercializing and institutionalizing of assistance to the unfortunate has invaded a similar sphere of social and emotional development. We no longer consider it appropriate to house the homeless or to feed the stranger who knocks upon the gate. Indeed, it is safe to assume that the stranger, in obvious distress, who accosts us on a city street and solicits a coin with which to purchase "a cup of coffee," or a hot meal, is not at all times in the dire straits he appears to be. In some instances he is employed at a fixed wage to ply his craft. Consequently, we harden our hearts and instruct our children to pass him by. But, what are the effects of this seeming indifference upon the child? And what can we substitute for the child to encourage his generous impulses and to avoid the corrosive influences of an impersonal society?

Obviously, the complex society of today cannot operate on the old system of voluntary services. When a fire breaks out in the middle of the night, we rejoice over the fact that we are no longer dependent upon the bucket brigade of men of good will but little skill to fight the fire or upon the hastily improvised tactics of the volunteer fire department. Nevertheless, old as well as young pay a price in spiritual coin for the comfort of returning to their slumbers with an easy conscience once they are assured it is not their house that is on fire. So, too, of illness. Hospitalization and professional medical attention are far superior to that which the home can provide, no matter how generous or devoted the neighbors may be; and few would exchange the benefits that derive from associated effort for the earlier types of individual and personal service.[19]

Not only are the opportunities for children and adolescents to participate responsibly in the life of the home and community fewer and less significant than was once the case, but there are positive influences today which encourage irresponsibility and the evasion of social and moral standards. Prior to the development of modern facilities of transportation, life in the city, as well as in the small town and rural community, involved much more of a community feeling than exists today. Cities were collections of neighborhoods in which families came to know each other in a manner no longer true of a period in which they move frequently or their members live in one section of the city and earn their living in another. This contributes to a sense of anonymity and frees the individual from the discipline of the observing eye as well as the tender concern of his neighbor.

Austin McCormack, formerly Commissioner of Welfare in New York City, once described the difference between the influences which play upon a school child in New York and those that controlled his childhood as a boy in a small New England village. The moment a child steps out of the school building in New York City he is amongst strangers and what he does or refrains from doing is seemingly unobserved. As a member of a gang, he and his comrades can "snitch" from the corner grocery and quickly lose themselves in the crowd, with little sense of having injured someone whose feelings are as theirs, whereas in the New England village, by contrast, the boy was known to everyone and the standards which his parents sought to have him adopt were obviously and consistently the standards of the community. Consequently, the temptation to deviate from the common code was quickly associated with public disapproval.

Such illustrations of community pressure are not intended to convey the notion that standards externally imposed are the most vital, or, for that matter, are essentially moral so long as they can

---

[19] For an informative and sensitive discussion of the difficulties which confront low-income groups in the modern city with respect to medical and dental care and health needs, see Helen Hall, "When Sickness Strikes a Family," *The Survey*, January, 1952, pp. 26–35.

be put on or taken off according to circumstances. On the contrary, genuine morality is an inner possession, a self-directive principle, a way of thinking, feeling, and acting toward people and with people which are as one's own. Its origin and development are social in the sense that morality grows out of membership and deep-rooted interests which one shares with his fellows. The home and the community must supply these necessary conditions, or, if circumstances render it difficult for these institutions to function with their one-time vitality, the school, as a supplementary institution, must obviously find ways of offsetting serious undernourishments of personality.

We are suggesting that there has emerged in American life a relatively new and distinctive stage of development for adolescents as well as for children. Young people have drunk deep from the fountain of youth, with results not altogether to their advantage or their inner satisfaction. Just as the nineteenth century witnessed the extension of the period of childhood, with a resulting appreciation of the potential significance of this stage, so the twentieth century is creating a unique and distinctive period of adolescence. This follows from fundamental changes in the proportion of young to old in the population, from the steady exclusion of young people from the labor market, from transformations in home and community which render difficult, often impossible, the active participation of children and adolescents in activities that have long served as a seed bed in which both to propagate and train qualities of mind and character indispensable for progress toward maturity.

Fundamental changes of this nature, particularly when they creep upon a people as a thief in the night, bring confusion and frustration, as many a parent will testify. But they need not yield pessimism. The lengthening of the period of adolescence holds genuine promise for the future of this age group and for society as a whole, provided we deal with it as creatively as we have done, on the whole, with childhood. Who would exchange our ways of dealing with children today for those employed when children were economic and social assets? Equally fruitful potentialities are doubtless lying fallow in adolescence. And just as we have unquestionably raised the level of our society and improved the quality of our living through the enrichment of childhood, so there is reason to hope that a creative recognition of adolescence as a new cultural stage will yield equally promising fruit.

School Enrollments Reflect Economic and Social Changes

Changes in the economic and social status of children and youth, to which we have called attention, are reflected in school enrollments. In 1910, for example, 18.4 per cent of all youth between the ages of ten and fifteen were employed; in 1920 the percentage of employed in this age group fell to 8.5 per cent, and by 1930 it fell to 7.4 per cent. On the other hand, this same period witnessed a rapid and dramatic increase in elementary school enrollments. Indeed, each decade prior to 1940 marked a steady increase in elementary school enrollments, although this was most marked prior to 1920. By 1920 elementary enrollments had begun to level off, although school attendance continued to rise significantly in the upper grades. Between 1930 and 1940 elementary enrollments decreased both in proportion to the total population and in actual numbers.[20]

World War II, however, brought a reversal of anticipated trends, and by 1947–1948 the "war babies" began their invasion of the elementary school. Between the school year 1947–1948 and 1956–1957 elementary school enrollments increased by 5,702,889 or 32.4 per cent.[21]

High school enrollments reflect a similar trend, although with the age of compulsory school attendance seldom higher than fifteen, enrollments for the age group of fourteen to twenty are subject to fluctuations in the economic picture. Nevertheless, the exclusion of young people from economic life has been reflected dramatically in secondary school enrollments. For example, in 1870 one in each 500 of the population was in high school; by 1930 the ratio was 1 to 22, and from less than 5 per cent of the total enrollments in 1900, high school enrollments have grown to the point where in 1950 they included more than one-fifth of the

---

[20] *Schools and the 1950 Census, op. cit.,* p. 165.
[21] *The Postwar Struggle to Provide Competent Teachers, op. cit.,* p. 106. The increase in secondary school enrollments for the same period was 2,534,499, or 39 per cent.

Youth and the World's Work · 109

total.[22] Again, in 1930 the high school population embraced 51
per cent of the population fourteen to seventeen years of age. By
1940 this had increased to 73 per cent. By 1950, due doubtless to
more favorable employment conditions in the decade 1940 to 1950,
this stood at approximately the same ratio as in 1940. The striking
manner in which schooling has come to replace out-of-school
occupations for adolescents is evident when we observe that in
1890 enrollments in all high schools, public and private, constituted but 2.5 per cent of the total enrollments in all public and
private schools, in contrast with 21.5 per cent in 1950.[23]

The rapid increase in the school population since 1890 has
brought severe growing pains to public education. By 1910 the
situation had become acute in the upper years of the elementary
school and the first year or two of the high school. The work of
these years was obviously ill adjusted to the needs of boys and
girls of varied backgrounds and widely differing life goals. Just
as early childhood had come to be recognized as a unique and
distinctive stage of development, and children were no longer
conceived of as adults in miniature, so now early adolescence was
receiving recognition as a period of growth requiring special
understanding. This, in turn, called for new educational materials
and types of experience and a new and more appropriate form of
school organization and administration. These new demands and
expectations gave birth to the junior high school, an institution
that undertook both to adapt its program to the distinctive characteristics of young adolescents and to provide a "terminal education" for those boys and girls who expected to enter upon a
vocation prior to completion of high school.

Today, few junior high schools include vocational curricula

[22] *Ibid.*, p. 166.
[23] *The Schools and the 1950 Census, op. cit.*, p. 167. According to a report issued
by the Census Bureau on December 30, 1957, and reported in the daily press, school
attendance was as follows:

The number of children enrolled in kindergartens and elementary schools in
October was 29 million, up 5,700,000 in five years. High school students numbered 9
million, a five-year increase of 1,800,000, and college and professional schools had
3,100,000 students, a boost of 1,200,000.

Both full- and part-time students were counted in the report.

The percentage of children five to thirteen years old who were enrolled in school
increased from 88.3 to 94.4 in the five years since 1952. Figures for other age groups
were: fifteen to seventeen, from 85.1 to 89.5; eighteen to twenty-four, from 15.0 to
20.2, and twenty-five to thirty-four, from 1.9 to 3.6 per cent. (*Washington Post and
Times Herald*, December 31, 1957.)

in their offerings. Indeed, vocational training of a specialized character in the senior high school is undergoing critical scrutiny. General and universal education has moved up the age scale, from the elementary school (once characterized as the common school) into the upper years of the secondary school and the lower levels of the college. Today, educators are discussing the need for a terminal education in the junior college in much the same terms that, forty years ago, they applied the concept to the junior high school. It is here, too, that these educators are raising the question of a general education appropriate to the needs of young people who are seemingly unable to pursue the type of curriculum traditionally designed for the few rather than the many. The educational terms employed and the objectives stressed are strikingly similar, but the students in mind are of late rather than early adolescence.

We conclude, then, that the past few decades have been of unusual significance in their influence, economic and social, upon the status of youth. Changes in the ratio of old to young, changes in the nature and kinds of employment opportunities, whether in the labor market or in the activities of home and community, together with statistics of school enrollments, all point to the fact that schooling is replacing work as a formative influence in the lives of growing boys and girls. This lends importance to the nature of the education schools should provide in the light of their enlarged responsibilities; and it is therefore crucial that the public direct its attention to the dangers implicit in the steadily widening gap between existing provision for education in the way of physical facilities, working capital, and adequately trained personnel, on the one hand, and the developmental needs of our youth, on the other.

Suggested Reading

Bode, Boyd H., *Democracy As a Way of Life* (New York: The Macmillan Co., 1943), chaps. II–IV.

Brownell, Baker, *The Humane Community* (New York: Harper & Brothers, 1950), chap. VI.

Hart, Joseph K., *Education in the Humane Community* (New York: Harper & Brothers, 1951), part I.

Rugg, Harold, and Marian Brooks, *The Teacher in School and Society* (Yonkers, N.Y.: World Book Co., 1953), chaps. 4, 6.

Stratemeyer, Florence, Hamden Forkner, Margaret McKim, and A. Harry Passow, *Developing a Curriculum for Modern Living* (New York: Bureau of Publications, Teachers College, Columbia University, 1957), chap. II.

/\.\/\./\

7

The School and the Changing
Status of Youth

The Status of Youth a Resultant of Plural Factors

Chapter 6 has drawn attention to the present status of young people in American society. The reader may think it paints too depressing a picture, one that overemphasizes the influence of economic factors and expresses the spirit of social determinism. Such is not the intention of the writer, although he does wish to face frankly conditions playing upon young people which create confusion and frustration for them as well as for their elders.

Economic factors attendant upon the transition from an agricultural and rural economy to one predominantly industrial and urban have assuredly played their part. But it would be an oversimplification to hold that the changes described are economic alone. Rather are they the resultants of many interpenetrating influences. Certainly we cannot ascribe to economic change alone the present-day concern for health factors in education—health of personality as well as health of body—or the recognized importance of distinctive stages in the development of children from infancy through childhood, adolescence, and on into adulthood— each stage unique in its possibilities for emotional and social growth in home, school, and community.

The present status of children and adolescents derives from a plurality of factors, each serving as cause and effect. To what, for example, shall we ascribe the lengthening period of compulsory school attendance? To the exclusion of young people from work in mine, factory, and farm by virtue of the increased use of machinery and the greater abundance of adult labor? Or to the passage of child labor laws which, in turn, have grown out of a sensitive appreciation of the stultifying effects upon the young personality of close confinement to the machine and back-breaking labor? Science, too, has doubtless contributed its part, particularly in clarifying what constitutes wholesomeness of personality. But science, in relation to economic life, is both parent and offspring, and, as a method of thinking, it stands in much the same relationship of cause and effect to the democratic spirit. Although science is cold and impersonal in many of its applications, it has, nevertheless, bettered an understanding of human nature and provided a solid basis of fact for a democratic faith in the potentialities of human beings in all walks of life and all classes of society. This, too, has found expression in the consistent raising of the age of compulsory school attendance and in the progressive realization on all levels of society that continued progress is contingent upon the general education and specialized training of its young.

We cannot isolate any one factor of change in the status of youth and ascribe to it exclusive priority over others. Were educators to attempt such a task, they would circumscribe and narrow rather than enrich and broaden the education of youth. Just as the causes of change are plural, so an education designed to meet the changing needs of youth must be many-sided: economic, social, psychological, moral.

We will now glance briefly at contemporary efforts to adapt education to the needs of youth as revealed in our previous analysis.

Minimum Essentials in a Context of Meaning

The most obvious effort is the attempt to give body to the three R's, or to what are variously called the "tools" or minimum essentials of an education. These attempts take cognizance of the fact that elementary school children enter school at an earlier age and remain in school for a longer period than was common some generations back. This means they are introduced to verbal symbols and abstractions before life outside the school has provided a groundwork in firsthand, concrete, and active experiences that are sufficient to give meaning and substance to these abstractions. To be sure, differences in the environment of the country and city child make for differences in what the Herbartians once termed the "apperceptive basis" for learning. But machinery, the specialization of labor on the farm, and the urbanizing of rural life have all narrowed these differences to the point where the rural as well as the urban child is dependent upon the school for experiences which will give significance to the tools of his education.[1]

By and large, it is the failure of the traditionalist to sense this need that prompts him to attack what he conceives to be "busy work," or "mere activity," or the "fads and frills" of the modern school. Both progressive and conservative are as one in recognizing the importance of a thorough grounding in the three R's, but they fail to see eye to eye with respect to the methods of achieving these commonly agreed upon goals.

Now, what holds true of "the primary adaptations" in the elementary school is equally pertinent on the secondary and college levels. Unless the bony structure of a verbal education is covered with healthy flesh and blood, it will fail of its purpose. Accordingly, liberal-minded educators on all levels are searching for ways of relating students to the community, not merely to help them to grasp better the full implications of theory, but to foster as well intellectual and social maturity.

Enriched experiences thus serve the purpose of vitalizing an otherwise abstract and verbal education. They function, too, as plural routes to learning, thus opening the doors of insight and understanding to the nonverbal as well as to the verbally minded pupil. A visit to the health department, a conference with a public official, or a moving picture of services rendered the people by the agencies of government may enable the "slow reader" or the concrete-minded boy or girl to grasp the functions and purposes of community agencies and the operations of government as

---

[1] For a more specific application of this point to the rural school, see Effie G. Bathurst and Jane Franseth, *Modern Ways in One- and Two-Teacher Schools* (Washington, D.C.: Office of Education, Federal Security Agency), Bulletin 1951, no. 18.

intelligently as will the pupil with the high I.Q. or the academic mind grasp them from the printed word. So, too, the boy or girl who, following an introduction to his community in the manner described, records his observations, impressions, and interpretations in an art form may testify to the value of that experience for him as eloquently as he who resorts to the pen.

To be sure, one medium need not preclude the other. The child who learns to converse in many tongues has, potentially, a "superiority of parts" over others. Not only has he provided himself with a plurality of possible channels of communications with his fellows, but, in addition, he may enjoy nuances of experiences often denied his less gifted comrade. This, too, validates the use of plural media in instruction.

Relating the School to the Community

Field experience and the increasing use of social service and work projects on the secondary school level likewise testify to the school's assumption of a new obligation: the obligation to guide youth in the direction of social maturity.

Social service projects may develop naturally out of classroom work or as an independent but nevertheless inherent part of the program of the school as a whole. An example of the first type is an erosion project carried on some years ago by a junior high school class in Montevello, Alabama.[2] Not content with a theoretical discussion of erosion, the teacher of the eighth grade encouraged her students to set erosion traps in order to measure the extent of erosion in their own community. Armed with this data, the children proceeded to determine the possible location of dams which might prevent the washing away of the soil and they assisted a farmer in the vicinity of the school to safeguard his property from injury. Their enthusiasm eventually enlisted the interest and cooperation of the local newspaper, which opened its columns to material gathered and prepared by the students bearing upon the cause and the prevention of erosion and listing the resources of government available to those who wished to use them.

---

[2] Alice V. Keliher, "The Montevello Erosion Control Project," *Curriculum Journal,* May, 1937, pp. 213–214.

A large city high school affords a second illustration. The science department of this school has established close relationships with the officials of the city's botanical garden. Students with science interests are permitted to serve as apprentices in the gardens, thus rendering valuable assistance to the experts, on the one hand, and receiving the stimulus of firsthand association with experts in the field, on the other.

Similar possibilities of a two-way relationship between school and community can be identified in most localities. Opportunities for service in public health departments, public libraries, museums, and social and civic agencies will be seen to exist in abundance once both public officials and educators envisage their potential contributions to education. Nor need this extension of function interfere with or handicap the present activities of these agencies. On the contrary, once the departments of government add to their service functions that of education, it may well follow that the one will give quality to the other.[3]

The program of the school as a whole can often be geared to the need of involving students in socially useful work with an eye to furthering their responsible participation in the wider community. For example, one school in New York City requires "community service" of all students registered in the senior high school. This varies in character and is related as nearly as possible to the needs and interests of the students. It may consist of actual work, under professional supervision, in a settlement house, a day nursery, or a hospital or service as a volunteer in an agency devoted to a social-civic purpose. This school likewise searches out opportunities for its students to engage in work projects with a social agency on weekends and vacations. The projects include jobs such as painting and repairing buildings for a fresh air camp for children or serving as junior counsellors in a summer playschool or a camp for underprivileged children.

The Midcentury White House Conference on Children and Youth emphasized the importance of involving young people intimately in the affairs of their communities. As a result of this conference in December, 1950, numerous communities through-

---

[3] For an elaboration of this point, see V. T. Thayer, Caroline Zachry, and Ruth Kotinsky, *Reorganizing Secondary Education* (New York: D. Appleton-Century Co., 1939), chap. VI.

out the country have inaugurated the practice of including representatives of young people on councils and boards dedicated to community improvement. In Michigan, a Youth Advisory Council on the Youth Commission has worked with the Commission on problems affecting the young people of the state; in Missouri, the Missouri Association for Social Welfare decided to include a youth member on its Board of Directors.

The *Progress Bulletin* of the National Committee on Children and Youth has served as a clearinghouse of information respecting developments within the states. These reports indicate that communities are discovering hitherto untapped resources for the involvement of youth in civic undertakings. The following incident is typical.

An outstanding example of what youth participation can mean to a community is the Marceline Youth Council. Part of a small community of 4,000, this organization of youth brought immediate results and gave the youngsters purpose, interest and accomplishments. Marceline, like other rural communities in Missouri, was confronted with the loss of its youth as they grew to adulthood. Containing two industries, no college, short on community facilities and general citizen interest in improvement, there was little outlet for youth or the desire to establish adult roots. A Marceline adult had been involved in the Missouri pre-White House Conference meeting, getting stimulus to attempt some organization in Marceline. A Coordinating Council was formed in January 1950, held its first White House Conference, following which in May, it issued a questionnaire to each junior and senior high school student in an attempt to uncover interest in community service during the summer. Upon completion of the survey, the Council called a meeting of all youth in conjunction with its own meeting. Later a separate meeting of the youth established their own Council.

One of the Youth Council's first projects was the establishment of a playground. . . . Shifts of young people worked mornings and afternoons supervising the children, umpiring baseball games, taking part in other activity. Programs were presented by young people every Monday night at Family Night suppers. When the playground closed in August, the Council had evolved plans for an improved and more extensive program the following year.[4]

---

[4] National Committee on Children and Youth, *Progress Bulletin*, January, 1952, no. 4, pp. 1–2.

Criteria Are Important

In all attempts to relate the school to the community, it is essential to keep in mind that the primary purpose of this relationship is educational; that is, to provide young people with specific occasions to participate responsibly in life about them and through this participation to acquire qualities of personality which further identification with others and with the concerns of an ever enlarging community. Not infrequently, schools have leaped suddenly from a state of virtual nonparticipation into one in which activities are so numerous and varied that their educational value has been lost. To extract their full educational value, community projects should, to every extent possible, (1) grow naturally out of class work and bear an obvious and direct relationship to the objectives of the course of study; (2) serve the needs of children rather than those of pressure groups or propaganda agencies outside the school (worthy as these may be); (3) afford opportunities for pupils to identify themselves emotionally as well as intellectually with institutions and agencies that are furthering the interests of the community as a whole; and (4) be keyed to the social maturity of the students who are asked to engage in them.[5]

Doubts Concerning the School's Role

Not all will agree that the school can offset the undernourishments in social development that have come with the disintegration of the one-time community. The late Joseph K. Hart was one of those who lamented the loss of the "organic community."

We have lost "the organic community, with the living culture it embodied" and the education that was inherent in that culture. . . . Of course, *life* goes on—and *for adults* it goes on more easefully. But for children the freedoms, the stimulations, the patternings, the joyful realizations that were instinct in the old-time community are mostly gone. We have compounded matters by providing for them the most expensive schools the world has even known; and, as if to show their

---

[5] For a more complete discussion of these criteria and others relevant to community projects, see Thayer, Zachry, and Kotinsky, *op. cit.*, pp. 220–226.

gratitude for our "sacrifices," they indulge themselves in adult apings and in juvenile delinquencies.[6]

Since the work of the school, according to Hart, "is almost wholly intellectual in intent and practice," he holds forth little hope that it will meet the challenge of changed conditions. Moreover, "habits and skills necessary to actual social living," he contends, "cannot be developed in schools, for the simple reason that such habits and skills are the product of real situations which cannot be got inside the schoolroom." [7] To be sure, says Hart, "The effort of the schools is laudable, and in some degree plausible. It is, generally speaking, an attempt to recover that wholeness in education that was once characteristic of life in the local community. But the results are not convincing. *Talking* or *reading* about the experiences of other times or other people cannot substitute for actual experiences. The school has a valid job, a real task, but it has not found out how to do that job, or fulfill that task." [8]

The sole remedy for our educational problem, as Hart sees it, is to revive community life. "The solution now lags," he believes, "because we have not enough community between the generations to give us spirit for the tasks of our age. It is here, in the community between the generations, that the problem must once more be localized, if it is ever to be solved." [9]

It is well to stress the interdependence of school and community and the grave need to devise instruments that will enable old and young once more to participate jointly in meaningful experience, experiences that will enable the former to absorb from these associations valuable insights, attitudes, and dispositions. This is not to say, however, that the school can afford to wait upon the invention of new social institutions or the revival of the one-time community. Rather, as an institution charged with meeting the needs of children and youth, it must explore new possibilities for the fostering of healthy social development. Not to do so is to admit defeat.

---

[6] *Education in the Humane Community* (New York: Harper & Brothers, 1951), pp. 20–21.

[7] *Ibid.,* p. 12.

[8] *Ibid.,* p. 29.

[9] *Ibid.,* p. 166.

Nor has the modern school ignored this challenge.

To transform the school into a community is one response. What this involves as a total program is too large a topic for this chapter, since it would necessitate a description of essential relations between home and school at various stages of child development, as well as adaptations of the school program in harmony with a generous conception of pupil, even parent participation. Brief mention should be made, however, of its implications for relations between home and school.

Parents Have an Advisory Function to Perform

In an earlier chapter, the school was defined as an institution created and maintained by the adult community in order to realize in the lives of young people, through associated action, what cannot be achieved by individuals acting separately. In other words, the school is a supplementary institution.

The growing functions of parents' associations illustrate this conception of the potential contributions of the school. Not only do these organizations serve as interpreters between the school and the parent body—explaining the school's curriculum to the parents and relaying the concerns of parents to the school—but, in many instances, they have become the means whereby parents solve their problems as parents through cooperative action.

Parent organizations have likewise come to realize that in union there is strength with which to face the problem of unhealthy environmental forces playing upon young people. In an age of commercialized amusement and organized crime, the individual parent is frequently helpless to protect his child from what he believes to be harmful influences. But when parents are united, their status increases. Amusement centers respond more sensitively to their suggestions. Newsstands are usually eager to improve the character of their selection of comic books and best sellers. Movie theaters solicit their endorsement of good pictures. When parents are organized, and with the advice and counsel of a wise school administration, they can establish good relations between the school and other agencies within the community that are concerned with the health and welfare of young people. On occasion, a broad-gauged health and guidance program, including health examinations and referrals, a counseling system in mental health and hygiene, and vocational guidance and advice, has had its origin in the more informal relationships of the school with the local medical association, mental hygiene society, labor unions, and employer associations of the community. When parents are organized they can develop a constructive interest in underprivileged sections of the community and demonstrate to the less discerning members of the community that conditions which make for diseased personalities are as disadvantageous to the well-being of the community as a whole as are breeding spots of physical infection.

The possibilities of cooperation between the school and parents are not limited to the extracurricular life of the school. Virtually every subject taught in the school represents the interests, often vocational, of competent and resourceful members of the community. One effective means of vitalizing instruction and of breathing unity and significance into topics that might otherwise remain foreign and remote is to draw upon these adults for the purposes of enriching the curriculum and giving to students firsthand evidence of ways in which activities within the school are representative of worthy adult interests out of school.

These are but a few of many ways in which the school and its parents, united, can both meet problems of "undernourishment" in the lives of boys and girls and contribute positively to the enrichment of their lives. To achieve these goals the school must envisage its responsibility as a community responsibility and conceive of its work with young people in terms broader than conventional notions of the development of the "mind." It takes seriously the established fact that healthy intellectual growth involves healthy emotional and social relationships as well. It implies a disposition on the part of the school to bridge the traditional gap separating the two. Finally, it assumes that the school, through its administrative machinery, will exercise initiative in bringing about this change.

Vocational Orientation in General Education

We have centered thus far upon the task of furthering the social maturity of young people. What, if anything, can the school do to offset the effects of inadequate participation in the economic concerns of home and community?

As we saw in Chapter 6, business and industry, as well as the professions, have steadily raised the age at which young people may enter these fields with other blind alley prospects before them. These trends, it was seen, are both the cause and the effect of compulsory school attendance laws and child labor legislation. It would be wrong, however, to conclude that young people are adequately protected from employment of a noneducative character at a time when schooling would be more profitable. Despite the fact that the White House Conference on Children and Youth in 1919, in 1930, and again in 1940 set a goal of sixteen years old as a minimum age for employment during school hours, by 1952 only seven states had attained this standard.[10] This, of course, enables large numbers of young people to substitute for schooling activities that hold forth little promise for their economic futures.

The increasing cost of education likewise requires many of our young people to engage in part-time work while pursuing their studies. According to data gathered by the 1950 census, one out of every seven youths between the ages of fourteen and twenty in attendance at school was either employed or looking for work. As the defense program continues to draw upon the labor force and employment conditions move into high gear, part-time jobs may well attract an increasing number of students in high school and college. This suggests that the schools envisage a new and promising function: that of entering into cooperative relations with employment agencies of the community and perhaps with groups of employers as well, with a view to making part-time work experience educationally valuable not merely for students enrolled in vocational high school but for those engaged in general education as well. A number of cities have already established junior placement bureaus which place high school graduates and dropouts. We are suggesting that, in addition, these bureaus should assist young people who wish to remain in school but must of necessity add to the family income or those who would profit in

---

[10] Utah, Virginia, Maryland, New Jersey, New York, Ohio, and Illinois. These states also provide against employment of youth under sixteen in factories or manufacturing work at any time. Agriculture and domestic services are exempted. Also, in Ohio and Virginia high school graduates are exempted.

the maturing process from work experience. In these cases, the employment bureau, upon the basis of information supplied by the school, should assist the youth to find a job appropriate to his abilities and needs, and either the school or the employment agency should exercise a supervisory eye upon the experiences of the student at work, helping him to interpret and to use these most fruitfully.

A cooperative arrangement of this character might very well strengthen the holding power of the school. Although it is true, as a general phenomenon, that a steadily increasing number of young people of high school age are attending school, the percentage of nonattendance is still too high and suggests a wastage of personnel that the country can ill afford, as well as a sad harvest of ultimate frustration and failure for those who, with appropriate schooling, might have lived contented and useful lives.

It is obvious that the holding power of the school has increased with the attractiveness of the curriculum. This accounts for the emphasis in recent years upon education for "life adjustment" and the earnest attempts to organize the work of the school so as to meet the growing needs of boys and girls in all the basic relationships of living.[11]

This implies a more generous conception than heretofore of both general and vocational education.

Units of work in the elementary school, for example, that introduce children to ways in which the need for food, clothing, shelter, and other basic requirements of living is met constitute the first step in economic orientation. Moreover, in the upper years of the elementary school and the period embraced by the junior high school, there is little distinction between projects that involve an economic as against a social-civic orientation. The erosion project mentioned earlier contributes to social insight and sympathy as well as to economic understanding. So, too, do work camps on the senior and the college levels, when organized as self-govern-

---

[11] For a description of the Commission on Life Adjustment Education for Youth and its recommendations, see *Life Adjustment Education for Every Youth* (Washington, D.C.: Office of Education, Federal Security Agency), Bulletin 1951, no. 22; *Life Adjustment Education in American Culture*, Proceedings of a National Conference Sponsored by the Office of Education and the Commission on Life Adjustment Education for Youth (Washington, D.C.: Office of Education, Federal Security Agency), Circular No. 335. Other material, including a bibliography bearing on life adjustment education, is available in the Office of Education.

ing communities and devoted to the performance of tasks that are clearly as much social and civic as economic in character.[12]

Nevertheless, as the student moves through the secondary school, subjects of study should provide an ever more specific orientation to economic life.

Although each subject in the curriculum, particularly the "general studies" or the "core curriculum," lends itself to the orientation of students to economic life, there is need for vocational information which eludes even these fields. Modern life is sustained by thousands of specialized occupational pursuits. No school can hope to acquaint its students with them all. The complexities of the situation suggest the need for information and guidance that are more specific than general education alone can provide. One means of bringing this about is a working arrangement between a guidance specialist and student advisors.

Utilizing the Summer Vacation

Cooperative relations between school and community might also help to solve the problem of the summer vacation which seemingly becomes ever more acute for large numbers of young people. Rural life has long ceased to be the dominant pattern in this country but it continues, nevertheless, to determine the character of the school year, with the result that large numbers of children and adolescents are confronted each summer with a long vacation which many find it difficult to use constructively. To be sure, for those who can afford it, the recreational camp helps to solve the problem, but a considerable proportion of young people are unable to take advantage of this. Nor is it possible for the average community to provide temporary jobs of a worth-while character either in private firms or in the various public, semipublic, and voluntary agencies for the large number of young people thus released from school.

These facts have led educators and laymen repeatedly to raise the question of an all-year school, with little tangible success. One difficulty is genuine doubt as to the wisdom of extending con-

---

[12] See Warren C. Seyfert, "Providing Work and Service Experience for Postwar Youth," *Forty-Fourth Yearbook,* National Society for the Study of Education (Chicago: University of Chicago Press, 1945), part I, chap. VII.

ventional schooling into the summer months coupled with the failure, as yet, to develop a convincing substitute for this schooling. Another difficulty is the added expense which an all-year school would necessarily involve at a time when many communities are already restive under what they consider to be inflated school budgets.

On the other hand, public concern over what seems to be an increasing proportion of children and adolescents who become delinquents suggests that serious thought be given to the needs of children in their out-of-school hours. Nor are we without valuable experience upon which to draw. For many years and in various sections of the country, private agencies have developed programs which schools might well adopt and enlarge upon. For example, in New York City, the Play Schools Association, a private organization, has long conducted a summer play school program with the consent of and with some assistance from the Board of Education in the way of staff and supplies. These play schools provide experiences in art and shop and in dramatics and music, together with excursions and trips of an educational and recreational character, as well as games and other "play" activities. For older children, an extension of this basic plan would include special interest projects in areas such as science, art, literature, dramatics, shop, and the like which might vitalize and enrich interests related to the work of the school year.

Here again private initiative has set an example which public schools, with appropriate modifications, might follow. In one school, for example, an ingenious teacher of science decided to experiment with a science work camp for young people in the upper years of the high school. She succeeded in interesting other schools in the idea, with the result that a summer group of nine girls and twelve boys, "scientists" all, was eventually organized. A farm in the northern section of Westchester County, New York, was found with readily accessible meadows, ponds, brooks, woods, a large dairy establishment, and stables.

First of all, there was work that had to be done in order to sustain the little community: work jobs, such as table setting, dish washing, housecleaning and laundry, care of the barn and stables, work on the grounds. All of these jobs were shared in "turnabout" fashion and helped to give a sense of responsibility and community living.

Secondly came the science projects, related in each instance to the interests of individuals. Some were carried on by a young scientist alone, others in association with one or more of his colleagues. As might be expected, these projects varied widely in character. Some were suggested by the immediate environment, as, for example, the construction of an incubator and a study of the embryonic development of the chick, or the chemical analysis of soils and plants. Others testified to a scientific curiosity previously aroused.

This type of project suggests what may be done with young people who can afford to bear the expense of a summer camp. (Work camps, to which we have already referred, often enable young people to earn a portion of their expenses.) Enough has been done, however, in developing summer programs with children and adolescents to establish the wisdom of their extension to larger numbers. Were schools open during the summer months for "special interest" groups and work projects of various types within the community, together with ample opportunities for play and recreation under supervision, the rewards of enriched and maturing experiences would soon become evident to all. Moreover, with the cooperation and assistance of parents a foundation might be laid for their eventual support by the public. Here, as in other developments of the program of the school, experimentation on a voluntary basis wisely antedates efforts at universal application.

Vocational Education in a New Role

Until recent years, vocational education centered all too commonly upon training in specific skills and techniques, evidently on the assumption that the responsibility of the school ended with the immediate preparation of the student for a job, or that once he possessed a skill, he would safely weather economic change. Neither assumption is valid today.

It was suggested in Chapter 6 that qualities of personality rather than a specific skill are increasingly important in determining vocational success. It is also true that rapid changes in methods and procedures within the vocational field lead to both the constant scrapping of old skills and processes and the emergence of new ones. Hamden L. Forkner has drawn attention to the rapid changes that are taking place in industry in this respect. Before World War II, he tells us, a person who aspired to become a welder was required to spend from four to six years as an apprentice. Under the pressure of war production, however, the period of training was reduced to approximately 180 hours, or about six hours a day for a month. Pattern making has followed a similar course. In industry and agriculture, continues Forkner, there are indications that training programs for all occupations below the semiprofessional level will be reduced to "short, intensive units immediately prior to employment." [13]

Because rapid changes occur in vocational as well as in professional practice, education for a vocation should enable the individual to meet the experiences of life with flexibility, to possess himself of a basic knowledge that has application to "families" of occupations. Since, moreover, the future of the individual as well as changes in occupation are unpredictable, education for a vocation should be as the hub of a wheel with many spokes.

Studies of the American Youth Commission in the 1930's led to the conclusion that the "differentiation of youth prior to the beginning of the senior high-school period is not advisable; that prior to that time the program of education should be fairly general and uniform for all, with emphasis placed almost entirely upon a general or liberal education. There will be, of course, individual exceptions to these generalizations and the schools should be prepared to take these exceptions into account." [14]

Obviously, there is no one rigid rule to govern the character of vocational education or training, even on the senior high school level. This will vary with vocations, the circumstances operating upon young people, and conditions peculiar to a community. Two factors, however, would seem to be of importance. One is to encourage all who are competent to continue their education to do so. The second is to help each student to acquire

---

[13] See Hollis L. Caswell and others, *The American High School: Its Responsibility and Opportunity* (Harper & Brothers, New York, 1946), chap. IX. Also relevant in this connection is James B. Conant's, *The American High School Today* (McGraw-Hill Book Co., Inc., 1959), pp. 30–32; 51–55.

[14] Homer P. Rainey and others, *How Fare American Youth?* (New York: D. Appleton-Century Co., 1937), p. 54.

a realizing sense of progress toward a life goal, whether this be a trade or a profession. For some, this will mean a continuation of general education but with an ever present emphasis upon economic orientation. For others, it will involve an earlier introduction to occupational skills with, if possible, some firsthand contact with a job.

Forkner suggests, in this connection, that the community be used as a laboratory. For example, the boy who wishes to become a meat cutter can be found a position with a local meat dealer, while continuing his educational program under the direction and supervision of the school. "A teacher would be assigned to supervise and direct the study and coordinate the job activities of all young people so engaged." [15]

Finally, in this brief discussion of ways in which the school can meet the needs of young people in their economic relationships, mention should be made of provision for the placement of youth in jobs, both while in school and upon graduation. In other words, the introduction of young people to economic life should involve not only preparation for economic participation, but guidance and direction in the period of transition from school into full-fledged economic activity.

From its study of possible relationships between schools and employment offices, the American Youth Commission concluded that it is of no great importance whether responsibility for junior placement be lodged in public employment offices or in schools, provided in each instance the right hand gives assistance to the left.

The Commission likewise drew attention to the need for co-operation in placement services between schools and employment agencies on more than a local basis. This is especially necessary in rural and small-town communities, if the advantages of guidance and placement are to reach all young people who can profit from them.

Once placement and guidance functions intermesh, out-of-school work during vacation periods as well as part-time jobs during the school year can be rendered educational.

---

[15] Caswell and others, *op. cit.*, p. 180.

Social Status and Equality of Opportunity

Before concluding this chapter, it might be well to return for a moment to a problem mentioned but scarcely discussed in connection with the ideal of equality of educational opportunity: the problem of social status and class lines.

American communities, as we saw, are marked by class lines. Moreover, the public school in its administration as well as its curriculum not infrequently tends to reinforce rather than to erase the influence of class distinctions. School discipline, school regulations, the awarding of grades and prizes, and participation in extracurricular activities have been found to be influenced by class status. Nor can it be denied that many communities in the United States conform more closely to this pattern than to that implied by our ideals of equality of opportunity and social mobility. Nevertheless, these ideals are deeply rooted in the minds and hearts of Americans and find sufficient exemplification in practice to constitute a solid basis of appeal in the event a school strives to give substance to them. Although psychologists and anthropologists are doubtless correct in their contention that status and class are the invariable characteristics of human society, and inevitable in a society as complex as that of the United States, there is, nevertheless, no popular mandate for the conclusion that membership in a social class should carry with it special privileges and immunities in an institution dedicated to the needs of all the people. On the contrary, the principle that institutions established by the public to serve the children of all the people should do so without discrimination is both universal and fundamental to our way of life.

What, more specifically, does this suggest?

Most obviously, it points to the necessity of eliminating the present waste of talent and ability. If it be true that only 5 per cent of young people in working-class families continue their formal education beyond high school, despite the fact that this group comprises one-half the youth population of high intelligence, the loss to society from each generation is serious.

One suggestion is to ease the financial burden of education for worthy young people who would otherwise have to shorten their education. This would involve an extension of the principle implicit in the G.I. Bill of Rights and the policy of subsidizing the education of potential scientists, medical specialists, and others needed for defense to all youth able and willing to continue their education.

Advisable as this policy is for a nation that is none too richly blessed in numbers of young people, it would leave unaffected a sizable proportion of the able who lack motivation for higher education. Financial difficulties have been found to prevent no more than one-half of the young people in the lower socio-economic groups from continuing with their education.

How can we motivate where motivation is wanting?

Havighurst and Rodgers have the following suggestions to make: [16]

1. Turn the school's selection and guidance procedures more specifically toward this end. "Many superior youths," they point out, "do not know that they possess superiority, and neither do their parents." While the authors do not suggest revealing I.Q.'s to pupils and their parents as a general rule, they are convinced that a discreet use of this information in special instances would encourage both parents and children to "set their sights" higher.

2. Localities should organize "A Community Scholarship Association" in order to "increase the social motivation of working class youth by staging events in schools, churches, and theaters that played up the value of scholarship and higher education. Speakers and films could be scheduled and public scholarship awards could be given, starting in high school." These authorities recognize that the financial assistance provided by such an organization "might not be as important as the social motivation it could create in the community," but the purpose in mind is to stimulate young people of the lower socioeconomic class in ways analogous to those now operating too exclusively upon the middle- and upper-class youth.

3. It is suggested that the colleges accentuate their efforts to make college life attractive to students from working-class families once they are in college. Able students from the latter are less likely to join fraternities and sororities and clubs than are middle- and upper-class youth and are thus deprived of a social life that

[16] In Byron S. Hollinshead, *Who Should Go to College?* (New York: Columbia University Press, 1952), pp. 163–165.

adds zest to their college work. Accordingly, special attention should be directed toward facilitating the adjustment and encouraging the participation of the "unorganized students" in the extracurricular activities of college.

Foster McMurray has drawn attention to the fact that American society is rapidly passing out of the stage in which but a small fraction of its population can be supported in the upper years of high school and college. This gives further import to the factor of motivation in education.

As our national income increases, as our standards of living rise, and as our technology changes more widely the conditions of production, two of the most necessary conditions for the higher education of a higher percentage of the population will be met. More families will be able to afford more education, and to a greater extent than ever before our productive machinery will not require the labor of youth. For somewhat different reasons, an economic depression might have the same effect. More and more youth will find it possible to go higher in the educational ladder. Therefore it becomes increasingly unrealistic to associate higher education with the privileges of the elite.[17]

To salvage the talents of the gifted and to encourage those possessed of rare ability to continue with their education beyond high school is obviously important. But how are we to interpret the term "gifted"? Gifted in academic intelligence? Or gifted in the sense that a young person exhibits promise in science and mathematics, the arts and crafts, the machine shop and school garden as well as the humanities? From the data reviewed in Chapter 2, it is evident that young people face the necessity of prolonging their schooling in the absence of equally profitable and valuable experiences out of school. This imposes upon educators the necessity of adapting the school curriculum to many types of minds and recognizing that the term gifted is now plural in its denotation. As Robert Ulich indicates in his *Crisis and Hope in American Education,* the secondary school is now engaged in educating at least five types of individuals: the humanists (for whom the classical and humanist curriculum of the traditional

---

[17] "Who Should Be Educated for What?" *Progressive Education,* February, 1950, pp. 111–116.

school was originally designed); the scientists, who face an alluring future in the expanding fields of science and mathematics; the executive group, consisting of those who may be expected to conduct the affairs of state and to hold positions of responsibility in business and industry (and, why not add, in organizations of labor?); the artisans (by which Ulich means the future artists and sculptors, as well as the occupants of semiprofessional positions, the practical engineers, laboratory workers, etc.); and, finally, the "workers" in the various trades and vocations. Each of these groups, with the possible exception of the last, includes young people of unusual ability, as well as those of a run-of-the-mine character. A school which is both efficient and democratic in its operations will attempt to guide its students toward goals appropriate to their individual talents and interests and to avoid associating ideas of superior or inferior status with curricular differentiation.

Much remains to be done in adapting the curriculum of the school to varying types of mind and to different levels of ability within the various groupings. How many commercial curricula, for example, are keyed to the fact that bookkeeping, typewriting, and shorthand are requisite for but one segment of the school population that will enter the commercial field?

At the same time that Ulich draws attention to the necessity of a multiple type of curriculum in secondary schools, each type keyed to different levels of ability, he stresses the importance, in a democracy, of providing unifying experiences which will generate common ideals and a sense of oneness in the school community. These experiences are, of course, one of the objectives of the "core curriculum," to which attention has been given in recent years. But more potent, perhaps, are the unifying interpretations of life that can emerge from a school festival, dramatic work, or assembly exercise in which, through the medium of music, great poetry, or the contagion of an inspiring personality, young people are helped to sense the depth and breadth of the human spirit and to envisage ways in which they can identify their lives with an overarching ideal of more than personal significance.

To guide youth so that they may feel at home and secure in their school and in the curriculum of their choice requires a professionally trained teacher. It is no easy assignment for a novice. In a heterogeneous community it demands of a teacher an adaptability and maturity of personality capable of transcending the common barriers of class and of entering understandingly into the lives of children of all classes. Although the job is analogous in many ways to the task of the teacher who works with the foreign-born, it is more difficult in a community of long-confirmed class lines. In each instance, too, the key to success depends in no small measure upon an instructor's eye quick to discover possibilities within a pupil upon which both teacher and pupil can capitalize.

To equip a teacher adequately for this task, teacher education must be more sensitive to the existence of class lines in American communities than is now common. Just as the composition of the "working class," or the "lower socioeconomic group," to use the sociologist's phrase, is most varied, ranging from "pockets" in our population that have known only poverty and stagnation for generations to comparatively recent immigrant groups (such as the recent influx of Puerto Ricans into New York City, the Japanese and Filipinos in Hawaii, the Mexicans in the Southwest), so an appropriate school program will differ in different class and cultural backgrounds. But, ironically, a school and its staff is frequently far more generous in its ministrations to the needs of the immigrant child than it is to the child of lower-class parents in the native population. This is particularly characteristic of long-established communities where warmth of understanding comes less readily.

But once understanding is assured, from it, as from Christian love, other things will follow.

Of these, enrichment of curriculum ranks high. When squared against the necessity of gearing the work of the school to the facts of gradual exclusion of young people from active participation in the world's work and to the trends to which McMurray draws attention, the prestige values of the traditional curriculum becomes somewhat unrealistic. Unrealistic because of the false assumption that this traditional curriculum constitutes the sole, valid preparation for professional school and college. Unrealistic, too, for the reason that college doors will soon be open to students of a wider range of vocational interest than at present.

Here again, McMurray draws attention to a suggestive trend:

In the past few years the status of labor in America has begun to change. On the one hand, the number of people in the laboring classes who require and use technical skill, intelligence, and knowledge of a high level is increasing rapidly. The use of human workers as faulty adjuncts to the machine is on the decline, and must continue to decline and eventually to disappear if the masses of the people are to enjoy functional status in an industrial society. And on the other hand, the social-political power of labor in America is already tremendous, and on the increase. It is possible that our political fortunes will be determined by organized labor, and even that the technical or managerial aspects of industrial direction will be taken over by labor. In a society which already has this character to a marked degree, it would be sheer folly to minimize deliberately the educational aspirations of the working groups.[18]

The enlarged role of the working classes in American society to which McMurray calls our attention, would seem to counteract, in part, the solidification of class lines emphasized by sociologists. Evidently, two contradictory influences are operating: (1) a greater diffusion of culture which may accentuate trends toward social mobility and (2) tendencies toward economic and social stratification. If this be true, it would seem imperative in a democracy for the school to encourage the first and to soften the effects of the latter. This it can do, in part, by furthering the intermingling of young people within the school and maintaining an open road for the development and expression of special interests and ability in both the regular and the extracurricular activities of the school.

To the extent that both types of activities are open to all students on a democratic basis, the school will contribute to the realization of these objectives. In recent years the public schools have come to see the immediate importance of more conscious effort in this direction, both in guiding students and in sensitizing the wider community.

Suggested Reading

Bruce, William, and A. John Holden, *The Teacher's Personal Development* (New York: Henry Holt & Co., Inc., 1957), chap. 14.

---

[18] *Ibid.*, pp. 115–116.

Caswell, Hollis L. (ed.), *The American High School: Its Responsibility and Opportunity* (New York: Harper & Brothers, 1946), chaps. I–IV, IX.

Davis, Allison, *Social Class Influence on Learning* (Cambridge: Harvard University Press, 1948).

Department of Elementary School Principles, *The Parents and The Schools* (Washington, D.C.: The National Education Association, 1957).

Hanna, Paul L., *Youth Serves the Community* (New York: Appleton-Century-Crofts, Inc., 1950).

Hollinshead, Byron S., *Who Should Go to College?* (New York: Columbia University Press, 1952), chap. VII.

McMurray, Foster, "Who Should Be Educated for What?" *Progressive Education*, February, 1950, pp. 111–116.

Stratemeyer, Florence, Hamden Forkner, Margaret McKim, and A. Harry Passow, *Developing a Curriculum for Modern Living* (New York: Bureau of Publications, Teachers College, Columbia University, 1957), chap. 10.

Ulich, Robert, *Crisis and Hope in American Education* (Boston: Beacon Press, Inc., 1951), chaps. III, IV.

.∧.∧.∧.

8

The Family and the School

Plural Characteristics of the American Family

If we are to believe the prophets of doom, the American family is in a bad way. Statistics of divorce have evidently transformed the traditional vow of husband and wife, "Until death do us part," into an empty phrase. Similarly, the steady rise in the rate of juvenile delinquency in the privileged as well as the underprivileged families bears witness to a deplorable neglect of parental discipline. In sparing the rod the modern parent has evidently succeeded only in spoiling the child. And, finally, the disappearance of work and the household arts of yesterday from the home, together with the contraction and subtraction of living quarters, no longer encourage the common activities which once enabled the members of a family to live fruitfully with each other.

That the American family is involved in serious difficulties few will deny. But to identify severe growing pains with disintegration is an oversimplification. It ignores both past history and future promise. In fact, there is no one fixed pattern of the American family to fade away; nor have the unique and changing conditions of American life since the early colonial period sanctioned either uniformity or permanence of structure. Whether viewed historically or contemporaneously, change and plurality of form constitute the essential characteristics of the American family.

Take, for example, the patriarchal family of Europe which our colonial fathers transplanted to this country. On New England soil this very quickly took on a form different in essential respects from that which developed in the South and on the western frontier.

Stubborn and strong-willed as were the Puritans they were not altogether successful in maintaining the authoritative status of the head of the house in the face of influences native to the frontier and a budding industrial system. Despite long hours of labor and low wages, the factory system in New England enabled both women and children to establish a degree of independence from the lord and master; and out of the frontier emerged a spirit of independence and a concept of religion that stressed the integrity and worth of each individual, both sufficiently potent to undermine the authoritarian status of the husband.

How far these influences have transformed the original pattern becomes evident from a hasty glance at relationships within the early Puritan family.

The Puritans looked to the Bible, as interpreted by the clergy, for their model of family relations. To women was assigned a status lower than that of men; for had not St. Paul written that women were "to be in subjection to their husbands, to reverence them, to be chaste and sober keepers of the home"? Children were of a still lower order. Rebellion and disobedience were grave sins which called for stern discipline, as we may infer from John Wesley's injunctions to parents: "Break your child's will in order that it may not perish. Break its will as soon as it can speak plainly —or even before it can speak at all. It should be forced to do as it is told, even if you have to whip it ten times running. Break its will, in order that its soul may live."

Katherine DuPre Lumkin quotes a seventeenth century writer as holding that children "are their parents' goods and possessions and that they owe to them all, even their own selves. . . . As the Lord our God hath made and created children through their parents: so hath He also made them subject under their power and authority of their parents to obey and serve them in his stead." [1]

The husband was the master in his house. In matters touching his family he exercised "more authoritie," as one writer put it,

---

[1] Katherine DuPre Lumkin, *The Family: A Study of Member Roles* (Chapel Hill: University of North Carolina Press, 1933). Also quoted in Bernard J. Stern, *The Family Past and Present* (New York: D. Appleton-Century Company, 1938), p. 195.

"than a king in his kingdom." Even as late as 1848, the Reverend J. N. Damforth was impelled to break into poetry in order to picture this New England ideal of family relationships:

> The father gives his kind command,
> The mother joins, approves;
> And children all attentive stand,
> Then each, obedient, moves.[2]

This pattern had one advantage: it dictated a clean-cut division of functions among husband and wife and children. Writing in 1800, Hannah More describes the respective duties of husband and wife as follows:

The dutie of the husband is, to travel abroad to seeke living; and and the wives dutie is to keepe the house. The dutie of the husband is to get monie and provision: and the wives, not vainly to spend it. The dutie of the husband is to deale with many men: and of the wives, to talke with few. The dutie of the husband is, to be entermedling: and of the wife, to be solitarie and withdrawne. The dutie of the man is, to be skilfull in talke: and of the wife, to boast of silence. The dutie of the husband is, to be a giver: and of the wife, to be a saver. The dutie of the man is, to apparell himselfe as he may: and of the woman as it becommeth her. The dutie of the husband is to dispatch all things without doore: and of the woman to oversee and to give order for all things within the house. Now where the husband and wife performeth the duties in their house, we may call it a Collegge of Quietness: the house wherein they are neglected we may term a hell.[3]

Hannah More realized that prior training would do much to equip a young woman for the position she should occupy. Consequently she gives this advice for furnishing her with the appropriate "stock of ideas, and principles, and qualifications and habits, ready to be applied and appropriated as occasion arise": "An early habitual restraint is peculiarly important to the future character and happiness of women. They should, when very young, be inured to contradiction. . . . They should be led to distrust their own judgment; they should learn not to murmur at expostulation; but should be accustomed to expect and endure opposi-

[2] Lumkin, *op. cit.* Also Stern, *op. cit.*, p. 209.
[3] *Ibid.*, p. 193.

tion. It is a lesson with which the world will not fail to furnish them. . . . It is of the last importance to their happiness in life that they should early acquire a submissive temper and a forbearing spirit." [4]

As suggested, regional differences and cultural differentiations that followed upon geographical location were shortly reflected in family structure. In the South, for example, "Where the long growing season and the stretches of good land suitable for staple crops facilitated the development of the plantation system on a slave basis, conditions converted the more successful setlers into replicas of the European feudal lords, and the plantations constituted recrudescences of the mediaeval manor." [5]

The family on the southern plantation was isolated, as was the pioneer family, but ". . . it differed in that it was the core of a village community of underlings with alien *mores* that could not be immediately assimilated to English Protestant standards. Consequently there began that long, piteous problem of interracial morality so entirely incapable of solution under the chattel regime and so lingering in its consequences to later generations." [6]

The lingering consequences of interracial morality likewise gave to a woman in the South a status qualitatively different from that of her northern and western sisters. Though subordinate and weak, a romantic glow enveloped her figure. The free woman's virtue, in contrast with that of her husband, was at all times to be above suspicion. In the South, too, the absence of a vigorous middle class encouraged sharp distinctions between the poor white family and that of the plantation aristocracy. Both law and custom, as well as religion, rendered the status of wife and children in the former little different from that in the North and West, whereas the easier conditions of existence for the latter softened and eased somewhat the position of woman and child.

The westward movement, together with the development of manufacturing and trade, changed the pattern of family life in the North earlier than in the agricultural South. Despite the lag in legislation designed to free woman from the exclusive domina-

[4] *Ibid.,* p. 193.
[5] Arthur Wallace Calhoun, "The Early American Family," *Annals of American Academy of Political and Social Science,* March, 1932, pp. 7–12.
[6] *Ibid.,* p. 8.

tion of her husband,[7] the free air of the frontier and labor for wages outside led to the gradual emancipation of women and children both in law and custom. Families on the frontier were constantly on the move, and mobility of population tended to undermine family solidarity. This weakening of ties and of authority was evidenced by lowering the age of parental consent for marriage. One observer writing in the 1850's bemoaned the fact that parental consent for marriage was no longer required of boys who had attained the age of fourteen, or of girls at twelve.[8] Marriage was becoming less an alliance of families and more a union of two individuals on the basis of mutual consent.

The factory system and, later, industrialization likewise contributed to the dignity of woman, despite what would seem today to be unbearable conditions of employment. Hard as her lot was, the girl who left the farm and lived on her own earnings in town enjoyed a measure of self-determination which she soon refused to surrender, unless recognized and respected by her prospective spouse. Work outside the home likewise freed the unmarried woman from dependence upon her relatives, with the result that in America, as in England, "the twelve pound look" of an unmarried woman eventually came to exercise a magic influence upon her married sister.

Children, too, eventually profited from economic change. At first they were an economic asset on the farm, and, later, they were a source of financial gain when hired out to a factory owner. But the lot of the children was still sad indeed. In time, however, the machine rendered them less useful as hands on the farm, and aided and abetted by child labor legislation, they were gradually excluded from factory and industrial plant. Thus children, too, became persons in their own right and childhood as a distinctive

---

[7] Thus Matilda Gage, writing in 1892: "So that even in this year 1892, within eight years of the Twentieth Christian Century, we find the largest proportion of the United States giving to the husband custody of the wife's person; the exclusive control of the children of the marriage; of the wife's personal and real estate; the absolute right of her labor and all products of her industry. . . . That woman is an individual with the right to her own separate existence, has not yet permeated the thought of church, state, or society." [*Woman, Church and State*, 2nd ed., (New York: The Truth Seeker Co., 1893), p. 339.]

[8] Quoted by Willystine Goodsell in, "The American Family in the Nineteenth Century," *Annals of American Academy of Political and Social Science*, March, 1932, p. 19.

and unique stage of development began to engage the attention of educators.

Just as transition and change characterize the American family historically, so significant differences in structure can be found today to exist side by side, differences which derive from rural as against urban living, from racial and national background, from divergences in religious belief and the implications of these beliefs for relationships among the members of a family, and from socioeconomic status.

Take, for example, the rural and the urban family. The mere fact that some of the original functions of the early American family are still performed in the rural family makes possible an interpenetration of interests that is difficult, if not impossible, to realize in an urban family that dwells in a city apartment. Members of the rural family can still cooperate in the raising and preparation of food; the city dwellers find it increasingly convenient to use the delicatessen and restaurant, with the result that the family kitchen shrinks to the size of a kitchenette, too small to permit of activities shared by parents and children.

Other functions, now virtually obsolete in the urban family, survive to some extent in rural areas: the care of the sick or seriously ill, the making of clothes, recreational and leisure-time activities, and religious practices.

Significant differences in family structure and customs likewise mark racial and national groups. The Italian and the Jewish families, for example, have resisted more successfully than some the pulverizing influences of contemporary society upon family solidarity. In the economic sphere, the sense of family membership expresses itself frequently in the organization of family cooperatives and mutually sustaining family investments. Not uncommonly, business firms and professional houses consist of father and sons, uncles and cousins, as well as more distant relatives. Family unity and the obligation to function as a brother's keeper weighs heavier upon these groups than upon many of the "older" American families.

Differences in socioeconomic status likewise yield contrasting family patterns. As we move up the economic scale, the contributions of wife and children to the support of the family tend to decrease in importance. Although this enables them to substitute interests that enrich their ways of living, these advantages often lie fallow. At the same time, for the family in the lower income bracket, the uncertainties of uninterrupted employment, unfavorable housing conditions, and impoverished community facilities of a cultural nature condemn children and adults to an existence of a lean and hungry character.

We conclude that the American family, viewed historically or contemporaneously, is multipatterned. It is characterized by diversity rather than uniformity. From this fact derives an important moral for education.

Contemporary Trends in Family Relationships

Before we attempt to draw this moral, let us observe some of the trends with respect to American families as indicated by the 1950 census.[9]

1. Of the nation's forty million families, one-half have no children under the age of eighteen. One-fifth of these families have one child under eighteen; one-sixth have two children under eighteen; and only 14.1 per cent have three or more children under eighteen.

2. Nevertheless, fertility rates are increasing. In 1940, the fertility rate was 281 per 1000 women of childbearing age. In 1947, this had risen to 367 per 1000 women of childbearing age. This increase was particularly large in urban areas, where the number per thousand rose by 47 per cent. Farm women continued, nevertheless, to lead urban women with a birth rate in 1947 of 459 children under 5 per 1000 women of childbearing age, as against 431 per 1000 in rural nonfarm areas and 321 in urban areas.

It is interesting to observe that college women are beginning to render questionable the argument that education results in reduced fertility rates. The record shows that in the period of 1940 to 1947 college women enjoyed the highest fertility rate for children under five. For example, the per cent of change from 1940

---

[9] Much of the data which follow are vividly illustrated in *A Chart Book, A Graphic Presentation of Social and Economic Facts Important in the Lives of Children and Youth*. This was prepared for the Midcentury White House Conference on Children and Youth by the Advisory Council on Federal Government Participation.

to 1947 in the number of children under five years per 1000 women of childbearing age was as follows:

For women with less than five years of schooling	25 per cent
For women with one to three years of high school	36 per cent
For women with four years of high school	48 per cent
For women with one to three years of college	55 per cent
For women with four years or more of college	77 per cent

In terms of numbers, nearly five million children under five years of age in 1947 had mothers who had a grammar school education; about eight million had mothers who had completed one to four years of high school; about one and one-half million had mothers who had completed at least one year of college.[10]

3. The age at which both men and women marry has fallen noticeably in recent years. Indeed, according to the Department of Commerce, the median age of marriage went down more from 1940 to 1950 than in the entire half-century prior to 1940. Thus, in 1890 the median age of marriage for women was 22.0 and for men 26.1. By 1940 the corresponding ages were 21.5 and 24.3, respectively. By 1950 the median age of marriage for women had fallen to 20.4 years and for men to 22.6 years.[11]

4. Not only are men and women marrying earlier than previously, but a larger proportion of the population fourteen years of age and above is entering into wedlock. In 1940, 60 per cent of Americans in this age group were married. By 1950, this percentage had risen to 68 per cent.

Early marriages tend to lower the age of childbearing. Since the average family consists of no more than three children, and the family waits about one year to have its first child, parents, on the average have had their last child within five or six years of marriage. This means, according to Kingsley Davis, that parents "reach this point at a very young age—an age much earlier than people ended reproduction in any previous civilization." [12]

---

[10] *Ibid.*

[11] Statement issued by the United States Department of Commerce, and reported in *The Washington Post* for June 2, 1952.

[12] Kingsley Davis, "The American Family: What It Is, and What It Isn't," *The New York Times Magazine*, September 30, 1951, pp. 18 ff.

5. As stated above, half of the children of the nation are in families of three or more children per family. Moreover, one out of five mothers with children under eighteen works outside the home. This is true particularly of mothers who had broken homes, but in 1949 it applied as well to nearly one-fourth of the married women who lived with their husbands. "Of the more than 21 million mothers with children under eighteen years of age in 1949, over four million worked outside the home. One and one-half million of these had children of pre-school age." [13]

6. One out of eight children is not living with both parents, and, in 1948, about two million children under eighteen, or 4.7 per cent of the total, were living with neither parent. "Among children living with only one parent, approximately 1,500,000 had a widowed parent, 900,000 had a divorced parent, and 1,500,-000 had a parent away from home," in the armed forces, employed away from home, severely ill and away from home, or those who had left the family by separation.[14]

7. An increasing number of children are born out of wedlock. Because of the difficulty of collecting information on this item, statistics of births outside of marriage are incomplete, but the Census Bureau estimates that in 1947, 30,000 of estimated 137,000 births outside of marriage were to girls seventeen years of age or younger. Of these 46 per cent were to white mothers and 54 per cent to Negro or other mothers.[15]

8. The divorce rate has been climbing for some years, most rapidly since 1930. On the other hand, the number of divorces has decreased since 1946 (from 610,000 in 1946 to 386,000 in 1949).

Divorces are most common in families with children above eighteen years of age and with childless couples. For example, "In 1948 there were eight divorces per 1,000 couples with children under eighteen, as compared with fifteen per 1,000 couples without children. Of marriages ended by divorce before the end of the first year, about 10 per cent involved a couple with a child. Divorces involving children usually occur in the early years of marriage. Two-thirds of the children affected are under 10." [16]

---

[13] *A Chart Book, op. cit.*, chart 2.
[14] *Ibid.*, chart 13.
[15] *Ibid.*, chart 14.
[16] *Ibid.*, chart 15.

Although divorce has increased, it is interesting to observe that the percentage of families who suffer from dissolution by death and desertion is lower today than formerly. Moreover, three out of four persons who are divorced remarry within five years.

With these data before us, and bearing in mind the caution we must exercise when speaking of the "American family," we turn to some implications for education.

Educational Implications of Changes in the Family

Let us begin with the most obvious characteristic of the family today: its decreasing importance as an economic unit. As we have seen, economic operations are carried on outside the home and family circle and in ways which involve old and young less and less in shared activities. That is, at one time the family as a whole cooperated in *making* a living. Today the burden of *earning* the family living falls more exclusively upon one or two of its members. The family as a whole thus functions more as a consuming than a producing unit. This profound change in family functions has transformed its role as a character building agency. The impact of member upon member is still one of the most potent in an individual's life and the family continues to be society's most fruitful source of spiritual nourishment, but the media used to serve these purposes are no longer those of yesterday.

Again, the family has become marriage centered. As Kingsley Davis points out, the family of today tends to be built around the married pair. Newlyweds prefer, if possible, to live by themselves, "not because Dorothy Dix advises it, but because certain conditions such as extraordinary geographical mobility and our perpetual social climbing, favor it." Furthermore, continues Davis, the young couple often establish themselves in a class different from that occupied by their parents. In one community studied, it was found that of the professional men, less than 10 per cent had fathers in professional pursuits, and of skilled workmen, only 39 per cent had fathers in the skilled trades.[17]

---

[17] Davis, *op. cit.*, p. 18.

The Need to Enrich Interpersonal Relationships

These two facts, the transformation of the family from a productive into a consumatory unit and its narrowing circle of intimate and continuous interpersonal relationships, are of vital importance to children. As grandparents, uncles, and aunts cease to exercise their one-time influence upon the child, the impact of parental and sibling influence grows in importance. Moreover, as the suburban lot or city apartment replaces the more spacious country home, the impingement of personality upon personality within the home becomes more intense. To fulfill its mission the family must learn to build personality through shared experiences that are less economic and more recreational and "cultural" in character.

Here, indeed, is an argument in favor of a liberal education for all potential parents. To give, one must first receive. Only as education assists individuals to develop inner resources of character and personality and the means for a continuous replenishment of spirit can the family meet adequately the challenge of present-day living. But let us also take note of the fact that the culture required to maintain a high level of creative living within the home must be congenial to more than one type of mind. Books and the reading of books is surely one means for "achieving the excellence of human nature," but education for parenthood involves resources richer and more varied even than those contained within books. The parent, unlike the teacher, cannot segregate his children into homogeneous sections and minister to the idea-minded to the neglect of the thing-minded child. Indeed, the wise parent soon learns that these qualities are intimately related to each other. Education for parenthood involves an introduction to many-sided interests, abilities, and skills out of which to provide a varied and fertile environment in which children can grow.

The role of the arts and crafts in this connection was brought home to the writer a few years ago upon meeting a former student. In response to the customary question, "And what are you doing now?" the latter replied, "Conducting a marriage clinic." Further inquiry revealed that this was a marriage consultation bureau to which disillusioned or maladjusted married couples might turn for advice prior to taking the last fatal step of divorce.

Of the numerous causes for ill-adjustment, this consultant found the absence of common interests loomed large. The hours spent together in the cramped quarters of a city apartment were unrelated to their professional or vocational activity. Leisure-time interests, rather than work, thus constituted the strategic and indispensable conditions of becoming each an integral part of the other. Without common interests and versatility in the creation of these interests, they tended to become bored and to drift away from each other. Accordingly, the consultant's success in salvaging a marriage turned largely upon his ability to suggest some constructive interest they might cultivate and share in common.

To be sure, the on-coming of children tends to fill this void. But the advent of children accents the importance of numerous and varied activities congenial to different talents and different ages, activities and interests which lessen the child's dependence upon outside attractions, bring friends into the home, and cement the ties between parents and children at each stage in the latter's development.

Helping Young People to Cope with Differences in Family Patterns

Earlier we said that the American family is one of plural patterns, each with its distinctive role of man, wife, and child. No one of these patterns is privileged today to exist in lonely isolation. Living side by side in one and the same community, we find a survival of the patriarchal family in which the husband is still the "head of the house," with the wife and children subordinate to his will. Next door may dwell a democratically organized family, one in which man and wife deal with each other on the basis of full equality, and problems and concerns involving children and parents are discussed and decided in family council. The children enjoy free and easy relations with their parents, viewing them more as sympathetic and understanding but older and wiser brothers and sisters must have been viewed in the traditional family than as the conventional father and mother. Farther down the street is still another family grouping, one in which the mother by virtue of a vigorous and dominating personality molds the wills of husband and children as a modern matriarch.

The children from these different homes play with one another, attend the same school, form friendships, and grow into adolescence and adulthood together. In the process of growing up each is impelled to evolve for himself an ideal of the kind of person he wishes most to make of himself and, ultimately, of the marriage partner he will select, as well as the quality and kinds of relationships he would like to prevail in his future home.

These questions are of more than passing importance in the life of the growing boy and girl. They constitute growing pains rendered acute by the contradictions and inconsistencies unique to contemporary society. As growing pains they are entitled to consideration in an institution dedicated to meeting the needs of youth. Lawrence Frank has drawn attention to the fact that "In coming to understand that all is not ideal in the adult world, and that there are discrepancies between pretensions and actual situations, they [adolescents] often become concerned about their own families, sensitive and worried about family customs and patterns and ways of living which must appear peculiar, different and embarrassing." [18] Often the stresses and strains at home, common to this period, cause adolescents to compare their families with those of their friends, and not always to the advantage of the former. Or they evolve an image of the family as an ideal against which they match their own family constellation and find it wanting.[19]

The curriculum of the school can help young people to clarify these problems. Class discussions, wisely and tactfully led, based upon literature, the social studies, and science may enable them to sense more objectively problems that have hitherto been personal and private, or seemingly peculiar to one's self alone. In addition, from reading and directed observation, they may find it possible to harmonize better ideal and reality. Here, again, the arts can play an important part both as therapeutic agents and as nonverbal means of interpretation and expression.

---

[18] "The Adolescent and the Family," in *Forty-Third Yearbook*, National Society for the Study of Education (Chicago: University of Chicago Press, 1944), part I, p. 249.

[19] *Ibid.*, p. 249.

The extracurricular life of the school can also be helpful in meeting life's problems. Some authorities see in the coeducational school and a curriculum which encourages the intermingling of both sexes in a wide range of activities an excellent medium for boys and girls to secure a rounded knowledge of each other, favorable to a sane appraisal of assets and liabilities, in contrast with the artificial and romantic notions that tend to derive from an exclusively "social" contact. Taken in connection with decreasing size of the family and lessened opportunities for boys and girls to grow up together in the same family, the creation of multiple occasions to work and play together under conditions that breed mutual understanding takes on significance.

Direct Study of the Family

Finally, there is a place in general education for the direct study of the family. From an historical and contemporary survey of its many patterns, the young person should be helped to see that as an institution it is not so much in a state of decay as it is in process of becoming society's most effective instrument for enabling people to be at home with each other, as Horace Kallen defines being at home. "People are at home," says Kallen, "with each other wherever they live together (each with his neighbor) in such a way that their togetherness strengthens and eases and frees the separate character of each."

This concept of what it means to be at home may enable young people to interpret the facts of divorce with a weather eye to their own futures. For those who know but one fixed mold of family life, statistics of divorce are indeed alarming. But the picture is incomplete until matched by the data of remarriage. Remarriage, following separation and divorce and widowhood for women, is about one-sixth greater today than it was early in the century. Of those individuals procuring divorce during the five years 1943 to 1948, 75 per cent were already remarried in 1948, and of those divorced earlier (between 1934 and 1943) approximately 86 per cent had remarried by 1948.[20] These data are not unrelated to one's potential role as husband or wife. Moreover, if it be true that the family is becoming ever more marriage centered, this

[20] Davis, *op. cit.*, p. 42.

signifies that its success turns increasingly upon the extent to which it satisfies the hunger for companionship in its many forms. To the degree that education fosters health of personality and skill in all the "arts of communication," it should contribute constructively to enriched family living.

Family Living in General Education

These brief comments on general education are intended to suggest that our schools can contribute more fruitfully than at present to the improvement of family life once they envisage their task as concerned with helping young people to meet their needs in all the relationships of living: person-to-person, personal-social, social-civic, economic. On the other hand, there is a place and a very important place for a more specific emphasis upon education for family living.

Take, by way of illustration, the introduction of home economics into the school curriculum. This occurred during the last quarter of the nineteenth century, a period in which immigration from Europe assumed startling proportions. Between 1881 and 1890, for example, the number of immigrants nearly doubled over previous ten-year periods; and in 1891 to 1900, despite the panic of 1893 and the subsequent depression, there were nearly one million immigrants in excess of the period 1871 to 1880. But what alarmed many Americans was the change in the sources of immigration. Hitherto, this was primarily northern Europe; the stream now originated in eastern and southern Europe and countries unacquainted with the domestic manners and customs of the more firmly rooted Americans.

Furthermore, the new immigrants tended to herd in cities. Immigration thus constituted the outward and visible sign of a shift in the location of new opportunities in American life. These were less on the open frontier and more in the growing cities of industrialism. But new opportunities exacted their price in disruptions of the home. The tenement house, with its cramped quarters, was unfriendly to both work and play within the home. Industry seemed bent upon attracting to itself the labor of women and children. For example, the number of women in industry doubled between 1880 and 1890, and according to the census of 1910, nearly 70 per cent of the girls between the ages of ten and fifteen who were engaged in gainful occupations were employed outside the field of domestic service.

These trends alarmed many who saw in them evidences of disintegration in the American family. Consequently, they called upon the school to introduce courses which would conserve the vital character of the home. Since the most obvious changes bore upon lack of training for girls in cooking, sewing, and household management, these subjects received first consideration. Eventually, however, it was realized that important as the physical and economic conditions of family living might be, satisfying home life derives equally from the impact of personality upon personality. Accordingly, by the 1930's, we find emphasis placed upon the psychological factors essential for healthy and happy family living.

Several factors contributed to this change. One was a growing awareness of the effect of small families upon the education of children. It means, for example, that young people are growing up with less experience in the care and the understanding of younger brothers and sisters. Young mothers, upon being questioned regarding the subjects or training in which they felt themselves most deficient, replied, "In child care and the psychology of childhood." The facts of divorce, to which we have already alluded, likewise suggested the importance of guidance in the development of healthy personality as one factor contributing to a satisfying home life. It thus became apparent that young people need assistance in acquiring the arts of personality adjustment.

Still again, we have come to realize that women today are tending more and more to enter into multiple activities outside the home, activities that have broadened their sphere of interests but which, nevertheless, complicate their functions within the home. Success or failure thus turns upon a woman's ability to foster common interests and to encourage creative relations between child and child, parents and children, husband and wife. Outside the home she is involved in civic and cultural projects of value to the community as well as in a job that enables her to contribute to the family income. Often she carries on two careers simultaneously. Or, as statistics indicate, she gives birth to her last child in her late twenties or early thirties and thus finds it possible to devote a major portion of her time and energy in middle age to interests outside the home, while continuing to meet her responsibilities as wife and mother.

Preparation for parenthood, for men as well as for women, is thus a many-sided affair, to which both general and special education have a contribution to make. When we realize that approximately one-half of the high school graduates end their schooling with graduation, the importance of an introduction to the nature and the essential requirements of a satisfying marriage relationship becomes obvious. Nor is it safe to assume that higher education for men and women, as traditionally conducted, will provide the requisite training.

A number of schools have found that firsthand experience with children, for boys and girls alike, under the guidance of experts yields excellent results. These institutions have found occasions to bring high school students into contact with young children in day nurseries or kindergartens. Here they not only learn to care for babies and young children physically, but to observe their behavior and to glean some understanding of how best to cope with problems of child rearing. When correlated with biology and introductory psychology, this experience has been found to contribute as well to self-understanding and an appreciation of the stages of growth and development through which they themselves are passing.

In addition to and sometimes supplementing laboratory experience, we find secondary schools and colleges providing courses in family life. These deal with items such as the history of the family, its meaning and purposes, its multiple forms in contemporary society, the functions and responsibilities of its various members, relations between the older and younger generations, factors essential in the selection of a mate, the seriousness of mismating, the physiology of reproduction, social and psychological adjustment within the family unit, the relations of the family to other community institutions, economic forces that affect family life, budgeting the family income, understanding the social, mental, and physical growth of children, and the religious and recreational aspects of family living.[21]

---

[21] See, for example, Ruth A. Talbot, "Studying Family Life Education," *Journal of Home Economics,* March, 1952, pp. 187–189; also see L. M. Springfield, "Family

Merely to enumerate these items is to suggest that their importance is not limited to one sex. This raises the question of ways and means of educating young men as well as young women for family life. Some colleges as well as secondary schools have sought to meet this problem through the organization of the regular courses in literature, science, social studies, and the like.

By and large, young parents are psychologically disposed to cooperate with the primary and the elementary school in programs of parent education that are keyed to each stage of the child's development. In the early years—in the nursery school, the kindergarten, and the primary grades—the teacher, at her best, functions as a substitute parent. Her mission is to introduce the child to a family larger and more varied than his immediate family and to guide him in the art of working and playing harmoniously with others. Under her guidance, he may come to recognize and appreciate differences in background and origin in his comrades and take the first steps toward adequate living in a heterogeneous culture. But these insights and techniques will lack effectiveness without the cooperation and understanding of the home. The school thus needs the assistance of the home just as the parents often need the wisdom which the teacher, as an expert, can bring to them.

One function of the school, as a supplementary agency, is to serve as a professional guide to parents as well as to their young. This it will doubtless do as quickly as teachers become professionally equipped for their task. The relationships thus fostered among teacher, parent, and child will vary as the latter moves from the primary school into the elementary school, and on into the secondary school. Each marks qualitatively different stages in child development and changed relationships with his peers and with adults. Each requires him to redefine his relationships with people in a world that for him stubbornly refuses to remain pegged down; and each spells for his parents as well as for him acute growing pains.

Nor is this a simple task for the school. As Esther McGinnis wisely remarks:

Life Class for High School Seniors," *Journal of Home Economics,* June, 1952, pp. 339–440.

To teach as though there were only one way to live, one standard, is false. Even nutrition, where standards can be most nearly exact, is applied according to the amount of money the family has to spend. What is needed to get along on at the subsistence level is one thing, on a comfortable level is another. Home economics students need to be able to live on either and do it skillfully.

It is even more vicious to teach as though one way of living were the "best way" or the ideal way. Too often, the so-called ideal way is derived from the home background of the teacher, who is usually from the middle class. The range of living in our country and in our communities is tremendous. To know many families from a variety of backgrounds is essential for a home-making teacher.

Family centered education is based on knowledge of the conditions under which families are living today.[22]

Ideally, each teacher should be equipped to play this difficult role, but, unfortunately, all too few are so trained today. Nor does the present shortage of professionally trained personnel hold forth the promise of immediate fulfillment. Forward-looking schools may be tempted, accordingly, to solve the problem of parent-school relations through the establishment of a department of parent education. Although this may have the advantage of bringing professional personnel into the school, it might also delay rather than hasten the application of knowledge at the point where it is most urgently needed, that is, in the immediate relationships of teacher, child, and parent.

From this hurried survey it should be clear that the American family is not so much in process of disintegration, as many fear, as it is on its way toward the assumption of new forms, forms which can assure its members, under the complicated conditions of modern living, new and potentially more satisfying relations than those of the past. At its best, the modern family is an intimate association in which each member not only respects the integrity and worth of the other but learns how to live so as to nourish his own nature through the means he employs in fostering the distinctive nature of others.

---

[22] "Family Centered Teaching," *Journal of Home Economics,* January, 1952, pp. 9–12.

Suggested Reading

Davis, Kingsley, "The American Family: What It Is and What It Isn't," *The New York Times Magazine,* September 30, 1951, pp. 18 ff.

Davis, Ruth, "A Program in Family Living," *Educational Leadership,* March, 1953, pp. 360–363.

Gruenberg, Sidonie, "Why They Are Marrying Younger," *The New York Times Magazine,* January 30, 1955, pp. 17 ff.

Lerner, Max, *America As a Civilization* (New York: Simon and Schuster, Inc., 1957), chap. VIII.

Robbins, Florence Greenhoe, *Educational Sociology* (Henry Holt & Co., Inc., 1953), chap. XVI.

Smith, B. Othanel, William O. Stanley, Kenneth D. Benne, and Archibald W. Anderson, *Readings in the Social Aspects of Education* (Danville, Ill.: Interstate Printers and Publishers, 1951), pp. 242–252.

Stiles, Lindley J. (ed.), *The Teacher's Role in American Society* (New York: Harper & Brothers, 1957), chap. 12.

/.\.\.\.\

9

Some Aspects of the Intellectual Task of the School

What Constitutes Literacy?

The reader who has followed the discussion thus far has doubtless asked himself, "What of the distinctively intellectual task of the school? Surely, education has to do with the training of the mind. Does the author suggest we by-pass this traditional function?"

Not at all. Changes in the social order carry with them an insistent moral for the "training of the mind."

Many of the items already discussed bear directly upon both the content and the method of education, suggesting at one time that the school put new wine into its old bottles, at another that it provide both new wine and new bottles. For example, the meager participation of young people in economic and social activities, to which we have repeatedly drawn attention, renders imperative new ways of introducing children to the three R's and the abstract concepts of advanced subjects if their teaching is to be vital. Similarly, as we have also emphasized, undernourishment in these areas requires the school to provide what the Herbartians termed an "apperceptive basis" for an understanding of otherwise abstract and meaningless principles in the sciences and social sciences. In short, the moral of earlier chapters is that to equip young people to face the contemporary world resourcefully, we must train their minds in ways more relevant than those of the past. The times require a unique facility in the "arts of communication," superior even to those developed in the traditional school, but they also require a broader recognition of what is meant by the "arts of communication." No longer can we identify these arts solely with the verbal arts. They include, as well, the fine and practical arts, the use of radio and television, cooperative relations with others in work and play. In fact, the arts of communication include any media which ease and free communication and deepen understanding among people.

This broader conception of the arts of communication in no way lessens the importance of verbal instruction, when conceived functionally. Take, for example, the concept of literacy as defined in the relatively simple agricultural and rural economy of yesterday and in the more complex society of today. A man was once considered literate if he could read sentences of a simple character and sign his own name to legal documents. Given the ability, in addition, to add and subtract, multiply and divide, or to perform the operations equivalent to those mastered easily by a child in primary school today, he was sufficiently schooled to meet the normal problems of living.

But the demands of an urban and industrial society require an ability to read and to write and "to figure" of a much higher order if one is to be self-sustaining.

Take a member of a labor union, for example. To participate responsibly in the decisions of his union an individual must be able to read and to ponder the economic reports submitted to the membership by the trained economists whom the union has employed to keep its members informed regarding economic trends and the bearing of these trends upon the cost of living and the intimate relation of the latter to prices and wages. Again, as an urban dweller, the individual of today depends upon his daily paper or trade journal for information regarding opportunities and responsibilities of which he would otherwise be ignorant. As a member of a committee to consider a problem of importance to his church or fraternal society or civic community, he must know how to search out, organize, and interpret information bearing upon a many-sided question. Unless he can find his way to a library and not become confused and lost once he is inside, he is severely handicapped. Moreover, he needs to be able to protect himself against undue credulity with respect to what he reads. Reading cannot safely be identified with believing. Accordingly, our citizen has to learn how to weigh evidence, detect bias, identify prejudice, and resist the wiles of the propagandist.

Nor is literacy solely a matter of reading and reflecting upon what is read. The radio and television have accentuated the importance of the spoken word. This, too, calls for a discipline and training in the art of listening: the ability to grasp an argument as a whole, not merely to hear one point or to become so preoccupied with one statement that the speaker's argument as a whole is misinterpreted. To the extent that the radio is used in political campaigns and to sell ideas and programs in other areas of living, it becomes important for the citizen to develop an immunity against its abuses and the ability to listen critically and objectively to what he hears.

Again, as the influence of technology continues to permeate and transform our lives and to render men daily more dependent upon science and the applications of science, a rudimentary understanding of the biological and physical sciences (as well as the "mathematics" of everyday life), to say nothing of science as a method of thinking, becomes ever more important.

Finally, literacy, under conditions of the present, would seem to involve an elementary acquaintance with media other than the verbal, whether written or spoken. An acquaintance with the graphic arts, too, ranging from the simplest illustrations in a daily newspaper to the most vivid methods of conveying statistical information, is essential in the equipment of a literate mind. In short, literacy involves a minimum degree of facility in finding one's way around in a world where communication through plural media is a condition of intelligent living.

Uses of the Past

Some would insist that we have omitted a most important aspect of functional literacy, knowledge of the past, since few problems can be dealt with adequately without knowledge of the background out of which they emerge. Indeed, it might be argued that no present event can be fully understood apart from its known connections with the past. What is a present problem indeed, other than a unique combination of factors out of the past, operating in the present and charged with tantalizing future implications? Were the concept of functional teaching adhered to consistently in determining what out of the past should find its way into the curriculum, there would be less sound and fury in educational circles regarding the place of history and the classics in general education. Unfortunately, neither the friends nor the foes of traditional materials are at all times loyal to the arguments they employ. Many, for example, ground their arguments on behalf of the inclusion of a generous background in history in the curriculum upon its functional value in the solution of contemporary problems. Upon winning their case, however, they proceed to introduce not a functional history, but a special privileged history, that is, segments of historical experience of interest and concern to an instructor or to a specialist, perhaps, but quite unrelated, so far as the student can detect, to his interests and needs. On the other hand, the ardent advocate of a plan in which contemporary materials in education take precedence over the classics and the "dead languages" is equally prone to assume that the values he seeks reside in an arbitrary subject matter rather than in the interplay between a student and subject studied. As the writer has stated on another occasion:

There is a necessary content out of the past to which schools should introduce their students—a content not to be selected and listed arbitrarily in school and college catalogue as a uniform and required curriculum for all, but chosen lovingly and fearfully by teachers who seek to marry the peculiar promise of the student and the rich resources of our culture. Material that constitutes an open sesame to life's values for one student may defy the most skillful teacher's efforts with another. And for a very good reason. Values as such reside in Greek or Latin or mathematics in the same manner only that indigestion dwells within cold mince pies. The individual in each case is an important contributing agent. Values require for their emergence a living interplay between a unique personality and an appropriate subject matter. Consequently there is no avoiding the necessity of selecting and adapting educative materials to groups and individuals. Indeed, it is precisely this selection and adaptation that defines the genius as well as the profession of teaching.[1]

---

[1] V. T. Thayer, *American Education Under Fire* (New York: Harper & Brothers, 1944), p. 178.

Once it is realized that values are the resultants of several variables it becomes clear that an "appropriate" subject matter will take character from time, place, and circumstance. In one community, or with one group of students, the struggle of the Romans to create and maintain a government responsible to the people and mindful of their needs will give perspective, depth, and meaning to present-day efforts at political reform which contemporary material might lack. So, too, a comparative study of the relations between members of a Roman family and the family patterns of students in the class might help the latter to understand and appreciate the evolution of the family and to consider by comparison and contrast the role of child and parent which they would create for themselves. On the other hand, in a less historically minded community by a class less gifted verbally, a more exclusive reliance upon contemporary patterns might bring the desired results.

Not only do values change their character from the interaction of subject matter and student, but they vary as well with method employed. Take, for example, a freshman course in history as described by Elliott Dunlap Smith.

Early in the course . . . the students are asked to study the essay on the Germans by Tacitus and to decide for themselves whether Tacitus had ever been in Germany, supporting their conclusions with evidence. Then they beat out in class, through the slow process of wrestling with their observations and their deductions, a judgment as to what validity the evidence of Tacitus has in giving them a picture of the Germans of that time, and what corrections and precautions they must take to bring their picture of the Germans into true focus. In the same way, the course proceeds, now exploring, for example, the bias of Gibbon, and now what is historical and what religious in the Acts of the Apostles.[2]

Viewed in the abstract, Tacitus is remote indeed from the immediate concerns of college freshmen. But when used as a conscious instrument for developing the ability to weigh and appraise the testimony of an observer, and to exercise critical judgment, time ceases to operate as a dulling factor. With quite a different

---

[2] Elliot Dunlap Smith, "General Education in Practice," *Journal of Higher Education,* October, 1951, p. 377.

class group, however, these same characteristics of mind may require for their stimulation material of quite a different nature and on an altogether different level. Common to all situations, however, is the need to cultivate a habit of mind which confronts each problem with the queries: "How did you come to be what you are? What are your forebears? Your origins? Out of what background do you arise? What answers have men given to you in the past? With what results? How do the circumstances of successful solution in the past differ from the present? What data, then, are familiar, perhaps constant, and what novel, suggesting a new approach and perchance a new solution?"

One function of the past then is to further perspective and to develop the habit of attacking a novel problem with an eye to its origins as well as its present context. Still another is to offset the limitations of parochialism and to accustom young people to the facts of diversity in life values. Nor need this realization lead, as some fear, to a serious undermining of purpose. Surely this is not the only alternative to a realization that what meets the deepest needs of one individual or one people may not do so for another. In a recent volume, *The Uses of the Past,* Herbert J. Muller asserts "that the admission of a principle of relativity and uncertainty should not simply be depressing."

It enables a higher objectivity, a fuller understanding of present and past. It enables wiser choices among the possibilities open to us—among goods that are no less real because they are relative, and that are more relevant than arbitrary absolutes. Above all, this principle encourages a positive faith in positive values: of liberality, breadth of spirit, hospitality to new ideas, willingness to adventure, humility in admitting one's own fallibility and the limitations of the human mind—of the tolerance that is indispensable for the pursuit of truth, for social harmony, and for simple humanity. If these are not the highest values, none are more essential for world order and peace.[3]

The "Times" and Methods of Thinking

Intimately related to the use of the past is a conscious emphasis upon methods of thinking which are keyed to a heterogeneous

[3] Herbert J. Muller, *The Uses of the Past* (New York: Oxford University Press, 1952), p. 43.

society and a period of history unique in rapidity of change, to a world in which values are plural and facts refuse to remain pinned down.

Serious consideration of these aspects of modern life suggests an appropriate emphasis in the intellectual task of the school. As the philosopher Alfred N. Whitehead has emphasized, the period in which we are living is unique in human history in that we can no longer assume, as men have safely assumed since Plato, that each generation will live amid conditions substantially the same as those which governed the "lives of its fathers and will transmit those conditions to mould with equal force the lives of its children." This follows from the fact, to continue with Whitehead, that in the past "the time-span of important change was considerably longer than that of a single life." Today, however, this time-span is "considerably shorter than that of human life, and, accordingly, our training must prepare individuals to face a novelty of conditions." [4]

The Changing Status of Facts

One moral to draw from Whitehead's analysis relates to the teaching of facts and principles. Too often these constitute the be-all and the end-all of classroom instruction. Consequently, when classes increase in size, as they have on all levels of education in recent years, the temptation to evaluate the results of teaching in terms of facts memorized is difficult to resist. (Witness the widespread use of objective tests of a predominantly informational character on the college as well as the secondary and elementary school levels.)

Change both enhances and decreases the importance of facts. To acquire the habit of asking, "What are the facts of today as against yesterday?" is one way of avoiding error or of becoming quickly out of date. This puts a premium upon the techniques of searching out, organizing, and marshaling facts in each and every field of study. On the other hand, the ever present possibility that the validity of facts is of short duration requires a constant checking and rechecking of their credentials. Nowhere is this more

---

[4] Quoted in John L. Child, *Education and Morals* (New York: Appleton-Century-Crofts, Inc., 1950), p. 113.

evident than in the field of science, where, presumably, the methods of procedure for identifying and validating facts and principles are most refined.

This suggests the importance of developing early the habit of regarding the facts of a situation with a healthy scepticism until they are rechecked, of accepting conclusions tentatively, of acting upon the basis of principles that one stands ready to revise in the light of new and more relevant data. Here, again, a word from Elliott Smith is pertinent.

It is usually stated that general education is good in proportion as it serves to broaden or deepen a student's understanding of life as a whole. Our experience has taught us that this criterion is misleading. It is not that the concepts are wrong but that it is wrong in tense. After all, even in college, students are young and have a long life ahead of them. In this changing, perplexing, and indoctrination-ridden world, they must learn much more after graduation than they can possibly learn in school or college; and for the most part they must be their own teachers. What is important is any program of general education, therefore, is less what the students learn at the time than how well their education fits them to go on learning in the future.[5]

An education that equips the individual to find his way in a precarious and uncertain world runs counter to the traditional emphasis and the original purposes of the school. In the colonial period, for example, the dominant purpose of the school was to transmit the truths which men rejected on peril of eternal damnation. Schools were established by religious denominations and religious communities to convey the facts and principles which alone might insure the salvation of their souls. Religious orthodoxy was all-important, since the nonconformist was universally assumed to be a menace to himself and to his community. To be sure, religious differences existed, and out of these differences there gradually emerged a quite different conception of the nature and purpose of the school. Sects differed in their conception of the truth but they were united in ascribing its source to an authority outside the experience of men. On this assumption, John Cotton grounded his conviction that the desire for liberty

---

[5] Smith, *op. cit.*, p. 374.

is but the sinful prompting of the natural man. On this assumption, too, the early Puritans justified their conviction that the "elect" should govern in both church and state in opposition to Roger Williams, who, appealing to the same authority, the Bible, argued on behalf of freedom of conscience and the separation of church and state. Neither questioned the assumption that truth is formulated for man rather than by man and is thus discovered rather than created.

This concept of truth as external long dictated the emphasis in schools. The methods of thinking employed and fostered bore little resemblance to those which spelled success on the farm, in trade and commerce, or in the budding new industries which quickly developed on American soil. Habits of mind symbolized by the term "Yankee ingenuity" seldom found their way into the classroom even when teachers themselves engaged in original research. Thinking was restricted, rather, to deductions from a known principle or an axiom stated in the textbook, much as a minister of the gospel develops the moral of his sermon from a quotation taken from the Scriptures. Firsthand experience, if recognized at all, was considered a poor second to the printed word, and children were taught that new truths are in reality old truths which have been lying dormant, much as the sleeping beauty of the fairy story awaited the reviving kiss of her lover.

Increasing Importance of Empirical Methods of Thinking

The gradual conquest of the frontier brought a change in methods of thinking which eventually penetrated the insulated walls of the school. In long-established and settled communities the practices which men follow successfully in agriculture, trade, and commerce, as well as in their associations with each other, assume the character of fixed principles or major premises in a syllogism from which the answers to individual problems can be deduced as they arise in the daily course of living. But when the farmer moves into new territory where new conditions of soil and climate confront him with novel problems and a contradiction of old precepts, the familiar axioms which have dictated when to plant, how to fertilize, and when to reap no longer hold good.

New premises are called for and qualities of inventiveness assume an importance not previously accorded them.

It is precisely this necessity of coping with new conditions and discovering new processes and techniques, together with a readiness of a restless people, constantly on the move, to accept the new on the basis of equality with the old, that has transformed the American continent. Necessity has been the mother of invention, and the inventive spirit has furthered not only the development of modern science and technology but also a conscious formulation of methods of thinking better designed to control the novel.

To be sure, this change in attitude toward the natural environment is not exclusively American. Its origins antedate the discovery and settlement of the new world, and its revolutionary achievements in thought and action are written large in European history. In America, however, men were confronted with a unique situation, the repeated opportunity and necessity to create and re-create the physical and social conditions of a civilized existence. Successive generations cleared the forest, tamed the soil, and organized new communities, thus creating their own political, social, and civic institutions as well as their own customs and laws, manners and morals. Having done so, they moved on to a new location where their children proceeded to repeat the process.

The American's experience with institutions, laws, and customs in evolution contrasts with that of his European brother. For the latter (until two great world wars transformed the face of his continent) institutions have seemed more firmly rooted in reality, if not constituting an essential aspect of reality itself. Since their origin dates from a period beyond the memory of man, it is easy to ascribe to them a fixed and eternal character. To challenge their validity is to adopt the ways of the upstart. The path of wisdom is for man to adapt himself to his institutions rather than to mold his institutions to his needs.

The Influence of the Frontier Upon Conceptions of Law and Morality

Not so with one who establishes his residence on virgin soil and builds a community in cooperation with others of somewhat different background. Here the customs, laws, and morals originate with the people who make up the community, and the habit of evaluating institutions by their effects upon people comes naturally. Man, in the best sense of the word, is thus the measure of all measures.

The American's notion that institutions are born of man and are designed to serve his needs led him also to change the age-old concept of the nature and purpose of law. Contrast, for example, the concept of law as expressed by the distinguished jurist, Chancellor Kent, in 1836 with that of Oliver Wendell Holmes some fifty years later. According to Chancellor Kent, "The law, as a science, is only a collection of general principles, founded on the moral law and in the common sense of mankind, and applied to particular cases as they arise, by the diligence of the bar and the erudition of the courts." [6]

Here the law is viewed as an externally formulated body of general principles derived from moral laws that are likewise essentially foreign to the native spirit of mankind. Consequently, the correct application to specific cases is more likely to follow upon a strict adherence to the rules of a syllogism than from a tender concern for what might be unique and individual circumstances involved in the case at issue. As the court sees it, justice is none too closely related to consequences. "Right for right's sake, though the heavens fall" marks the decisions of a just judge.

Doubtless it was reaction against a too rigid application of justice so conceived which prompted one jurist to remark that the wise decisions of western courts followed more from an ignorance of precedents than from their knowledge of the law!

By 1881, the year in which Oliver Wendell Holmes published his lectures on *The Common Law*, the practical conditions under which Americans had created their institutions had prepared many to accept a more dynamic and experimental conception of law. As Holmes observed,

The growth of the law is legislative. And this in a deeper sense than that what the courts declare to have always been the law is in fact new. It is legislative in its grounds. The very considerations which

---

[6] From *An Address*, Boston, 1836, p. 6. Quoted in Richard D. Mosier's *Making the American Mind* (New York: Kings Crown Press, 1947), p. 63.

•

judges most rarely mention, and always with an apology, are the secret root from which the law draws all the juices of life. I mean, of course, considerations of what is expedient for the community concerned. Every important principle which is developed by litigation is in fact and at bottom the result of more or less definitely understood views of public policy; most generally, to be sure, under our practice and traditions, the unconscious result of instinctive preferences and inarticulate convictions, but none the less traceable to views of public policy in the last analysis. And as the law is administered by able and experienced men, who know too much to sacrifice good sense to a syllogism, it will be found that, when ancient rules maintain themselves . . . new reasons more fitted to the time have been found for them, and they gradually receive a new content, and at last a new form, from the grounds to which they have been transplanted.[7]

As with law, so with certain aspects of morality. Diversity in background, characteristic of most American communities, has fostered a competition for men's loyalties in matters spiritual as well as things material, and the principle that "by their works ye shall know them" has seemed to many as appropriate to apply in choosing between rival conceptions of the good life as in other areas.

At the same time, Americans have been and still are an intensely religious people. Moreover, they are disposed to take their religion seriously. Despite the differences that separate Protestant from Catholic, or Catholic from Jew, even Protestant from Protestant, one common assumption has run through the faith that each one holds: the assumption that religion is both the source and the indispensable undergirding of morality. From which it follows that only a valid religion can yield a valid morality!

Here would seem to be the seeds of an inevitable conflict; and, indeed, rivalry and conflict there has been. On the whole, however, a spirit of tolerance and the disposition to live and let live in matters of religion characterizes the American today, in contrast with an earlier insistence upon orthodoxy and a none too gentle handling of the nonconformist. If we ask ourselves how this has come about, the answer is found in the use of two concepts of morality, without an overly conscious awareness of their con-

---

[7] Quoted in Max Lerner, *The Mind and the Faith of Justice Holmes* (Boston: Little, Brown & Co., 1945), pp. 54–55.

tradiction. The one, sectarian and authoritarian in character, regulates relations within the family and parochial group, dictating how one should spend the Sabbath, whether he should smoke or drink, play cards or dance, practice birth control. The other, secular and more specifically public in its applications, is a morality of common agreements which the individual and his neighbors have worked out together and come to accept as standards with which to channel their common interests, resolve conflicts, and, in general, to ease and free relations with each other.

In this manner American communities have narrowed the range of sectarian morality and widened that of the secular.

Doubtless the emergence of the nonsectarian school aided and abetted this trend. Originating in the Middle Colonies, it quickly spread into the North and the South and the rapidly expanding West. Characteristic of its instruction was a centering upon elements of faith common to all religious groups within the community and the by-passing of tenets upon which its patrons disagreed. This formula was followed by Americans in the development of public education in communities as multicolored as the traditional coat of many colors.

None the less, nonsectarian instruction perpetuated two assumptions in education, relevant and appropriate as they might have been a century ago, which many challenge today.

Contributions and Limitations of Nonsectarian Education

First, it assumed that pupils are to remain passive in the learning process and that teaching is a procedure in which the ideas of the instructor or the assertions of the textbook are to be conveyed to the mind of the student without change en route. Mansfield's *American Education,* published in 1851, put this neatly as follows: "What is the business of the teacher? . . . His position is strictly that of a conveyor of knowledge—moral and intellectual—to a yet unoccupied and growing mind. To do this successfully, requires that his instruction should carry to that waiting mind a conviction of its *truth,* and that he should also *connect* that truth with the *duties* of life."

Secondly, nonsectarian instruction assumed that items of controversy were to receive silent treatment in the school. In short, a device which originated in the effort to avoid the heat of controversy in a society religiously plural and highly sensitive to creedal differences was extended as well to other areas of significant difference. Were this principle adhered to logically, nothing but the commonly agreed upon would find a legitimate place in the curriculum of the school, and young people would emerge from the classroom, as, indeed, they have done all too frequently, wanting in the discipline of effective methods for coping with problems upon which men disagree or the final answers to which are known only to the future.

An Intellectual Discipline Relevant to a Pluralistic Society

As indicated earlier, the principles by which people direct their lives in a one-patterned society easily become identified with the inner structure of the universe. Once these life patterns become plural, however, a stubborn insistence that my neighbor mold his life according to my sacred convictions may do violence to convictions equally sacred to him. It may even threaten the integrity of his personality. At the same time, there is no avoiding the fact that we both live in an interrelated society, one in which interests overlap and the way in which each lives his life becomes of increasing moment to others. How then, can we manage not only to dwell together in comparative peace, but to transform our associations into mutual benefit?

Lawrence Frank provides one answer in an article entitled "Responsible Living." Having developed the thesis that contemporary changes in our political, economic, civic, and social life render less obvious today a single path of duty, or responsible living, he insists that this confusion is not altogether bad. Characteristic of today is an increasing sensitiveness to the consequences of our actions upon the lives of those affected by them. Not only is the "right" less easily identified in specific situations than it once was, but each of us is less content to follow the maxim of right for right's sake regardless of the consequences to others. That is, the situation or context of a problem as well as a general principle looms large in arriving at a decision. As Frank puts it:

"What today seems significant is that we are increasingly evaluating what people do or refrain from doing, not as measured by impersonal rules and conformity to super-human standards, or obedience to legal and moral codes, but by its meaning and significance for others as personalities. We are realizing that, in whatever we do, we should have, to use an old Quaker word, a *concern* for others—a feeling of sensitive awareness of what we are doing to and for others, how others feel and what we may be evoking from them." [8]

Now, if we seek a formula with which to justify and explain this increasing tendency to resolve moral issues and conflicts of interest in terms of the effect of one decision as against another upon the personalities involved rather than in the logical deductions from an abstract principle, we find it in the concept of a democracy of absolutes.

Applying the Golden Rule to Absolutes

But this concept is double-edged in its application. It guarantees to each individual or group freedom to think and to act in accordance with its own absolutes in private life and parochial relationships. But once men venture into the public market place, their absolutes are required to discard their royal and sovereign robes and to clothe themselves in a garb befitting a democracy in which loyalties are free to compete on an equal and fair basis. In other words, when absolutes overlap or conflict, they are to be evaluated in terms of their potential contribution to the general welfare rather than by their pedigrees.

Seeing the World Through the Eyes of Others

The first step leading toward peace and understanding in a world of plural values is thus an application of the Golden Rule to absolutes. But this is only the first step. Second is the disposition and habit to enter sympathetically and appreciatively into the lives of our neighbors, with a view to seeing the world as nearly as possible through their eyes.

---

[8] Lawrence Frank, "Responsible Living," *The Standard*, January-February, 1951, p. 208.

There was a time when traveling abroad was considered to be the last stage in the completion of a formal education. This was intended, at its best, to confront the student with the customs and manners and life values of a people different from his own. The hope was that the values he was ultimately to make his own would be ripened and seasoned from observing the customs and codes of others. Rich in possibilities as travel is, the experience of a critical comparison and contrast of values cannot be safely left to the last days of schooling. Rather should the discipline begin in the primary school, with the young child's friendly interest in people who differ from his own, and continue as an intercultural education through the elementary and secondary school and college. It is this that gives plausibility to recent emphasis upon a curriculum based upon the "great books" in school and college and the central place of the humanities in general education. But it is also this purpose which reveals the limitations in one arbitrary list of books for a student to read. Not only will a relevant selection of books vary with individuals and local circumstance but the "great books" taken alone are insufficient. To them should be added opportunity for enrichment of experience in art and music, the science laboratory and industrial shop, and, above all, firsthand contact with people under conditions that further seeing life as others see it.

William James once remarked that no one has adequately refuted another's philosophy until he not only has laid bare the principles of the rival system, together with their limitations, but has also clarified what caused his opponent to see life as he does. So it is with all conceptions of life with which one must come to terms. As Lawrence Frank has said, wherever men live they encounter persistent problems of living. The different answers they devise for these problems constitute their assumptions about nature and the world. But since all experience is limited, no assumption does full justice to the needs or the potentialities of living of all people in all times and places. This should humble the claims of any system of values. To acquire the disposition and skill as well as the courage to sift and winnow from the past and the contemporary scene that which will mature and ripen and render ever more relevant one's own life assumptions is the never ending purpose of a liberal education. Perhaps it was this realization which led Pascal to remark, "Thought makes the whole dignity of man; therefore endeavor to think well—that is the only morality."

The application of the Golden Rule to all contenders for truth and an honest attempt to afford a fair field for all rivals for men's loyalties comprise two aspects of an intellectual discipline keyed to a pluralistic world. A third is what Max Otto has termed creative bargaining.[9]

The Art of Creative Bargaining

The term creative bargaining is not altogether a happy one to apply to the process we have in mind since there is a tendency to identify bargaining with the disposition to accept half a loaf today with the expectancy of further gains tomorrow. (Perhaps creative consensus would be a better term.) Bargaining, or compromise, so conceived testifies neither to growth in the understanding of the needs and interests of others nor to change in the evaluation of one's own position. It suggests merely a shrewd adaptation of means to inflexible ends. What Otto has in mind envisages the possibility of a wiser and more generous formulation of objectives resulting from conference, deliberation, investigation, and an earnest attempt on the part of the participants in a discussion to put themselves in the place of others.

There are, to be sure, occasions when creative bargaining cannot run its full course, and education in the art of compromise requires full recognition of this fact. The dispute between England and Iran in 1952 over the disposition of Iranian oil illustrates this point. England held firmly to "the sanctity of contracts" and refused to concede Iran's right to unilateral cancellation of its obligations under international agreement. Iran was equally adamant in upholding the principle of national sovereignty. The possibilities of agreement hinged entirely upon the ability of neutrals to persuade both to by-pass their absolutes and to give serious consideration to the consequences of an indefinite deadlock not only upon themselves but upon the entire free world.

---

[9] "Creative Bargaining," *The Standard*, March, 1951, pp. 263–269. See also Max Otto, *The Human Enterprise* (New York: F. S. Crofts & Co., Inc., 1940), chap. V, and by the same author, *Things and Ideals* (New York: Henry Holt & Co., Inc., 1924), chap. V.

Agreement in cases of this character involves an appeal to an overarching ideal more compelling than the principles in conflict or to an aroused sensitiveness to the context of the problem sufficient to bring about the weighing of principle against contingent circumstance.

The controversy over the teaching of religion in public schools illustrates further the difficulties which often beset creative bargaining. According to the principle of separation of church and state, as interpreted by the Supreme Court, public schools are forbidden to engage in religious instruction. This does not preclude, however, an objective and impartial study of religion. Nevertheless, few communities are willing to subject religious tenets to comparative study. They are satisfied only when school authorities indoctrinate their pupils in one or another religious faith or in a "common core" of religious doctrine. Lacking a willingness to subject religious tenets to a scrutiny similar to that applied to the principles of politics, or economics, most schools have found it expedient to exclude from the curriculum all study of issues in religion upon which men do not see eye to eye.

Nor is religion unique in this respect. In recent years numerous groups have come forward to censor textbooks and to control the manner in which teachers deal with controversial issues. They wish no unbiased or impartial weighing of evidence, since, as they see it, there is but one side to a question. Failing to appreciate that the issues upon which people divide often constitute the growing points of society and thus afford the young, when properly handled, most fruitful opportunities from which to acquire methods of thinking and ways of living of inestimable value in the contemporary world, they seek to confine the classroom either to the innocuous or to questions of a hothouse variety.

Pressure groups within the community and well-meaning but overly ardent or intolerant advocates of special causes likewise present obstacles to the educational handling of controversial issues and mooted questions, since they generate an emotional atmosphere that precludes suspending judgment, pending a calm and dispassionate hearing of all points of view. Often, too, in the discussion of an issue the members of a class generate a heat that militates against light. Under these conditions the instructor performs a valuable service when he insists upon a "cooling off period," or discontinuing discussion until the group can demonstrate a proper degree of maturity.

The atmosphere which permits or forbids the educational handling of critical issues in the classroom pervades the community as well as the school. Fortunately, schools start with an initial advantage in that the average community gives lip service, at least, to the principle that it is the school's function to educate people to have an open mind. But, like a wayward pupil, it needs to be reminded of its convictions and the implications of these convictions.

The principal of one school reports a happy incident of this character. A teacher in social science succeeded in stimulating discussions of controversial issues to the point where they overflowed the classroom and extended into the homes of his students. A number of parents found their convictions challenged and protested to the principal that the classroom was being used to promote false and dangerous notions. They demanded either an end to discussion or an acceptable weighing of conclusions.

Instead of yielding to this pressure, or advising the teacher to "go slow," the principal invited the irate parents to spend an evening in his home and there to meet the offending teacher. This they agreed to do. In this informal atmosphere, the parents were led to state their objections to the procedures of the classroom. The instructor described the objectives he sought and reviewed some of the questions discussed. In the discussion which followed he inquired, innocently, of the group how they would have dealt with one of these questions. The suggestions that followed were in no way unanimous, and before long an animated debate was in progress. So rewarding, indeed, was the evening that it concluded with the organization of the group into a discussion club!

Not all community objections eventuate so happily. Few instructors are as successful in calming worried citizens or in helping them to see that in areas of controversy the function of the school, as the representative of the public at large, is to promote understanding rather than to grind the ax of any one segment of community opinion.

Collective bargaining between capital and labor constitutes one field of creative bargaining. The "Quaker Way" of dealing with knotty problems testifies to its extension in still other areas where the interests or the ideas of one impinge upon those of another. Morris Llewellyn Cooke has described the manner in which this method is gaining ground in the work of committees and commissions in government and "is being adopted by numerous directors of public and private organizations in various parts of the country."

In striking contrast with traditional methods of debate and reliance on majority rule, which, according to Cooke, assume "there exists a divergence of interests rather than a common purpose," the Quaker Way concentrates upon the importance of a consensus.

The first step is to divorce the individual as nearly as possible from emotional identification with one position as against another. For this reason, in a Quaker meeting,

. . . a subject is introduced not by presenting a resolution but by "reading a query." This is usually done by the chairman—or "Clerk of the meeting," as he is known in Quaker groups. Such a departure from parliamentary order is by no means a petty one, for by this simple device, the issue seems to come from the group as a whole instead of being sponsored by one faction within it.

Various points of view on the subject are expressed by individual members—whoever wishes to contribute. But strong words, provocative language and repetitive discourse are taboo: members are encouraged to speak just once on a given point, and only after careful thought. And, most significant of all, the individual speaks not simply as a man, expressing his own conscience but as the voice of the group addressing itself to the issue at hand. If a contrary viewpoint is raised, it is considered as if it were one's own for the purpose of treating it objectively. "Getting under the weight" of the other man's doubts is the term the Quakers sometimes use to describe this attitude of respect for a minority viewpoint.

If conflict at any point become so heated as to make an agreement doubtful, the Clerk may halt discussion and ask members to consider the subject for a while in thoughtful silence.[10]

According to Cooke, the President's Commission on Water Resources Policy, of which Cooke was chairman, "never took a vote and no record was kept of its proceedings. The report itself

---

[10] Morris Llewellyn Cooke, "The Quaker Way Wins New Adherents," *The New York Times Magazine*, June 17, 1951, p. 21.

is its record." Other committees and commissions which, according to Cooke, either have operated or now operate in accordance with this "Quaker principle" are the Joint Committee on the Organization of Congress in 1948–1949, The Committee on Economic Development, the International Monetary Fund, and the Acheson-Lilienthal committee of the State Department on atomic energy.

These illustrations suggest that a new and more democratic method of conference, deliberation, and decision are in process of evolution, methods more sensitively attuned to a complex and interdependent society than are the older methods of debate in which protagonists for one side strive to overwhelm those of another. They also render clear that success in arriving at a consensus turns upon a discipline in cooperative thinking no less rigorous than the individualistic procedures of the past. Just as the schools have sought to develop in their students the skills and techniques requisite for the one, so it is now incumbent upon them to provide opportunities for the acquisition of the other —and to determine when the one is appropriate and when the other. For this reason, it may be helpful to identify the crucial factors that make for either a consensus or a generous understanding of problems upon which honest men disagree.

Crucial Factors in the Conference Method

First is the habit of insisting upon a knowledge of relevant facts. To be sure, the method of debate is not unmindful of the importance of facts, but it stresses a selection and organization of data favorable to the winning of converts. The method of conference, in contrast, is less biased, since the question under consideration has been posed as a query, not as a bone of contention.

When facts seemingly conflict or differences in their implication become obvious, there is need for further data. A wise moderator, at such a time, will assign the task of further research to individuals who most need training in objectivity, with the injunction that they are now the servants of the group, not partisans!

It is one thing, of course, to sense the need for additional data with which to clarify a problem and another thing to gather, organize, and present them. What the latter involves will vary with the nature of the problem under study. It calls for the exercise of many different skills, techniques, and methods. Intelligent participation in problem solving, be it individual research or group study, rests upon both prior and supplementary training in methods that are pedagogically different: the methods of the laboratory, of historical inquiry, of the social sciences, of weighing values. To acquaint students with these methods and to enable them to determine when one as against another is called for is one of the functions of general education.

Some years ago, a class in elementary science undertook to dissect a chicken as a practical means of identifying the organs of the body and its bony structure. Not only was the flesh removed but the skeleton was taken apart as well. This being done, several pupils suggested that the bones be restored to their original position. No sooner said than attempted, and with success—up to one final bone. This stubbornly refused to reveal its original position. Where did it belong? One theory after another was proposed, tested, and found wanting. The discussion elicited by this process was exciting and vigorous but no satisfactory solution emerged. As the end of the period approached closer and closer, tension and frustration mounted. Finally, one boy exclaimed, "Let us vote on where it belongs."

This experience afforded the teacher a rare opportunity to impress upon the children the difference between the type of situation in which voting may lead to a satisfactory solution and one in which it is valueless. When different methods are thus involved, the school can be helpful in leading pupils to appreciate the circumstances under which one method or the other is applicable.

But let us return to our unsolved problem. The need for additional facts temporarily halts discussion. Emotional squalls may also inhibit intelligent consideration of points at issue. When these occur, it is the responsibility of the moderator to order a cooling-off period.

Not all cooling-off periods succeed in a permanent reduction of temperature, but, in education, particularly, the values sought derive less from the ultimate solution of a problem than from the habits distilled in the process. The discipline of recognizing when emotion is blocking intelligence is one of the lessons a school can impart. For a class to observe that it lacks sufficient maturity with which to continue a discussion may constitute in itself a valuable educational experience.

Finally comes the stage of summing up or concluding a discussion and evaluating what has been done. Here again each situation is unique and the concluding session will take its character from this fact. The class may have discovered that the problem must continue as an open question, that circumstances do not permit of a definitive conclusion, or that the best authorities on the subject are themselves divided. Other problems are equally inconclusive as regards evidence but the circumstances may require action on the basis of a tentative judgment. Still other discussions may have ended in a consensus, but even in these instances the participants should have learned that time plays tricks upon certainty, and what seems altogether evident today may be under suspicion tomorrow.

Whatever the outcome of a specific discussion, the training it yields is not complete until its members have summarized and appraised what has happened. The urgency of this training is evident to anyone who observes the reaction of many who listen to a lecture or a discussion on the radio or television. How eagerly they seize upon one point with which they agree or disagree to the neglect of all others! They have lacked experience in considering an argument as a whole, or the relation of one item to its qualifying context. But, if we reflect upon the future use of the radio and television as media for the discussion of critical issues, the discipline of listening so that one acquires what John Locke termed "a round-about knowledge" of a topic assumes increasing importance. Consequently we must turn again to the school for the development of the art of listening, an art that comes only from the repeated necessity of listening and reporting fairly and objectively upon what one has heard and summarizing for others as well as for oneself the "pros" and the "cons" of a discussion.

Cooperative thinking, as we have hurriedly described it, demands the exercise of a number of functions for which the school can train its students: (1) the functions of a moderator, whose duty it is to subordinate his own feelings and to insure a fair hearing for all points of view, to keep his finger upon the pulse of the group, and to identify occasions when additional facts are required, a cooling-off period is advisable, or the time is ripe for concluding the discussion; (2) the function of fact-gathering or resource leader; (3) the function of an observer and critic of the discussion; and, (4) the function of a direct participant whose thinking has been refined and tempered by repeated practice in these other functions.

Opportunities to develop these habits, dispositions, and skills abound both in classroom and the general life of the school, wherever, indeed, ideas and interests come into conflict. When so used, conflict and disagreement constitute happy occasions for developing the habits of mind and character upon which our contemporary world places a premium. For, to repeat, we live in a world of rapid change in which confirmed ways of thinking, feeling, and acting are constantly being challenged. It is a world of increasing interdependence, of chain reactions, in which no man and no people can safely live in lonely isolation. It is a world of variegated communities and plural cultures with their contrasting and contradictory life values but a world, nevertheless, in which men of different codes and standards must traffic with each other in accordance with principles and procedures which promote a community of interests. Given this kind of a world, an important task of the school would seem to be to develop the logic and the ethics of thinking which might encourage even the lion and the lamb to deal with each other in peace and good will.

The Curriculum and Methods of Thinking

Little has been said about the content of the curriculum. This is indeed relevant to any consideration of the intellectual task of the school. It is unwise, however, to assume an arbitrary and dogmatic attitude with respect to the essential content of education above the level of "primary adjustments" or the minimum essentials of the elementary and early years of the secondary school. Most people would agree that each and every individual is handicapped severely in modern life if he lacks facility in elementary mathematics, is unable to read simple material in the vernacular, is unable to express himself clearly in oral and written language, or is ignorant of the facts and principles of science which enter into everyday living. But precisely at what point requirements for all students on the secondary level in the various fields of knowledge should end is by no means conclusive. In a world of shifting emphasis in the demands of society and the needs of young people, it is likely that the answer to the question of when general education should end and special education begin will always vary with time and place and individual. Consider, for example, the suddenness with which educators as well as the public at large have awakened to the serious consequences which may ensue as a result of the neglect of science in the schools. Revolutionary changes in technological development at home and abroad bear directly upon what constitutes an appropriate curriculum in school and college.

Nor is the problem clarified by insisting merely that the "permanent studies" should comprise the heart of the curriculum, since this in no way solves the problem of what specific content within these studies is appropriate today in contrast with yesterday. Probably the best we can do is to seek agreement on the broad fields which should be included in the program of each school, leaving more specific definition of content within each field or area to the results of a cooperative study by curriculum planning groups within each state and locality: teachers, administrators, students of adolescent development and of society, experts within the various fields. By and large, there is unanimity of belief that these fields should include language and literature, the social studies (history, sociology, geography, psychology, anthropology), mathematics, foreign languages, science, the fine and practical arts. To these conventional fields many would add, either as special courses or as inherent parts of the above, types of experience which loom large in importance from a functional analysis of significant "relationships of living": personal-social, social-civic, economic, as well as problems of personal development.

In recent years there has been much discussion and some experimentation having to do with "erasing subject matter lines." Much can be said on behalf of this trend as a corrective for the insulation of subjects which characterizes instruction in many schools, an insulation, incidentally, more or less inevitable when the preparation of teachers becomes overly specialized or, at the other extreme, teachers are required to teach subjects for which their preparation is inadequate.

Nor are the conventional divisions within a given field, such as science, or mathematics, or the social sciences, pedagogically justified in all instances. Mathematics teaching, for example, might well improve were algebra, geometry, trigonometry, and calculus taught with less emphasis upon rigid sequence and greater attention to the evolving structure of mathematics and the ongoing life of students. Just as, outside the school, the psychologist sometimes advances his work best when he draws upon biology or physiology, or the physiologist upon chemistry, so, within the curriculum of the school, learning is often enriched and vitalized by crossing over or "erasing" traditional subject matter lines.

The theory of the "core curriculum" illustrates the point we are marking. Where this has been most successful, attention has centered upon helping young people to understand and to cope with "growing pains" within relationships of living commonly omitted from or insufficiently emphasized by the traditional subjects. Consequently, by concentrating upon life problems without necessary reference to the lines which separate science from social science, literature from art, history and economics from psychology, students are helped in facing their "developmental tasks" more effectively than in a school which adheres faithfully to traditional subject matter divisions. Furthermore, within the subjects themselves, certain areas of investigation are dependent upon materials drawn from other subjects. For example, a problem in the social studies having to do with public health cannot be solved without drawing upon science, and many problems in science cannot be solved without the aid of mathematics. Good teaching, in other words, often requires ignoring rather than adhering to the dictum that each subject should stick to its last.

Granted this, it is nevertheless true that greater rather than less emphasis should be given to the pedagogical differences in the methods and procedures used in science as against social science, or mathematics, or literature, and the arts. Each of these disciplines involves the use of a unique and distinctive set of intellectual tools which the student must acquire. The procedures in solving a problem in a laboratory science—the method of gathering data, testing an inference, or validating a conclusion—differ significantly from the procedures employed in resolving an historical question, or the relevance of one moral principle as against another in a conflict between individuals. Again, language and mathematics represent quite distinctive methodologies in logic and the analysis of experience. The art approach and the realm of values in literature yield still other disciplines. To help young people acquire the self-directive methods of thinking appropriate to each is one of the most important contributions of education. Without this discipline and these methods, one's knowledge scarcely goes beyond the level of information about specific items of little permanent value.

It seems, then, that the world we live in assigns to the school the responsibility of fostering an intellectual discipline unique in the history of civilization. An analysis of trends with respect to the life tasks, vocational, social, cultural, indicate the importance of training all youth in ways of thinking and ways of living peculiar to today. Traditionally, our schools have emphasized the acquisition of information and the passive acceptance of principles which, insofar as they were applied, served the function of major premises in a syllogism. It is not contended that training in deductive logic lacks value. Quite the contrary. Skill in the use of the syllogism has its place as does the intellectual wariness which comes from practice in determining what is implied and what is not implied in a general principle or a proposition. Indeed, this discipline is most relevant to certain phases in what John Dewey termed a complete act of thought. Consequently, we are not urging less emphasis upon controlled thinking of an essentially deductive character. Rather are we suggesting that this is but one aspect of a larger discipline which the student must make his own.

Secondly, we have called attention to the importance of types of intellectual experience that take their character from the nature of the world in which we live today: a world of rapid change, a world of heterogeneous communities and plural cultures, and an interrelated world of chain reactions.

Finally, we have stressed the importance of equipping young people with the intellectual tools peculiar to the different fields or disciplines represented in school and college. As against the tendency in some quarters "to erase subject matter lines" we have urged the conscious acquisition of what are clearly distinctive methods of work on the assumption that one important contribution of general education is the ability of the student to progress on his own steam in the solution of problems, each of which may require the use of an appropriate method.

Suggested Reading

Alberty, Harold, *Reorganizing the High School Curriculum,* rev. ed. (New York: The Macmillan Co., 1953), chap. XII.

Childs, John L., *Education and Morals* (New York: Appleton-Century-Crofts Co., 1950), chap. VIII.

Hullfish, H. Gordon, and others, *Educational Freedom in an Age of Anxiety* (New York: Harper & Brothers, 1953), chaps. 5, 8, 10.

Kerlinger, Fred N., "The Authoritarianism of Group Dynamic," *Progressive Education,* April, 1954, pp. 169–173.

Otto, Max, *The Human Enterprise* (New York: F. S. Crofts and Co., 1940), chap. V.

Raup, R. Bruce, and others, *The Improvement of Practical Intelligence* (New York: Harper & Brothers, 1950), chaps. II–IV, VI–VII.

PART III

Conceptions of Learning in Their American Setting

/\.\/\.\/\.\/\.\

/\\.\\.\\.\\

10

Our Colonial Inheritance

Early Motives for Establishing Schools

Frequent mention has been made of the influence of religion upon American education. This was particularly true of the colonial period in all of the colonies, but its manifestations in New England were perhaps most conspicuous and most dramatic, for there it was that the vision of the Holy Commonwealth long dominated both civil and ecclesiastical establishments. For a period, indeed, church and state were united, with the church the dominant partner. "We came hither," wrote Cotton Mather, in his *Magnolia*, "because we would have our posterity settled under the pure and full dispensations of the gospel; defended by rulers that should be ourselves."

Historians have cautioned us not to read too generous or enlightened a conception of the nature and purpose of education into early legislation on compulsory education in Massachusetts or, for that matter, in other New England colonies which followed the example of Massachusetts. The Beards, for example, emphasize that the acts of 1642 and 1647 [1] did not represent the intention of the state to assume responsibility for the education of all children as much as it represented a theological determina-

---

[1] The act of 1642 required parents and masters to teach children and apprentices to "understand the principles of religion and the capital laws of the country." The act of 1647 ordered towns of fifty householders to appoint a master "to teach all children as shall resort to him to write and read" and towns of one hundred householders to set up a grammar school to prepare youth for the university.

tion to impose upon all the sectarian creed of the Puritans.[2] The fact that this education was ordered by the state, they insist, was of little significance since the state and the church were one.

Again, we should bear in mind that although the religious motive loomed large in legislation, other interests were also operative. The New Englander was determined that children acquire the means of self-support. Consequently, all compulsory educational legislation provided that parents or guardians who failed to teach their children the elements of some lawful calling, labor, or employment should be deprived of their guardianship and the children apprenticed to someone more responsible.

Observe also that although the state enacted legislation, enforcement was left to localities. Moreover, as was indicated in Chapter 4, state legislation respecting the establishment of schools followed upon rather than antedated prior action by localities.

Nor is it without significance that the Puritan adopted universal education as a means of perpetuating orthodoxy in preference to the device of Governor Berkeley of Virginia for achieving the same end, namely, keeping the masses in ignorance. Two important phrases occur in the preamble to the law of 1647: (1) "It being one chief object of that old deluder Satan, to keep men from the knowledge of the Scriptures, as in former times by keeping them in an unknown tongue . . ." and (2) "that learning may not be buried in the graves of our fathers in Church and Commonwealth. . . . It is therefore ordered. . . ."

The interests of scholarship were highly valued by the Puritans, and despite the later failure of towns to obey the education laws, an abiding respect for books and the fruits of learning long characterized the people of New England.

Granted significant differences between the motives of the Puritans and those which animated the advocates of publicly supported schools in the nineteenth century, the lines of connection between the two are nevertheless evident. The early religious determination to use the schools as a means of insuring religious orthodoxy and civic conformity is not unrelated to the later objective of using them for moral and civic purposes. In each instance schools are viewed as instruments for realizing in the lives

---

[2] Charles and Mary Beard, *The Rise of American Civilization* (New York: The Macmillan Co., 1930), vol. I, pp. 179–180.

of the younger generation the vision of the good life as envisaged by the older.

Time has done much to transform the objectives of both school and college since the colonial period. Nevertheless, Americans still conceive of the school as the custodian of the morals of the young, and one of its purposes—indeed, a primary purpose—is to raise the young in the paths of virtue. Consequently, when the rate of juvenile delinquency increases, there is a natural tendency to hold the school as well as the home responsible.

To the moral purpose of education we may also ascribe the fact that the school, in contrast with other institutions of government, has been kept relatively free from political manipulation. Not that politics and favoritism have been totally excluded from the public school! That is too much to expect of an American community. But this is more nearly true of the school than perhaps of any other public agency, with the result that when evidence of political influence becomes clear the public is easily persuaded to "turn the rascals out."

As we have seen, the ideal state for the Puritan was one in which the church and state were merged, but with the religious influence dominant. In the early church the elders were the elect and the elect ruled.

Not until the revision of the charter in 1691 was the right to vote in Massachusetts extended to nonchurch members. With a widening of the suffrage, however, and the rise of a wealthy merchant class, the foundations of the Holy Commonwealth began to yield to the acids of secular influence. Nevertheless, something of the earlier spirit has persisted in the American's conception of the missionary function of his way of life, so that a genealogist might trace without too much difficulty a relationship between faith in the "manifest destiny" of the American Republic and the earlier conviction that "the God of Heaven had carried a nation into a wilderness upon the designs of a glorious transformation."

It was this intense conviction also that gave vital importance to education, since upon each generation rested the responsibility of fostering, but not altering, the basic structure of the state. Consequently, we have the rare phenomenon of a devoted people establishing within a few short years of their sailing into Boston harbor a complete system of schools—an elementary school to educate all young people sufficiently to enable them to read and understand the Bible and the religious and civil laws; a secondary school to equip the future leaders of church and state for college; and a college that would insure an educated ministry as well as an adequately prepared professional class.

Education, even dogmatic education, has a way of stimulating people to think for themselves. Education in early New England was no exception to this rule, with the result that serious differences in theology soon manifested themselves, a fact which did much to populate new communities with heretics and dissidents. Challenging official doctrine was not only a personal sin; it undermined the health of the community as well. Consequently, when Roger Williams and Anne Hutchinson, as well as less well-known folk, began to propagate offensive ideas they were driven into the wilderness to fend for themselves.

On the other hand, the New Englander was a Protestant. As such, he was committed to the proposition that salvation is an individual matter, dependent not upon official intermediaries between God and man, but upon direct relations between each person and his Maker. This imposed upon one the obligation to read and interpret the Bible for himself, with its possibilities of deviation from the straight and narrow path of truth. Successive generations proceeded to exploit this opportunity to the full. But this possibility also demonstrated the importance of censorship and meticulous attention to methods of teaching which might insure the acquisition of truth and avoidance of error.

Colonial Influences in Contemporary Education

Were it possible for a colonial schoolmaster to visit a modern classroom, it is doubtful that he would recognize it as a school. Imagine, for example, the horror with which an Ezekiel Cheever might view the activities of teacher and pupil today, or the qualities of relationship between the two which a competent teacher strives to develop. Would he not conclude that the "old deluder Satan" had at last succeeded in his designs upon education?

Nevertheless, there still survive from the colonial period a number of assumptions in education which exercise a formative influence upon the minds of many, educator and layman alike.

Man's Dual Nature

Take, for example, the assumption that man's nature is dual in character, that a distinction of kind exists between body and soul. This continues to operate as a basic assumption for many and has yielded abundant fruit in education. Originally it was grounded more in theology than in philosophy and psychology, although in the hands of Jonathan Edwards, theology and philosophy united to prepare the mind for the later more distinctly psychological distinctions between mind and body which, as formulated by John Locke, dominated educational thought and practice in America well down to the end of the nineteenth century.

According to the colonial conception of man, the traditional conflict between good and evil is reflected in the constitution of each individual, with the body and its impulses oriented toward evil and the soul alone aspiring to higher things. Moreover, in this contest, the devil seems to have an initial advantage, since children are born in sin and are thus natively disposed toward evil. Consequently, Cotton Mather could describe the child as a "little viper" and John Wesley, as we indicated in discussing the family, was prompted to enjoin parents to "Break your child's will in order that it may not perish. . . . Break its will, in order that its soul may live." [3]

As we page through the literature of the seventeenth and eighteenth centuries, to which children were customarily introduced, we can detect little that was designed to develop in them what the psychologists of today emphasize as all-important, namely, a sense of inner confidence and security. Imagine, for example, the inspiration they must have derived from Cotton Mather's "A Token for the Children of New England, or some examples of children in whom the feare of God was remarkably budding when they died in several parts of New England." Or consider the manner in which their eyes would turn eagerly toward their own future

---

[3] Quoted in William Heard Kilpatrick, *Source Book in the Philosophy of Education* (New York: The Macmillan Co., 1923), p. 334.

after reading Janeway's "Tokens for the Children: An exact account of the Conversions, holy and exemplary Lives and Deaths of several young Children." What picture was a child expected to form of himself as he encountered these words in a manual widely used in an infant school of something more than a century ago?

> Yes, I was ever born in sin,
> And all my heart is bad within.

A textbook entitled *Youth's Instructor,* published as late as 1757, carried this introduction for the eager youth to read: "Lord, what is man: Originally, dust, engendered in sin, brought forth in sorrow, helpless in his infancy, extravagantly wild in his youth, mad in his manhood, decrepid in his age; his first voice moves to pity; his last commands grief." [4]

It follows from this conception of man's original nature that discipline is a first essential, and discipline must be from without rather than from within if the young are to succeed in following the straight and narrow path of virtue. Discipline and hard work are necessities from the earliest years.

We can appreciate how general and persistent this concept of childhood has been, not only in this country but in others as well, when we consider the manner in which Charles Dickens was moved to use his pen in order to arouse the public to a more humane conception of child nature and a reform in methods of schooling.

Observe the satire in this passage from *Old Curiosity Shop:*

"Don't you feel how naughty it is of you," resumed Miss Monflathers, "to be a wax-work child, when you might have the proud consciousness of assisting to the extent of your infant powers, the manufacturers of your country; of improving your mind by the constant contemplation of the steam engine; and of earning a comfortable and independent subsistence of from two and nine pence to three shillings per week? Don't you know that the harder you are at work the happier you are?" (Chapter XXXI).

And Mrs. Pipkin in *Dombey and Son:*

"There is a great deal of nonsense—and worse—talked about

---

[4] Quoted in Newton Edwards and Herman G. Richey, *The School in the American Social Order* (Boston: Houghton Mifflin Co., 1947), p. 122.

young people not being pressed too hard at first and being taught and all the rest of it, sir . . .

"It was never thought of in my time, and it has no business to be thought of now. My opinion is; keep 'em at it" (Chapter XI).

Nor is this view of human nature, to say nothing of child nature, inactive today. It is implied by the common expresson, "You can't change human nature" and by the suggestion so commonly heard in these days of public concern over juvenile delinquency that more frequent visits to the wood shed on the part of father with his offending son would bring desirable results.

On February 17, 1954, the *Washington Post and Times Herald* carried the following headline: "Impish Little Angels in Famed Choir Get 2 Paddle Pats for Each Demerit."

There followed an account of methods adopted in the Cathedral School of New York City together with the headmaster's justification of the new practices. "We, as Christian masters," he is quoted as saying "must completely deny the secular idea that a boy should not be punished for his offenses. If he is not punished, his selfish ego will know no restraint and his soul as well as his body will be placed in dire jeopardy."

Probably more significant than this one incident is the revival in certain theological circles of the doctrine of an innate depravity, although a substitute for this ancient term may be used. Take, for example, the concept of morality as expounded by the eminent theologian, Reinhold Niebuhr, in his *Moral Man and Immoral Society*. According to Niebuhr, individual people may succeed in climbing to moral heights but groups, as groups, find it virtually impossible to do so. This follows from the fact that an individual can tame and discipline his natively selfish impulses through the exercise of reason, which impels one toward consistency, the equating of one's own desires with the claims of others, together with the sympathy and the imagination which enables an individual to put himself in the place of another. With groups, however, reason is not sufficiently potent to achieve these ends. The result, as Niebuhr sees it, is that in relations between groups might alone can establish the right.[5]

Two contradictory theories of child development thus confront

---

[5] See Reinhold Niebuhr, *Moral Man and Immoral Society* (New York: Charles Scribner's Sons, 1932), chap. II.

the modern parent and teacher: one which continues to emphasize the native tendency of children to kick against the pricks and to become "soft" unless acclimated to hard work and effort with or without, perhaps better without, interest; and the other which stresses the importance of fostering in the young an inner confidence and an inwardly directed discipline, both of which are furthered not hindered when a child, in a friendly and nourishing atmosphere, is encouraged to identify himself with the manners and the morals of the society in which he is to live, move, and have his being.

Without Orthodoxy the Health of the Community Is Endangered

That orthodoxy in religion is an essential for individual morality and the well-being of the community is a second assumption which originated in the colonial period, an assumption which continues to function as an operative principle in contemporary education.

As a policy of governments, the colonial conviction that the health and welfare of the community require uniformity in religion was in no way original with the American colonies. Consequently, when Nathaniel Ward announced that "All Familists, Antinomians, Annabaptists, and other Enthusiasts shall have free liberty to keep away from us," he was but applying to Massachusetts a policy of which the Puritans themselves had been victims. As they had been dealt with, so they proposed to do unto others!

Nor was this principle confined in application to Massachusetts. Although the religious faith it safeguarded varied from colony to colony, the principle of orthodoxy was applied generally. In time, however, it gave way to one of live and let live, and, eventually, to the concept of noninterference by the state in matters of religious conviction, or, as we now term it, the principle of separation of church and state.

The assumption that morality derives from and is dependent upon religious conviction continues, however, to influence the minds of many educators and laymen, with one essential difference between today and yesterday. The assumed *necessary* relationship between creed and moral behavior has become less specific. Few Protestants will insist today that their own version of Protestantism (Baptist versus Methodist, Presbyterian versus Congregationalist, etc.) is alone in its underwriting of morality, and, obviously, members of the Jewish faith can hardly agree with the dictum of the Catholic Bishops of America to the effect that "Only the life of Christian faith can guarantee to man in his present state the moral life; and the Christian life is lived in its entirety only through the one true Church of Christ." [6] Rather is it more common today to concede that although men may legitimately disagree as to the validity of one faith as compared to another, nevertheless, religious faith in some form is considered essential for morality. That is, in place of the earlier insistence upon religious faith in the singular as a condition of morality men today tend to substitute the necessity of religion in the plural.

It is this assumption that religion and morality are inseparably related which explains the determination of many earnest people "to bring God into the school," although professing neutrality as to the concept of God thus introduced and denying any attempt to foster the acceptance of one religious faith as against another. As Professor Butts has pointed out, there has been a growing demand in recent years "to re-establish the notion that the states may and *should* promote religion as a matter of promoting the public welfare." [7]

Eliminate the Controversial from the Classroom

To teach with an eye to orthodoxy implies the exclusion from the classroom of views which run counter to prevailing opinion. Only as doctrines to be refuted may the latter receive attention in the classroom. It is not surprising, therefore, that the principle we are considering finds application as well in areas other than

---

[6] Statement by the Catholic Bishops of America on "Secularism and the Schools" (*New York Times*, November 16, 1952.)
[7] "The Relation Between Religion and Education," *Progressive Education*, September, 1956, pp. 140–142. This entire issue is of interest in that it presents varying points of view regarding the place of religion in public schools.

religion. It is to this principle that we must ascribe responsibility for the assumption, widely held, that since education is a public function and teachers are the hired agents of the public, they should instill in the minds of children only ideas approved by the public. In practice this means that the school board, or groups in the community to whom the school board owes its selection, should determine what doctrines might legitimately be fostered in the school. It is this conviction, evidently, that prompts a southern community, dominated by the white population, to insist that schools teach nothing which runs counter to the "southern way of life," prompts members of patriotic organizations to insist that schools promote their version of Americanism; prompts leaders in business to urge that both textbook and teacher deal with the history of American economic development and the issues of contemporary economic society in ways designed to insure adherence to the principle of "free enterprise"; or prompts lay groups of every shade—reformist, conservative, radical—to look to the schools for the spread of their doctrines.

Nor are liberals in education in agreement as to where the line should be drawn in dealing with problems of this character, even when teaching for "understanding" as against "conviction." Some hold that on all issues upon which men disagree the proper educational objective is to develop the method or the discipline which emerges best from wrestling with problems that cannot be answered by looking in the back of the book; that is, to teach how to think but not what to think. Others contend that an institution established and maintained by the public is under obligation to develop an allegiance to the basic principles of the society which sustains it. This second group would argue that although the individual problems which thus confront a democracy should receive only objective consideration (and students be permitted, nay, encouraged to arrive at their own conclusions), there should emerge, nevertheless, from study and discussion a common loyalty to the principles of democracy and the methods of free inquiry without which a free society cannot long exist.

To the problems which inevitably emerge from these rival conceptions of the function of the school, we shall return in the chapters dealing with freedom to learn and freedom to teach.

To Read Is to Believe

Closely allied to teaching for conformity is the tendency to identify reading with believing. This, too, as indicated in Chapter 1, is an inheritance from the colonial period but it has received sufficient nourishment in later periods of our history to insure its continued health and vigor today.

Doubtless it is the early prominence of the Bible in men's thinking on the issues of life and the central position given to religious materials in the curriculum to which we must ascribe responsibility for the assumption that what one reads he is both prone and expected to believe.

On this view, a major purpose in schooling is to stock the mind with the facts and principles from which one might later in life deduce the appropriate solutions to life's problems. Accordingly, when difficulties present themselves, or disagreements among men arise, the first step in the direction of an ultimate resolution of points at issue is to identify the relevant precept, principle, or major premise which might serve as a starting point toward a happy solution. In the relatively simple Protestant communities of the past, the Bible served as this fountainhead of basic principles. Nor has it lost this position altogether, as evidenced by the common tendency for people today, when confronted by a burning issue, such as that of the segregation of the races, to quote the Scriptures in support of their position. In a similar manner, when Roger Williams wrote his treatise on *The Bloody Tenent of Persecution etc.* and John Cotton replied with *The Bloody Tenent Washed and Made White in the Blood of the Lamb etc.,* only to be answered by Roger Williams in *The Bloody Tenent Yet More Bloody: By Mr. Cotton's Endeavor to Wash It White in the Blood of the Lamb etc.,* both grounded their positions in the words of the Scripture.

Not so long ago, the study of the law followed this method, and aspiring lawyers read the law for the purpose of familiarizing themselves with the principles of the law in its various categories, together with their applications in the past, which later as judges and advocates they would be called upon to apply to individual cases as these might arise.

Advocates of a return to "the old books" in education, or to a curriculum similar to that which prevailed in school and college during the nineteenth century, ground their position in a manner similar to that under discussion. Thus Walter Lippmann, in the *American Scholar* some years ago, charged that those responsible for education during the past forty or fifty years "have progressively removed from the curriculum of studies the Western culture which produced the modern state." He further charged,

That the schools and colleges have, therefore, been sending out into the world men and women who no longer understand the creative principles of the society in which they must live;

That, deprived of their cultural tradition, the newly educated Western men no longer possess in the form and substance of their minds and spirits, the ideas, the premises, the rationale, the logic, the method, the values or the deposited wisdom which are the genius of the development of Western civilization;

That the prevailing education is destined, if it continues, to destroy Western civilization and is in fact destroying it; . . .[8]

More recently, in his *The Public Philosophy,* Lippmann returns to the attack upon contemporary education, charging that it fails "to transmit the moral system" and "the psychic structure" of civilized society, but follows instead the "Jacobin heresy" of catering to the native impulses.[9]

Thus far, our attention has centered upon certain aspects of colonial thought and practice which continue to influence men's minds and to give character to education today. Some readers will doubtless cherish these as a valuable inheritance. Others will consider them as atavistic in nature, appropriate and relevant, perhaps in their time, but as handicaps to progress today.

To what we have stressed should be added items discussed in earlier chapters. Thus friends of public education recognize their indebtedness to the early New Englander for his conviction that the education of all young people is a public as well as a private obligation. Significant also is the fact that from the beginning, local communities as well as the state, sometimes prior to the

---

[8] "Education vs. Western Civilization," *The American Scholar,* Spring, 1941, pp. 184–193.
[9] *The Public Philosophy* (Boston: Little, Brown & Co., 1955), chap. VII.

state, assumed this responsibility, thus assuring a high degree of local initiative in education and the disposition to adapt this education to needs peculiar to the local community.

Finally, we should not forget that many aspects of the colonial mind were more European than American in origin. Under the impact of conditions in the New World, together with a gradual loosening of ties with Europe, quite different conceptions of man and his destiny came into being.

These changes were reflected, eventually, in education. Material success and material well-being led to new demands upon the school, both elementary and secondary, and, eventually, the college. Gradually the elementary school began to enrich its offerings and the grammar school, with its exclusive emphasis upon classical and literary materials, gave way to the academy and, later, in the nineteenth century, to the high school. Both these institutions endeavored to serve interests and needs of a wider range than those recognized by the grammar school.

To these developments we now turn.

Suggested Reading

Boorstin, Daniel J., *The Americans: The Colonial Experience* (New York: Random House, 1958), chaps. 1–5.

Butts, R. Freeman, and Lawrence A. Cremin, *A History of Education in American Culture* (New York: Henry Holt & Co., Inc., 1953), chap. 2.

Childs, John L., *Education and Morals* (New York: Appleton-Century-Crofts, Inc., 1950), chap. VIII.

Drake, William C., *The American School in Transition* (Englewood Cliffs, N. J.: Prentice-Hall, Inc., 1955), chaps. I, II.

Meyer, Adolphe E., *An Educational History of the American People* (New York: McGraw-Hill Book Co., 1957), chaps. 2, 3, 4.

/\.\/\.\/\.\

11

Education and the Conquest

of the Continent

An Expanding Economy Transforms the Colonial Mind

The religious motive loomed large in colonial America, but it was by no means the only one to influence education. Even the Mayflower, on its memorable voyage in 1620, included among its passengers a considerable number of adventurers whom William Bradford characterized as an "undersirable lot." Indeed the Mayflower Compact was, in part, designed to prevent this group of "undesirables" from realizing their boast that once on shore they would "use their liberties" as they wished. In the South, the desire to improve one's fortunes in a material way clearly overshadowed spiritual aspirations. Likewise in the Middle Colonies, which set an example in religious toleration novel for the period, the lure of economic success commonly competed with the religious motive. Moreover, in all of the colonies, the inducements of material success became ever more attractive with each succeeding generation.

Only in New England did the vision of the Holy Commonwealth succeed for a considerable period in dominating the policies of state as well as church. But even here, eventually, preoccupation with the conditions of salvation gave ground before the attractions of the world of the flesh and the devil. Nor were these attractions lessened by the happy discovery that the Puritan virtues were evidently designed to insure worldly success as well as the salvation of the soul. From the practice of these virtues the spiritually elect soon found themselves possessed of the power and the influence of the materially elect.

As a background for understanding developments in education in the latter part of the eighteenth century and throughout the nineteenth century, we should bear in mind the influence of the frontier or, better, perhaps, the effects of the conquest of the continent upon successive generations of individuals who faced a continuing invitation to better their stations in life through the development of natural resources that gave no hint of exhaustion. Hard as life was on the frontier, it afforded the underprivileged, the oppressed, and the submerged an opportunity to share in the goods of this world. Under these conditions class lines became less rigid. In the South, the young surveyor of limited means could gain entrance into the planter class and, eventually, become an outstanding representative of Virginian aristocracy. In New England, the son of a poor candlemaker, by judicious use of the Puritan virtues of temperance, order, resolution, frugality, industry, honesty, etc., rose to a position not only of wealth and influence in the business and professional communities but of leadership in the affairs of state. Innumerable experiences of this character on the part of innumerable individuals soon gave to life a tang and a glow which rendered tolerable what might otherwise have been intolerable conditions of hardship. The expression "While there is life, there is hope" became more than a happy phrase with which to assuage disappointment; it described a confirmed attitude toward discouragement, even defeat, in an atmosphere in which failure was never final.

To be sure, there were regressions and depressions in the development of the economy of the colonies as well as of the later Republic; but, despite the "ups" and the occasional severe "downs" throughout the years, Americans have lived consistently in a steadily expanding economy. All this has contributed to a gradual change in man's conception of himself and the human drama. The virtues of religious individualism, as we have said, were transformed into the conditions of worldly success. What Benjamin Franklin records in his autobiography as his own observations and conclusions were shared by many others:

"Revelation," he writes in his Autobiography, "had no weight with me, as such; but I entertained an opinion, that though certain actions might not be bad, *because* they were forbidden by it, or good, *because* it commanded them; yet probably these actions might be forbidden *because* they were bad for us, or commanded *because* they were beneficial to us, in their own natures, all the circumstances of things considered."

For many, the nature of the Deity likewise underwent significant change. Less emphasis was placed upon the stern and forbidding qualities of a jealous God and more upon his characteristics as a beneficent planner, the designer of the universe, who operates in accordance with laws and principles that make of this the best of all possible worlds. Thus Alexander Pope could pen for the American as well as for the Englishman with little fear of contradiction:

> All are but parts of one stupendous whole,
> Whose body Nature is, and God the soul; . . .
> All Nature is but art, unknown to thee;
> All chance, direction, which thou canst not see;
> All discord, harmony not understood;
> All partial evil, universal good:
> And, spite of pride, in erring reason's spite,
> One truth is clear, whatever is, is right.[1]

Nowhere was the swing of the pendulum, from the concept of man's innate depravity to one of optimistic faith in his possibilities for a continuous progress toward perfection, more evident than in the intellectuals of New England. "For two hundred years," writes Parrington, "the dogmas of Calvin had lain as a heavy weight on the mind of New England," [2] By 1850, however, Calvinism had found a formidable rival in French liberalism and its New England expression in Unitarianism, a religion which Parrington describes as "essentially a humanistic religion, rational, ethical, individual, yet with deep and warm social sympathies." [3]

---

[1] *Essay on Man.*

[2] Vernon Parrington, *Main Currents in American Thought* (New York: Harcourt, Brace & Co., 1927), p. 321.

[3] *Ibid.*, p. 327.

Both within and outside formal membership in this faith came an upsurge of confidence in God's love and man's potentialities for perfection, which, when married to the spirit of social reform, led to passionate and far-reaching attempts to transform the institutions of this world into forms more appropriate to man's new status. All the passionate determination which once seemed bent upon establishing the Holy Commonwealth in New England now centered upon removing impediments to progress—economic, political, social—or conditions which hamper expressions of that infinite worth of which each individual soul is possessed.

Nor was this liberal and reformist spirit confined to New England. The influence of a William Ellery Channing or a Theodore Parker, a Ralph Waldo Emerson, a Henry Thoreau, or a William Lloyd Garrison was welcomed by kindred souls in all sections of the country. There, too, soil and climate, material and spiritual, were favorable to visions of a potential heaven on earth.

Typical of this new faith in man and his universe were the writings of Ralph Waldo Emerson. Contrast, for example, the following selections from his essays on *Fate* and *Culture* with the quotation on page 192 from the introduction to the *Youth's Instructor:*

The book of nature is the book of fate. She turns the gigantic pages leaf after leaf, never re-turning one. One leaf she lays down, a floor of granite; a thousand ages, and a measure of coal; a thousand ages, and a layer of marl and mud; vegetable forms appear; her first misshapen animals, zoophyte, trilobium, fish; then saurians, rude forms, in which she has only blocked her future statue, concealing under these unwieldly monsters the fine type of her coming king. The face of the planet cools and dries, the races meliorate, and man is born. . . .

We call these millions men; but they are not yet men. Half engaged in the soil, pawing to get free, man needs all the music that can be brought to disengage him. If love, red love, with tears and joy, if want with his scourge, if war with its cannonade, if Christianity with its charity, if trade with its money, if art with its portfolios, if science with her telegraphs through the deeps of space and time, can set his dull nerves throbbing and by loud taps of the tough chrysalis can break its walls and let the new creature emerge erect and free, make way and sing paeon. The age of the quadruped is to go out, the age of the brain and of the heart is to come in. . . . And if one shall read the future of the race hinted in the organic effort of nature to mount and meliorate, and the corresponding impulse to the better in the human being, we shall dare to affirm that there is nothing he will not overcome and convert, until at last culture shall absorb the chaos and gehenna. He will convert the furies into muses, and the hells into benefit.[4]

Evidences of the New Spirit

These changes did not come over night; nor was the rate of change identical in all colonies. The normal expectation of the early immigrants to this country was, of course, to perpetuate the ways of life they brought with them. Only gradually did differences in soil and climate become manifest in developments as divergent as the plantation aristocracy of the South with its tobacco-cotton-slave economy and the more fluid society of the North which rested by contrast upon trade and commerce, manufacturing, farming, and free labor. In less than a century following the first settlements, differences between American and European society as well as significant contrasts among the colonies themselves had become evident. Important as the latter were to become in subsequent relations among the sections, one trait was common to all, an optimism which expressed itself in developments both novel and revolutionary.

One was the extension of the suffrage and the gradual participation of ever larger numbers in the affairs of government. The first step in this direction was the elimination of the religious test for both voting and the holding of public office. A second was a modification in the property qualification for voting and office-holding. In 1789, only four states permitted nonproperty holders to vote, with the result that less than one-fifth of the male population of the original thirteen states was privileged to vote. Then came the admission to the Union of new states, each with liberal provisions for manhood suffrage: Vermont in 1790, Kentucky in 1792, Tennessee in 1796. Ohio, in 1803, required that voters be taxpayers, but abolished this requirement in 1804. By 1840 the battle for manhood suffrage had been won.

Other evidences of the new spirit were prison reform, the

---

[4] *The Prose Works of Ralph Waldo Emerson* (Boston: Fields, Osgood and Co., 1870), vol. II, pp. 323, 402.

gradual humanizing of the criminal code, and agitation on behalf of the freeing of the slaves.

Political and social reform was, of course, an outgrowth of economic developments. Again, with the possible exception of the South (in which the plantation system created new divisions of class as well as caste) birth and family origin tended to lose importance, and individuals were judged more in terms of what they demonstrated themselves to be than in terms of background. This was particularly true of the frontier, where it was not always wise to inquire of the stranger what brought him to his present location! On the frontier, too, work ceased to be a mark of class distinction or something to be avoided and became more a badge of honor. The employer commonly worked side by side with his employee and took pride in his ability to do more or better than what he asked his helpers to do. The "hired man" or the "hired girl" was not considered a hireling or a member of a subordinate class. Rather was he or she one temporarily dependent upon earning the means with which to achieve independence. Accordingly, it was more common than not for the "help" to eat at the same table and to share in the activities of the family in which they occupied more the status of assistants than of servants.

Since the East, with its unquenchable thirst for manpower, was faced constantly with loss of population to the West, these characteristics of an open society soon operated to undermine old ways and to bring about "low visibility" of class lines there as well.

To these characteristics of a dynamic and changing society we should add the influence of science and conditions favorable to empirical methods of thinking, in contrast with those which lean heavily upon authority. Yankee ingenuity and inventiveness were in no way confined to New England, although they flourished there in abundance. As Americans moved west they encountered ever new conditions of soil and climate and people of novel backgrounds and life assumptions. Consequently, they were called upon repeatedly to modify old precepts and principles and customs in order to sow and to reap to advantage and to evolve fruitful ways of living with their fellows. Major premises once accepted as fixed and final became subject to modification in the light of new situations or a context different from that which once gave them validity. As indicated earlier, these factors of change not only encouraged methods of solving problems other than by an appeal to authority, but tended to generate as well a confidence in the creative power of men's minds and an unwillingness to accept what is as necessarily what must be.

In certain important areas of life there thus occurred a change in both the nature and the location of truth, as men envisaged the truth. No longer was it a proposition or a principle external to men's interests, or which came to them from tradition and the past. Rather was it conceived to be a product of man's inventiveness and oriented in large measure to the future.

This is not to say that tradition and precedent and external truths were wholly discarded and a new logic substituted for the old. More accurately, we should say that this was characteristic of only certain areas of experience. For the bulk of individuals, two contradictory schemes of values and methods of thinking came to dwell together in one and the same person (as for many today), with now one dominant, now the other.

In no place, however, were the potential conflicts between the old and new less well recognized than in school and college. Indeed, by and large, the methods of thinking fostered by the schools tended to lag behind those employed outside the school in business, in politics, and in social relations. Even in the teaching of science emphasis was placed more upon the acquisition of facts than upon scientific methods of inference and discovery.

John Locke As a Formative Influence

One way in which to appreciate developments in the curriculum and the evolution of educational method in the late eighteenth and the nineteenth centuries is to observe the influence of John Locke's philosophy and psychology upon men's minds. Not only was Locke the founder of modern psychology, but his theory of how the mind operates was designed specifically to provide a theoretical foundation for changes in society as fundamental as the substitution of representative government for government based upon the concept of the divine right of kings to rule; of toleration in religious thought and the separation of church and state; of an education for the young which stressed the importance of direct observation of the world about them and the encouragement of many-sided interests, in contrast with the narrow and exclusively bookish practices of the pedagogues of his day.[5]

In his *Jefferson and His Time,* Dumas Malone tells us of requests which Jefferson, when serving as minister to France, made of his friend Trumbull for the procurement of busts and pictures. High on this list were life-sized busts of Bacon, Locke, and Newton, which he wished copied for him as a picture. His reason was that these "are the three greatest men that have ever lived, without any exception, and as having laid the foundations of those superstructures which have been raised in the physical and moral sciences." [6]

Observe that these three men were distinctive, in turn, for the development of an inductive logic, a mathematical and scientific explanation of the operations of the universe, and an empirical explanation of the operations of the mind. They developed ways of thinking, in other words, that were hospitable to an open universe and none too friendly to tradition and custom.

Jefferson and his associates in the American Philosophical Society (which included in its membership the leading minds of the period) doubtless first encountered Locke's ideas as students in the academy. Central in the curriculum of the academy was Isaac Watt's *Improvement of the Mind,* a popular rendition of John Locke's *The Conduct of the Understanding.* For generations this document served as a practical logic for all who passed through the academy. When we reflect that this included the future teachers of America as well as the future statesmen and leaders in the professions and business, it is difficult to overemphasize its influence on the American mind.

What were some of these formative ideas?

The Mind at Birth As a White Sheet of Paper

First was Locke's denial of innate ideas, "some primary notions . . . characters, as it were, stamped upon the mind of men, which

---

[5] Locke's *Two Treatises on Government* were written with a view to justifying the revolution which brought William and Mary to the throne of England. Other writings to which the liberal minds of the period turned repeatedly for inspiration and guidance were his *Letters on Toleration, The Conduct of the Understanding, Essay on the Human Understanding,* and, of course, *Thoughts on Education.*

[6] Boston: Little, Brown & Co., 1951, vol. II, p. 211.

the soul receives in its first being, and brings into the world with it." [7]

Locke's purpose was to refute the rationalists in philosophy who assumed that the mind is so constituted that it accepts, without proof or prior experience, the truth of certain logical principles or axioms as well as those practical and moral principles which constitute the foundation of universally accepted moral values. As evidence of his position, Locke argued that the recognition and acceptance of "innate ideas" come not at birth but with maturity and experience. He also contended that far from being universally accepted, moral principles, in particular, vary with time and place, or, as we would say, with cultures.

In modern terms, what Locke denied is the existence of instincts or inborn tendencies to think, feel, and act in ways predetermined and unrelated to the experience of the individual, a concept of human nature of revolutionary significance for a people, long accustomed to rigid distinctions of class, now ready to exploit the resources of a new continent.

From whence come, then, the obvious differences in talent and interest and ability which clearly mark off one individual from another?

Locke answers, "From experience. . . . Let us suppose the mind to be, as we say, white paper, void of all characters, without any ideas; how comes it to be furnished? Whence comes it by that vast store which the busy and boundless fancy of man has painted on it with an almost endless variety? Whence has it all the materials of reason and knowledge? To this I answer in one word, from experience; in that all our knowledge is founded, and from that it ultimately derives itself." [8]

Once furnished with simple or unorganized ideas and impressions, the mind has the power to organize them in such a way that they come to picture or represent the external world of objects, events, and ideas, through the powers of perception, memory, imagination, reason, etc. Thus to experience in its raw or original form, Locke adds the contribution of "ideas of reflection" or the operations of the mind upon simple ideas.

---

[7] John Locke, *An Essay Concerning the Human Understanding*, Book I, chap. II, sec. 1.

[8] *Ibid.*, Book II, chap. I, sec. 2.

All Men Are Essentially Equal

Locke's theories, when combined with cultural influences in America, in various ways gave character to American education well on down to the end of the nineteenth century. Most conspicuous, perhaps, is the encouragement Locke gave to the individual's own experience, in contrast with inheritance, in determining his worth. This gave to and received support from the concepts of equality native to the frontier where daily experience seemed to confirm the principle that a man should be judged in terms of what he reveals himself to be rather than by what he inherits either in worldly goods or social status from his forebears.

It was this basic assumption, as we have seen, which induced Horace Mann and others to labor on behalf of a system of tax-supported public schools open and free to all. As these educational pioneers saw it, a democratic society can do no less for its children than it does for its adults. What free land and open economic opportunities were for adults, free schools might become for children. Naive as Mann's assertion may seem to the effect that "there is by nature little or perhaps no distinction among men with respect to their original power of intellect," we may question seriously whether the American people would have developed public school systems as we have them today but for an assumption of this character in preference to the notion prevalent in the early part of the twentieth century that each individual is endowed at birth with a fixed quantum of intelligence.

On the other hand, the concept of an essential equality among individuals may also imply that the failure has only himself to blame, and although the school's doors should be open to all on equal terms, this does not imply that it should attempt to make a silk purse out of a sow's ear. In other words, in this analogy between the school and free land, it also follows that the child should fit himself to the curriculum, not the curriculum to the child! Consequently, just as it has taken time for the public to hold society as well as the individual responsible for poverty and other social disadvantages which beset men in the complicated world of today, so the school, thanks to an individualistic psychology, has been slow to adapt its program to the varying needs of those who are to benefit from it.

There Is a Typical Mind

Secondly, Locke's psychology assumed that all minds are essentially alike, an assumption which gave support to the notion that education, both in content and method, can properly be the same for all. Do we need to know how the mind works or how one best learns? Then examine one's own learning experiences. As our parents and teachers dealt with us, and as we responded, so may we conclude the children entrusted to us will respond to our treatment of them. Thus educators derive their ideas of method and the kinds of knowledge most worth while largely from analogy. Since, moreover, teachers have tended to be verbally minded, it was natural that they should favor the verbally inclined over other types of mind and find them easier to instruct. Likewise, with the advent of intelligence tests—instruments which have consistently been skewed in favor of the verbally intelligent—educators as well as laymen have been prone to infer that the verbally intelligent are genuinely the more intelligent.

The assumption that minds are essentially alike influenced educational theory and practice until relatively recently. William James once remarked that the significance of individual differences received little recognition in psychology until Fechner's work in 1863. Not until the last decade of the nineteenth century do we find Edward L. Thorndike and other psychologists calling attention to their significance for education.

Mind, as Locke envisaged it, is twofold in its operations. In its original state, as we have seen, it is analogous to a white sheet of paper waiting to be written upon. Once impressions are received from the various senses, however, it proceeds to give order and pattern to them. In this way it comes to reflect, or to know, albeit partially, the outside world.

Here are two characteristics of mind which developed eventually into two contradictory theories of its nature. One group— Rousseau, Pestalozzi, G. Stanley Hall, etc.,—transformed Locke's notion of the original powers of the mind into "original tendencies" and inner drives which those responsible for the education of the young are to observe and follow. A second group concentrated upon the essentially passive and receptive nature of the mind and thus envisaged the responsibility of the adult as that of furnishing the growing individual with appropriate information and ideas which are to form his character.

Learning Becomes a Receptive Process

It was this second interpretation of the nature of mind and of learning which largely characterized schooling throughout the nineteenth century, and this interpretation is not without influence today. The child's mind was likened to a wax sheet upon which the educator and his textbook are to write what he should know or likened to a cabinet full of pigeonholes in which one files bits of information which reside there until needed. Consequently, schooling was neither expected nor required to concern itself with what immediately appeals. Its values were oriented toward later life. The significance of schooling and what one learns in school were to be taken largely on faith.

There was much in the cultural setting in the early days of the Republic to give support to this conception of education. The advent of manhood suffrage had drawn attention to the importance of acquainting young people with the nature and the operations of our political institutions and, as the guardians of the status quo saw it, with the principle of both private and public morality without which a stable society cannot endure.[9]

Moreover, the purposes which prompted parents to send their children to school, as, indeed, the motives of young people themselves in subjecting themselves to education, gave weight to a conception of learning as basically a receptive process. The school was envisaged as a means for bettering one's station in life. This gave to learning the appearance of an instrument for purposes practical and ornamental and to culture an external aspect. It was something one might acquire more or less as he buys a new suit of clothes with which to improve appearance and to gain status, rather than the cultivation of interests and talents genuinely one's own. For a time, indeed, it was considered a sign of weakness or inefficiency in a teacher were he to gear instruction to the interests of his students. Effort for the sake of effort was considered valuable since it developed traits of persistence, a

---

[9] See Richard D. Mosier, *The Making of the American Mind* (New York: King's Crown Press, Columbia University, 1947), chaps. II, III, IV.

valuable asset in life.

This schoolmaster's attitude is well expressed in Dr. Alexander Hill's defense of the classics, as recorded in John Adams' *Modern Developments in Educational Practice*. The worthy doctor valued the classics, as he evidently taught them, for the discipline they provide "of working at a subject which offers in itself no temptation to work." From the schoolboy's point of view, the "only motive for learning his lesson is that his master tells him to do so." And this, concludes Dr. Hill, "should always be sufficient." [10]

Basic to Locke's psychology was the distinction between mind and body. The sense organs are physical and are stimulated by physical events, but the ideas conveyed by them to the mind are nonmaterial impressions or pictures of the real world outside.

This gives crucial importance to the sense organs since, in the first instance, it is they and they alone which enable us to know the outside world. Decrease their number or impair any one of them, and the nature of reality as we know it undergoes change.

Keep the Channels of Inquiry Open

This carries with it profound implications. For example, in his *Conduct of the Understanding*, Locke, in concerning himself with ways in which men fail to reason correctly, mentions among other things "the want of having that which we may call large, roundabout sense" or "a full view of all that relates to the question, and may be of moment to decide it." In this, he continues, the angels have a permanent advantage over man, being endowed "in their several degrees of elevation above us" with "more comprehensive faculties; and some of them perhaps, having perfect and exact views of all finite beings that come under their consideration can as it were in a twinkling of an eye, collect all their scattered and almost boundless relations; a mind so furnished, what reason has it to acquiesce in the certainty of its conclusions!"

But man is mortal and his senses necessarily limited, a fact that carries a moral quite different from the dogmatic and authoritarian spirit which Locke undertook to undermine. In

---

[10] John Adams, *Modern Developments in Educational Practice* (London: University of London Press, 1922), p. 209. (Published in the United States by Harcourt, Brace & Co.)

religion, it favored the point of view that each individual and each sect sees through the glass but darkly, and although each may have found rays of valuable insight, other individuals and other sects may also have contributions to make toward a larger and more comprehensive vision of the truth. From this it follows that he who genuinely seeks the kingdom of heaven will encourage freedom of religious belief and the right, nay, the obligation, to subject all views to critical inspection. This is similarly true in areas other than religion. No longer was it wise to identify the well-being of the state with orthodoxy, be it political, economic, social, or what not.

We are not saying that it was Locke's philosophy alone which brought about this change in intellectual orientation. Nor are we suggesting that the climate of opinion veered immediately or conclusively from one direction to its opposite. One has only to look about him today to realize that the old habits still persist. What we are saying is that in Locke liberals found a philosophical and psychological justification for freedom of thought and expression, which, in conjunction with other trends of the period, enabled them, eventually, to incorporate the principle of freedom of thought and expression in the constitutions of both state and national governments. Here also were sound reasons to justify the intellectual's pursuit of a "round-about-knowledge" in contrast with narrow specialization—as evidenced in Benjamin Franklin, Thomas Jefferson, and other members of the American Philosophical Society—and the support of studies in physics, mechanics, astronomy, mathematics, etc., together with the implications of these studies for the development of the natural resources of the country.

New Life Values and the Curriculum

Not even the schoolmaster could withstand completely the intellectual trends of the time or the determination of the people to use education for ends practical as well as theoretical. As a result, by the end of the eighteenth century the primary and elementary school, as well as secondary school and college, had taken steps to liberalize the curriculum. In the former, arithmetic shortly edged out religion as the third R (although readers with heavy emphasis upon morality and the virtuous life continued to provide a generous substitute for the earlier emphasis upon items of creed). In quick succession came the addition of history, civics, and geography, together with the subdivision of reading into grammar, word analysis, spelling, oratory, etc. By the end of the nineteenth century, the typical elementary school pupil found himself occupied with some ten or more subjects: reading, writing, spelling, arithmetic, geography, history, nature study, physiology or hygiene, music, and drawing.[11]

Benjamin Franklin's announcement of his plan for the Philadelphia Academy, published as early as 1749, expresses very well the new conception of education that was to characterize both the academy and its eventual successor, the public high school, for decades to come. Concerning the studies he would offer, Franklin said, "it would be well if they could be taught everything that is useful, and everything that is ornamental," but since "art is long and their time is short . . . it is therefore proposed that they learn those things that are likely to be most useful and most ornamental; regard being had for the several professions for which they are intended."

How varied were the offerings that eventually found their way into the academies of the country may be inferred from the fact that in 1837, the academies of the state of New York reported some seventy-five or more subjects as included in their curricula.[12]

Nor did this picture change materially as the public high school, roughly from 1830 on, came to replace the academy. Indeed, the difference between the academy and the high school, until well after 1900, was essentially that of control and sources of support rather than curriculum. What specifically an individual school decided to teach was a matter of local self-determination. College admission requirements, at this stage, were of little concern to the secondary school educator.[13]

---

[11] Ralph W. Tyler, "The Curriculum—Then and Now," *The Elementary School Journal,* April, 1957, pp. 364–374.

[12] See Alexander Inglis, *Principles of Secondary Education* (Boston: Houghton Mifflin Co., 1918), p. 180.

[13] Up to the year 1800, Latin, Greek, and arithmetic were the only subjects required for admission to the leading American colleges. Between 1800 and the outbreak of the Civil War, five new subjects were commonly added: geography, English grammar, algebra, geometry, ancient history. As Elmer Ellsworth Brown tells us in his pioneer work on *The Making of Our Middle Schools,* the disposition of

All of this was very well until the college preparatory function of the academy and the high school began to assume importance. By 1890, however, the lack of uniformity in school programs had become a serious problem for administrators of school and college alike. Some agreement seemed essential in order to determine which subjects or phases of subjects were appropriate for treatment on the college level and which for secondary school; and, with respect to the latter, some principle or principles of organization had to be established if order were to be brought out of chaos.

No one was more insistent upon drawing the attention of the profession and the lay public to this problem than Charles W. Eliot, President of Harvard University. In an address before the Massachusetts Teachers Association in November, 1890, President Eliot asserted that it was literally impossible to determine what work was being done in the secondary schools of the United States.[14] Indeed, he went on to say, it was equally impossible to answer the same question with respect to the state of Massachusetts, or even a municipality, such as Boston, so great were the differences among schools. In rural areas also "an extraordinary variety of conditions and results" might be found.

This condition resulted, according to Eliot, from a number of causes: (1) the absence of an "elaborate system of national or State superintendence, and no permanent bodies of experienced inspectors"; (2) local control and administration of education, with each municipality or town conducting its affairs with little cooperation or coordination among communities; (3) the nonexistence of any accepted standards for schools to follow.

This situation prompted the educators of the country to organize a number of national committees, charged with the responsibility of bringing order out of confusion: the Committee of Ten on Secondary School Studies, 1891; the Committee of Fifteen on Elementary Schools, 1893; the Committee on College Entrance Requirements, 1895. From the work of these committees a remarkable degree of agreement resulted on such mat-

---

the secondary schools for a considerable period was to add subjects to their programs "at their own sweet will." (New York: Longman's, Green & Co., Inc., 1914), pp. 232–233.

[14] *Educational Reform, Essays and Addresses* (New York: The Century Company, 1898), pp. 179–194.

ters as the appropriate subjects to be taught, the order of their appearance in the curriculum, and the length of time each should be pursued. Out of the three committees concerned with secondary school and college there also eventually evolved standardizing agencies whose influence still continues.

Classroom Method Takes On New Form

Thus far we have centered upon curriculum developments which had their origin in the liberalizing influences of the nineteenth century. The educational picture would not be complete were we to omit developments in classroom method in this same period.

At no time in their history have American schools been blessed with an adequate supply of professionally trained teachers. In the early days (a situation to which we seem to have returned in recent years!), teachers were largely transients in the profession. They were young people who were using teaching as a means of accumulating resources with which to pursue a more desirable career, individuals who were on the verge of retirement, or those who were none too successful in other lines of work who had turned to teaching as one way of recouping their fortunes. Few, in consequence, would claim to know more than the textbook or presume to teach without its assistance.

In addition, teachers who are transients in the profession do not contribute to a stable teaching staff. Consequently, American schools have been faced from the beginning with a heavy turnover in teaching personnel. To this we must add the fact of rapid growth in both rural and city population, with cities springing up overnight and rural schools expanding rapidly into city school systems. Under these conditions it was but natural for textbook writers to prepare their books with an eye to offsetting or supplementing the deficiencies in the knowledge of both the teacher and the pupil and for supervisors and administrators (once these officials came into existence) to see in the text an instrument for insuring some degree of continuity in the pupil's education.

Developments in educational theory and their reflection in practice contributed to the same end. The advocates of the Pestalozzian method, for example, felt constrained to prepare manuals and texts which would indicate how specific subject matter was to be taught under the new method. As object teach-

ing developed, books were written which indicated in detail procedures for teacher and pupil to follow. The Herbartian theory,
which came into prominence near the end of the last century,
likewise called for revolutionary changes in content and method.
Readers, geographies, arithmetics, etc., were carefully written so
that a teacher, without too clear an understanding of the five
steps of Herbartian procedure, might nevertheless teach in a
fairly acceptable manner.

To make the contents of the textbook the be-all and the end-all
of instruction is, of course, to substitute uncritical acceptance of
what is read for what might otherwise become food for thought.
And who will say that this has not characterized much of the
teaching and learning in the schools? Taken together with the
wax-tablet concept of the mind and the cultural influences to
which we have drawn attention above—all favorable to the notion
that teaching exists for the purpose of instilling in the minds of
the young the information, the principles, and the ideals deemed
important by adults—we can understand how Locke's psychology
was transformed into one encouraging education for conformity.

From Individual to Class Instruction

Prior to 1800, instruction in both elementary and secondary
schools was prevailingly individual. The master's chief occupation seems to have been that of whittling goose quills, and although school legislation usually required pupils at twelve or
thirteen years of age to whittle their own pens, we are told that,
like many laws of today, these regulations were seldom enforced.
The results were wasteful of time for both master and pupil. Not
only was the former unable to give attention to the latter's study
habits, but the practice of calling pupils to the master's desk to
recite individually severely limited the amount and the character
of the attention available for each individual.

This system persisted much longer than is generally supposed.
As late as 1855, Grimshaw, writing in *Barnard's Journal,* deplored
the waste of time resulting from "the old-fashioned and false"
method of individual instruction.[15]

The invention of steel pens and blackboards enabled resource-

---

[15] S. C. Parker, *History of Elementary Education* (Boston: Ginn & Company,
1912), p. 88.

ful teachers to take the first steps toward group instruction, the former by freeing the teacher from his traditional task of whittling pens and the latter by making it possible for the master to gather together pupils who were at the same point in their progress in order to clear up common difficulties or to present new material. Henry Barnard has recorded his surprise upon viewing a blackboard for the first time. It was the winter of 1813–1814. While still a student at Harvard, Barnard visited a Boston school and there saw a group of pupils gathered about a blackboard undergoing what he described as "analytical and inductive teaching."

Considerable credit must be given to Joseph Lancaster and his fellow monitorians for developing in minute detail the methods of group instruction. Under his direction, pupils were organized into small groups, usually of ten, with an older pupil in charge of each group. Thus supervised, the children were marched to and from class in military fashion. They recited in unison in answer to questions posed and responded as one to instructions such as "hats off!" "show slates!" etc.

David Solomon, in his *Joseph Lancaster,* describes Lancaster's method of saving time in the taking of attendance.[16] To each pupil was assigned a fixed number. Corresponding numbers were written in a row on the wall. To determine absences it was necessary only for the class to take positions, each pupil under his own number.

Steps in learning were organized in similar detail. For example, the monitor's manual in arithmetic consisted of examples and a key which revealed not merely the complete solution of the problem but the steps by means of which the answer was to be obtained. If the question were one of simple addition, the monitor would find instructions of this character: "First column 7 and 9 are 16, and 3 are 19, and 5 are 24. Set down 4 under 7 and carry 2 to the next column"; after reading this instruction the monitor would so instruct the class.[17] Evidently by repetition rather than from explanation proficiency was expected to result.

Crude and mechanical as was this method of instruction, with

---

[16] David Solomon, *Joseph Lancaster* (New York: Longmans, Green & Co., Inc., 1904), p. 9.
[17] *Ibid.,* p. 12.

its tendency to confuse overt performance and memorization with genuine learning, its results were startling when compared with individual instruction. David Solomon records an incident of a worried father who was impelled to call upon his pastor to stop the practices of the monitorial school attended by his son for the reason that the master must be engaged in magic. How else might one account for his son's making such rapid progress in mastering arithmetic!

Not only are we indebted to the monitorial system for many of the practices still employed in group instruction, but it must also be credited with rendering feasible the idea of free public schools manned by professionally trained teachers, since the cost of group instruction by any other method would have seemed impossible, if not fantastic, in its drain upon the taxpayer. For example, in Philadelphia, in 1819, there were ten monitorial schools, each with one teacher in charge and an average of 284 pupils per teacher. As late as 1834, in the same city, the average number of pupils per teacher was 218.

To be sure, the followers of Pestalozzian methods likewise contributed to the art of group instruction, but an analysis of these contributions as well as those of Herbart and Froebel would reveal numerous items of indebtedness to the monitorians.

Take, for example, Pestalozzian methods which, in theory, start from quite different premises, the theory that learning should begin with the actual experiences of children and proceed by carefully graded oral instruction to systematic and organized knowledge. Children's experiences were thus to replace exclusive dependence upon books and the teacher's direction of learning activity was to replace the passive method of hearing lessons.

These ideals brought profound changes in elementary courses of study. Arithmetic was reorganized on the basis of object teaching so that pupils passed gradually from the observation of sensible objects to an understanding and manipulation of abstract numbers. "Mental arithmetic" assumed a prominent place in schoolwork. Object teaching likewise led to oral instruction with heavy emphasis upon oral language training. Geographies of a "dictionary-encyclopedia" type were replaced by home geography; and natural science as an outgrowth both of object teaching and oral language received recognition.

When we turn, however, to the methods of teaching into which Pestalozzian procedures quickly crystallized, we encounter a dismal formalism. It is said that a French-Swiss officer once remarked to Pestalozzi, when the latter was explaining his methods, "I see, you want to mechanize instruction." Whether or not Pestalozzi believed his psychological procedure was identical with mechanical routine there is no doubt of the fact that his followers, at least, succeeded in mechanizing instruction. And they mechanized it in the direction of formal group work, which, in the hands of the average teacher, became deadly routine. Parker states of oral instruction that a proper method of questioning became the sole requisite and a teacher's knowledge unimportant. Frequently, a teacher "simply questioned the children about their experience and told them nothing." [18]

The Herbartians Professionalize Instruction

Important as Pestalozzi's influence was upon classroom teaching, it is probably to the Herbartians that chief credit should be given for professionalizing teaching procedure. By 1890, as we have seen, a number of factors had combined making it imperative to create order out of the chaos which characterized both the curriculum and the administrative structure of the schools. Conspicuous among the leaders in education who devoted themselves to this task was G. Stanley Hall. Others who were to exercise a determining influence for some decades to come were Charles DeGarmo, Frank and Charles McMurry, William C. Bagley, and John Dewey. A number of these men had studied in Germany and had become ardent disciples of Johann Herbart. All were profoundly impressed with the latter's theories even when, as with John Dewey, they constituted a foil for their own thinking. In 1892 they joined with others in forming the National Herbart Society, which, under the name of the National Society for the Study of Education, still functions as one of the leading educational organizations in the United States devoted to the scientific study of education.

Herbart was in agreement with John Locke in denying the existence of the innate faculties with which Pestalozzi begins. He

---

[18] Parker, *op. cit.*, p. 329.

even went farther in that he denied the existence of the mind as a substance or as an entity which receives impressions (except as a logical entity used to explain the fact that the first impressions are responded to either by attraction, repulsion, or indifference). Sensations thus received respond in one of these three ways to subsequent impressions and thus, purely through association, a self is created. What men speak of as the mind is nothing other than the ordering and the organization of the experiences one has encountered since birth. "The 'furniture' of the mind," on this view, writes Dewey, "is the mind." [19]

Obviously, this conception of the mind carries to an extreme Locke's assumption of the nature of experience and contradicts the notion of an inner nature or an original contribution on the part of the individual in giving character and quality to his experience. What one becomes or makes of himself is manifestly the result of the ideas or the experiences presented to him and the method (the laws of association) employed in their presentation.

The effects of the Herbartian movement upon education were twofold: (1) to direct attention to the appropriate content of study and (2) to standardize methods of instruction. Had the pedagogues of the period applied the doctrines of Herbart to children in the *concrete* rather than to children in *general,* they would doubtless have been impressed with the significance of individual differences in backgrounds and interests and the consequent necessity of organized instruction in harmony with these facts. This possibility, however, was not grasped for some time. Rather was the importance of the teacher's activity accentuated and the "method of the recitation" used to mold the performances of children in groups, in accordance with the laws of thought.

Out of these efforts came the Herbartian "steps" in teaching and learning. These "steps" or stages influenced the ordering and the presentation of materials in textbooks and the details of procedure within the classroom. The "Inductive Lesson" as developed by Professor Bagley will serve as one example.[20] This included five steps: (1) preparation, which called for questions and answers and was to consume no more than one-fifth of the

---

[19] John Dewey, *Democracy and Education* (New York: The Macmillan Co., 1916), pp. 81–84.
[20] William C. Bagley, *The Educative Process* (New York: The Macmillan Co., 1907), chap. XIX.

period; (2) presentation, in which the pupil was to acquire the facts from textbooks, lecture, or other means; (3) comparison and abstraction, which called for the question-and-answer method again, with the time varying depending upon whether one or more generalizations were sought for; (4) generalization, which consisted in the summing up in a class definition the results of previous labor and which was to consume no more than three or four minutes; and, finally, (5) application, either direct or indirect, which might be elastic in method as well as in the time involved.

Beginning roughly with 1890, the Herbartian influence tended to dominate theory and practice in the normal schools and teacher training institutions of the United States. Despite the fact that it led in many ways to an enrichment of the curriculum, through its emphasis upon history, literature, and the arts and brought into prominence the concept of interests as central in education, its basic assumption of education as an activity to be controlled and directed from outside the learner resulted inevitably in what came to be called "lock-step methods" of teaching.

It would seem, then, that education in the period under review moved out of one type of formalism, through an intervening period of liberalism and expansion, only to end in another period of formalism. Under the influence of an expanding economy and the evolution of new political and social institutions, together with a philosophy of rugged individualism, schools on all levels came to serve a multitude of interests and purposes. These developments were reflected in an increase in the number of subjects taught in both elementary and secondary schools as well as in a broadening of the curriculum and the purposes of the college. Moreover, just as the classical grammar school gave way to the academy, so the academy, as a private institution, in the nineteenth century, began to give ground to the public high school, a reflection of public recognition of the increasing importance of education. Following the Civil War compulsory school attendance gradually replaced voluntary attendance on the elementary school level; and the number of graduates from secondary schools, particularly in the latter part of the century, increased substantially. Indeed, in the 1890's the number was sufficient to create demands for uniformity and standardization of the curriculum of the latter and to promote common agreements between colleges and secondary schools on conditions of admission to college.

These new demands for a reorganization of education, together with efforts to bring about standardization, resulted from the marriage of new psychologies of learning with emerging factors in American society. These factors of change will be discussed in the chapter to follow.

Suggested Reading

Butts, R. Freeman, and Lawrence A. Cremin, *A History of Education in American Culture* (New York: Henry Holt & Co., Inc., 1953), chap. 6.

Commager, Henry, *The American Mind* (New Haven: Yale University Press, 1952), chaps. I–IV.

Drake, William E., *The American School in Transition* (Englewood Cliffs, N.J.: Prentice-Hall, Inc., 1955), chap. X.

Meyer, Adolphe E., *An Educational History of the American People* (New York: McGraw-Hill Book Co., 1957), chaps. 7–10.

Thut, I. N., and J. Raymond Gerberich, *Foundations of Method for Secondary Schools* (New York: McGraw-Hill Book Co., 1949), chap. 6.

CHAPTER

12

Inner Development As a Criterion

for Education

Rousseau and the Doctrine of the Original Goodness of Man

As we have seen, the Lockian conception of the mind dominated educational thinking during the period of the conquest of the continent. According to Locke, all knowledge begins with sense impressions and all of the complexities of mental life are traceable, ultimately, to those objects of sense outside the organism which instigate mental activity. If one ignores what Locke termed ideas of reflection, or the power of the mind to work over the original impressions of sense, to combine them in diverse ways, and thus to create objects of imagination as well as to draw inferences from them respecting matters that have no counterpart in the real world, it is easy to credit the nature of an individual's personality primarily to environmental influences. This some successors of Locke proceeded to do, notably Helvetius and his colleagues in France and, somewhat later, the extreme Herbartians in this country and abroad. By the end of the nineteenth century, in the hands of the latter, the concept of education as essentially a formative process had not only assumed prominence as a theory but had found expression in the details of the curriculum, in methods of teaching, and in the administrative structure of the school.

· 224 ·

Beginning roughly with Rousseau, however, a different conception of original nature found expression which was to provide new criteria for educative materials and methods. This lodged the beginnings of education squarely within the nature of the child, making of his nature and his needs the basic considerations in the educative process. Here, once again, we have a matching or mutual reinforcement of psychological theory and cultural factors.

Attention was drawn in the last chapter to the new confidence in man and his inner nature which developed in this country during the first half of the nineteenth century. It was also suggested that the supreme confidence in the individual, the affirmation of the integrity and worth of personality, which prompted Emerson to make the following assertion, found little concrete application within the actual practices of the schools: "No law can be sacred to me but that of my nature. Good and bad are but names very readily transferable to that or this; the only right is what is after my constitution, the only wrong is what is against it." [1] Much the same can be said of England and the continent. Contrast, for example, the schoolmaster's concept of child nature as pictured by Charles Dickens with that of William Wordsworth in his ode, *Intimations of Immortality*.

> Not in entire forgetfulness,
> And not in utter nakedness,
> But trailing clouds of glory do we come
> From God, who is our home.
> Heaven lies about us in our infancy!
> Shades of the prison house begin to close
> Upon the growing Boy.
> But he beholds the light, and whence it flows;
> The Youth who daily farther from the east
> Must travel, still is Nature's Priest;
> And by the vision splendid
> Is on his way attended;
> At length the Man perceives it die away,
> And fade into the light of common day.

---

[1] *The Prose Works of Ralph Waldo Emerson, Essay on Self-Reliance* (Boston: Fields, Osgood and Company, 1870), p. 244.

Nevertheless, as early as 1762, in his *Emile,* Rousseau had outlined a program of education keyed to the developing nature of the child, which, once the situation was ripe, was to influence profoundly both the practice and the science of education. We will glance briefly at some of his germinal ideas.

In contrast with the notion that children are born in sin and thus are originally corrupt in nature, Rousseau boldly proclaims the original goodness of man. Thus the opening words of the *Emile:* "God makes all things good; man meddles with them and they become evil."

It follows that the native impulses and desires of the child should constitute the criteria to observe in planning his education, rather than the demands of society. The child, like the man, is an end in himself. That is to say, man is too noble a being to serve as a mere instrument of others. Consequently, in planning the future of the young person it should be borne in mind that "men are not made for their stations but their stations for men." [2]

As applied to children, this implies both a respect and a reverence for child nature and, in consequence, a revolutionary approach to education. Educators became concerned not with preconceived subject matter or preordained ground to be covered, but with the selection and adaptation of learning experiences in harmony with the evolving characteristics of children. "Thus are we taught by three masters. If their teaching conflicts, the scholar is ill-educated and will never be at peace with himself; if their teaching agrees, he goes straight to his goal, he lives at peace with himself, he is well educated. . . . What is this goal? As we have shown, it is the goal of nature. Since all three modes of education must work together, the two that we can control must follow the lead of that which is beyond our control." [3]

This principle of adapting educational materials and methods to child nature accounts for the program which Rousseau outlined for the education of his Emile. Since the child's first impulses and desires are sensuous and relate to his physical well-being, his early training should concentrate upon the physical.

---

[2] For an excellent analysis and summary of Rousseau's thought, see M. B. Ellis, *Julie, or the Nouvelle Héloïse, A Synthesis of Rousseau's Thought* (Toronto: University of Toronto Press, 1949).

[3] Jean Jacques Rousseau, *Emile* (New York: Everyman's Library, E. P. Dutton & Co., Inc., 1925), p. 6.

To substitute books for sense experience "does not teach us to reason, it teaches us to use the reason of others rather than our own; it teaches us to believe much and to know little." [4]

Until the age of twelve, then, Rousseau would have Emile's education confined primarily to physical activity and the manifold active relations with his sensible environment. Similarly with other stages in his development. His intellectual education (in the sense of coping with abstract ideas and principles) should not begin until he is from twelve to fifteen, and from fifteen to twenty he should receive his moral and social training. By this time, it is assumed, the senses and the brain have developed to the point where it is appropriate and necessary to temper the heart. "Man's proper study is that of his relation to his environment. So long as he knows that environment through his physical nature, he should study himself in relation to things; this is the business of his childhood; when he begins to be aware of his moral nature, he should study himself in relation to his fellow-men; this is the business of his whole life, and we have now reached the time when that study should begin." [5]

It is interesting to observe that although Rousseau would organize education in accordance with stages of development common to children *in general*, he nevertheless repudiated Locke's concept of a typical mind, thus anticipating the educator's concern for individual differences by more than a century. Each mind, he insists, has a form of its own which carries a moral for the teacher's efforts, if he would be successful.

Perhaps, however, his idea of an education appropriate for members of the female sex was less progressive! Since women, in his view, are not constituted in character or temperament as are men their education should be different, and, since men are the stronger the education of the girl should prepare her for a role subordinate to man. [6]

To Rousseau must be given credit (some would insist blame!) for formulating in suggestive terms a concept of education in striking contrast with that prevalent in his day. Children, accord-

---

[4] *Ibid.*, Book II, p. 90.
[5] *Ibid.*, Book IV, p. 175.
[6] See *Emile*, op. cit., Book V, pp. 321 ff. for a detailed outline of the education of Sophie, Emile's future wife.

ing to his theory, were no longer to be viewed as adults in miniature. Their minds are unique and peculiar to them, and their
development proceeds in stages which manifest themselves in a
serial and predetermined order.

From today's vantage point, Rousseau's insight into child nature may seem naive. In appraising its importance, however, we
should distinguish between the specific applications of his doctrines, as he made them, and their later influence upon the history of education.

His basic principle was that nature is right, and, in consequence, the wise parent and teacher will follow its lead. Two conclusions from this premise have exercised a determining influence
upon education: (1) that the child's spontaneous and natural interests and impulses are essential ingredients in his education; (2)
that the child and the adolescent, in the course of their progress
toward maturity, pass through identifiable stages, each with characteristics of its own, which must be given opportunities for expression if development is to be healthy.

This concept of child development and its translation into
educational procedures may be divided into two phases, one
which antedated developments in biology and the doctrine of
evolution, the other biological and evolutionary.

Preevolutionary Conceptions of Inner Nature and Education

Both Pestalozzi and Froebel are representative of the first phase.

Pestalozzi, for example, pictured the child's nature after the
analogy of the seed of a tree, on the assumption that within the
seed the mature tree exists in miniature.

Sound education stands before me symbolized by a tree planted
near fertilizing waters. A little seed, which contains the design of the
tree, its form, and its properties, is placed in the soil. The whole tree
is an uninterrupted chain of organic parts, the plan of which existed
in its seed and root. Man is similar to the tree. In the new-born child
are hidden those faculties which are to unfold during life. The individual and separate organs of his being form themselves gradually
into unison, and build up humanity in the image of God. The education of men is a purely moral result. It is not the educator who puts

new powers and faculties into man, and imparts to him breath and life. He only takes care that no untoward influence shall disturb nature's march of development. The moral, intellectual, and practical powers of man must be nurtured within himself and not from artificial substitutes. Thus, faith must be cultivated by our own act of believing, not by reasoning about faith; love, by our own act of loving, not by fine words about love; thought, by our own act of thinking, not by merely appropriating the thoughts of other men; and knowledge, by our own investigation, not by endless talk about the results of art and science.[7]

In practice, Pestalozzi's theory of education found expression in object teaching, an effort to educate the child in the first instance through the senses, since these develop and require discipline prior to other faculties, such as memory, imagination, reason. In practice, too, contradictory results followed from Pestalozzi's efforts. On the one hand, the emphasis upon the child's firsthand observations led not only to fundamental changes in the organization of subject matter and the content of learning experiences, but to carefully graded lessons as well. As a result, the curriculum of the elementary school was enriched by the addition of materials in science, geography, arithmetic, oral language, etc. On the other hand, Pestalozzi's concept of general faculties of the mind which evolve in a serial order, but are assisted in so doing by the stimulation of outside material, lent itself to a concept of formal discipline (the notion that once the faculties of memory, reason, etc., are trained and disciplined by one sort of material they will function efficiently in any situation calling for their exercise). This was, of course, grist for the mill of the traditionalist who might then justify the teaching of his subject by virtue of its disciplinary value, when hard pressed to demonstrate its relevance on any other basis.

Similarly, in the realm of method Pestalozzian emphasis upon object teaching and the art of questioning associated with it was twofold in its educational effects. It opened the door of the classroom to the outside world of objects and events, but, in the course of time, it also degenerated into a barren verbalism, a trend fostered rather than retarded by the publication and distribution

---

[7] Quoted from Paul Monroe, *A Text Book in the History of Education* (New York: The Macmillan Co., 1905), pp. 611–612. By permission of The Macmillan Company.

of "Pestalozzian methods" with detailed instructions for teachers
to follow. Take, for example, the following language lesson conducted by Pestalozzi himself and reported by one of his students.
The lesson was intended to develop ideas by means of gradually
enlarged sentences.

> Thus he would ask: "Boys, what do you see?"
> (He never addressed the girls.)
> Answer: "A hole in the paper."
> Pestalozzi: Very well, say after me:
> "I see a hole in the paper.
> "I see a long hole in the paper.
> "Through the hole I see the wall.
> "Through the long, narrow hole I see the wall.
> "I see figures on the paper.
> "I see black figures on the paper.
> "I see round black figures on the paper.
> "I see a square yellow figure on the paper.
> "By the side of the square yellow figure I see a round black one.
> "The square figure is joined to the round figure by a large black
> stripe, etc." [8]

Pestalozzi's influence upon American education probably dates
from the publication of Warren Colburn's *First Lessons in Arithmetic on the Plan of Pestalozzi,* published in Boston in 1821. This
was followed by descriptions in American periodicals of European
practices. Henry Barnard, for example, used his *American Journal* and the Connecticut *Common School Journal* (1838–1842)
toward this end. Most potent, however, was the influence of Oswego, New York, during the superintendency of Edward A. Shel-
don. Under the latter's direction, Pestalozzian methods were not
only introduced into the Oswego schools, but, through his efforts,
they were widely publicized. In 1866, the Oswego training school
was established, to be followed by others throughout the country,
all devoted to the spread of the new gospel.[9]

---

[8] Quoted in Samuel Chester Parker, *A Textbook in the History of Modern Elementary Education* (Boston: Ginn & Company, 1912), p. 326.

[9] For a comprehensive description of Pestalozzian theory and practice in this
country and Europe, one can do no better than to read Samuel Chester Parker's
account in *A Textbook in the History of Modern Elementary Education* (Boston:
Ginn & Company, 1912), chaps. XIII–XVI.

Froebel and the Kindergarten Influence

A second conspicuous illustration of the doctrine of inner development is that of Froebel and the kindergarten movement. Although a few kindergartens were established in this country between 1850 and 1875, the movement did not assume significant proportions until about 1875.[10]

Froebel, like Pestalozzi, believed that each child contains within himself the germs of his future possibilities and, therefore, a major purpose of education is to adapt instruction to the laws of development. Froebel, moreover, conceived of child nature as the offshoot of the divine nature which unfolds according to the laws of self-activity but which, at the same time, is dependent upon the quickening influence of outer conditions for adequate expression. Hence the mission of the school as a kindergarten. Education, when truly conceived, consists in no more than the proper relating of the inner and the outer, with the latter subordinate to the former. When given adequate outlet for its divine energy and appropriate materials with which to concern itself, the child's inner nature will develop in a healthy manner. When thwarted, stunted growth and perversion follow.

It thus follows that for Froebel educative materials and activities serve a divine purpose. As described in his *The Education of Man*, "Education consists in leading man, as a thinking, intelligent being, growing into self-consciousness, to a pure and unsullied, conscious and free representation of the inner law of Divine Unity and in teaching him ways and means thereto." [11]

This involved for Froebel differing emphases and different activities at different stages in the child's development but with one common purpose throughout: to relate the individual to the whole. In practical terms, this consisted in engaging cooperatively in the activities of the social environment. In childhood, this was accomplished quite largely through play in which phases of domestic life were imitated; in boyhood, by participating in the work of the home, as well as sharing vicariously in racial experi-

---

[10] For an interesting description of Elizabeth Peabody's pioneer efforts in the establishment of kindergarten education in this country, see Louise Hall Tharp, *The Peabody Sisters of Salem* (Boston: Little, Brown & Co., 1950), chap. 25.

[11] Friedrich Froebel, *The Education of Man*, Hailmann translation (New York: D. Appleton and Company, 1897), p. 2.

ences through story and song. It was assumed that through this process of sharing, actually and vicariously, the spiritual truths which objects and activities and stories symbolize would emerge in the consciousness of the child.

Although Froebel outlined an educational program which should extend beyond the first years of childhood, it is with the kindergarten that his name is most commonly associated. To him, however, should be credited certain germinal ideas of far-reaching importance.

In the first place, he envisaged each child as a sacred personality, a replica of the Infinite Spirit. This inspires reverence for child nature as such. Childhood and youth, as unique stages in development toward maturity, are thus possessed of laws and characteristics uniquely their own, which must be known and followed by those responsible for child rearing in a manner analogous to that of a skillful gardener who tends his plants with an ever watchful eye upon the inner conditions of healthy growth. In the best sense of the term, education is thus to be child centered.

Secondly, the conditions requisite for healthy development constitute a regimen or a discipline binding equally upon guardian and child. Discipline is thus taken out of the category of mere external pressure, or the arbitrary imposition of the will of a superior upon the will of a weaker individual, and assumes instead the character of an overarching ideal to which teacher and pupil alike must subordinate themselves.

Finally, Froebel introduces a concept of growth that is social rather than individualistic in nature. It is through *shared* activities and *participation* in the concerns of the family and the community that one becomes a *personality,* a concept which contrasts with the idea of maturity as a goal of self-containment.

These ideas have profoundly influenced education, not merely on the kindergarten and primary levels but at later stages as well. On the other hand, a number of difficulties were quick to emerge from the Froebelian concept of education. These derived from the fact that two sets of criteria were employed in selecting and organizing educational experiences for the child. One, his needs as empirically observed; the other, these needs as metaphysically interpreted. Theoretically, what best serves the interests of the child, as determined by the direct observations of the "skilled gardener," also functions best to liberate the infinite nature within the young person, as determined by metaphysical insight, and vice versa. In practice, however, both the observations and the conclusions drawn from them by empirical observers have often been in disagreement, whereas in the realm of pure thought and mystical experience, no such stubborn obstacle confronts the individual engaged in its operations. It was not strange, therefore, to find the Froebelians following the easier path and selecting the activities of the kindergarten more by reference to their symbolic or metaphysical value than their appropriateness to child nature as determined by observation and experiment.

Although in the mind of one and the same individual there may be no inconsistency between educative materials selected from actual observation and experiment and those logically approved by means of mystical insight into the purposes of the infinite, this seldom holds true of different interpreters. Mysticism as a method of curriculum building and as a means of constructing helpful teaching procedures suffers from the same difficulty as mysticism in other areas of life; it is satisfactory and reassuring only to the individual translator of the deliverances of the ultimate reality. Consequently, it is not strange that efforts were made to discover criteria for education, free from philosophical presuppositions—that is by resort to science.

G. Stanley Hall and the Child Study Movement

Few individuals in the course of their lifetime have exercised greater influence upon American education than G. Stanley Hall, President of Clark University from 1888 to 1920. Under his leadership, able scholars representing all fields of higher education were attracted to Clark University, giving to this institution an enviable status for many years. Hall's advice was sought on educational questions from all parts of the Union, with the result that directly, as well as indirectly, through his students, his ideas found wide application. To the theory and the practice of education he brought contributions from his knowledge of many fields—biology, history, geology, comparative psychology, etc.—as well as the conclusions from firsthand observation and study of children. Quite appropriately he earned the title of father of the child study movement in this country. Both he and his students addressed thousands of questionnaires to all manner of individuals in all sections of the country, seeking data bearing upon childhood experiences which might serve as a basis of comparison with the results of direct observation of children. Finally, he had the courage to draw conclusions from his investigations which seemed warranted by the data, even when these conflicted with traditional and conventional ideas.

Not only did Hall and his students devise many of their own methods and procedures, they utilized as well theories and inferences drawn from other fields. Thus, from biology they derived the recapitulation theory and from psychology the theory of instincts, two theories which served as lenses through which they read and interpreted many of the data derived from their own investigations.

According to the biological theory of recapitulation, each individual, prior to birth, passes through well-defined physical stages reminiscent of that line of evolution to which he belongs. Thus, at one stage in its development, the human embryo possesses a fishlike tail and gill slits which shortly disappear to be replaced by still other nonhuman characteristics in its progress toward its eventual human structure.

Now, if we assume, as did Hall and his followers, that the cultural and historical development of western civilization reappears as stages of development—intellectual, emotional, social—in the lives of young people as they move from infancy to adulthood, we have what became known as the cultural epochs theory. In shorthand terms this theory affirms that "ontogenesis recapitulates phylogenesis."

Observe, also, that for this school of thought, the stages of individual development which parallel racial history manifest themselves more or less suddenly (a saltatory conception of development) and in an order or series (serial development) similar to their appearance in history. These stages, as described by one follower of Hall, are (1) prehistoric; (2) patriarchal; (3) tribal; (4) feudal, with absolute monarchy; (5) revolutionary, with constitutional monarchy; (6) republic or self-governing. According to the same author, the corresponding stages in the development of the individual are: (1) infancy; (2) childhood; (3) preadolescence; (4) early adolescence; (5) middle adolescence; (6) late adolescence.[12]

One more item requires mention, the doctrine of catharsis, according to which the suppression or repression of tendencies characteristic of one stage may affect unfavorably development in a subsequent stage. More positively stated, the undesirable original tendencies must be given expression either because they are necessary preliminaries to, or correlates of, other quite different impulses or because free expression in early life safeguards the individual from their appearance in later life.

The cultural epochs theory, together with this doctrine of catharsis, carried revolutionary implications for education with respect to the content of the curriculum, methods of discipline and guidance, and the administrative structure of the school. Its greatest impact upon education in the United States was in the last decades of the last century and the first quarter of the present century, although, in modified form, a number of its tenets are still evident in the theories of Freud and Jung as applied to individual guidance and therapy.

The Curriculum Takes Its Cue from Nature

In 1901 Hall delivered an address before the National Council of Education on the topic "The Ideal School As Based on Child Study," [13] which states in short compass the applications of his conception of the nature of the child to the curriculum and the organization of the school. Thus he observed that during the years from eight or nine to puberty "there is a decreased rate of growth, so that the body relatively rests; but there is a striking increase of vitality, activity, and power to resist disease." This stage, he believes, corresponds to the period of human development well above the simian and before the historic period, "when our early forebears were well adjusted to their environment." It does not suggest, therefore, an emphasis upon reasoning, creative thinking, appeals to judgment or originality, but it is admirably adapted to

---

[12] R. W. Pringle, *Adolescence and High School Problems* (Boston: D. C. Heath & Company, 1922), pp. 16–17.
[13] *Proceedings and Addresses*, National Education Association, 1901, pp. 474–488.

"drill, habituation, and mechanism." Accordingly, the teacher will seek to establish the fundamentals of an education in reading, writing, arithmetic, etc. "Accuracy, which, when out of season, is fraught with so many dangers for mind and body, is now in order." Arithmetic should be mechanized, "with plenty of mental exercises, and later with rules and processes for written work, with only little attempt at explanation." He complains that the geographies have not respected the unity of the child's mind and in their presentation of facts they have not considered connections with each other or the "nascent stages of growth." The subject should be organized on the basis of the fact that the child's interest in primitive life and animals culminates in the ages of nine to ten, and interest in trade and government does not appear until from sixteen to twenty. Singing is very important at the age we are considering, "but far more time will be given to rote singing than to singing from notes, especially at first. The chief aim will be not to develop the power to read music, but to educate the sentiments, and especially to attune them to love of home, nature, fatherland, and religion—the four chief themes of songs in all ages, past and present." The hand must also receive training in these years since it is "in a sense never so near the brain as now" and "muscular development never so conditions mental." This age is also most favorable for beginning the study of foreign languages, although these will be taught by ear and mouth. "The child has a natural desire to express himself in many vocal forms other than the vernacular, for it is the age when all kinds of gibberish, dog Latin, and inventive words culminate. It represents the stage when human speech evolved fastest." These natural urges toward oral expression furnish also the cue for the teacher's dominant method of instruction. It will be by the "short-circuit from ear to mouth, which existed for unknown eons before reading and writing, and not chiefly on the long circuit and, biologically, very recent brain-path from eye to hand." Not much writing, accordingly, should be required of the child but he should hear and talk for hours each day. The story is of great importance and the ability to tell stories is a prime requisite in the teacher. "The ideal storyteller will prefer twilight or evening, with at least the dim light that gives the imagination a chance over sense, perhaps with flickering flames to objectify his themes. He will

then weave the almost hypnotic charm of 'Once upon a time.' "
The stories selected will correspond with the age the child is
recapitulating: "the tales of Ulysses, Orestes, Siegfried, Thor,
King Arthur and his knights, the wanderings of Aeneas and Tele-
machus, perhaps some tales from one or other of the great ethnic
Bibles, some of the soul-transforming myths of Plato—such as
Atlantis, the cave, the two steeds—Hercules at the cross-roads,
perhaps some legends from Ancient India, Reynard the Fox,
something from Grimm and Simrock."

Such, in meager outlines, are Hall's suggestions for a curriculum for children during the period which extends between the
ages of eight and nine and the onset of puberty. With the dawn
of adolescence a rich curriculum and varied educative experiences
become essential. In this stage "To drill merely is to arrest."
Facts, "ideas, laws and principles should be in the very atmosphere, for they are now the ingenious youth's native breath,
his vital air."

Methods of discipline and teaching advocated by Hall and
others during the elementary school period likewise take their
cue from nature. This leads to quite different procedures at different stages; at one time the most rigorous disciplinary measures
are applied and at another time a *laissez faire* let alone policy is
followed. Thus, when speaking of the methods employed during
the period from eight or nine to puberty, Hall contended that to
explain instructions yields only self-consciousness and conceit.
"Obedience should be a law, if not a passion." Even with respect
to morals and conduct the chief duty of the child at this age is to
obey.

In a similar vein, Pringle advises against an appeal to the higher
reasoning powers during the period of preadolescence. To get the
best results, he insists, instruction in this period should be dogmatic and authoritative, even mechanical. "So far as the fundamentals are concerned, it is a case of drill and inculcation rather
than true teaching." [14]

On the other hand, with the dawn of adolescence, not only do
rich and varied experiences become imperative, but the manner
of their presentation is of strategic consideration. To drill at this
stage is to retard development. Now is the time for encouraging

---

[14] Pringle, *op. cit.*, p. 19.

the reasoning powers, thoughtfulness, and reflection.

To the layman the applications of the catharsis theory were shocking. Take, for example, the property instinct and its implications for parent and teacher as discussed by Kline and France, and quoted by Hall:

> Selfishness is the corner-stone of the struggle for existence, deception is its very foundation, while the acquiring of property has been the dominant factor in the history of men and nations. These passions of the child are but the pent up forces of the greed of thousands of years. They must find expression and exercise, if not in childhood, later. . . . It does no good to make the child perform moral acts when it does not appreciate what right and wrong mean, and to punish a child for not performing acts which his very nature compels him to do, is doing that child positive injury.
>
> During the period of adolescence, generosity and altruism spring up naturally. Then why try to force a budding plant into blossom? Instruct them by all means, teach them the right; but if this fails, do not punish, but let the child be selfish, let him lie and cheat, until these forces spend themselves. Do not these experiences of the child give to man in later life a moral virility? [15]

The Secondary School Becomes the Common School

As we have said, the culture epochs theory exercised its greatest influence in the last decades of the last century and the early years of the present century. This was a period of extreme growing pains in education on both the elementary and secondary levels. Prior to this time the elementary school had been the "common school" in the sense that only a fraction of its graduates anticipated further education. Consequently, it was under no impelling obligation to organize its curriculum with an eye to work which followed in the secondary school. Nor would this have been an easy task, considering the chaotic condition of curricula in the latter. From 1890 on, however, it became ever more evident to observers that the high school was in process of becoming the common school, insofar as that term implies the enrollment of

---

[15] G. Stanley Hall, *Aspects of Child Life and Education* (Boston: Ginn & Company, 1907), pp. 266–267.

the bulk of the school population within a given age range and the point at which most young people terminate their formal education.

On the other hand, the number of pupils who were dropping out of school between the first and last years of the secondary school was creating general concern. According to data provided by Alexander Inglis, the first year of public secondary schools in 1914–1915 included 40.86 per cent of all pupils enrolled in these schools, whereas the fourth year included only 13.99 per cent, a fact which suggested not only that something was wrong with the holding power of the secondary school but also with the elementary school for failing to equip pupils adequately for work on the secondary level.[16]

Several demands upon educators emerged from this situation: a demand for a reorganization of the curriculum in the upper years of the elementary school which would provide learning materials more relevant to the interests and future intentions of this age group and a demand for a reorganization of the secondary school keyed to the fact that it was no longer concerned exclusively with a selected school population but in its first years at least should minister to the needs of all graduates of the elementary school.

Thus was the stage set for the apostles of G. Stanley Hall to insist that a new school unit was required, one adapted to the age commonly embraced by the upper years of the elementary school and the first two years of high school. Many objectives contributed to the reorganization of the elementary and secondary schools in this period, objectives such as the need for economy of time in education and provision for some form of vocational education for boys and girls who were to terminate their education at this point, but the psychological need to adapt education to the characteristics of early adolescence was of general appeal. Thus a new school unit, the junior high school, came into being, one which, it was hoped, by virtue of its administrative structure and its curricular and extracurricular offerings, would meet the unique needs of young people—intellectual, emotional, social, moral, and vocational—in the early years of adolescence.

---

[16] Alexander Inglis, *Principles of Secondary Education* (Boston: Houghton Mifflin Co., 1918), p. 121.

Nor were administrators slow in meeting their responsibilities. Within a few short years fundamental changes were inaugurated in the curriculum, the methods of teaching, and the types of activities in which young people might engage. For example:

1. It was observed that in this stage irregularities in physical growth are common, together with rapid changes in aptitudes and interests. This suggested a broad sweep of subject matter in contrast with narrow and specialized concentration upon one area or one field, with the result that general science, general history, general mathematics, general literature, and "try-out" courses in the arts and crafts were substituted for special subjects such as physiology, ancient history, etc.

2. It was observed that this period was one of budding social interests, marked by new relationships between the sexes, keen sensitiveness with respect to group approval or disapproval, especially of one's peers. These interests suggested the wisdom of socializing the work of the school at this point through the introduction of extracurricular activities, special-interest clubs, assemblies, dramatic work, etc., and utilizing the social motive in the teaching of the regular subjects through the project method and the "socialized recitation."

3. In this period intellectual interests were seen to center upon the concrete and the immediate rather than upon the abstract and the remote, with the implication that instruction should foster the development of the practical rather than the theoretical reason.

4. Since individual differences in interests and life goals become prominent in this period, it was concluded that this called for a differentiated curriculum. In practice, however, this eventuated all too often in provision for individual differences in interests and life goals as viewed by the administrative office: a commercial curriculum, an industrial arts curriculum, or a general and a college preparatory curriculum, each with a specialized purpose but from which it was often difficult for a pupil to transfer to another curriculum.

5. Finally, the junior high school period was seen to be one in which young people are concerned with the immediate environment, which, as the educator saw it, suggested vocational education for those who would terminate their education at this point.

Thus came into being *terminal courses* to serve a function not unlike that assigned today to the junior college.

A large measure of credit must be given to psychologists for the emergence of the junior high school and the stimulus for a reorganization of education on all levels. In all fairness, however, we should add other factors such as (1) the concern of social reformers over the wastage in education which resulted in large numbers of dropouts in the early years of the secondary school and (2) the insistence of business and industry that the vocational needs of youth receive attention. To this latter insistence we shall return in our next chapter.

An Appraisal of the Culture Epochs Theory

How shall we appraise the contributions of the culture epochs theory?

Most obvious were its positive contributions to the enrichment of the curriculum, particularly in the elementary and the junior high school periods. Not only was new subject matter introduced which served a wider range of interests, but methods of teaching were vitalized and what were once considered "fads and frills"— art, music, dramatic work, club-like activities—now attained the status of essentials.

On the other hand, the presentation of appropriate materials and the use of methods keyed to a given stage of development were assumed to exercise a magical influence. That is to say, the child's response was supposed to spring forth as a jack-in-the-box, by virtue of a pre-established connection between inner nature and outer stimulus. For example, Indian life was studied in the early years of the elementary school, not so much because primitive life, in its simplicity, serves as a happy introduction to an understanding of the operations of a modern community, such as the providing of food, clothing, and shelter; but rather because it affords channels of expression for atavistic tendencies in the life of the young child.

Moreover, the fact that stages of development were conceived of as inborn tendencies to think, feel, and act in ways characteristic of racial experiences gave an aspect of inevitability and imperativeness to child behavior. Since John or Mary's behavior was thus known in advance, teachers easily forgot John and Mary as individuals in order to lay their plans for children in general. Thus the explanation for misbehavior on the part of an individual child was sought for in the past history of the race, which was thus reasserting itself rather than in the circumstances peculiar to that child's environment. (See the quotation from Kline and France on p. 238.) This theory was not at all helpful in advancing the diagnosis of growing pains in children, although it doubtless had the advantage of easing the conscience of a negligent parent whose child might give indications of waywardness!

The uses to which subject matter might be put were also limited by this theory. Movements and events in history easily yielded to the interpretation that what is, or, at least, what has been, is right inasmuch as these were manifestations or expressions of a cosmic process in which human beings function more or less as pawns, not as responsible agents.

It was this interpretation of history, indeed, which prompted an outstanding educator of the time, Charles McMurry, to introduce "project teaching" in the study of history and literature. The project differed from the daily recitation in that it concerned itself with the solution of a problem, the understanding of a movement in history, a masterpiece in literature, or the operations of a social, industrial, or economic institution as a unified experience in contrast with the daily nibbling process of assign, study, recite characteristic of the daily recitation. From the standpoint of the pupil, it was purposive, designed to capture his interest and to enlist his continued efforts until either a solution of the problem or a unified understanding emerged. Secondly, the project departed from conventional teaching in that it employed "plural routes to learning," research in textbook and library, yes, but other media as well, such as the arts and crafts, music, kitchen, and shop, etc.—whatever might contribute a real-life character to the study.

The obvious advantages which the project method brought to teaching led to its widespread adoption and later development into "units of work" of both an academic and real-life character. It also contributed to the spread of free, informal, and diversified procedures within the classroom, thus rescuing teaching from rigid and lock-step methods. As its originators conceived of it, however, the project had other purposes to serve as well. It was designed to enable young people "to gather up and organize" the world's experience and wisdom by reliving, so to speak, "the actual evolution of the main life processes in a practical world" and thus to bring to a focus in the mind of the pupil a progressive revelation of the world, past and present.[17]

The kinship of the project, so conceived, to the theory of recapitulation is clear, as well as the danger it entailed that school experiences might be used for the purpose of having children relive the experiences of others with a view to identifying themselves with their purposes and ideals. What better way might one devise for forming the minds of the young in harmony with the status quo?

A second contribution of the culture epochs theory consisted in fostering an objective attitude toward children. Once children ceased to be adults in miniature and were thought to pass through stages unique and peculiar to them, it was natural to conclude that both the causes and the significance of their behavior were to be appraised and dealt with in a manner different from that warranted by similar behavior in adults. Theft and lying in a child, for example, were no longer conclusive evidence of a criminal nature. This encouraged the development of a professional attitude toward children. Absurd as we now believe the explanation of lying and stealing to be, as put forth by Kline and France, it nevertheless suggested methods of diagnosis and treatment relevant to children. As confidence in the theory of recapitulation weakened, psychologists were encouraged to seek the explanations of delinquent behavior in the circumstances which play upon children, in the situation rather than in heredity. Contrast, for example, the explanation of Kline and France, as quoted, with that later offered by Frederick H. Allen, and reported in *Mental Hygiene,* for October, 1927. According to Allen, an analysis of the histories of some sixty instances of stealing on the part of children led to the conclusion that feelings of inadequacy were the cause, feelings which grew out of life situations, such as physical characteristics that marked the child off from others (obesity, speech defects, undersize, etc.) or certain habits such as

---

[17] For example, Charles McMurry, *Teaching by Projects* (New York: The Macmillan Co., 1920), p. 4.

bed-wetting or masturbation; racial prejudice; the presence of brothers and sisters who seemed more gifted or attractive; immorality and desertion of parents; overly repressive discipline; economic factors.

As we have seen, the culture epochs theory, together with the notion that stages of development are saltatory in character, rather than gradual in transition, seemed to justify, psychologically, school units, each organized with special reference to stages of development.

Both experience and careful observation of children eventually undermined the validity of this conclusion. It was found, for example, that children of the same chronological age are not necessarily at identical points in their development, intellectual, social, or emotional. Consequently, even though we may grant the validity of stages of development (which educators do, although not as recapitulations of the past), individual children of one and the same age may differ significantly in maturity. That is to say, the age at which characteristics of certain stages may appear should not be taken too literally. Likewise, the assumption that administrative units must correspond to age range should be taken with liberal grains of salt. Other factors peculiar to the community, such as its size, the geographical distribution of the school population, and the like, are as relevant as an assumed stage of development. Relevant as the junior high school was to conditions of some years ago, factors which were nonexistent at that time are today suggesting new groupings of administrative units. Thus the increasing tendency of young people to continue both their general and their vocational training beyond the period served by the conventional senior high school is leading to the emergence of new units, such as a six-year elementary school, a four-year junior high school and a four-year senior high school, the latter embracing what were formerly the last two years of high school and the first two years of college.

The Sum of the Whole Matter

What, by way of conclusion, shall we say of the concept of inner development and the culture epochs theory?

For one thing, the biological foundations of the recapitulation theory no longer sustain it in the form accepted and applied by its child study advocates. It is now established that although an individual embryo roughly repeats, in the course of its development, the phylogenetic series, there are large omissions and gaps in this series. Moreover, studies in heredity have thrown doubt upon the theory of acquired characteristics which underlies the notion that the individual inherits and thus relives the cultural experiences of his ancestors. Furthermore, a detailed comparison of cultural periods with stages in the development of the individual finds only superficial resemblances between the two. It would appear, then, that the validity of the cultural epochs theory varies inversely with a detailed knowledge of history and a careful and meticulous observation of child development.

A somewhat similar fate has befallen the theory of instincts as inherited habits, or as specifically organized ways of thinking, feeling, and acting which derive from inheritance rather than from experiences in the lifetime of the individual. As a result of Edward L. Thorndike's insistence, for example, that instincts as natively organized responses be described in terms of the *specific* elements within a situation to which *specific* responses in the individual are related, Hall's instincts began to shrink in number. Later observations of infant behavior have reduced the number of instincts still further. Moreover, those instincts which seem to have survived have lost their specific characteristics, with the result that the "instincts" of love, fear, and anger are described as variable ways of responding to varying circumstances.

Finally, in the psychology of John Dewey, instinctive behavior as "impulse" becomes a source of novelty and change in behavior! Although recognized as first in time, in the life of an individual, impulses lack specificity and meaning prior to their interaction with the surrounding medium. Thus Dewey writes as follows in his *Human Nature and Conduct:* "In conduct the acquired is the primitive. Impulses although first in time are never primary; they are secondary." Since impulses in their original expression are without form and acquire form only through interaction with an individual's surroundings, "the *meaning* of native activities is not native; it is acquired, . . ." and so "we need to know about the social conditions which have educated original activities into definite and significant dispositions before we can discuss the psychological element in society." [18]

Does this mean that educators have abandoned the concept of stages of development? Not at all. It is still recognized that childhood is a unique period of growth and development and that children, as they move from infancy into childhood and adolescence and on toward the mature status of adulthood, pass through relatively distinct stages of emotional and social development, a knowledge of which is helpful for parent and teacher alike. Roughly speaking, these stages are infancy, a narcissistic period, a latency period with its gang interests, a hero-worship period, a heterosexual period. Each of these stages is marked by emotional and social characteristics sufficiently definite to carry a moral for the guidance and education of the individual. But observe that they are no longer conceived of as "instincts" but rather as the resultants of an *interplay* between the impulses and urges of the individual and factors cultural and environmental. They are thus idiomatic as well as cultural in their expressions and cultural as well as native.[19]

As the concept of instincts as racial urges which reappear in the lives of growing individuals weakened in the minds of educators, new influences were quick to assert themselves. The junior high school, as we have seen, owed its inception in large measure to the doctrine of culture epochs and the assumption that administrative school units should parallel stages of development. But we have also pointed out that a second motive was to provide a terminal education for that large proportion of young people who were to conclude their schooling at a point between graduation from the elementary school and entrance into the senior high school. Educational planning of this character had its source not so much in the psychology of adolescence as in the response of educators to economic trends. American society was rapidly becoming industrialized. Industry called for workers, and the educa-

---

[18] See John Dewey, *Human Nature and Conduct* (New York: Henry Holt & Co., Inc., 1922), part II. Also John Watson, *Behaviorism* (New York: The Peoples' Institute, 1924), chaps. V, VI.

[19] For a helpful discussion of the growth process in these terms see Robert J. Havighurst, *Developmental Tasks and Education* (New York: Longmans, Green & Co., Inc., 1952).

tion of future workmen, as the hardheaded businessman or industrialist conceived of it, called for habit training and the development of skills. This, in turn, had use for a psychology of "adjustment," a psychology, in short, less sentimental and romantic than that of inner development.

And, once again, the times brought forth the man!

Suggested Reading

Butts, R. Freeman, and Lawrence A. Cremin, *A History of Education in American Culture* (New York: Henry Holt & Co., Inc., 1953), chap. 10.

Carroll, Herbert A., *Mental Hygiene: The Dynamics of Adjustment* (Englewood Cliffs, N.J.: Prentice-Hall, Inc., 1951), chap. 2.

Cole, Lawrence E., and William Bruce, *Educational Psychology* (rev. ed.) (Yonkers, N.Y.: World Book Company, 1958), chap. 1.

Dewey, John, *Human Nature and Conduct* (New York: Henry Holt & Co., Inc., 1922), parts I, II.

Eby, Frederick. *The Development of Modern Education* (Englewood Cliffs, N.J.: Prentice-Hall, Inc., 1952), chap. 23.

Erickson, Erick H., *Childhood and Society* (New York: W. W. Norton & Company, Inc., 1950), chap. 7.

Havighurst, Robert J., *Developmental Tasks and Education* (New York: Longmans, Green & Co., Inc., 1953).

/\\.\\.\\/\\

13

Education As Adjustment

Industrial Development Creates New Problems

On October 3, 1876, Thomas Huxley delivered an address in Baltimore, Maryland, on the occasion of the opening of Johns Hopkins University. He spoke of the impression he received as an Englishman in landing upon the American shore for the first time and "traveling for hundreds of miles through strings of great well-ordered cities, seeing your enormous actual and almost infinite potential wealth in all commodities, and in the energy and ability which turn wealth to account."

It was not so much the evidences of bigness and matchless natural resources, however, which impressed Huxley most, since he realized that "Size is not grandeur, and territory does not make a nation." Rather was he moved to inquire of this country's future:

The great issue, about which hangs a true sublimity, and the terror of overhanging fate, is what are you going to do with all these things? What is to be the end to which these things are to be the means? You are making a novel experiment in politics on the greatest scale which the world has yet seen. Forty millions at your first centenary, it is reasonably to be expected that at the second, these states will be occupied by two hundred millions of English-speaking people, spread over an area as large as that of Europe, and with climate and interests as diverse as those of Spain and Scandinavia, England and Russia. You and your descendants have to ascertain whether this great mass will hold together under the form of a republic, and the despotic reality of universal suffrage; whether state rights will hold out against

centralization, without separation; whether centralization will get
the better, without actual or disguised monarchy; whether shifting
corruption is better than a permanent bureaucracy; and as population
thickens in your great cities, and the pressure of want is felt, the
gaunt spectre of pauperism will stalk among you, and communism
and socialism will claim to be heard. Truly America has a great
future before her; great in toil, in care, and in responsibility; great in
true glory if she be guided in wisdom and righteousness, great in
shame if she fail. I cannot understand why other nations should
envy you, or be blind to the fact that it is for the highest interest
of mankind that you should succeed; but the one condition of success,
your sole safeguard, is the moral worth and intellectual clearness of
the individual citizen.

By the turn of the century, some of the questions so forcefully
posed by Thomas Huxley had become even more imperative than
they were in 1876. The trend toward industrialization had reached
a point where it was clear that a predominantly rural and agricultural economy was to be superseded by an urban and industrial
economy. As Professor Arthur Schlesinger put it, "rural America,
like a stag at bay, was making its last stand." [1] By 1890, three-fifths
of the population of the North Atlantic states had become city
dwellers, and in sections of New England and the Middle Atlantic
states many rural areas were falling into decay. Moreover, this shift
from rural to urban living was proceeding at an ever accelerating
pace.

These changes were of significance to education in that they
testified to fundamental transformations in the lives of people and
thus had an impact upon children. Parents who had been accustomed only to rural life were now moving to cities in large numbers, there confronting not only the necessity of engaging in new
vocations but of rearing children under circumstances novel and
disturbing to adults and children alike.

Large numbers of the foreign-born were also coming to the cities.
Prior to 1880, the bulk of immigrants had come from Great Britain
and the north of Europe. The eighties marked a change in this tide
and the beginnings of immigration from southern and eastern Europe, where customs, institutions, and habits were sufficiently dif-

---

[1] Quoted in Newton Edwards and Herman G. Richey, *The School in the American Social Order* (Boston: Houghton Mifflin Co., 1947), p. 452.

ferent from those encountered in this country to create severe growing pains. Between 1881–1890, for example, 75.6 per cent of all immigrants into the United States came from the countries of Great Britain, Germany, Ireland, Norway, Sweden, Denmark, and Canada. By 1901, this proportion had shrunk to 21.3 per cent. In the same period, however, the percentage of immigrants from Austria-Hungary, Italy, Russia, and Poland increased from 17.6 per cent of the total to 68.5 per cent.[2]

How different were the ways of living thrust upon these immigrants may be seen from the fact that in Europe they had lived primarily in rural areas and small villages and had earned their living, in the main, as farm laborers, an occupation from which they hoped to free themselves upon coming to America. Once here, they flocked to the cities or to mining towns, there to share slum conditions of living with relatives and friends and there, too, to create complicated patterns of diversity out of what had once been relatively homogeneous communities.

Finally, a sizable proportion of the immigrants were illiterate (12.9 per cent, according to the twelfth census, as compared with 5.7 per cent of native whites, and 1.6 per cent of native whites of foreign parentage),[3] competent only to enter unskilled occupations. Strangers in a strange land, subject often to exploitation at the hands of unscrupulous employers, living under inadequate housing conditions, these people, in striking proportions, nevertheless, strove manfully to give their children the advantages of a free education.

One more factor of concern to educators early in the century requires mention in order to appreciate the task confronting the schools. Not only were new technological developments absorbing large proportions of a population once accustomed to rural life in this country and abroad, but change was invading the home and undermining the family through the employment of women and children. Thus, in 1900, 18.2 per cent of all children between the ages of ten and fifteen years of age were engaged in gainful occupations, of whom about one-sixth, or 17.2 per cent, were under twelve years of age. Moreover, according to the census of 1910, 70 per cent

[2] Thomas Sewall Adams and Helen L. Sumner, *Labor Problems* (New York: The Macmillan Co., 1905), p. 73.
[3] *Ibid.*, p. 89.

of all girls between the ages of ten and fifteen who were engaged in gainful occupations were so engaged outside the home.[4]

To the credit of Americans, it should be said that these conditions weighed heavily upon the conscience, and eventually, laws were passed with a view to improving both working and living conditions and, in the case of children, limiting hours of labor and encouraging attendance at school.

The passage of compulsory school attendance laws had the effect of rendering more complex the task of education. Into the schools there now flocked large numbers of young people of a type who had previously received little or no education. For them an exclusively academic curriculum on either the elementary or secondary level no longer seemed adequate. New subjects as well as new criteria for the selection of materials within the traditional subjects seemed essential. Thus "civics" no longer concerned itself with matters exclusively political but undertook as well to acquaint young people with the agencies and institutions and the problems of the community. Thus "community civics" came into being. Similarly, in the elementary school, particularly, the need for health education was obvious, education that would safeguard the health of children even when this involved correcting the erroneous practices and ideas of parents. Still again, as a result of the alarming exodus of women from the home and an increase in child labor, particularly of girls, home economics (chiefly cooking and sewing) gained entrance into the curriculum, as did shop of a practical character for boys.

The changes in American society to which we have drawn attention affected education on all levels. But the contrast between programs of education keyed, on the one hand, to the inner nature of the young person and, on the other, to the demands of society were most obvious on the junior high school level. Here genetic psychology was emphasizing the dynamic and instinctive potentialities of the young person, with the clear implication that nature was to be followed; whereas life outside the school, in home and community, in business and industry, stressed the importance of education for adjustment, one that would give specific and detailed attention to the formation of desirable habits and skills and techniques.

---

[4] *Ibid.*, p. 27.

Confronted with this necessity of choice, educators turned to a psychology that would further education for adjustment.

The Rise of Behaviorism in Psychology

In discussing Herbart and the Herbartians, it was pointed out that the fundamental postulates of this movement lent themselves to a concept of learning in which the schoolmaster conceives of his task as that of forming the character of youth. Since the mind and the personality of the individual are nothing other than the organized experiences that have come to him (the ideas presented to him and the method of their organization), it is easy to conclude that all learning is habit formation. Although Herbart and his followers explained the details of the mental life in terms of psychic phenomena (mental states), there is little difference in spirit between their conception of learning and that implied in the assertions of John Watson, except that the latter conceives of all learning in physiological terms. Thus, according to Watson, there is nothing within to develop. Let an individual begin life with the right number of fingers and toes, plus the few elementary movements which are present at birth, and we need nothing more "in the way of raw material to make a man, be that man a genius, a cultured gentleman, a rowdy, or a thug." [5]

What Watson is saying, in the above reference, is that human behavior is best explained in purely physical and physiological terms. At the time of his writing, this seemed a logical conclusion to draw from developments in psychology. With the rise of a physiological psychology, there seemed less and less occasion to explain human nature and behavior by reference to mental states or to the mind as a nonmaterial entity. Briefly summarized, the stages in this process (shall we say the manner in which psychologists came to lose their minds?) were as follows:

1. Mind as an all-embracing substance, an immaterial agency in contrast with body as a physical substance, shrinks to the status of a collective noun. In Herbart, for example, it designates an association and organization of ideas with no more objective reality than the woods over and above the trees which comprise its existence.

---

[5] *Psychological Care of Infant and Child* (New York: W. W. Norton and Company, Inc., 1928), p. 41.

This was also the position at which William James had arrived when he demonstrated in his *Principles of Psychology* that each "passing thought" includes within itself all that is essential in order to explain the operations of the mental life.[6]

2. Further observation and analysis of mental activity seemed to establish the fact that what were once described as mental states, or ideas, are dependent upon an underlying physical or neural activity. Given interference with the latter, such as a blow upon the head, consciousness seemingly disappears for a time, but the physical processes and neural activity continue to function without dependence upon mental activity. This tended to place mental phenomena in a position subordinate to the physical, but at least they were tolerated for a time as "epi-phenomena" or psychic correlates of the physical with a capacity to register if not to initiate and control behavior.

3. As so often happens, however, when the lion and the lamb lie down together, the lamb shortly disappears. So it was in this instance. Before long, a dominant school of psychology arose, of which Watson was one, which repudiated mental states and attempted to explain all behavior in purely physical terms (physiology, physics, chemistry).

In this transition from a psychology of mental states to a psychology of behaviorism or physiological processes, few played a role more decisive than Edward L. Thorndike.

Thorndike Investigates the Doctrine of Formal Discipline

Early in his career, Thorndike, as we have seen, subjected the concept of instincts, as conceived by G. Stanley Hall and his followers, to critical examination. If instincts actually exist as inherited tendencies to think, feel, and act under given circumstances, he insisted, then an observer should be able to identify the specific situations in the environment which cause or accompany their manifestations and also the specific responses of the individual to these stimulating conditions. That is to say, instincts should be subject to description in terms of specific responses to specific situations. Confronted

---

[6] New York: Henry Holt & Co., Inc., 1890, vol. I, pp. 360–373.

by this necessity to be definite and precise, the cohorts of the instinct psychology and the culture epochs theory began slowly to fold their tents and to disappear over the educational horizon.

The guns which Thorndike leveled at the formal disciplinarians in education were equally devastating. It will be recalled that in Chapter 11 we spoke of the conservative influences in education which, near the end of the nineteenth century, sought to bring order out of chaos in the curriculum of the secondary school and in relations between school and college. One purpose of the Committee of Ten, in its report issued in 1893, was to identify the subjects most appropriate for study by young people "who are going to college, for those going to a scientific school, and for those who, presumably, are going to neither," and to determine how these subjects might best be taught.[7]

In answer to the first question, the Committee took the position that there should be no essential difference in the content of subjects taught for those who intend to continue their education upon graduation and those who do not so plan. The principle enunciated was that an education best designed for the noncollege bound is also best for the college bound, although a careful reading of the recommendations of the various subcommittees suggests that what the Committee really meant was precisely the opposite. Thus, out of the list of subjects endorsed by the Committee (English, the classics, foreign language, mathematics, science, and history), only minor provision was made for the fact that some students would not be going on to college.[8] The reason for this was that despite differences in their educational plans, the two groups were essentially alike in that they constituted "a small proportion of all the children of the country."[9]

This conception of the secondary school as an institution designed to serve only a selected group was shortly to undergo significant change.

---

[7] *Report of the Committee of Ten on Secondary School Studies* (New York: Published for the National Education Association by the American Book Company, 1894), p. 17.

[8] The Committee did recognize the possibility of electives in bookkeeping and commercial arithmetic. It also suggested that "if it were desired to provide more amply for subjects thought to have practical importance in trade or the useful arts, it would be easy to provide options in such subjects for some of the science in the third and fourth years of the English program."

[9] *Report of the Committee of Ten on Secondary School Studies, op. cit.,* p. 51.

In defense of its policy of limiting the curriculum to a few, well-selected subjects, the Committee stated: "Every youth who entered college would have spent four years in studying a few subjects thoroughly; and, on the theory that all the subjects are to be considered equivalent in educational rank for the purposes of admission to college, it would make no difference which subjects he had chosen from the programme—he would have had four years of strong and effective mental training." [10]

The assumption that the educational values of one subject can be equated with the values of another was challenged by one member of the Committee, James H. Baker, President of the University of Colorado. Baker pointed out that the recommendations of the majority assumed as valid the doctrine of "formal discipline," which held that the mind is possessed of general powers—memory, imagination, reason, etc.—which, when trained by appropriate materials, will function better thereafter in all situations calling for their exercise.

Were this doctrine valid, the task of education would be relatively simple. All the preparation a schoolman would need to insure the effectiveness of schooling would be to identify the mental powers most important for training and the subject matter best adapted toward this end, knowing the future would take care of itself.

But suppose that the assumption of general powers or faculties is without valid foundation, that we have only specific memories, not a faculty of memory, that we engage in individual acts of reasoning but have no faculty of reason which we can employ in general. Then should we not, as educators, seek to identify the specific items of information, the most important habits, skills, and techniques employed in adult life, and help young people to become possessed of them?

Herculean as this task might seem, some educators, under the influence of a behavioristic psychology, concluded that it was of necessity the only practical alternative to the "false doctrine" of formal discipline.[11]

---

[10] *Ibid.*, p. 53.

[11] See, for example, Franklin Bobbitt, *How to Make a Curriculum* (Boston: Houghton Mifflin Co., 1924), chap. II. Bobbitt identified the objectives of the curriculum with the specific activities which make up or ought to make up the lives of men and women in the major fields of human action.

Here are two conflicting theories of learning with quite different implications for the curriculum and methods of teaching, two theories which Thorndike and other investigators were quick to subject to investigation and experimentation. From his studies, Thorndike concluded that there are no general powers, such as those of reasoning, memory, etc., which when trained by one sort of material and in one situation will thereby function better with other materials and in other quite different situations. He concluded that there is no reason to believe, for example, that the discipline which comes from memorizing Latin verbs will improve the functioning of memory in other areas. On the other hand, Thorndike succeeded, as did others, in identifying certain situations in which "transfer of training" clearly takes place. From careful analysis of these occasions, he concluded that instances of improvement followed from the presence of "identical elements" present in the two situations, from identical procedures, or from both. Thus an actor who has memorized his part in one play may discover that he learns his part in a second play more easily or in a shorter period of time by virtue of similarities in content or of certain tricks and devices with which he has become familiar.

All Learning Becomes Habit Formation

Observe that this explanation of improvement in learning by means of identities of content and identities of procedure assumes that learning situations are reducible to specifics of stimulus and response!

It is this assumption which constitutes Thorndike's contribution to educational psychology, an assumption eagerly received and employed by educators concerned with both curriculum construction and methods of teaching since it seemed to insure for education advantages similar to those being derived at the time from the employment of scientific management in business and industry.

The crucial factors in learning thus became for a period what Thorndike termed S→R bonds; that is, original and innate tendencies within the individual to respond favorably to certain specific situations and to be indifferent or hostile to others. Out of these original *connections* between situations to which one is innately sensitive and the responses which one makes to the situations in a manner *native* to the individual, each person, it was believed, develops his personality and character. As Thorndike wrote in his *Educational Psychology:*

Any man possesses at the very start of his life that is, at the moment when the ovum and the spermatozoon which are to produce him have united—numerous well-defined tendencies to future behavior. Between the situations which he will meet and the responses he will make to them, pre-formed bonds exist. It is already determined by the constitution of these two germs, that under certain circumstances he will see and hear and feel and act in certain ways. His intellect and morals, as well as his bodily organs and movements, are in part the nature of the embryo in the first moment of its life. What a man is and does throughout life is a result of whatever constitution he has at the start and of all the forces that act upon it before and after birth.[12]

Observe the three components in each learning situation: the S, or situation to which one is natively disposed to respond; the R, or response, also, in its elements, of an inherited character; and the connection, or bond between the two, which also derives from inheritance. These S→R bonds vary in degrees of complexity and specificity of response, and in accordance with the degree of response they are termed reflexes, instincts, and capacities.

The reader will observe a similarity between Thorndike and Herbart in that for both the education of the young consists in control and direction of a meticulous and detailed character. From this point of view the difference is one of vocabulary rather than of spirit. Thorndike, however, avoids the terminology of earlier psychologists. Mental states, impressions, ideas conceived of as something distinct from physical reactions are no longer mentioned. Attention centers rather upon response units, or S→R bonds, which may be viewed either as mental or physical or, perhaps, better as the two in one.

There is, however, one significant difference between the two. For Herbart, there are no inherited ideas. All derive from experience. For Thorndike, on the other hand, the manner in which one responds to the experiences of life finds its explanation, ultimately,

---

[12] Edward L. Thorndike, *Educational Psychology,* Briefer Course (New York: Teachers College, Columbia University, 1917), p. 2.

in his stock of inherited tendencies to respond to specific situations. These tendencies, Thorndike terms original satisfiers and annoyers. As he puts it, "The original basis of the wants which so truly do and should rule the world is the original satisfyingness of some states of affairs and annoyingness of others. Out of such original satisfiers and annoyers grow all desires and aversions; and in such are found the first guides of learning." [13]

Thorndike's Influence on Education

It was not long before Thorndike's influence in education rivaled that of G. Stanley Hall. Indeed, few men have succeeded in extending their influence more widely than did he. As with Hall, from Thorndike's classroom and laboratory, future teachers and supervisors and administrators and research workers went forth to translate his ideas into practice.

On the surface, at least, the S→R bond concept of learning simplifies the task of instruction. All learning, we are told, reduces itself to a matter of relating situation elements to response units already given. It follows that what one learns is less a novel experience than a matter of making explicit associations with which one is already endowed, of encouraging one group of associations and discouraging others. Two basic laws of learning thus emerge for parents and teachers to apply: the *Law of Exercise or Use* and the *Law of Effect*. That is, repetition tends to perpetuate and give prominence to an S→R bond; failure to exercise tends to push these connections into the background. Secondly, learning experiences which are accompanied by or followed by feelings of satisfaction tend to become confirmed, whereas the opposite is true of those not so favored.

From these two basic laws, Thorndike derived certain subsidiary laws of learning which he sought to validate in the laboratory.[14] An analysis of these laws and their application reveals that they are formulated from the standpoint of the observer, or the manipulator of learning situations, rather than from that of the learner.

---

[13] *Ibid.*, p. 50.

[14] The laws of Multiple Response, of Set or Attitude, of Partial Activity, of Analogy, and of Associative Shifting (*ibid.*, chaps. X, XI). For a detailed examination of these "laws," see V. T. Thayer, *The Passing of the Recitation* (Boston: D. C. Heath & Company, 1928), chap. VI.

Take, for example, the manner in which a child is taught the meaning of the abstract idea of "fiveness." This consists first "in having the learner respond to the total situation containing the element in question with the attitude of piecemeal examination, and with attentiveness to one element after another." [15] By naming five boys, five girls, five pencils, etc., and having the learner respond in such a way as to favor "the partial and predominant activity of 'how-many-ness' as far as may be," it is thought that a bond is ultimately established between the element "fiveness" and the response to "fiveness" on the part of the learner. A second way in which a connection between the desired element in the situation and the response may be effected is by means of dissociation of varying concomitants. By associating a response of five to a variety of situations such as five pencils, five boys, five girls, etc., which differ in all respects except in the element five, this element of "fiveness" finally becomes distinctly associated with the response. Thirdly, "fiveness" may be learned by having a child respond to situations which "pair by pair, present the element in a certain context and present that same context with *the opposite of the element in question,* or with something at least very unlike the element in question." [16] Thus a child being taught to respond to one-fifth of a pie, a cake, or the like will have the bond between situation and response brought out and strengthened by contrasting five pies, five cakes, etc.

But, again, observe that nothing new has been learned! According to Thorndike the response of "fiveness" is in the nervous system as an inherited potential response, and the association of the correct response with the proper element in the situation needs only to be made explicit by exercise and effect. Unless the response were already there, the teacher's efforts would be futile.

Thorndike's psychology encouraged the use and development of intelligence tests with which to discover the native equipment of children and thus to determine in advance of their education the possibilities and the limits of this education. For a time, it looked as though these tests might be used in a manner fatalistic to the futures of many. There were, for example, school systems in which alert supervisors undertook to administer intelligence tests

---

[15] Thorndike, *op. cit.,* p. 159.
[16] *Ibid.,* p. 160.

to children in the primary grades with an eye to their assignment in groups graded according to "native intelligence," a procedure which it was hoped would render teaching more efficient. In the course of time, however, confidence in the tests as indicators of inherited as against acquired ability weakened somewhat, and they came to be used instead as instruments with which to gauge a child's present working capital, without dogmatic inference as to its original source.

The Curriculum Centers Upon the Acquisition of Specific Habits

Thorndike's psychology of learning came as manna from heaven to harassed superintendents and supervisors who, during the first quarter of the century, were unexpectedly confronted with the problems of mass education. Into their schools were flocking large numbers of young people of varied backgrounds, interests, and abilities. For these young people the times seemed to suggest an education in habits and skills relevant to a society in which neither they nor their parents were as yet adjusted. School systems were increasing in size more rapidly than adequately trained teachers could be found to man them. At the same time, business and industry were capturing the imagination of people with manifestations of efficiency that seemed to follow from the applications of scientific management to the details of the manufacture and distribution of goods, results which clearly followed from the detailed analysis of processes and the applications of a psychology of habit formation to the acquisition of skills and techniques. Why not apply these same methods, it was asked, to the task of education, thus simplifying the work of both teacher and taught? The steps required for so doing were relatively simple. Identify the relevant facts and skills children need to acquire, together with the abilities requisite for their acquisition, provide teachers with suggestions for inculcating these facts and skills, test from time to time the effectiveness with which both teacher and children have followed the plans thus formulated. Do this faithfully and an effective education will be assured.

This new emphasis in the selection and organization of subject matter received support in 1918 from the Report of the National

Commission on the Reorganization of Secondary Education. This commission stated the functions of the secondary school in the form of life objectives. Its preliminary statement read as follows: "In order to determine the main objectives that should guide education in a democracy, it is necessary to analyze the activities of the individual. Normally he is a member of a family, of a vocational group, and of various civic groups, and by virtue of these relationships he is called upon to engage in activities that enrich family life, to render important vocational services to his fellows, and to promote the general welfare." [17]

There followed a more detailed breakdown of these three areas and a formulation of the fundamental principles which should guide educators in the reorganization of subjects and of curricula. These "cardinal principles" were health, command of fundamental processes, worthy home membership, vocation, citizenship, worthy use of leisure, and ethical character.

Curriculum Construction Becomes "Scientific"

With the areas of education thus defined, research workers, wedded to a psychology of adjustment, began the task of organizing subjects of study in terms of "scientifically determined specific objectives."

The methods resorted to in order to realize this "simple" program were not impressive when viewed from the perspective of today. The professed aim was to be "scientific," precise, and definite. But what does scientific mean when it is a matter of determining the important facts and principles within a given field for a child to master, as well as the appropriate habits and skills for him to acquire? The methods of business and industry were, of course, to serve as a model. For example, job analysis was the method followed in business and adopted with evidences of success in vocational education. It seemed natural, therefore, to apply the techniques of job analysis and activity analysis to other aspects of education as well.

There is one significant difference, however, between vocational education and general education. In the former, the specifics of the job were known. In the latter, the components of the job as well as its purposes had to be defined, unless tradition were to be

---

[17] Bureau of Education, Bulletin, 1918, no. 35.

followed. What, for example, were the habits and skills most appropriate for attainment in first-year English? Or the most relevant processes to teach in arithmetic? Or the most significant facts and principles in a course in science or the social studies?

Search for an answer to questions of this character led to some interesting solutions. One method followed was to cull from contemporary magazines and newspapers references to the subject being organized, such as history or general science, in order to determine from frequency of mention the relative importance of facts pupils were to digest. Another was to question members of a faculty, or a parent body, regarding the abilities or traits of character which adults deemed it most important for a child to acquire. In one instance, the appropriate materials for a course in physics were validated by asking parents of children what applications of the principles of physics they had made in their daily lives. Whatever the method, the general tendency was to emphasize subject matter which pertained to adult life rather than to child life or adolescence and to accept the existing state of adult culture as the criterion for determining what adults of tomorrow should know.

Nor were the applications of education as adjustment in any way confined to trade and vocational school, on the one hand, or to the curriculum of elementary and secondary schools, on the other. Just as early in the century it was assumed that large numbers of pupils who were then pouring into the secondary school would conclude their education upon graduation from the junior high school, so in the 1920's and the 1930's, the junior college developed as a terminal institution designed to serve that mass of students which was now engulfing the senior high school and beginning to encroach upon the lower levels of college and professional school.

To meet these new demands upon education, terminal courses were devised for the junior college much as they had originated earlier for the junior high school. These courses operated in large measure on the assumption that the vocational preparation afforded should be of a specific character, leading to the acquisition of specific skills and operations.

In support of this assumption were several trends in industry, business, and the professions to which educators called attention. One was a trend toward the upgrading of certain types of work in such a way that entrance to occupations which once called for little if any preliminary training now required considerable preparation. Thus a contractor frequently evolved into an engineer or a domestic servant into a trained nurse. Secondly, many professions were being subdivided into parts, each part requiring a period of intensive preparation, and, thereafter, tending to exist in its own right. Dentistry, for example, had come to include not only the profession of the dentist, but that of the orthodontist, the research dentist, the dental nurse, the dental hygienist, the dental mechanic. Thirdly, there was evidence to indicate that individuals moved from one occupational level to another with less frequency than formerly. A dental mechanic, for example, might improve his status as a dental mechanic in salary and position, but he tended to remain a mechanic and not to become a dentist.[18]

A similar point of view influenced the organization of courses in general education in the first two years of college and the lower division of universities. An example of the general education course is the survey course which evolved out of the laudable desire to give unity and consistency to the student's education by means of an overview of representative fields of knowledge or an equally complete introduction to the facts and principles and activities within a functional area of living. Probably the most ambitious effort along this line was that of Colgate University, where students in the freshman year were required to devote two-thirds of their time to five survey courses: a survey of the physical sciences, the biological sciences, the social sciences, the fine arts, and philosophy and religion. It was the ambition of Colgate, in this way, to enable the student at the beginning of his college education to survey "the whole domain of human knowledge."[19] Although other institutions were less ambitious in their hopes for the accomplishments of a student in one year, the plan of enabling students by means of survey courses to "master the leading ideas, and significant facts in the principal fields of knowledge" was widely adopted.

Still other institutions adopted the method of introducing students to "functional areas of living." Stephens College, a girls'

[18] Robert J. Leonard, "Professional Education in Junior Colleges," *Teachers College Record*, May, 1925, p. 729.
[19] See statement of President Cutten in the *Thirty-first Yearbook*, National Society for the Study of Education, part II, pp. 46–47.

college in Missouri, attracted wide attention to its curriculum which was organized on this plan. Under the direction of W. W. Chaters, surveys were made of the activities in which women engage and the problems and needs they encounter in the course of their lives. These were classified under seven different categories of activities and problems, following which courses were devised with an eye to enabling the students to acquire the facts and principles and skills essential for effective functioning as women.

Observe that the assumptions underlying these approaches to the organization of the curriculum were similar to those followed in the applications of job analysis to vocational education. In each instance, the student was viewed as primarily a recipient of ideas, skills, and habits defined for him. To insure their acquisition, the educator leaned heavily upon behavioristic psychology and the statistical and scientific tools which its devotees had developed for identifying and selecting from the activities of men those items which, when viewed objectively and quantitatively, seemed of most importance.

It was not long before the limitations in these methods of determining what knowledge is of most worth became evident. Nevertheless, the determination to apply scientific method to the organization of the curriculum had the advantage of bringing to the forefront of educational discussion a search for the criteria that should operate in defining the task of the school. Up to this time, the question had not been faced squarely. Writers of textbooks tended to reflect the interests of advanced students in the field rather than the growing needs of young people. Although the areas defined by the Cardinal Principles of Secondary Education were vague and even subject to abuse, they represented an attempt to define the task of education in a manner relevant to the needs of both the student and his society. The result was that the curriculum of both elementary and secondary schools, and, eventually, that of the college, became for educators a central problem of study and experimentation.[20]

---

[20] See, for example, the *Twenty-sixth Yearbook*, National Society for the Study of Education, Parts I, II. Also Harold Alberty, *Reorganizing the High School Curriculum* (New York: The Macmillan Co., 1947), Chaps. IV–VII.

Teaching Methods Take Character from Scientific Management

The psychology of adjustment and attempts to introduce the spirit and methods of scientific management into the school not only led to new methods of curriculum organization but they revolutionized teaching procedures and classroom methods as well.

Both Pestalozzi and Herbart, as we have seen, did much to professionalize the task of the teacher. Their efforts, however, centered pretty much upon the acts of the instructor. The Herbartian steps, in particular, were detailed descriptions of what the teacher should do in promoting learning on the assumption, to be sure, that this was in harmony with the laws of learning. Under the S → R bond, or stimulus-response concept of learning, attention centered more specifically upon a meticulous direction of the activities of the child.

One of the first attempts in this direction was the supervised study movement. This resulted from both psychological and sociological considerations. On the psychological side attention was directed toward the acquisition of study habits in contrast with exclusive emphasis upon the recitation.

On the sociological side, educators had become impressed by the large number of pupils who lacked facilities for study at home. Investigations of home conditions seemed to establish a one-to-one relation between home conditions for study and quality of schoolwork. These facts, together with accumulated evidence that home assignments were often poorly given and inadequately understood by children, gave support to the suggestion that schools should develop methods of instruction which would bring the entire learning activity of the student under the direction and control of the teacher.

Nor were these arguments restricted to school people. Among laymen also the suspicion grew that reciting a lesson is the least important aspect of schooling.

Supervised study, or the "directed period," as it was sometimes called, involved three steps: review, study, recite. Not infrequently, the conscientious administrative officer insisted upon specific time limits for each phase!

One advantage in supervised study quickly became evident. By transforming the classroom into a place for supervised study as well as for reciting, attention began to center upon difficulties which students encounter in learning and the work habits appropriate to each field of study. Studying, in other words, became professionalized, and manuals and texts, as well as directions for study within the conventional textbook, began to make their appearance.

Supervised study soon drew attention to the need for lengthening the conventional class period, and, somewhat later, instruction was organized in terms of units of work, and the daily recitation period was abolished altogether. Thus the time consumed in completing each phase of a unit was variable, depending upon the nature of the unit or topic under study. In these cases, as in the Morrison Plan and in what became widely known as the "contract plan," emphasis still centered upon what William Heard Kilpatrick has called "pre-digested subject matter" (information, ideas, principles, habits and skills, all carefully planned in advance) but there was, nevertheless, more generous provision for individual differences in rate of learning and even for differences in interests and abilities than existed under the traditional system of recitation.

Investigations of the results of supervised study, in contrast with the conventional recitation, clearly established its value, but they also indicated that further improvements in method were still needed, for, although the poor student obviously did better, good students either did no better or actually did worse! Analysis of these unexpected results led to the conclusion that methods of work differ from one individual to another and that what is best for one is not of necessity best for another. These conclusions led to a second development in methods of teaching—individual instruction.

Experiments with individual instruction took on different forms but two types, in particular, received wide attention, not only in this country but abroad. These two were known as the Dalton and the Winnetka plans. They are representative of the period in their efforts to model instruction on characteristics of business life and a psychology of adjustment.

Common to both plans was provision for each pupil to progress at his own rate. For certain purposes, primarily social education, the class group in each instance retained its organization. In the Dalton Plan, as conducted by its originator, Helen Parkhurst, administrative provision was made for group conferences once a week. In other schools adopting the plan, more numerous conferences were held. On occasion, in Miss Parkhurst's school, certain assignments in certain subjects were deliberately planned so that pupils might work together, as in conducting experiments in science, or the writing and production of a play in which teachers and pupils in English, history, and the arts might cooperate. Since, however, the original purpose of the Dalton Plan was to provide for individual progress, these cooperative and group ventures were not easily devised. In the Winnetka Plan, pupils were both expected and encouraged to go it alone. Assignments were completely individualized. Subjects were organized in the form of tasks, or "goals," in such a way that pupils, by following directions, might proceed alone. When a goal, or a logical portion of a goal, was completed, the pupil took a self-administered test in order to determine whether or not he was ready to submit to the teacher's examination, which was the final criterion for determining his mastery of one step and his fitness to advance to the next.

In the Winnetka Plan there was no effort to relate the achievements of a pupil in one subject, such as arithmetic, to his achievements in another, such as history or geography. Thus it frequently happened that a child might be working on fourth-grade arithmetic at the same time that he had advanced to the fifth or sixth grade in another subject.[21] Under the Dalton Plan, the conventional time schedule of subjects was also abolished, thus giving a pupil the opportunity to work on a subject in which he might be less able or slower for a longer period of time than would be necessary for a subject which he could master more easily or quickly. For example, he might report to the science laboratory on a given morning and work there continuously for the entire day, thus completing a number of "contracts" in advance and saving time for subjects upon which he might work more slowly.

---

[21] In describing the Winnetka Plan in the *Twenty-third Yearbook* of the National Society for the Study of Education, part II, p. 257, Superintendent Washburne cited one case of a gifted boy who was one year and six months ahead of his grade in arithmetic and two years and two months ahead in language.

However, he was not permitted to undertake a second month's contract in any one subject until the month's contracts for all subjects were completed.

Characteristic of both the Dalton and the Winnetka plans was the careful preparation of assignments, directions for individual progress, self-testing devices, and the final tests administered by the teacher to determine a pupil's competence to move from one "goal" or "contract" to another. In short, as their advocates envisaged their plans, partial learning and the conventional marking systems, which sanctioned partial learning, were replaced by an emphasis upon mastery. What was required in the way of assimilative material might vary among individuals. But no one was presumed to advance from one task to another until he had assured himself and his instructor that he was ready to do so.

Both plans, as we have said, drew their inspiration from the business world. The Dalton Plan emphasized the importance of budgeting time and entering into a "contract" to perform an agreed upon task. The Winnetka Plan divided the day into two parts, a period of hard work in which the child, like his father, worked individually at a job and a period of recreation and group activities in which he functioned as a social being. Under both plans, group and social activities, as well as art, music, and leisure-time activities, were assigned primarily to the afternoon portion of the day. However, the Dalton Plan was somewhat more flexible, or, shall we say, less consistent, than the Winnetka Plan in that work in the "common essentials" was frequently motivated by having pupils engage in group projects.

Schools adopting either of these plans found it necessary to abolish the conventional time schedule for recitations and to abandon the assumption that all pupils should begin and end a semester's assignment in a subject at one and the same time. Not all schools considered it wise to carry the plan of individual instruction to such an extreme. Accordingly, we find a number adopting the concept of mastery and individual progress while retaining the conventional class organization. The "unit method" of instruction followed at the University of Chicago Laboratory School, under the direction of H. C. Morrison, represents one such attempt.[22] Morrison's influence, as that of Carleton Wash-

---

[22] The Morrison Plan was described in H. C. Morrison, *The Practice of Teaching in the Secondary School* (Chicago: The University of Chicago Press, 1926).

burne and Helen Parkhurst, was far-reaching. His was essentially the Herbartian psychology and method applied to instruction on the secondary level. Although he developed different techniques for the teaching of understandings than for appreciations and skills, his influence was probably greatest in the teaching of what he called the science technique (the teaching of "understandings" in science, history, mathematics, etc.). This consisted of five steps, or stages: exploration, presentation, assimilation, organization, and recitation.[23] It was in the assimilative period that provision was made for individual rates of learning as well as for individual interests and abilities.

Still another plan was that of H. L. Miller, at one time Principal of the University High School in Madison, Wisconsin. Miller's plan, like Morrison's, combined individual and group instruction but was outwardly more conventional in that it did no violence to time schedules and systems of grading.[24] Once the teacher had introduced a class to a fundamental principle in mathematics, a basic understanding in science, a period in history, or a book such as *Ivanhoe*, a series of "contracts" would be laid before the pupils. All pupils who satisfied the requirements of the course would have to master the first contract. The remaining contracts were organized in an ascending series, each with a corresponding grade. Completion of the first contract was necessary for the grade of F(air), the second for a G(ood), and the last for an E(xcellent). Following the assignment was the working period, or a period of "directed study." In this period, which might consume some days or weeks, each student proceeded at his own rate and in accordance with his ability. It was a period also in which the teacher might give special attention to individual differences in abilities and interests.

Following the working period under both the Miller and the Morrison plans, the class would be brought together for group purposes: discussion, individual reports, group recitation, and the like, as the subject and the unit might require or suggest.

We thus see that both the psychology of learning and conditions within American society during the first third of the cen-

---

[23] For an excellent presentation of Morrison's Plan in short compass together with a critical examination of the plan, see Alberty, *op. cit.*, pp. 233–239.

[24] See H. L. Miller and R. T. Hargreaves, *The Self-Directed School* (New York: Charles Scribner's Sons, 1925), Chap. II. Also the *Twenty-fourth Yearbook*, National Society for the Study of Education, pp. 52–57.

tury, speaking broadly, cooperated in developing types of curriculum organization and methods of teaching which emphasized education for adjustment; the acquisition of information; habits, skills, and techniques; and even those dispositions and attitudes which scientific investigations of society seemed to validate.

Administrative Reform Reflects Corporate Organization

These were developments within subject matter and method. The spirit of science and business efficiency were equally potent in bringing about administrative reforms. Originally, the people in public assembly administered their schools as they conducted other affairs of the community. Here they voted to establish a school, to employ a teacher, and to provide the essentials of maintenance. In time, it seemed advisable to delegate the details of administration to a committee or to an individual. Before long, however, this method, too, proved inadequate for the proper conduct of the school, and a specially designated officer came into being charged with the responsibilities of an executive secretary or school superintendent. In Connecticut, for example, "school visitors" or a "school committee" undertook the task of preparing courses of study, supervising methods of instruction, and enforcing discipline, but eventually these functions were delegated to one individual. However, the inferior service rendered by laymen resulted, in time, in the selection of a trained educator with the title of superintendent.[25]

Other states followed much the same general pattern. Thus in the South, today, where the county form of government obtains, it is still common for the county board to select a school committee, or school board, together with a trained educator (sometimes selected by the school board and in some instances by the county board) who serves as the executive secretary of the board or as superintendent of schools.

The school committee has also set the pattern for the administration of city school systems. Since our cities have commonly enlarged through the absorption of communities that were once

[25] Frank P. Graves, *The Administration of American Education* (New York: The Macmillan Co., 1932), pp. 407–408.

independent, school systems have grown by a similar process. Often these new additions insisted upon maintaining a direct interest in their schools, with the result that the central board of education became an aggregate of semi-independent committees, each tending to put the interests of its own district first. In other instances, a central board was established with control over the schools as a whole. In either case, it was the general practice to perpetuate district or ward representation, with the result that city boards of education increased in size with the growth of the city. As late as 1902, for example, the Philadelphia board of education was composed of some five hundred members.

It soon became obvious that large boards with parochial representation and the inevitable log-rolling methods of arriving at decisions on critical matters could result only in the demoralization of the schools. Committee administration of matters such as the purchase of school supplies, employment of teachers, selection of textbooks, etc., not only fostered inefficiency but encouraged graft and favoritism.[26] Maladministration of public education became one aspect of what Lincoln Steffens, writing early in the century, characterized as the "shame of the cities," and the rescue of the schools from the clutches of special interests was one of the leading objectives of all who labored for reform.

In their search for ways and means of bettering school administration, reformers turned to business organization as a model. Nor is it strange that they did so. Both the conduct of large business corporations and their structure seemed at the time to possess those characteristics in which the schools were sadly lacking, and as a result of these lacks school systems declined to their low estate. In contrast with the large board of education, whose operations involved waste of time, log-rolling, and, all too often, the subordination of the public interest to special interests, the governing boards of corporations were small in size, evidenced a singleness of purpose, and concerned themselves with the formulations of policy as distinct from the details of adminis-

---

[26] Samuel T. Dutton and David Snedden point out that in the city of Rochester, New York, lay members of the board of education once served on the following committees: finance, qualification and employment of teachers, organization of schools and grievances, textbooks, library and apparatus, repairs, buildings, supplies, fuel and fire fixtures, printing, free academy salaries, janitors and law apportionment. [*Administration of Public Education in the United States* (New York: The Macmillan Co., 1915), p. 141.]

tration. Superintendents of schools, as the executive officers of boards of education, were commonly checked in their administration of details by the self-seeking and petty interference of laymen. Boards of directors of corporations defined general policies, assigned the task of their execution to a manager, and encouraged him from that point on to exercise initiative and independence.

A similar comparison can be made of the internal structure of the business corporation. The general manager appointed the heads of departments on the basis of merit, and department heads were held immediately responsible to the manager for results. In the discharge of their duties no considerations of politics or special favoritism stood in the way. Centralized responsibility and control, clearly defined functions, and single-hearted concentration of each functionary upon his own sphere of duties seemed an ideal and a method worthy of incorporation in the conduct of public affairs.

Out of these contrasts came pretty much the general pattern of school organization and administration as we have it today in the United States. The large board has been replaced by the small board, which, in ideal at least, concerns itself with the formulation of policy rather than the details of administration. Ward or district representation has given way largely to city-wide or non-geographical representation, either by appointment or election. Within the school system, there are clear-cut divisions of labor and authority which run from the board of education to the superintendent and from him to associate or assistant superintendents, to principals, to heads of departments, to teachers. There are some variations, to be sure, in the internal structure of administration and supervision. For example, in one city or county, assistants to the superintendent, as supervisors, may be assigned responsibilities on a geographical basis, and in another, assignments may be along functional lines, as, for example, elementary schools, junior high schools, senior high schools, etc., or some division of the curriculum such as elementary education, home economics, physical education, and the like.

These changes unquestionably resulted in more efficient administration. Supplemented and assisted by legislation designed to protect the schools from interference, either from members of the board when acting as individuals or from outside pressure groups, school systems and school officials are today relatively free to concentrate upon their educational functions in a manner often denied them in the past. Not until approximately the second quarter of the century did the question of the appropriateness of an organization of education in harmony with the structure and purposes of business disturb educators or the general public. With the advent of totalitarianism abroad, however, especially the rise of Mussolini in Italy and Hitler in Germany, and the challenge these dictators hurled at the "effete" democracies of the West, evidences of misgivings developed. Educators, like others, began to question themselves seriously as to the meaning of democracy and democratic education. From this it was but a step to inquire: How relevant is the administrative organization of the school to the purposes of a democratic education? Is the organization of an education on an essentially authoritarian and autocratic pattern best designed to prepare young people for responsible participation in democratic life? What changes would follow in the administration of the school as well as the conduct of the classroom if public schools undertook literally to raise young people for responsible participation in a government of the people, by the people, and for the people?

To many, the answer to this question involved the application of a psychology of learning and a response to factors in American life different from education for adjustment.

Suggested Reading

Alberty, Harold, *Reorganizing the High School Curriculum,* rev. ed. (New York: The Macmillan Co., 1953), chap. IX.

Butts, R. Freeman, and Lawrence A. Cremin, *A History of Education in American Culture* (New York: Henry Holt & Co., Inc., 1953), chap. 6.

Drake, William E. *The American School in Transition* (Englewood Cliffs, N.J.: Prentice-Hall, Inc., 1955), chap. XII.

Kolesnik, Walter B., *Mental Discipline in Modern Education* (Madison, Wisconsin: University of Wisconsin Press, 1958).

Thorndike, Edward L., *Educational Psychology,* Briefer Course (New York: Teachers College, Columbia University, 1917), chaps. I, X.

Watson, John, *The Ways of Behaviorism* (New York: Harper & Brothers, 1928), chaps. II, V.

/\\/\\/\\/\\
.•.•.•.•.

14

Education in an Interdependent
World: Theories of Learning

Theories of Learning As Expressions of the Culture

Thus far we have considered four psychologies of learning in their American setting, together with their influence upon classroom and school. The first was called the *mind-substance* theory, since it conceived of the mind as an all-embracing substance, analogous in one of its aspects to a container or a receptor of experience and in another aspect to an active agent endowed with faculties or powers which work over original impressions, giving order and character to them. In each instance man is viewed as dual in nature, consisting of body and soul. Body is a physical substance and operates in accordance with the laws of the material world; the mind, or the soul, in contrast, is an immaterial substance (defined in terms precisely the opposite of material substance) which, by virtue of its power to receive and organize sensations and ideas, can mirror and even anticipate objects and events in the external world. It thus serves as the directive agent in the partnership.

A second theory emphasizes the importance of *inborn tendencies,* instinctive ways of thinking, feeling, and acting which make their appearance at well-defined stages of development in the life of the individual as he progresses from infancy to adulthood. We characterize adherents of this conception of learning as the *follow-nature* group, since the nature and the sequence of instinctive expressions dictate what is appropriate in the way of learning experiences and the methods of instruction employed by those responsible for dealing with the young.

A third conception of learning, the theory of *mental states* (clearly represented by the Herbartians), rejects the concept of the mind as an entity separate and distinct from its content. Rather does it consider this relationship as similar to that of a woods to its trees. That is to say, the mind lacks objective reality. It is nothing more or less than a collective noun. On this view, the operations of the mental life are explained entirely by means of the laws of association. Mental states (sensations, perceptions, images, ideas, etc.) are, however, intimately associated with the nervous system, so intimately, indeed, that psychologists soon observed that no psychic state can make its appearance without neural activity, although physical processes obviously can perform their functions with or without consciousness. This observation shortly led many to pose the question: "Is consciousness anything other than a spectator of events, an epi-phenomenon, and thus an impotent by-product of physical activity?"

Finally, in *behaviorism,* or what we have termed education for adjustment, we have a psychology which endeavors to explain all learning in terms of the acquisition of habits. In Thorndike (whose views serve more as a transition from a psychology of mental states to behaviorism than as an outright expression of the latter) there is no open disavowal of dualism or of mental states, although the new units of learning ($S \rightarrow R$ bonds) are clearly designed to avoid the issue of mental versus physical and to center attention in learning solely upon the conditioning of the nervous system. There is, however, one significant difference between Thorndike and behaviorists such as John Watson with respect to the originals of learning. According to Thorndike, these are inherited. Consequently, it is to heredity that we must look to determine the limits and the possibilities of education in the individual; whereas Watson stresses the influence of environmental factors. For both, however, all learning is habit formation; all learning, from the simplest physical act to the most original and seemingly creative intellectual activity. Education, accordingly, is conceived of as an operation in which one generation gives character to its successor through carefully controlled and directed exercises. To improve himself, man must learn to lift himself by his own bootstraps!

Each of these theories of learning has influenced American education at one time or another, depending upon cultural factors that are at one time dominant and at another time recessive, and each is represented in the educational forum of today. For example, John Locke's individualism seemed admirably adapted to frontier conditions and a period when nature was lavish with its resources. Similarly, a psychology of inner development flourished during a period when cultural factors seemed to confirm man's confidence in the innate goodness of original nature in contrast with the corrupting influences of society. Finally, with the rapid transition of a rural and agricultural economy into one urban and industrial, learning became identified with "conditioning," which is essentially a one-way process. Having before him direct evidence of his ability to change his society fundamentally by means of the machines of his own invention, man studies himself and concludes, "Lo! I, too, am a machine!"

We come now to still another concept of learning, one that has profoundly influenced methods of teaching, the selection and organization of learning experiences, and the administrative and supervisory practices of the schools in the past half-century. No one term is used consistently to identify it, because its assumptions are drawn as much from philosophy as from psychology. Although many individuals less well known than Charles Pierce, William James, John Dewey, and William Heard Kilpatrick are entitled to credit for its formulation and its applications, these four, within the disciplines of logic, philosophy, psychology, and education, are most conspicuously associated with it under various designations such as, "pragmatism," "instrumentalism," "functionalism," "experimentalism." Kilpatrick frequently employed the term "organismic learning." Within the field of education, the term progressive education was used for many years to identify methods and procedures which looked to "organismic learning" for their justification, although the term "progressive" has also been used to describe practices which can be justified only by distorted interpretations of this theory of learning. To avoid confusion we shall employ the terms "organic learning" and "experimentalism." [1]

In line with our previous procedure, let us glance briefly at factors in American society which seem relevant to a psychology of learning which emphasizes interrelationships and interdependence.

Economic Developments Undermine Rugged Individualism

First were the obvious changes of an economic and political character which, since the turn of the century, have undermined policies of isolation of the United States in relations with other nations and concepts of laissez faire and rugged individualism in economic and political relationships at home. World War I probably marked the first general realization on the part of the American people that the modern world no longer permits either nations or individuals to live unto themselves alone. Despite the disillusionment and temporary reversion to isolationism which followed upon a war none too successful in its attempt to make "the world safe for democracy," the rise of Hitler and Mussolini soon brought people consciously once again into the mainstream of world events. Few question today that we live in what Wendell Willkie termed One World, even though this world be as a house divided against itself. World War II and international events since have taught young people in the most remote backwoods settlements that a decision of a foreign office in some small nation, the name of which they do not know, or the manner in which a colonial power deals with its subject people may decide whether they are to lay down their lives that others may live.

Nor are international issues related solely to those of war. What was known early in the century as "dollar diplomacy" has evolved

---

[1] A somewhat parallel development to that described here was the theory of Gestalt psychology developed by two German animal psychologists, Wolfgang Kohler and Kurt Koffka, based upon a theory of learning first announced by Max Wertheimer in 1912. This conception of learning, called organismic psychology by Wheeler, like the philosophical reasoning of Dewey, challenged Thorndike's views and had an important influence upon the formulation of what we are characterizing broadly as "organic learning." For an account of these developments, see Ernest R. Hilgard, *Theories of Learning* (New York: Appleton-Century-Crofts, Inc., 1956), chap. 7.

into relationships among people of a thousand and one varieties. Since the creation of the United Nations with its Economic and Social Council (to mention but one of the organs of the United Nations), all manner of previously existing international agencies concerned with the economic and social welfare of peoples have come into one organization, an agency which knows no rigid national boundaries. A plague in India, for example, quickly brings relief in the form of vaccine gathered from all parts of the world through the instrumentality of the World Health Organization. Similarly, through the efforts of other organizations of international membership (such as UNESCO in education) individuals and associations of individuals from all parts of the globe are learning to merge their interests and to work together in the realization of common purposes. Thus are men in the process of laying the foundations of an international morality through the welding of interests which bind the people of one nation to the people of another as with Lilliputian threads.

In 1893, in an epoch-making article, "The Significance of the Frontier in American History," [2] Frederick J. Turner drew attention to the official closing of the American frontier. Americans, he pointed out, now faced a future in which free lands and easy access to seemingly inexhaustible natural resources would no longer play the role they had played so significantly in the past. One consequence of this fact has been a closing of the familiar avenues of retreat for the nonconformist, the radical, and the dissenter, when community patience has reached the breaking point.

Within two or three decades of Turner's article, the consequences of uncontrolled exploitation of the nation's natural resources gave rise to the conservation movement on both state and national levels. Rugged individualism and laissez faire in other areas was also on trial. The evils of unrestricted conditions of employment for women and children particularly, but of men as well (freedom of contract!), suggested to liberals, who had hitherto objected to governmental interference in matters economic, the necessity of legislation designed to control conditions of work and, in the case of children, to raise the age at which they might

---

[2] First published in the *Report of the American Historical Association for 1893*.

be employed and to compel attendance at school prior to this point.

Similarly restrictions were placed upon the relationships between the large and the small businessman. Large-scale operations with their requirements of large capital were rapidly changing the status of the "independent producer" and the small businessman. By 1937, corporate activity had reached the point where it controlled 96 per cent of mining, 92 per cent of manufacturing, 89 per cent of transportation, 84 per cent of finance, and 100 per cent of communication.[3]

Within the field of corporate organization, moreover, the trend toward the separation of management from ownership was creating a novel situation in American business and industry. For example, in its study of *The Distribution of Ownership in the 200 Largest Non-Financial Corporations,* the Temporary National Economic Committee discovered that ownership in American corporations was widely diffused but control narrowly limited, with the result that the individual shareholder, or owner, had very little to say, if anything, with respect to the management and direction of the corporation in which his funds were invested.[4]

It would seem that the individual operator of a business or a factory in the "free enterprise system" had lost his status as a self-determining individual. Rather did he find himself on the outer fringe of a rapidly revolving wheel over which he had little control. Nor are the rewards of industry (if we may change to the present tense) as directly traceable to individual responsibility and merit as was once the case. Success or failure of a product or an enterprise has become more and more dependent upon unforeseeable factors. Witness, for example, the distress of the producers of silk in Japan following the invention of rayon and nylon in the United States. Economic operations now go on in a

---

[3] Cited by the Temporary Economic Committee, *Economic Prologue, Investigations of Economic Power,* part II, p. 96. Hearings before the Temporary Economic Committee, Seventy-fifth Congress, Third Session (Washington, D.C.: Government Printing Office, 1940).

[4] *Investigations of Concentration of Economic Power,* Monograph 29, Seventy-sixth Congress, Third Session, Senate Committee Print (Washington, D.C.: Government Printing Office, 1940). See also Max Lerner, *America As a Civilization* (New York: Simon and Schuster, Inc., 1957), pp. 284–296, for a contemporary picture of corporate organization.

highly sensitive and delicately balanced economic society, with the result that a disturbance in one basic industry, or abnormal conditions in one section of the globe, bring maladjustment and distress in another. Rugged individualism and self-determination have given way before a closely interknit and interdependent economic society.

Large organizations of capital were followed by large organizations of labor and the emergence of a variety of organized interests, all of which recognized that the individual alone is relatively helpless, but, through association, his integrity might be insured and many of his interests and needs realized. Only through union and collective bargaining did it seem possible for the workingman to reap the advantages of "freedom of contract" and to insure for himself and his family the benefits of wages and conditions of work in harmony with the American ideal of a constantly rising standard of living.

These advantages and others have come with the growth of the union movement, but at the sacrifice of other values and of independence in other respects. Relations between employer and employee have been depersonalized, and, often, there is an absence of identification of the worker with his work. Compliance with agreements and regulations which have in mind the protection of the worker have frequently had the additional effect of undermining pride in craftsmanship and quality of performance.

The facts of interdependence have led liberals also to abandon the earlier notion that the best government is one that governs least and to substitute for it the ideal of government as a mutual insurance association, or an agency by means of which individuals may meet and serve needs through associated action which cannot be met and served when individuals operate on their own. Thus state legislatures and the national Congress have been prevailed upon to pass all manner of legislation (health laws, social security acts, provisions for unemployment insurance, laws defining standards for the manufacture and distribution of goods, minimum wage legislation, etc.) including measures which bring relief to business and industry in times of distress (such as the establishment of the reconstruction finance corporation, or an act authorizing the President to declare certain sections of the country as disaster areas in times of misfortune and to bring to them the assistance which only the resources of the national government can provide).

As we review these many developments, it seems that a realization of interdependence suggests a sense of futility and weakness on the part of the individual when he attempts to operate alone. Often he is as a grain of sand caught up in a complex air current and blown about hither and yon with little power of resistance. That is, the trend of events have deprived him of his one-time imperial status and assurance of social significance. No longer is he the architect of his own fortunes or the creator of his own universe. He is, as John Dewey once described him, the "lost individual." Often he is confused and bewildered by the complexities of events. The loyalties and the conditions which once gave him "support, direction and unity of outlook, have well-nigh disappeared." Even the captains of finance and industry are no longer captains of their own souls, since they, too, are involved in "impersonal and socially undirected economic forces." They may succeed in promoting corporate and collective results, and reap profits, but these rewards lack the satisfaction "which comes from a sense of social fulfillment." They, too, "are impelled hither and yon by forces beyond their control." Consequently, on all levels of society the "most marked trait of present life economically speaking is insecurity." [5]

A Social Concept of the Individual Emerges

On the other hand, there has developed a respect for the individual which is altogether different from that which characterized the era of rugged individualism. People are viewed as persons. In a manner unique to the present their differences are respected, even encouraged, as are the differences which mark one group off from another. Equality is no longer identified with sameness, but rather with an equal right for the expression of differences. Thus, in relations between personalities and groups new conceptions of what constitute "right relations" have come into being. The cultural background of an individual or a group becomes an important factor in the determination of "the right" or in the

---

[5] John Dewey, *Individualism Old and New* (New York: Milton, Balch and Company, 1930), chap. IV, on "The Lost Individual."

solution of a moral problem, even to the extent of modifying at times the definition of the abstract principle which once dictated its answer.

These changes have found expression in a conception of democracy that stresses essentially a distinctive type of relationship between individuals and groups in contrast with the earlier individualistic emphasis of democracy. The rise of modern democracy in Europe was associated with efforts (1) to free individuals from restraints by removing the shackles of absolute government and sometimes by escaping from government altogether, since this was associated with the imposition of the will of a monarch or a class foreign to the interests of the governed; (2) to gain freedom of operation in trade and commerce; and (3) to rise in the world without the limitations of class distinctions. In America, these characteristics of the democratic ideal were further encouraged by the isolation and loneliness of frontier existence and the remoteness of government and organized social institutions. Similarly, in our economic development conditions were for a long time favorable to the concepts of laissez faire, with the result that for a considerable period in our history all branches of government—legislative, executive, and judicial—cooperated in perpetuating the ideal of the individual as self-sustaining and self-sufficient and of society as little more than a collection of these individuals.

The Concept of Democracy Revised

In the period under review, this conception of the individual had begun to yield sour fruit, with the result that the meaning of democracy was brought under critical review. In both philosophy and psychology the social nature of growth and development began to receive attention hitherto denied to it, and the nature of society was redefined. In contrast to the concept of society as a mere collection of individuals or as an entity separate and apart from the individual, society was now conceived of, in one of its essential aspects, as habitual and confirmed ways in which people think, feel, and act in association. Just as the concept of democratic government was redefined, so, also, the concept of government in general, underwent redefinition. No longer was government envisaged as a necessary evil or an organization external to the interests of the individual, or merely as a referee between rival and competing interests. Rather was it recognized as analogous to a mutual insurance society or as an indispensable instrument for realizing interests and values and meeting needs through associated actions which individuals on their own resources alone could not realize.

Democracy was seen as placing emphasis on the recognition of the worth and integrity of the individual. This assumption continues as a be-all and an end-all; but the new definition is unique in its insistence that only through relationships, that is, through qualities of relationship between individuals and groups, can the democratic ideal be realized. Democracy is thus no longer a political or an economic ideal, merely; it has evolved into a social and a moral ideal, "signifying the possession and continued use of certain attitudes, forming personal character and determining desire and purpose in all the relationships of life." [6]

Science Emphasizes Interrelationships

Not only have changes in political, economic, and social relations given rise to a social conception of the individual, but science, too, has contributed toward this same end. In biology, for example, the concept of traits once basic to Thorndike's explanation of behavior in terms of S → R bonds is no longer viewed as analogous to the unit characters in the Mendelian theory. Traits are now believed to be the resultants of relationships between inner and outer factors, an interpretation which renders untenable the once rigid division between heredity and environment.

An early contributor to this change in the conception of the nature of heredity was Professor H. S. Jennings of Johns Hopkins University. In a little volume widely read and entitled *Prometheus, or Biology and the Advancement of Man*,[7] Jennings reviewed the results of research into the nature of heredity which seemed to refute the theory that the central factor is the presence in the germ plasm of "determiners" or the carriers of heredity carefully

---

[6] For this description of democracy as a moral ideal, see the address prepared for delivery by John Dewey at the celebration of his eightieth birthday and reprinted in Irwin Edman, *John Dewey, His Contributions to the American Tradition* (New York: The Bobbs-Merrill Company, Inc., 1955), chap. VIII.

[7] New York: E. P. Dutton & Co., Inc., 1925.

insulated from outer influence. As against this view, Jennings pointed out that the carriers of heredity are genes, or minute chemical packets within the germ cell. The chemical action of these genes, moreover, can be influenced by conditions outside as well as inside the germ cell.

Take, for example, the development of the frog. This begins as a single cell. Under normal conditions one-half of the germ cell develops into the right half of the body and the other half into the left half. It is possible, however, to induce other results. If the two halves are severed, each will develop into an entire animal. Moreover, at one stage in the development of the young salamander, it assumes the form of a sphere. Under normal conditions certain known cells in this sphere will produce the brain, others the eye, the skin, the spinal cord, etc. But whether or not these sections will actually do so depends not only upon materials within the cells but also upon conditions outside the cell and *relations among cells.* At a certain period in development there begins a "differentiating influence" which "creeps" from cell to cell and determines the nature of the chemical process which will occur within these cells. This differentiating influence is of such a character that it predisposes the structure of each cell to develop in harmony with or to conform to the structure of the cells differentiating prior to it. However, if prior to the operations of this influence, a disk of cells is cut off and turned either sidewise or completely around, the differentiating influence creeps in an opposite direction, with the result that cells which should have formed skin develop into spinal cord, and those that should have formed eyes grow into midbrain, or some other structure, as the case may be. Likewise, a small piece of prospective skin transplanted to the center of the eye-producing region will transform itself into an eye, or a prospective ear transplanted to another region will grow into skin or spinal cord, "as its place in the pattern requires."

To be sure, there comes a time in the process of growth when plasticity ends, when the fate of the cell may be said to have been determined. Nevertheless, Jennings concluded that what a given part of the germ plasm will produce is not determined solely by the genes, or chemical packets within the cell, but is rather the product of the reaction of the genes upon each other and the *surrounding medium.* In other words, characteristics or traits emerge from interrelationships. Growth is an affair of the medium as well as of the individual; and, as Jennings emphasized in concluding, our environment determines what in our heredity will function, and our heredity determines what we shall be sensitive to in our environment.

This conception of inheritance as an interrelationship, or as essentially a two-way process, contributed to the development of a psychology strikingly different from that which assumes that we come into the world endowed with a fixed number of inherited "connections" between "situations" in our environment and "response units" within our nervous system. It also suggested to educators a new approach to education if this education were to meet the needs of young people in a society characterized by change and interdependence.

A Psychology of Organic Behavior Competes with a Psychology of Adjustment

The psychology which emerged rejects the concept of a mind as analogous to a blank sheet of paper upon which experience writes, a container to be filled, or a substance endowed with faculties that grow and develop under the stimulus of external application. Insofar as the term *mind* serves a purpose, according to this view, it is best thought of as a verb rather than a noun. It is a name for a distinctive type of behavior, behavior of an *organic* character, which occurs when objects and events take on meaning and significance (implications for the future) which the individual thus anticipates and seeks to control or direct in ways friendly to ends and purposes envisaged. It is, in short, a process of minding.

Mind, for this school, moreover, is but one form of organic behavior, organic behavior conceived of otherwise than as adjustment or mere habit formation of a one-way type of reaction. It contrasts with behaviorism as implicit in Thorndike and explicit in Watson. The orginals of behavior, as we saw in Thorndike, are $S \rightarrow R$ bonds (observe the direction of the arrow!) or original and innate tendencies to respond in specific ways to stimuli of a specific character. In Watson, emphasis is placed upon the original plasticity of the organism, but plasticity in the sense of a readiness to take on form and character from external pressure and direction, more or less as putty responds to the pressure of the hand. The concept of an organism here presented, in contrast, emphasizes the two-way character of behavior. The baby, in responding to its parents, transforms them as well as itself! What distinguishes an organism is the fact that a unique type of interplay or transaction between itself and its surroundings is a condition and means of its survival and prospering, an interplay in which both undergo change.

This conception of an organism and of organic behavior flatly repudiates the analogy between a machine and an organism. A machine functions properly only so long as its parts remain unchanged. An organism, on the other hand, continues to function only by virtue of a continuous alteration and re-creation of its parts (organs, tissues, cells, fluids) in response to changes it is at the same time effecting in its surroundings.

John Dewey introduced the idea of interaction (or, as he later expressed it, *transaction* between inner and outer) with the publication in 1896 of a paper on the reflex-arc concept in psychology. In this paper he attempted to refute the conventional idea of stimulus-response as essentially a one-way process in which an external stimulus impinges upon a sense organ, passes through a central system, and emerges as a response, which, when repeated frequently, creates a channel, so to speak, in the nervous system of a reflex or habitual character. As against this conception, Dewey showed that activity (stimulus and response) constitutes a cycle (a "reflex current") in which the response may seek out or "constitute" the stimulus. That is, one gives character to the other.

In other words, it is the nature of organic behavior on all levels, from the reaction of the simplest organism to the human being involved in an act of original and creative thought, to engage in transactions with the environment, both tangible and intangible.

Take, for example, an act of perception in which an object is "recognized." This is more than the mere reception of impressions which mirror qualities "out there." It is similar rather to the interpretation of a puzzle picture, which presents itself at first as a meaningless arrangement of lines on a piece of paper but, in the course of study, gradually acquires form and shape and finally stands out clearly as a tree with a beautiful lady seated upon one of its branches! So the familiar objects of our environment gradually take on the characteristics by which they are known as a result of a give-and-take relationship between ourselves and them.

Thinking Conceived of As an Interrelationship

It is this fact of a mutually creative relationship between the individual and his environment that the earlier psychology of habit formation neglects. Take an act of reflective thought, for example. According to Thorndike and the behaviorist, an original and creative act is neither original nor creative in any genuine sense. Inspect it carefully, break it down into its constituent parts, and we find that it is composed of "preformed bonds." For Thorndike an act of thought is little different except in its complexity from reflex action. As Thorndike put it, "We trust to the laws of cerebral nature to present us spontaneously with the appropriate idea and also to prefer that idea to others." [8] Watson describes thinking as "talking to oneself"; that is, as a purely physiological process of an habitual character. To the experimentalist, these explanations are inadequate in that they attempt to explain a total process in terms of merely one of its aspects. One distinctive characteristic of thinking, for example, is the use of meanings. Items of present experience point to, imply, and suggest things not present. Let us suppose that I am driving along an unfamiliar highway and come to a fork in the road. Which route shall I take? To decide this question, I look for "signs," highway markings and others. I trace in imagination, with what data I can muster, the consequences of one choice or the other, and, finally, test in action the decision arrived at. In other instances, the past may function in such a way as to give certain characteristics to present data (such as an established principle or a cherished ideal or a precept which has often demonstrated its applicability to similar situations) and to charge these data with future implications.

For the experimentalist, then, thinking is a unique type of

---

[8] Edward L. Thorndike, *Educational Psychology*, Briefer Course (New York: Teachers College, Columbia University, 1917), p. 172.

interrelationship, roughly analogous to other forms of give-and-take behavior between an organism and its environment. It is a relationship, however, on a much higher level than one of physical contact. In thinking and the higher forms of learning, the environment includes things absent as well as things present, the remote as well as the immediate. Thinking originates in a disturbed situation. The customary flow of events is halted. In a complete act of thought, there follows an attempt to locate the difficulty, to define the problem. Then follows a process not unlike trial-and-error behavior. Suggested ways of resolving the difficulty present themselves and are examined in terms of what they promise. Those which seem to meet the conditions of the problem, that is, pass this inspection, are tried out and tested. If inadequate, they are rejected, and new candidates in the form of inferences and hypotheses are examined. This procedure continues until a final solution is found.

According to the experimentalist, thinking, as we have described it, "is the method of an educative experience," [9] and, conversely, the most effective methods of learning are identical with the method of reflective thinking. Consequently, he would have the subject matter of instruction planned with this in mind.

The scientist goes farther. He believes that when learning follows the method of reflective thinking, which is also the method employed in science, it not only develops an intellectual discipline most relevant to the nature of modern life, but it lends itself as well to the development of democratic values. And, to achieve this result, he insists, is a primary responsibility of the school. John L. Childs writes:

In their attempt to care for democratic values, in the sphere of education . . . the experimentalists hold that children should be accepted as persons and treated accordingly. They affirm that to treat an immature human being as a moral end requires that he be educated in such a way that he will progressively develop into a self-directing person, equipped to make an intelligent manifestation of preference, and qualified to share in the determination of the social arrangements under which he lives, including the ends for which he spends his

[9] John Dewey, *Democracy and Education* (New York: The Macmillan Co., 1916), p. 192.

energies. In the development of democratic attitudes and skills, as in the development of scientific attitudes and skills, the experimentalist holds that it is essential for the young to practice that which we would have them learn and become. It is at this point in education that the scientific and democratic procedures meet as one, for both call for a person who can think, who has respect for evidence and consequences, and who is willing to bring his ideas of truth and value to the test of group examination, criticism, and validation. In fact, the self-correcting procedures of scientific inquiry and the self-governing procedures of democratic living, both internalize authority within the shared experiences of ordinary men and women, and they call for the nature of the young in that pattern of morality and character which is the correlative of these co-operative human procedures.[10]

The experimentalist's concept of learning, as we have seen, rejects a dualism in which a mind as an immaterial substance receives impressions in some mysterious way from the sense organs and then proceeds to give form and character to them. It also rejects the concept of mental states together with its description of learning as no more than an association of ideas. This, it holds, differs from the psychology of behaviorism only superficially. Change the vocabulary by substituting "the laws of cerebral nature" for the "laws of association" and the difference between the two fades away.

A New Theory of Instincts

On the other hand, the experimentalist likewise refuses to accept the concept of instincts as inner drives, or organized systems of responses which come to us from inheritance. He conceives of original impulses as unorganized and unformed, but which, in interaction with the culture (as the anthropologist conceives of culture) or the "ordered relations" of the environment, take on a form and character that is both new and old. It is this that led Dewey to assert that "the meaning of native activities is not native, it is acquired," and, again, "we need to know about the social conditions which have educated original activities into

---

[10] *The Experimentalist Educational Theory,* Bode Memorial Lectures, 1957 (Columbus, Ohio: College of Education, The Ohio State University), pp. 14–15.

definite and significant dispositions before we can discuss the psychological element in society." [11]

Dewey's position is thus a means between two extremes. In contrast with education as adjustment, he emphasizes the importance of seeing in native impulses the possibilities of novel response to environmental factors. Instead of following nature, he would encourage an accommodation between native impulse and cultural factors. Take language, for example. The unformed utterances of the child are soon channeled in such a way as to conform to the verbal expressions of his family and community. He speaks the words with the accent and the meaning others give to them. But not without variation! He adds his own enunciation, and he may also give to his words shades of meaning slightly different from common usage, a deviation which, in some instances, is adopted by others. In this way the language we use is both idiomatic and common to the group to which we belong.

So it is with other responses of the young person to his culture. No generation follows exactly in the footsteps of its elders. In these variations of response which individuals make to the customary and the traditional as well as to the novel in their environment reside the possibilities of change and progress. Consequently, the wise parent and teacher is sensitive to the potentialities within novel responses of the young as well as to the nourishing and sustaining effects of identification with group patterns, whether these be in the interpretation and use of objects and events or in the realm of manners and morals.

The above is but a sketchy presentation of the experimental or organic concept of learning. Basic to its understanding is the concept of a "transaction" between an organism and the environment as a condition of survival and development. On all levels, from the responses of a simple one-celled organism to the most complex organisms this involves an *adaptation* of a give-and-take character to the environment, adaptation in the sense that the organism and its medium are engaged in a mutually transforming relationship. In the evolutionary process this mutually responsive relationship goes hand in hand with structural developments or changes in the

---

[11] John Dewey, *Human Nature and Conduct* (New York: Henry Holt & Co., Inc., 1922), pp. 90–91.

organism. On all levels, organisms have interests or goals which they seek to realize consciously or unconsciously. With the acquisition of distance receptors (eyes, ears, nose, etc.) these interests come to involve the future as well as the immediately present and the distant as well as the tangibly near. With these acquisitions also, the environment takes on new qualities. Eventually, too, the past contributes to the nature of present experience. In man, gestures and symbols and language enable the remote in time as well as space, the future as well as the past, to function in the present, and the interests of others as well as of oneself become an inherent part of each individual.[12]

As the experimentalist sees it, this conception of organism renders inadequate previous explanations of learning either in terms of a mind as distinct from body, which receives and organizes experiences, or the concept of stimulus and response (body without mind) as a conditioning process. That is to say, as viewed by the experimentalist, the organism, as body, has more mind in it than the behaviorist will grant, and, as mind, the organism has more body in it than the traditional conception of mind permits. This is true, whether we view the responses of the organism from within or in response to external stimuli.

Consider, for example, the relationship between the blood stream and the organs of the body. This can be described only as a form of communication, a highly sensitive relationship in which the blood is kept in a relatively uniform and stable condition by various organs which "filter, refine, elaborate, detoxify, add, remove or otherwise regulate its composition," [13] and the blood, in turn, conveys to the same organs (the lungs, kidney, liver, etc.) what they require for their healthy functioning.

In much the same manner the organism communicates with its external environment. Breathing, wrote Dewey many years ago, is an affair of the atmosphere as well as of the lungs.

---

[12] The experimentalist thus agrees with those psychologists who maintain that awareness of one's identity is impossible without awareness of an external reality, that "only through a recognition of that part of the universe which is 'not I' can the self be discovered " See Franz Alexander, in a review of *On Shame and the Search for Identity* by Helen Merrill Lynd (New York: Harcourt, Brace & Co., 1958) in *The New York Times Book Review,* March 30, 1958, p. 22.

[13] See Lawrence K. Frank, *Nature and Human Nature* (New Brunswick, N.J.: Rutgers University Press, 1951), chap. III on "Our Internal Environment."

Learning Viewed As a Unique Form of Communication

Learning, too, is a form of communication. It is purposive in that meanings and goals operate as selective factors in relationships between "inner" and "outer," the individual and his environment. Were we to employ the term *mind* in this connection, we should say it signifies the *process of "minding,"* a process in which objects and events suggest future consequences in such a way as to influence present behavior. Again, learning is a process in which experiences in the past operate along with factors in the present with an eye to their future implications. To continue in paradoxes, learning may be described as a process in which an individual maintains his integrity, continues to be himself, by consistently reconstructing and remaking himself and his environment into something different. When an organism ceases to learn, it dies.

So much for the theory of learning as an interrelationship. We now turn to its practical applications.

Suggested Reading

Berkson, I. B., *The Ideal and the Community* (New York: Harper & Brothers, 1958), chaps. 1–2.

Childs, John L., *American Pragmatism and Education* (New York: Henry Holt and Co., Inc., 1956), chaps. 3–5.

Dewey, John, *Individualism Old and New* (New York: Milton, Balch and Company, 1930), chaps. IV, VIII.

Edman, Irwin, *John Dewey, His Contribution to the American Tradition* (New York: The Bobbs-Merrill Company, Inc., 1955), chap. III.

Frank, Lawrence K., *Nature and Human Nature* (New Brunswick, N.J.: Rutgers University Press, 1951), chaps. III, IV.

Hilgard, Ernest R., *Theories of Learning* (New York: Appleton-Century-Crofts, Inc., 1956), chaps. 6, 7, 8.

Kilpatrick, William Heard, *Philosophy of Education* (New York: The Macmillan Co., 1951), chap. II.

National Society for the Study of Education, *General Education, Fifty-first Yearbook* (Chicago: University of Chicago Press, 1952), part I, chaps. II, III.

/\.\/\.\/\.\

15

Education in an Interdependent World: Educational Practices

The Child Becomes a Participant in Educational Planning

A wise teacher once remarked that the verb "teach," in the sentence, "I teach John Latin," governs two accusatives. Consequently, to teach well, one must know "John" as well as the subject "Latin" in order to make the most of the potential relationships between the two. At its best, the experimentalist's conception of learning has contributed fruitfully to the potentialities of a creative interrelationship between student and subject matter.

First and foremost, it emphasizes the importance of encouraging the pupil's active participation in his own learning; of bringing about his identification with the task in hand by virtue of its known bearing, directly or indirectly, upon his interests, needs, and future hopes and plans.

Writing early in the century, John Dewey stated that the subject matter of instruction has two aspects,[1] one for the scientist as scientist, the other for the teacher as teacher, each involving a somewhat different organization. For the scientist, that organization of a subject is best which enables its user to solve problems, to locate new problems, and to "carry them through to a verified

[1] John Dewey, *The Child and the Curriculum* (Chicago: University of Chicago Press, 1902), p. 30.

outcome." For the teacher, on the other hand, the relevant organization of his subject is that which best relates to the child's experiences at a given stage of development. In other words, the teacher's major concern is with "the subject-matter as a related factor in a total and growing experience."

It proved to be but a step from a sense of direction and identification on the part of the pupil to firsthand participation in the planning of his program. The improved attitude toward school and its responsibilities on the part of young people, once their interests were enlisted, led many teachers, early in the century, to engage in radical departures from tradition. On the assumption that facts, skills, habits, attitudes, and ideals are best acquired in the context of a practical endeavor, or in the solution of a "real-life" problem, a number of schools resolved to abolish traditional subjects and to substitute "projects." For example, in place of separate periods for arithmetic, reading, spelling, geography, etc., one class group in an elementary school might concern itself with a study of family life, another might conduct a school store, still another might center upon city living. Not uncommonly, these "areas of interest" became as conventionalized as "subjects," with the result that children of a given age would be expected this year to be interested in the same type of project, or "center of interest," as were children of the same age last year. Nevertheless, these centers of interest, in the eyes of their practitioners, had the advantage of providing vital occasions for development in reading, writing, arithmetic, art, music, industrial work, etc., as incidental learning which comparea more than favorably with the old subject matter curriculum.[2]

In the hands of a skillful teacher, one keenly aware of the bones to be covered by the flesh and blood of active learning, the project method of teaching, particularly on the elementary school level, yielded superior results. However, with an unskillful teacher, the active participation of pupils in the planning of a project often led to the selection of trivial activities and to the partial mastery of the facts and the skills which incidental learning was

---

[2] For two excellent accounts of project teaching in its early stages, see Ellsworth Collins, *An Experiment with a Project Curriculum* (New York: The Macmillan Co., 1923), and Margaret E. Wells, *The Project Curriculum* (New York: J. B. Lippincott Co., 1921).

to achieve. In these instances only skewed development could result. In one well-known school, for instance, it was the practice of teachers and pupils at the opening of each school year to decide "cooperatively" upon the units of work or the major themes of the year. In one class group the unit might be primarily of a science character; in another, historical or literary. The result was that although the learning of the pupils within each area of interest was impressive, pupils in the science units experienced little history and the historically minded group learned little science.

"Progressive" Practices Criticized

Extremes of this kind were certain, of course, to bring a reaction. Indeed, experimentalists have been as severe in their criticisms of the project method thus employed and its successor, the "activity curriculum," as conservatives. Professor Boyd H. Bode, for example, was a consistent critic of incidental learning, pointing out that although it has its values, it is likely to be "too discontinuous, too random and haphazard, too immediate in its functions, unless we supplement it with something else," [3] and John L. Childs, while emphasizing the values in the activity curriculum which come from the fact that it enables children to learn by employing the methods of scientific thinking, also warns that "In our zeal for pupil initiative, pupil planning, and pupil problem-solving, we must never forget that education is a deliberate effort to provide the young with a course of experiencing which makes the maximum use of these meaningful and charged stimuli of the culture." [4] Since one all-important function of education is to enable the young, in Dewey's words, "to traverse in a short life-time what the race has needed slow, tortured ages to attain," Childs concludes that there is "an irreducible difference between a form of inquiry in which the aim is to introduce the young to that which is already known and functioning in the life of a people, and the pattern of research in inquiry in which the aim is to discover knowledge which no one has as yet achieved." [5] To the method

[3] *Modern Educational Theories* (New York: The Macmillan Co., 1927), pp. 150–151.
[4] *The Experimentalist Educational Theory*, Bode Memorial Lectures (Columbus, Ohio: College of Education, Ohio State University, 1957), p. 25.
[5] *Ibid.*

of the project and the activity curriculum, then, Childs would add "more effectual procedures by which the young can master well-organized bodies of knowledge. In some fields the logical order of the materials to be learned may have to be given priority." [6]

Other critics have directed their attacks upon what they consider to be a superficial interpretation of the nature of scientific method as embodied in the activity curriculum. No scientific problem is solved, they insist, without heavy indebtedness to the past. Granted that thinking begins with a problem, it follows, nevertheless, that a full understanding of a serious problem and the suggestions in the way of inferences and hypotheses for its solution involve the use of funded experience. Scientific method, as exemplified in a complete act of thought, thus involves both deduction and induction; and for induction to contribute fruitfully to the solution of problems, a thinker may have to draw heavily upon the accumulated results of generations who have gone before and have provided the present generation with the assumptions and systems of belief which constitute an indispensable framework for inquiry and valid reasoning today. [7] This in no way lessens the importance of a pupil's identification with the task in hand or his participation in planning but it renders questionable the assumption that he is an equal partner in determining what knowledge is worth while. The relation of an apprentice to a master craftsman is not an unwise analogy in this connection.

These criticisms of experimentalism as practiced by its overly enthusiastic disciples are of value in calling attention to the twofold nature of experience as originally described by Dewey. It is not Dewey but his so-called followers who have neglected the part that racial experience plays in learning. Consider, for example, these words with which Dewey concludes his discussion of *The Child and the Curriculum:* "The case is of the child. It is his present powers which are to assert themselves; his present capacities which are to be exercised; his present attitudes which are to be realized. But save as the teacher knows, knows wisely and thoroughly, the race-experience which is embodied in that

---

[6] *Ibid.,* p. 26.

[7] For a searching criticism of the experimentalist's conception of experience and its implication for scientific method, see I. B. Berkson, *The Ideal and the Community* (New York: Harper & Brothers, 1958), chap. II.

thing we call the Curriculum, the teacher knows neither what the present power, capacity, or attitude is, nor yet how it is to be asserted, exercised, and realized." [8]

Developmental Tasks and the Curriculum

To restore a balance which the project method and a curriculum devised by pupils and teachers "on the spot" was in danger of losing, a group of educators, in the 1930's, undertook to survey the task of the school with an eye to defining the "needs" of pupils, or what were later termed "developmental tasks." This represented an effort to avoid the extremes of a one-sided emphasis upon the individual, his nature and his interests, and an equally one-sided emphasis upon the "demands of society." As a result of its study, this group concluded that curricular experiences should meet the following criteria:

First, they must relate meaningfully to the prevailing desires, inclinations, and quests of the particular students for whom they are designed, since needs are personal in reference. Curricular experiences, in other words, must have identifiable connection with the individual student's desires for a sense of security, of belonging, of achievement, and the like, and must contribute to their fulfilment in socially desirable ways.

Second, they must be relevant to significant current social, economic, political, and cultural trends as they bear upon the adolescent, since needs are also always social in reference. In other words, they must further the individual's adjustment within the basic relationships of living.

Third, they must further the realization of democratic values, since education cannot meet needs without giving direction to their expression. Curricular experiences must be conducive to the growth of that kind of personality which is capable of democratic living under modern conditions.[9]

In line with this concept of needs, various subject matter committees within the field of secondary education associated with

---

[8] Dewey, *op. cit.,* p. 40.
[9] The Commission on the Secondary School Curriculum, in V. T. Thayer, Caroline Zachry, and Ruth Kotinsky, *Reorganizing Secondary Education* (New York: D. Appleton–Century Company, 1939), p. 415.

the Commission on the Secondary School Curriculum undertook to examine the resources of their fields—science, social studies, mathematics, language, literature, art—with a view to suggesting materials and methods appropriate for meeting the needs of young people in the areas of immediate personal-social relationships, social-civic relationships, economic relationships, and in personal living.[10]

The attempt to provide educational experiences for young people with an eye sensitive at once to individual and social criteria soon influenced the organization of courses of study and the curriculum in both the elementary and secondary schools. Nor was it without influence upon college curricula.

This was a particularly fruitful period of experimentation in College education. Colleges such as Sarah Lawrence, Bennington, Bard, and Black Mountain, although not large, nevertheless attracted wide attention for their departures from conventional curricula and methods. Others, such as Reed College, Stephens College, Goucher College, together with curricular experimentation in the lower divisions of state universities (Wisconsin, Minnesota, etc.), elicited equal attention, although the emphasis in these cases was less than with the first group upon what might be called the adolescent study approach. Somewhat later, curricular revisions at Harvard, Yale, Princeton, and others invited critical study in higher education circles.

The "Needs" of Youth Versus "Social Functions" As Criteria for the Curriculum

The depression of the 1930's, with its disastrous effects upon American youth, stimulated studies of the status of American youth on a nationwide scale. Of these the studies conducted by the American Youth Commission were particularly influential. A preliminary report of the work of this commission, entitled, *"How Fare American Youth?"* [11] revealed clearly that the schools

---

[10] *Ibid.*, chaps. IV–IX. See also *Science in General Education, Art in General Education, Mathematics in General Education, Language in General Education, The Social Studies in General Education, Prose Fiction in General Education: A Bibliography of 1500 Novels* by Elbert Lenrow. All of these volumes were published by D. Appleton–Century Co., New York.

[11] By Homer P. Rainey, Director of the American Youth Commission (New York: D. Appleton–Century Co., 1937).

of the nation were far from meeting the needs of young people. Out of these studies came numerous suggestions for improving education from elementary school through college.

As might be suspected, the programs which emerged were not always in agreement in their appraisal of the relative influence of the "requirements of society" and the concerns and interests of young people, one group tending to emphasize the importance of "social functions" to which youth should be introduced and the other the needs of young people as defined above.

Once the essential social functions were determined, that is, what came to be called the *scope* of the curriculum, the next task was to plan an appropriate *sequence* of experiences through which pupils, grade by grade, might become oriented within each function or area of living. This led to the planning of "centers of interest" or "units of work" for each year. It was at this point that the seeming inability of educators to maintain a balance between social adjustment and individual development became evident. Ideally, as Harold Alberty has pointed out,[12] the social-functions approach to curriculum re-organization affords an opportunity to resolve the conflict between an adult-centered and a child-centered approach to curriculum planning. The scope of the curriculum would thus emerge from an analysis of the various relationships in which young people are involved and the sequence from an identification of the needs of young people within these areas at various stages of their growth and development.

Guidance Programs Enlarge Their Responsibilities

Obviously, not all instructors are competent to meet the varied responsibilities imposed by the social-functions approach to the curriculum. To aid them and to round out or supplement their efforts, many schools have established guidance departments. Originally, guidance was chiefly vocational and narrowly academic in its functions. These services remain of importance, as contemporary emphasis upon identifying and stimulating the gifted ren-

---

[12] *Reorganizing the High School Curriculum* (New York: The Macmillan Co., 1953). See Chapter VIII for an excellent description of procedures followed in curriculum organization.

ders clear. It is now recognized, however, that these functions can be performed more effectively when seen in the context of emotional and social development. For this reason, guidance has enlarged its sphere of responsibility in recent years to include an understanding of the emotional and social development of children and adolescents, profiting from the insight which has come out of the mental hygiene movement and the contributions of child guidance clinics and research into child and adolescent development. What are commonly spoken of as "traits" of character and personality are no longer viewed as relatively independent entities (cooperation, reliability, honesty, or the reverse) which an individual either acquires or inherits and carries around with him in fixed quantities. Rather are they conceived of as qualities of relationships, the outcomes of interplay between oneself and others, and thus flexible and subject to change as conditions change. The conditions of health of personality are thus seen to be the conditions of mutually creative communication between a child and others—parents, siblings, playmates, etc. High on the list of essentials for mental health are firsthand assurance to a child that he is accepted and loved, that he is needed and that others are thus dependent upon him in certain essential respects, that he is recognized for his achievements in some area of importance and significance in the eyes of others, and that he is free, in the sense that he feels he is progressively acquiring the "know-how" with which to walk on his own feet and to make his own decisions. Maladjustment, on the other hand, is related to the absence of one or more of these factors and is evidence of the fact that one's relations with others are badly snarled.

This concern for the emotional and social aspects of growth and development, of health of personality, explains the emphasis educators have placed upon the "whole child" in recent years. As so often happens, this phrase is easily misinterpreted in its applications. It does not mean that the school should now undertake to provide all of the young person's education, thus replacing or invading the territories of home, church, and the like; although it may mean that the school should, on occasion, seek to offset serious deficiencies in these areas. It does mean that what the school undertakes to do should contribute positively to health of personality. It means, too, that in the professional preparation of teachers, knowledge of personality development should be acquired in addition to knowledge of subject matter so that the verb "teach" may, in fact, govern two accusatives.

Once health of personality is identified with desirable qualities of relationships with people, stages in a child's development may be seen in a light quite different from that which impressed G. Stanley Hall and his associates. No longer are they viewed as inner drives of an hereditary and self-contained nature. Rather are they stages in emotional, social, and intellectual development which are at once personal and social, individual and cultural. Highly significant as they may be within a given cultural setting, they are nevertheless idiomatic as well, subject to modification and reinterpretation in their applications to an individual child.

As normal and general characteristics of growth and development, however, they are helpful in defining the functions of the teacher-as-guide at different stages in the progress of young people from early childhood to adulthood. In the kindergarten and the first grade, for example, they would indicate that the teacher's role, in part, is that of a substitute parent, the head of an enlarged family who thus renders easy that first critical step of the child from the intimate relationships of his own family to the more impersonal relations of the larger community. As the child moves up into the elementary school, the functions of the guide change, becoming analogous to the role of an admired older brother or sister, who, by virtue of his or her skill in many areas, constantly reveals new and intriguing interests and transmits the "know-how" of new activities. With early adolescence, the young person tends to identify with an adult outside the family and to clothe him (or her) with qualities of personality he (or she) would like to make his (or her) own, a fact which calls for wisdom and discretion on the part of the older person thus selected. Finally, in late adolescence, the relations of student and instructor become more nearly those of adult and adult.

Each of these stages carries a moral for the teacher-pupil relationship; each has an obvious bearing upon the type of personality in the teacher which makes for success at one stage as compared with another.

The Core Curriculum

As we have said, the depression which began in 1929 and extended throughout the 1930's stimulated investigations into the status of American youth. The results of these studies led many to doubt that the curriculum of the conventional secondary school lent itself readily to meeting the needs of young people, viewed either from the standpoint of social functions and social processes or of needs that are personal-social in character. Nor did the conventional time schedule seem to provide sufficient time in which to engage in learning experiences of a "real-life" character. Out of these doubts and a determination to transform education into ways more vital and functional, the core curriculum emerged.

Harold Alberty, one of the leading authorities on the core curriculum, points out that the term "core curriculum" is used to describe practices which range from preoccupation with new groupings of subjects or combinations of subjects ("unified studies") to radical attempts to provide an "experience curriculum," "which draws upon all fields of knowledge in order to meet the needs, solve the problems, and extend the interests of students." An illustration of the more conservative approach is the not infrequent "fusion" of history and English and the less frequent merging of science and mathematics. A further step, called the culture-epochs core, is to organize the work of each year in all subjects studied so as to contribute toward an understanding of an historical period, or a significant phase in cultural development. For example, some years ago, the Horace Mann School for Girls in New York City adopted as a general theme for its three upper years Modern Civilization and Culture. Under this heading, the tenth grade concentrated upon American Civilization and Culture; the eleventh grade upon Other Modern Civilizations and Cultures (Russia, Germany, China, Great Britain, France, etc.); the twelfth grade upon Modern Problems and Issues in America. An effort was made to use each subject (English, social science, science, mathematics, the fine, industrial, and household arts, and music) so as to give students a complete picture of society in each of these periods. Work was planned cooperatively by teachers drawn from several fields, and each course was conducted by a "coordinating teacher."

A third general type of core curriculum described by Alberty is the contemporary problems core, which, in contrast with the historical approach, is contemporary in its emphasis and attempts to "relate the functions of living" to a broad "integrating theme" in each grade.[13]

An illustration of a core curriculum organized around adolescent needs is that adopted in 1945 by the Ohio State University School for the three years of the junior high school. In the seventh grade the problems dealt with centered on Personal Living; in the eighth grade, on Personal-Social Problems (problems related to being with others); and in the ninth grade, on Social-Civic-Economic Problems (problems of living in and understanding society).[14] This approach had in mind the organization of the total curriculum in a way basic for all students and organized without reference to conventional subject matter lines.

Alberty has listed the following criteria for the organization of a curriculum of this character:

1. The ideals and values of democracy, and the implied characteristics essential for good citizenship, provide the direction for curriculum reorganization.

2. The needs, problems, and interests of the adolescent, which grow out of his interaction with the culture, provide the basis for the learning activities which make up the curriculum.

3. The common needs of the adolescent can best be met by teacher-student planned units based upon broad problem areas which draw upon all pertinent fields of knowledge, and which provide for most of the values, understandings, abilities and skills needed by all.[15]

Proponents of the core curriculum conceive of it as a most effective means for meeting the needs of all students, the college-

---

[13] See, for example, Prudence Bostwick and Charles Reid, *A Functional High School Program* (New York: Hinds, Hayden and Eldredge, Inc., 1947). A few categories illustrative of this functional approach are: Orientation to the School, Home and Family Life, Community Life, Contemporary Cultures, Vocational Orientation, Resource Development, Conservation and Use, etc. See Harold Alberty, "A Proposal for Reorganizing the High School Curriculum on the Basis of a Core Program," *Progressive Education*, November, 1950, pp. 57–61.

[14] *A Proposal for a Core Curriculum in Grades Seven, Eight and Nine* (Columbus, Ohio: The Ohio State University School, 1945).

[15] Alberty, *Progressive Education, op. cit.*, pp. 57–61.

bound as well as students with more immediate vocational intentions. They would make this dual provision possible by substituting for the present system of majors and minors in the secondary school a division on the lines of general and special education. General education would meet the needs of all students through the core curriculum; special education would be that portion of the curriculum "in which individual interests, vocational competencies and requirements for advanced study are made." [16] One authority recommends that the core curriculum in the elementary and junior high school should absorb a major portion of the school's program. In the senior high school, however, more liberal allowance should be made for special interests. "One-third of the day in the tenth, eleventh, and, if necessary, the ninth, and one-half of the twelfth grade program could be used for work experience, vocational or commercial education, and college preparatory courses. Outside of the general education program there would be no requirements for graduation and each student's program would be tailored to meet his own special needs." [17]

Under the impetus of the Eight-Year Study in the 1930's,[18] there were sound reasons to believe the core curriculum would receive wide adoption in the secondary schools of the country.

Despite its assumed advantages the data bearing on the adoption of the core program are disappointing. In an article on "The Core Program" in the December, 1953, number of the *N.E.A. Journal,* Ralph W. Tyler reported that it is used most commonly in junior high schools. For example, according to a survey conducted by the Office of Education in 1949, 36 per cent of all core courses were in use in the seventh grade, 30 per cent in the eighth, and 20 per cent in the ninth grades, leaving only 14 per cent in all other grades. Secondly, the number of schools using the core curriculum is not impressive: 11 per cent of the larger

[16] Lavonne Hanna, "Proposals for the Secondary School Curriculum," *Progressive Education,* November, 1950, pp. 62–67.

[17] *Ibid.,* p. 67.

[18] Through a cooperative arrangement between some 300 colleges and 30 secondary schools, operating under the general direction of The Commission on the Relation of School and College of the Progressive Education Association, these 30 schools were to be freed for a period of eight years from the usual requirements for admission to college in order that they might experiment with the curriculum of the secondary school. See Wilford M. Aiken, *The Story of the Eight-Year Study* (New York: Harper & Brothers, 1942).

junior and senior high schools of more than 500 pupils and 2 per cent of those enrolling fewer than 500 pupils. Finally, the fields drawn upon in organizing the core are limited, 73 per cent combining English and social studies and only 7 per cent combining social studies, English, and science.

One explanation for this timid departure from tradition may be found in the conservative influences in American education which have come to the fore since World War II, influences we shall want to consider in a chapter devoted to contemporary criticisms of public education.

The Concept of Democracy Examined

Mention has been made of the fact that prior to World War II, both theories of learning and the dangers to American democracy posed by the rise of totalitarian governments abroad led to soul searching on the part of educators in this country. To what extent, they began to ask themselves, do classroom procedures and the administrative structure of the schools contribute toward the conscious realization on the part of young people of the principles of democracy and their applications in daily living? The answer was not always flattering to the school. Nor were many individuals in or outside school systems any too positive in their own minds as to why they preferred democracy to nondemocratic forms of government.

Obviously, in order to educate for democracy, clarification of its meaning as applied to relationships among people becomes essential.

Three of its aspects are relevant here. First and foremost, it implies the attribution of worth to the individual—respect for the integrity of his personality in "the conviction that personality is the center of value and that all social organizations get their significance from their promise to enhance the individual: to guarantee the sacredness of his person, to safeguard his rights, to extend his opportunities." [19] In a heterogeneous society, this means respect for differences, differences in origin and background, differences in interests, abilities, and skills. It implies the right of a child to grow up with a sense of security and an inner

---

[19] John Dewey, "Education and Social Change," *The Social Frontier*, May, 1937, p. 238.

self-respect by virtue of what he himself is, rather than to be judged and classified in terms of a stereotype or factors of origin over which he has no control. It means freedom of thought and inquiry and the right of individual conscience.

Secondly, democracy contrasts with both totalitarianism and rugged individualism. The first assumes (shall we say, requires?) that an individual realizes himself best by merging his interests in the interests of the whole and subordinating his convictions and his talents to the requirements of a central authority. The second places the individual above society and its institutions and is in essential agreement with Emerson's conception of the relation of the individual to the state, as expressed in his *Essay on Politics:* "To educate the wise man, the State exists; and with the appearance of the wise man, the State expires. The appearance of character makes the State unnecessary. The wise man is the State. . . . He needs no library, for he has not done thinking; no church, for he is a prophet; no statute-book, for he has the lawgiver; no money, for he is value; no road, for he is at home where he is; no experience, for the life of the creator shoots through him, and looks from his eyes." [20]

Democracy, on the other hand, implies a mutually creative relationship between society and the individual, the whole and the part, in which society and its institutions find their justification in promoting the distinctive nature and the well-being of the individual, and the individual, in turn, validates his right to be unique, his self-expression, through his contributions to the whole or through the creative impact of his gifts upon the self-expression of others. A democratic personality by its very nature is thus a social personality and the democratic ideal a moral ideal.

Finally, the democratic ideal, when applied to the resolution of conflicts and disputes between individuals and groups, relies upon the use of intelligence rather than upon force and the attempt to solve problems and to resolve differences through the process of creative compromise discussed earlier.[21]

---

[20] *The Prose Works of Ralph Waldo Emerson* (Boston: Fields, Osgood and Company, 1870), vol. I, p. 529.

[21] For a fuller discussion of the democratic ideal and its bearing upon "desirable directions of growth" together with its implications for classroom and school, see Thayer, Zachry, and Kotinsky, *op. cit.*, chaps. III, IX.

Using the Classroom to Educate for Democracy

The attempt to use the classroom as one means of educating for democracy carries a moral for the organization of teaching materials and teaching procedures. To employ a conventional term, a "lesson" commonly involves at least three phases: assignment, study and work period, recitation and evaluation. Although subjects differ, the study of each utilizes these steps. Within each step, moreover, there are ample occasions for the promotion of democratic ways of thinking and acting.

For example, the assignment period has as a major purpose an introduction of the task at hand in such a way that the student will understand its importance and be encouraged to identify himself with the work ahead. A skillful teacher is skillful by virtue of his ability not only to relate new experiences to old, but to sense the varied reactions of members of his class to the new undertaking; to hold in reserve more than one route for individuals to follow; and to invite the participation of members of the group in the selection of routes in accordance with their interests, needs, and abilities. This does not mean that the uninformed are to pass upon what the informed only can know or that the apprentice is to substitute for the master. It does mean, however, that there are areas in which the pupils can participate with profit in defining the part they will play in their own education. One aspect of this education, indeed, consists in learning to distinguish between those occasions in which one may legitimately cooperate with the master in outlining the course he is to follow and when he must accept and follow instructions more or less on faith. For the teacher, it also means an attempt to apply the results of contemporary research into the nature of group behavior and the comparative effects upon motivation of democratic, autocratic, and laissez faire methods of leadership.[22]

The working period likewise affords opportunities for democratic practices. It is in this period that both individual and group interests may be served. There is, of course, in every subject a common body of information, principles, and skills to master, but

---

[22] Kurt Lewin, Ronald Lippitt, and Ralph K. White, "Patterns of Aggressive Behavior in Experimentally Created Social Situations," *Journal of Social Psychology,* May, 1939, pp. 271–279.

each subject offers in addition abundant opportunities for interesting side excursions which can be made in such a way as to enrich the group as well as the individuals engaged in them. Often the problem or topic under study lends itself to committee work. This is of increasing importance today in the light of the tendency of Americans to solve their problems, political, social, civic, scientific, etc., through cooperative research. This should suggest to educators the importance of helping young people to acquire the discipline and the techniques of cooperative research and committee activity which alone will render committee activity effective rather than wasteful.

Within the committee as well as in the class recitation period, there are ample opportunities to employ the techniques of democratic group discussion, discussion in which each student will have some occasion to function as discussion leader, as participant, as observer and critic, and as research worker who gathers data for the group in an objective spirit, irrespective of his own conclusions and prejudices.

Finally, in the evaluation period, members of the group should be encouraged to review their work with a critical eye to their failures as well as their successes. In this phase, as in others, students may be led to understand the nature of a problem, the manner in which it has grown out of the past, how it implies a disturbed or unsatisfied present, and, in the process of its solution (whether finally solved or not), the way in which it may give character to the future. Thus, too, will they come to appreciate the vital importance of experimental thinking and freedom of inquiry in a democracy and, indeed, the dependence of free institutions upon freedom of thought and, in consequence, the imperative need that this freedom be a disciplined freedom.

In this hasty summary of ways in which a lesson period may be used to further the understanding and appreciation of democratic values, there is no intention to discount the importance of thorough intellectual accomplishment. On the contrary, it is assumed that the conscious use of democratic procedures will not only lend vitality to learning but foster and encourage intellectual discipline.

Applying Democracy to Administrative and Supervisory Relationships

Attempts to use the school in the interests of democratic thought and action (over and above the direct study of the origins, development, and nature of democracy and its methods) have not been confined to the classroom. They have led to new relationships between faculty and students [23] and new departures in the administrative and supervisory functions of school officials.

Basic to these changes is a conception of democratic leadership which contrasts with leadership in both an autocratic society and one characterized by heavy accent upon individualism. Traditionally, the leader is thought of as one gifted with a dominant personality, one who by virtue of a strong will and an aggressive personality can impose his will upon others or through the exercise of magnetic qualities can induce others to identify their wills with his. In either case, the leader is thought of as one who determines for others what they should think and the course they are to follow.

The democratic leader is of a different breed. He conceives of his relationships with the members of his staff less as one between superior and inferiors and more as one between functionaries in which each is charged with a distinctive task and each complements the other in the realization of an overarching ideal. As against the notion, then, that he has a will or a program to impose upon others, he seeks for mutually stimulating and creative relations between his colleagues and himself. In the formulation of policies, as in their execution, he realizes that he, as supervisor or administrator, by virtue of his central position has one function to serve and the members of his faculty have other functions; but when each contributes in the light of these different points of view, decisions are likely to be more relevant than when each operates without reference to the other. In his relations with individual teachers, heads of departments, or other functionaries, he encourages initiative and originality while acting, when need be, as a constructive critic who, by virtue of his more varied experience or his central position, is likely to be sensitive to factors

---

[23] Reference is made, of course, to forms of student government which we cannot discuss fully here but which might well engage a chapter.

of which the specialist is unaware. As chairman of a meeting or as a conference leader, he is "permissive," if by this term is meant one who fosters a free play of ideas and suggestions while retaining the privilege of using his central position to call attention to neglected aspects in suggestions made and to round out the limited, partial, and often slanted proposals of those who speak from one vantage point only. In the school situation again, it is the leader's responsibility to foster harmonious relations among the members of his staff through mutual understanding and appreciation, to keep alive the overarching purposes and philosophy of the school, and to stimulate his colleagues to identify themselves with this philosophy in such a way as to promote all possible unity within difference. Finally, an administrator should conscientiously provide his colleagues with the essential tools of their craft and earnestly strive to safeguard them from unnecessary interference and distraction in the performance of their distinctive functions.

This conception of a democratic leader differs in a number of respects from that common in the management of industrial and business corporations. The specific pattern of organization, however, will vary with different school situations. In a small school, little in the way of formal structure may be required. The spirit is all-important. In a large and complex situation, on the other hand, faculty participation in the formulation of policies may call for a formal organization of the faculty, together with the establishment of joint faculty-administrative committees.

Logic would seem to suggest an extension of the principle of functional representation to the composition of boards of education. It must be admitted, however, that neither the small board which came into existence early in the century nor experiments in group representation on boards of education for public schools have entirely realized the ideals of their advocates. As George Counts pointed out as early as 1928, the small board often lends itself to the influence of pressure groups and even to capture by special interests. To offset this, Counts suggested [24] that boards be constituted in such a way as to insure "to each legitimate interest . . . an opportunity to make itself heard." But in this respect also results have not been altogether happy. Not infrequently one

---

[24] *School and Society in Chicago* (New York: Harcourt, Brace & Co., 1928), chap. XV.

group has combined with other groups to realize its limited and selfish purposes in accordance with the principle, "If you will scratch my back, I will scratch yours!"

This, of course, defeats the primary purposes of group representation. These purposes can only be realized when representatives of groups recognize that their primary obligation is to the institution or the school system as a whole and that as members of the central governing body they are selected *from* a group because of the special contributions they can make to the whole. This obligation they can discharge only when they contribute out of their special backgrounds and unique associations what is relevant in the formulation of general policies and serve in turn as successful interpreters of these policies to their groups. If this ideal be out of the reach of frail human beings as at present constituted, a substitute procedure might insure nonparochial representation on boards of education (that is, selection of members of the board from the community at large) with conscious provision for group representation upon advisory bodies—representation from parents, the professional staff, the community at large, civic organizations within the community. The form and structure matter less, although they are not without importance, than the general understanding on the part of the public at large of the primary function an educational system is to serve in a democracy. As the writer stated some twenty-five years ago:

We thus conclude that it is not solely in its relation to the learner that the school should observe the precepts of education. In all of its dealings it should bear witness to its major function. This implies the fostering and creation of living arrangements which permit of an intelligent sharing of experiences. It means an organization of such a character that each one participating performs his own special work with a full realization of its implications and effects upon his associates and the larger aims of which he is a means. In short, a school system should typify and exemplify in its operations as a whole and in the functioning of its parts the process which is the be-all and the end-all of its existence. It should stand forth clearly as an educational institution. And to make these purposes manifest is the distinctive function of school administration.[25]

---

[25] V. T. Thayer in William Heard Kilpatrick and others, *The Educational Frontier* (New York: The Century Company, 1933), p. 256.

Suggested Reading

Alberty, Harold, *Reorganizing the High School Curriculum,* rev. ed. (New York: The Macmillan Co., 1953), Chaps. V–VIII, XVI.

———, "A Proposal for Reorganizing the High School Curriculum on the Basis of a Core Curriculum," *Progressive Education,* November, 1950, pp. 57–61.

Association for Supervision and Curriculum Development, *What Shall the High Schools Teach?* (Washington, D.C.: National Education Association, 1956), chap. V.

Berkson, I. B., *The Ideal and the Community* (New York: Harper & Brothers, 1958), chaps. 2, 13.

Bruce, William, and A. John Holden, *The Teacher's Personal Development* (New York: Henry Holt & Co., Inc., 1957), parts II, III.

Dewey, John, *The Child and the Curriculum* (Chicago: University of Chicago Press, 1902).

Krug, Edward A., *Curriculum Planning* (New York: Harper & Brothers, 1957), chaps. III, IV.

Lury, Lucile, and Elsi J. Alberty, *Developing a High School Core Curriculum* (New York: The Macmillan Co., 1957), chaps. II, III, VI.

Shane, Harold G., and others. *The American Elementary School* (New York: Harper & Brothers, 1953), chap. II.

PART IV

Critical Issues in Contemporary

Education

/\./\./\./\

ΛΛΛΛ

CHAPTER

16

Public Education Under Fire

Early Criticisms of the Schools Primarily Local

It is commonly assumed that the strength and vitality of a democ-racy derive from the responsive character of its institutions to the will of the people served by these institutions. In contrast with the conformity of mind and will upon which the survival of an autocracy depends, ideally, at least, it is the governed who govern in a democracy. Criticism thus constitutes the life blood of a free society.

If this be true, the American public school has received gen-erous injections of good red blood in recent years. Nor is there evidence that the original springs of vitality are in process of dry-ing up! The flood of articles and books devoted to the failures of public education increases steadily in volume and threatens at times to become a veritable torrent.

Prior to 1950, indictments of failure gave the appearance of local origin and seemed to testify to a widespread but healthy concern of the friends of public education that instruction in the schools be brought to higher levels of efficiency. The enforced resignation of Dr. Willard Goslin from his position as Superin-tendent of Schools in Pasadena, California, in the fall of 1950, indicated that criticism was neither exclusively local in origin nor designed merely to improve and to strengthen the public schools.

One of the first to draw attention to a national pattern in these attacks and to identify individuals and organizations fostering them, together with their obvious motives, was Robert Skaife of the National Commission for the Defense of Democracy Through Education. In a series of articles written for the *Nation's Schools,* beginning in January, 1951, Skaife undertook to expose the propaganda methods and procedures of these "critics" of public education.

Nevertheless, the public at large was slow to realize the nature of these assaults upon the public schools. As Archibald Anderson pointed out in 1952, "Even when a particular controversy broke out in a particular school district, there was a tendency to regard this as an isolated phenomenon because the pattern of issues involved, and the relationship between issues were old and familiar." [1]

Early criticisms bore down most conspicuously upon the assumed failure of the schools to ground their pupils in the three R's. Not only is this a recurrent argument, repeated generation after generation, but it is also one that educators realize lends itself to easy refutation, if statistical evidence of childrens' accomplishments can be accepted in preference to the undocumented inferences of parents and teachers who seem forever disposed to prefer the past to the present.

For example, as early as the 1920's, Caldwell and Courtis, in a volume entitled *Then and Now in Education,* conclusively answered this argument for their generation. Having come into possession of examinations administered to school children in Boston in 1845, the authors arranged to subject children of the 1920's to the same tests. Despite the fact that in the 1840's only superior pupils were privileged to undertake these examinations, whereas the children examined by Caldwell and Courtis were taken from the run-of-the-mine, the children of the 1920's clearly demonstrated a superiority of performance over those of 1845.

---

[1] In a paper read before Section Q, American Association for the Advancement of Science, St. Louis, Mo., December 31, 1952. For further information respecting the nature and source of attacks upon the schools, see publications of the National Commission for the Defense of Democracy Through Education of the National Education Association, 1201 Sixteenth St., N.W., Washington, D.C. Ernest O. Melby and Morton Pruner in *Freedom and Public Education* (New York: Frederick A. Praeger, Inc., 1953) have also compiled a representative series of articles and addresses in this area.

Contemporary Criticisms of Public Education

But what of today?

Again, research validates the new over the old. Thus William H. Burton pointed out in 1952 that over 275 separate studies were then available in magazines and master's theses to establish the fact that the schools "are teaching the Three R's today far more efficiently than ever before in history. The children, generally, have far greater skill than their parents and forbears. Modern methods are measureably superior to those used formerly, or, 'in my day.' " [2]

In 1951 a thoroughgoing survey was conducted by a graduate seminar in education at Ohio State University under the direction of Professor Harold Alberty. From its review of the major experiments and research studies bearing upon the effectiveness of instruction in the basic skills "in the present-day curriculum as compared with the older and more traditional practices," the seminar concluded that "The evidence of growth in basic skills, both at the elementary and the secondary levels, reveals clearly that in the modern curriculum these skills are achieved as well or better than in the conventional curriculum. This is true for the basic skills discussed here, namely, skills in reading, arithmetic, and language." [3]

A comparison of high school and college education at mid-century with that at the turn of the century leads to a similar conclusion. Critics of modern education have either forgotten or are ignorant of the conditions which prompted the National Council of Education in 1892 to appoint a Committee of Ten, under the chairmanship of Charles W. Eliot, with instructions to bring order, if possible, out of a chaotic and confused situation. This committee was confronted with the absence of any consistent policy on the secondary level for preparing students either for college or "for life." Subjects taught varied from school to school. There was no uniformity as to time allotments, and grade placements of topics or subjects pursued in one institution did not

---

[2] See "Get the Facts: Both Ours and the Other Fellows," *Progressive Education,* January, 1952, pp. 82–90.

[3] *Lets Look At Our Schools* (Columbus, Ohio: College of Education, Ohio State University, 1951, pp. 21–29. Selections from this study are also included in Melby and Pruner, *op. cit.,* pp. 227–232.

have any obvious relationship to time allotments and grade placements in another. Writing in the *Arena,* for June, 1890, on "The
Gap Between Common Schools and Colleges," President Eliot
stated, "The elementary or common-school system, in both city
and country, is tolerably organized in many States; but between
the elementary schools and the colleges is a wide gap very im-
perfectly bridged by a few public high schools, which conform
to no common standards and are under no unifying control. The
masses of the rural population—that is to say, three quarters of
the American people are unprovided with secondary schools."

Speaking of his own state, Massachusetts, one of the leading
states of the period, Eliot continues, "The plain fact in Massachusetts is that not one tenth of the schools called high habitually
maintain a course of study which enables the pupil to prepare
himself for admission to Harvard College, or to any other college
in the State which enforces its requirements for admission as
stated in its catalogue. If this is the condition of things in what
may be called an urban State, what must it be in a rural one?" [4]

An examination of the nature of instruction afforded in college
prior to the turn of the century is equally fatal to the argument
that the salvation of American education depends upon restoring
to the colleges "the kind of education in the liberal arts which
American colleges had furnished well into the nineteenth century." [5] The plain fact is, as Professor Frank Freeman has demonstrated, "Comparisons of entrance requirements, college curricula,
textbooks, and methods of instruction" support the conclusion
that "Until 1890–1900, the courses and the teaching in most
colleges in this country did not make as great demands upon
the mental abilities of their students as do the average academic
high schools of today." [6] As to the "sound intellectual discipline"
the liberal arts were supposed to convey, the record seems to
indicate, continues Freeman, that "College education, down
through the 19th Century, was largely a matter of memorization
and repetition of textbook lessons in the classical languages, gram-

[4] Reprinted in *Educational Reform, Essays and Addresses* (New York: The Century Company, 1898), p. 199.

[5] See Stringfellow Barr, "The Education of Freemen," *The New Republic,* August
13, 1942, pp. 248–250.

[6] From a paper read before the Academy Conference of the American Association
for the Advancement of Science in Philadelphia, December, 1951.

mar, rhetoric, some logic and philosophy, some mathematics; and, in some colleges, a bit of French, German, and elementary English. The sciences, and the arts, and the humanities properly understood, certainly were not dominant in secondary or in college education up to the decade 1890–1900."

In describing the intellectual discipline provided by colleges in this period, Henry James remarks, in his biography of Charles W. Eliot, that college teaching consisted in "drilling rudiments into boys who, most of them, brought no enthusiasm for the particular subject in the classroom . . ." and from whom the college "exacted . . . as little as possible." [7]

Since the decade 1890–1900 our high schools and colleges have expanded phenomenally. Enrollments have increased, new curricula have been added, and the education afforded is far richer and varied than ever before in the history of this nation or, for that matter, of any other. To be sure, rapidity of growth is not always best for quality. That the standards of education in high school and college today are not what they should be, the educator should be the first to concede. Moreover, in seeking to minister to the needs of individuals who no longer constitute a selected group, school and college alike have increased the complexity of their tasks immeasurably. It is one thing, however, to recognize that meeting the requirements of both quality and diversity in education have not kept step with each other, or that in attempting to serve all types of minds (those whom Robert Ulich suggestively classifies as humanists, scientists, executives, artisans, workers),[8] equal and exact justice is not meted out to all, and quite another thing to attribute this failure to the "excesses of progressive education."

It is reasonable to conclude, then, that there is little evidence to sustain the charge that the quality of education in high school and college today is inferior to that of yesterday. Moreover, with respect to the elementary school, the results of comparative study indicate further that the children of today are mastering the fundamental processes—reading, writing, arithmetic—at a much earlier chronological age than ever before and on a level of pro-

---

[7] Quoted by Freeman from Henry James, *Charles William Eliot* (Boston: Houghton Mifflin Co., 1930).

[8] See Robert Ulich, *Crisis and Hope in American Education* (Boston: Beacon Press, Inc., 1953), chap. III.

ficiency superior to that of which their parents and grandparents are prone to boast.

To refute the criticism that our schools no longer teach the fundamentals of an education is not difficult if we confine ourselves to the record. To bring conviction to the public mind when the will to believe is being undermined steadily by the repetition of inaccuracy, often outright falsehood, is in no sense the same. Recent years have taught the educator that educational discussion is no exception to the rule that persistent repetition of error can overcome well-documented truth.

Education Is Said to Cost Too Much

Closely allied to the charge that public schools are neglecting the fundamentals is the indictment of waste and extravagance. Education, we are told, costs too much.

This is, indeed, a serious matter, since the criticism comes at one and the same time that many communities are attempting to float bond issues and to levy special taxes with which to better salaries, erect new school buildings, and to improve facilities, all of which is rendered imperative by rapid increases in the school population, so characteristic of the last decade, as well as the excusable neglect of the war period.

It is obvious, of course, that accusations of waste and extravagance are best checked when examined concretely and specifically. It is possible that individual communities here and there may have spent more for materials and supplies or for building construction than the circumstances warranted. If so, this can be determined by careful and objective investigation. Surely the professional educator, as well as the taxpayer, should be concerned to see that a dollar's value is received for every dollar spent. Toward this end, laymen and professional men can be of help to each other, the educator interpreting to the layman the physical necessities of an effective education and the layman contributing his practical knowledge as businessman, architect, or contractor to insure most economically the translation of these needs into actual construction.

This practical method of cooperation, however, is not always followed. It assumes a genuine concern for the promotion of public education on the part of the layman, whereas the criticism of waste, unfortunately, is often otherwise motivated and the indictment is kept in the realm of the general rather than the specific. Thus the public is informed that modern education, or "progressive education," inevitably involves waste with its fads and frills and its "activity curriculum." That "public education costs more money every year" was asserted over and over again in the campaign waged against Superintendent Willard Goslin in Pasadena, but one specific objection to the Goslin budget, seldom mentioned openly, was his plan to improve the educational facilities available for the underprivileged children of the city, namely, the Mexican and Negro children.

Public Education As an Undesirable Monopoly

It is but one step from the contention that public education costs too much to the argument that public schools are both unnecessary and unwise. In support of this position we find a curious assortment of individuals and groups, who, nevertheless, possess in common one objective: the substitution of private or parochial schools for the existing system of public education.

An ardent advocate of the abolition of public schools several years ago was Robert Cyrus Hoiles, the owner of some ten newspapers in Texas, California, Colorado, New Mexico, and Ohio.[9] Hoiles utilized news items and educational events to promote the thesis that "Government schools are leading us to socialism and communism." "It is impossible," he contends, "for tax-supported education to teach American principles. They can only teach foreign principles, collectivism, fascism, might-makes-rightism and the end justifies the means."

Hoiles combined opposition to all taxation without individual consent with the contention that government schools are inevitably the agents of "collective ideas." In an editorial criticizing the American Association of School Administrators, he states, "These men, of course, do not want free enterprise in ideas. They

---

[9] A description of the campaign waged by Hoiles is found in an article by Lewis C. Fay, Sunday Editor of the *San Antonio Light*, written for *The Nation's Schools*, August, 1952, under the title "Abolish Public Schools." Statements ascribed to Hoiles are derived from this source. I include Hoiles in this discussion because his views are more widely held than many realize.

want a complete monopoly in ideas just as the government of Russia does. And a complete monopoly on ideas is necessary in a dictator form of government." The obvious moral "is to have private schools that can teach voluntary ways of doing things. . . . If we had private schools, people would buy education just as they do bread." Nor, seemingly, would there be cause for regret if some parents decided not to buy education for their children, since "Government was more 'moral' 75 years ago when there was a higher percentage of illiteracy than today. . . ."

Hoiles' position is not unrelated to a position now being advocated by representatives of both Protestant and Catholic sects desirous of securing public funds in support of nonpublic schools. These individuals and groups hold that to restrict public funds exclusively to public education encourages a "dangerous monopoly" in education. They further contend that sound public policy runs counter to government assumption of functions that constitute the "appropriate tasks" of other social institutions and agencies.

This second position is ably argued by Robert C. Hartnett, editor of *America*. In an article on "The School in the American Community," Hartnett points out that

the state can fail to perform its proper functions in two ways: one, through lack of initiative, as when it allows the economically powerful to exploit the economically weak, or allows private interests to pillage the natural resources of society or in any one of a dozen ways permits the benefits and burdens of social life to be apportioned without regard to social justice . . . [and, two, through] excessive and too far-reaching interference in the free areas of social organization. In trying to redress the balance in favor of social justice, the state often extends its coercive arm much farther into such fields as education, health, and social welfare than is at all necessary or compatible with the nature of a free society. Ideally, the state should always aim to assist social institutions and agencies to perform their appointed tasks, rather than to *replace* them with public (i.e. political) agencies (italics in the original).[10]

Since Hartnett assumes that education is one of the "appointed tasks" of the church rather than of the state, it would seem that

[10] *America*, April 9, 1952, pp. 65–68.

the American people have erred in establishing public schools. Or to employ his own words, "The States have substituted a system of public education, incorporated into the structure of State governments, for what might have become a flourishing non-political educational system, assisted and regulated by the States."

A partial correction of this mistake would be made were the state to assist private as well as public schools. This policy, in the eyes of many, seems to follow also from government recognition of the legal right of parents to send their children either to public or to private schools. Thus Father William E. McManus, of the Department of Education of the National Catholic Welfare Council, has pointed out that the United States Supreme Court, in 1922, overruled the State of Oregon in the latter's attempt to compel all children to attend public schools. He therefore concludes that unless the state lends support to private as well as public education, this right becomes an "empty right," and, indeed, does positive injury to private education by creating a monopoly of public education. "When the state supports the public schools only," insists Father McManus, "it does an injustice to all non-public schools, which, by the state's own testimony do for the state the very same service as the public schools but yet receive no public support." [11]

The Schools Are Agents of Irreligious and Subversive Influences

The contention that public schools constitute a monopoly of a questionable, if not dangerous, character is not restricted to the level of theoretical discussion. What some seek to establish as a theoretical possibility others are busily proclaiming as fact.

This takes us to the charge that public schools have become the instruments of subversive influences bent upon "undermining" the American way of life in economics, politics, and religion.

Critics within this category constitute a varied group: members of the clergy—Protestant and Catholic—who indict the sec-

[11] From an article entitled "Should Public Funds Be Used to Support Parochial Schools?" published in the magazine section of the New York newspaper, *PM*, August 24, 1947.

ular school not only for neglect of religious instruction but for indoctrination in a "secularistic philosophy"; defenders of "true Americanism" who would believe that textbook writers and many teachers are planting in the minds of the young ideas of a collectivistic hue; and opponents of progressive education, convinced that the modern school is raising young people who know neither law and order nor respect for parental authority.

An exhaustive discussion of these criticisms is impossible within the limits of one chapter. A few illustrations will have to suffice.

Let us begin with indictments emanating from the clergy. These range from the thesis that education without religious indoctrination renders moral education impossible [12] to the charge that our schools "are dominated by naturalistic religion" [13] and the equally violent assertion that they are turning out "millions of uncontrolled delinquents."

The object of these charges would seem to be to convince the public that it is in its own interest to lend support to church schools and to replace the present policy of neutrality in matters of religious conviction with one of positive indoctrination. Religion, writes Henry P. Van Dusen, must be made "to permeate all teaching without exception and on all levels of education." [14]

When this more positive approach is not feasible, the advocates of religion in public education would encourage programs of religious instruction on released time. In either case, a transformation in the character of teacher training is called for, since, according to Bishop Pike, formerly Dean of the Cathedral of St. John the Divine, in New York City, "virtually every school teacher these days has been trained in the dogmatic theology of . . . naturalistic religion, whatever may be the extent of his Sunday devotions. As a result, some of our Christian school teachers are not aware that there is a conflict between two sets of dogmas. . . ." Pike, in common with other critics of secular education, would "provide for our public school teachers who are church people a thorough theological orientation so that it may be reflected in

---

[12] See the *Statement on Secularism and the Schools* by the Catholic Bishops of America, printed in *The New York Times*, November 16, 1952.

[13] Bishop James A. Pike, formerly Dean of the Cathedral of St. John the Divine, in *Bulletin of the General Seminary*, June, 1951, pp. 21–37. The quotations attributed to Bishop Pike are taken from this bulletin.

[14] See *God in Education* (New York: Charles Scribner's Sons, 1951), p. 78.

their teaching of secular subjects, just as the faith of the naturalistic humanists is reflected in their teaching."

Should these efforts fail, it is suggested that Protestants reverse
their traditional policy of support for public schools, set up
church schools, and agitate for the public support of nonpublic
schools. Indeed, Pike's words suggest that but for the dictates of
expediency these steps might be taken immediately. "While at
present," he writes, "being realistic about where we stand in the
development of these matters, such a plan would not be wise,
since it would give a disproportionate advantage to one group in
our community, yet if in fact other groups develop substantial
school systems, this might provide an entirely democratic and
entirely reasonable plan. Perhaps federal and state amendments
would be required, but we are not beyond amending constitutions
in this country when the majority of the people wish such amendments."

It is but a step from the charge that public schools are unwisely
excluding religion from the curriculum and, in consequence, neglecting the moral and spiritual development of the young to the
charge that they have become the pliant tools of alien influences
in American life. This fear of subversion was particularly acute
during the early 1950's, when Senator McCarthy was engaged in
his investigations of communism. Although this indictment has
not been as conspicuous since 1956 as before, it nevertheless continues frequently enough to merit brief attention.

For a time, a number of organizations thrived upon this indictment. Prominent among these was Allan Zoll's National Council
for American Education. Zoll's pamphlets found their way into
communities of virtually every state in the Union. Their purpose
may be inferred from the title of one pamphlet, *"They Want
Your Child."* Our schools, it was stated, "were founded to preserve the American form of government and the American institutions of freedom and individual liberty. It can safely be asserted that ninety per cent of the texts and teachers in our schools
today are in considerable measure subversive of these basic American principles." [15]

---

[15] Other pamphlets distributed by the National Council for American Education
include *Progressive Education Increases Delinquency, How Red Are the Schools?
Private Schools: The Solution to America's Educational Problem.*

Among those lending support to charges of subversion have been prominent radio commentators and journalists. Consider, for example, the obvious suggestion that emerges from these words of advice to parents from George Sokolsky:

> You need to know what a teacher believes. The teacher says that it is none of your business. The teacher says that the Constitution, under the Fifth Amendment, protects a citizen in his beliefs. That is absolutely true. A citizen can believe anything he likes: That the moon is made of green cheese, that Karl Marx is as great an historic figure as Moses, Jesus, Aristotle, and Plato; that John Dewey was the greatest philosopher of all time. That is a teacher's private business. . . . No child need be sent to a school whose teachers offend a parent's beliefs. The child must have a certain amount of "education," according to the law. That may require the parents to pay for the upkeep of two schools. Many do.[16]

Charges of subversion in education also received support from a number of educators who claimed firsthand acquaintance with the doctrines and influence of John Dewey, William Heard Kilpatrick, and their associates. One of these "experts," Dr. Felix Witmer, professed to speak out of seventeen years of teaching experience at the New Jersey State Teachers College in Montclair, New Jersey. Witmer resigned from this institution to devote himself to writing and lecturing. As one admiring editor put it, what he had to reveal "exploded over the national scene like wellplaced time bombs."

One of his articles on "The Initiators of Operation Socialism," began with these words:

> Have you ever read a book on "curriculum development"? No one should blame you if you haven't. If you have, you may understand a little better what has happened to the schools in your community, and how it has come about.
>
> As the years went by and your children passed through the grades, you may have noticed that a change was going on. Subject matter, teaching methods, types of study, everything changed. If you put two and two together, you realized that the emphasis shifted from the individual to the group.

---

[16] "Do You Know the Teachers? What Do Teachers Know?" *Rochester Times-Union,* December 28, 1951.

Your children learned that the Communist Manifesto ranked among the great works of world literature and that the Soviet Union was an "economic democracy." Competition, it seems, had become old hat. "Attitudes" and "group relationships" were the thing.

Just who was responsible for the changes you could not say. "Trends of the times" hardly seems to be a penetrating explanation. Fact is that a relatively small group of educators, who had gravitated toward Columbia Teachers College, have in the course of 20 years turned thousands and thousands of teachers into missionaries of the collectivist, i.e., socialistic, creed. These thousands of converts have brought about the change.[17]

Textbooks Are Subjected to Lay Censorship

From the above it is clear that one source of criticism of public education bears upon the manner in which controversial issues of a political and economic nature are handled in the classroom. Textbooks and teachers alike, it is said, are indoctrinating for a new social order. Consequently, "patriotic citizens" are urged to purge public education of both textbooks and teachers who are seemingly bent upon undermining American institutions. This follows, since the valid purpose of education, in the words of one enthusiastic partisan, should be that of "instilling traditions which are not subject to re-examination."

Efforts to control the selection and rejection of textbooks have extended as well to topics that schools are permitted to consider in the classroom.[18]

Equally serious, perhaps even more serious, has been the growing tendency of governing boards, on state as well as local levels, to limit the choice of textbooks, reference materials, and the content of teaching to that which promotes an uncritical acceptance of the status quo. Typical of these efforts were the criteria for the

---

[17] See "The Initiators of Operation Socialism," *National Republic*, June, 1953, p. 13.

[18] One example has been the decision of school authorities, in a number of instances, to prohibit the study of the United Nations and its agencies. Thus, in January of 1952, the Board of Education of Los Angeles forbade the distribution of a booklet entitled, "The E in UNESCO," despite the fact that this booklet had been prepared by its own curriculum department and was intended only to furnish information for its teaching staff. Organizations responsible for this veto of a study of the United Nations and its agencies are The Liberty Bells, The Daughters of the American Revolution, and The Minute Women of the U.S.A., Incorporated.

selection of textbooks as unanimously adopted by the Denver School Board in December, 1952. No textbook or other instructional material, declared this Board, might be used unless it was first established that its "author supports the principles of American Constitutional government" and "the nature and content of the material are consistent with the principles of American Constitutional government."

Of these trends, George F. Kennan, former ambassador of the United States to Russia, was moved to remark:

> I have lived more than ten years of my life in totalitarian countries. I know where this sort of thing leads. I know it to be the most shocking and cynical disservice one can do to the credulity and to the spiritual equilibrium of one's fellow men. . . .
>
> In this way, we begin to draw about ourselves a cultural curtain similar in some respects to the Iron Curtain of our adversaries. In doing so, we tend to inflict upon ourselves a species of cultural isolation and provincialism wholly out of accord with the traditions of our Nation and destined, if unchecked, to bring to our intellectual and artistic life the same sort of sterility from which the cultural world of our Communist adversaries is already suffering.[19]

Continuing Effects of Attacks Upon the Schools

Periods of hysteria come and go. Unfortunately, however, their aftereffects are not always healthy. The number of teachers in American schools whom the patriotic groups succeeded in identifying not merely as Communists but, as Senator McCarthy phrased it, those "who think as communists," was small indeed; but the procedures employed in searching them out and depriving them of their positions have tended to weaken instruction and to deprive young people of the opportunity to develop that intellectual discipline which comes only from wrestling with problems to which the immediate answers are unknown. Indeed, there is evidence of a cultural lag on the part of the schools. Outside educational institutions, the courts have rendered a number of significant decisions designed to reaffirm the constitutional guarantees of freedom of thought and expression. Consequently, there

---

[19] From an address delivered on May 15, 1953 at the University of Notre Dame, on the occasion of the dedication of the new I. A. O'Shaughnessy Hall of Liberal and Fine Arts.

has come about an obvious relaxation in the public mind that permits a freedom of thought and expression which once seemed on the point of eclipse. Within the field of education, however, this is less evident.

Writing in 1951, the Committee on Tenure and Academic Freedom of the National Education Association stated that the "Presence in the school curriculum of items to which a partisan group is sensitive" is causing a greater degree of voluntary censorship than ever before." The committee asserted further "that voluntary censorship by administration and teachers—to avoid conflict with groups—is far more insidious than the overt acts of boards and legislatures."

These statements describe the situation of some years ago. But who will say that they are completely inaccurate as of today? Nor should we forget that restrictive acts of boards of education and state legislatures with respect to the selection of textbooks and teaching materials, in many instances, remain unrescinded and thus continue to influence the function of teaching.

Suggested Reading

Alberty, Harold, and others, *Lets Look At Our Schools* (Columbus, Ohio: Ohio State University, 1951).

Association for Supervision and Curriculum Development, *Forces Affecting American Education* (Washington, D.C.: National Education Association, 1953), chaps. III, VI.

Bestor, Arthur E., *Educational Wastelands: The Retreat from Learning in Our Public Schools* (Urbana, Illinois: University of Illinois Press, 1953).

Burton, William, "Get the Facts: Both Ours and the Other Fellows," *Progressive Education,* January, 1952, pp. 82–90.

Haefner, John H., "The Battle of the Books," *N.E.A. Journal,* April, 1953, pp. 227–228.

Hook, Sidney, "Can We Trust Our Teachers?" *Saturday Review,* April 18, 1953, pp. 11 ff.

Melby, Ernest, and Morton Pruner, *Freedom and Public Education* (New York: Frederick A. Praeger, Inc., 1953).

Scott, C. Winfield, and Clyde M. Hill, *Education Under Criticism* (New York: Prentice-Hall, Inc., 1954).

Thayer, V. T., *Public Education and Its Critics* (New York: The Macmillan Co., 1954).

/.V.V.V.\

17

Today's Challenge to Education

The Intellectuals Indict the Schools

In the fall of 1957, Russia succeeded in launching Sputnik I, the first man-made satellite to revolve around the earth. This epoch-making event testified dramatically to advances in education which the Russians had achieved within a few short years and suggested that they were now in the lead of the United States not only in attempts at the "conquest of outer space" but, perhaps, in other significant areas of scientific development as well. This had the effect of fanning into bright flames the smoldering criticisms of public education by influential groups of intellectuals— publicists, journalists, devotees of the liberal arts—who had long contended that the "new education" weakens the intellectual fibre of American youth.

Statistical demonstrations of the fact that the three R's are taught more effectively today than yesterday carry little weight with these critics, since, as Harold W. Dodds, former President of Princeton University, has insisted, public schools "can and should be better; more effective in strengthening and educating the muscles of the mind for leadership toward a stronger and wiser democracy." [1]

---

[1] "Your Youngster and the Public Schools," *The American Magazine,* January, 1954, pp. 15 ff.

Universal Education Is Said to "Sacrifice Quality"

President Dodds is not without appreciation of the contributions of public education or of the complex task which confronts it in this country. He recognizes that with "our wide variety of racial origins and cultural backgrounds, we should be a vastly more divided country today had there been no universal public schools." Nevertheless, he also believes that in performing the essential task of educating young people of all types of mind and cultural background, in ways, often, that reflect the limitations of community sentiment, standards in public education have been lowered. Inadequate salaries and facilities, faith in mass-production methods of instruction, and an anti-intellectual philosophy of education contribute to the same result. In consequence, work is geared to the slow or to those of low ability and the "above average student, and often the average student, finds himself spending long periods marking time."

In contrast with the relatively sober and thoughtful criticisms of President Dodds are the more extreme indictments of an Albert Lynd, an Arthur Bestor, and a Dorothy Thompson.[2] Writing in the *Ladies Home Journal* for February, 1953, Miss Thompson asserts that popular education has deteriorated, classroom behavior and discipline has worsened, and children are not learning what they should. In her judgment the subject matter of instruction and methods employed in schools of today are less valid than those of a generation or two ago. Accordingly, she pleads for a return to the simpler curriculum characteristic of her day on the assumption that education is concerned with the training of the faculties of the mind, and these faculties, essentially the same for all children, are best developed when resort is had to the materials and methods that have "stood the test of ever-changing time."

The Educators Accused of Corrupting Education

This emphasis upon both a philosophy and a psychology of educa-

---

[2] Albert Lynd, *Quackery in the Public Schools* (Boston: Little, Brown & Co., 1953); Arthur Bestor, *Educational Wastelands: The Retreat from Learning in Our Public Schools* (Urbana, Illinois: University of Illinois Press, 1953); John Keats, *Schools Without Scholars* (Boston: Houghton Mifflin Co., 1958); H. G. Rickover, *Education and Freedom* (New York: E. P. Dutton & Co., Inc., 1959).

tion which hardly accords with the results of scientific research can, perhaps, be excused in a Dorothy Thompson. It is more surprising to encounter an identical thesis in the writings of professional scholars. *Educational Wastelands,* written by Arthur Bestor, Jr., of the University of Illinois, is a violent indictment of education as now carried on in public schools and of the "anti-intellectual" influence of the "educationalists"—a term Bestor applies to the faculties of schools of education, superintendents and principals and local administrators of schools, and the "bureaucrats" in state departments of education and the United States Office of Education. "On every hand," he cries,

there is evidence of the debasement which the teaching profession is undergoing at the hands of the interlocking directorate of professional educationists. Forced to undergo the humiliation of piling up credits in sterile courses in pedagogy, virtually forbidden to align himself with scholars and scientists in his chosen field, ceaselessly indoctrinated in an "official" educational philosophy, subjected to minute control and supervision by a professional educational hierarchy, the public school teacher cannot hope to resist administrative dictation or to secure a real voice in the formation of educational policy. Though large numbers of able teachers oppose the anti-intellectual trend in education that is so obvious today, they are powerless to do anything about it. The educational directorate has seen to that. . . .

Across the educational world today stretches an iron curtain which the professional educationists are busily fashioning. Behind it, in slave-labor camps, are the classroom teachers, whose only hope of rescue is from without. . . . American intellectual life is threatened because the first twelve years of formal schooling in the United States are putting more and more completely under the policy-making control of a new breed of educator who has no real place in it—who does not respect and is not respected by—the world of scientists, scholars and professionals.[3]

Bestor's remedy is the familiar one of avoiding the evils of one extreme by rebounding violently to another. The preparation of teachers at present, he feels, is lopsided. It overemphasizes pedagogical training and shortchanges academic education in the

---

[3] Bestor, *op. cit.,* pp. 120–121.

fields the student expects to teach. Therefore, argues Bestor, reduce departments of education to what amounts to a single chair in pedagogy (concerned, evidently, with the psychology of learning, classroom methods, teaching, and the "adapting of instruction to students of differing intellectual capacity") and lodge all other responsibilities in a Faculty of Teacher Training consisting of members of the academic departments of the college of liberal arts.

Bestor would also reduce conventional requirements in the preparation of teachers, which, he believes, now emphasize unduly pedagogical training and deny to students adequate preparation in subjects they expect to teach.

Following the appearance of Sputnik I, both the indictment and the remedy as proposed by Bestor became headline items in the daily newspapers and received generous space in the country's leading magazines.[4] Typical of these renewed attacks were the remarks of Professor Merle A. Tuve of the Carnegie Institute of Technology. According to Professor Tuve, a decision on the part of school boards and state legislatures to eliminate requirements in educational psychology, practice teaching, and similar subjects as a requirement for the certification of teachers "would have great effect in strengthening our schools."[5]

Professor Karl Bigelow of Teachers College, Columbia University, was quick to answer Professor Tuve. In a letter to *The New York Times* on March 30, 1958, Bigelow pointed out that "the number of semester hours in professional courses, including student teaching, required for certification ranges from twelve (four states) to twenty-seven (one state), with eighteen (twenty-one states) the most usual figure, and the average as 18.9. The average requirement, 18.9 is 15.2 per cent of the average total 124."

Many who believe that teacher training institutions would do well to review their offerings will, nevertheless, agree with Bigelow's conclusion that it is not excessive "to expect a prospective teacher to devote 15.2 per cent of four or five years of college work to considering what education is for, what adolescents are

---

[4] An illustration of this unusual generosity is an article by Lydia Stout entitled, "What Strangles American Teaching," *The Atlantic Monthly*, April, 1958, pp. 59–63.
[5] In an address delivered at St. Albans School, Washington, D.C., as reported in *The Washington Post and Times Herald* for March 25, 1958, as well as in *The New York Times* and other widely read newspapers.

like and how learning may be promoted, and to trying their teaching wings under expert supervision."

Competition with Russia Reveals a Neglect of Science and Mathematics

Scientific progress in Russia has also drawn public attention to the comparative emphasis upon science and mathematics in the public schools of these two nations. On first view, this comparison is far from favorable to the United States. For example, it has been pointed out that a graduate from a Russian high school has studied physics for five years, chemistry for four years, biology for five years, astronomy for one year, mathematics for ten years (including trigonometry) and foreign language for five years.[6] In contrast, the American high school operates on an elective system which permits even students who plan to attend college to study no more than one year of science and two years of mathematics above the offerings in the elementary school. Moreover, it is charged, so low have mathematics and science fallen in the esteem of students in high school that only 12 per cent study algebra and geometry; 9 per cent, chemistry; and less than 5 per cent, physics.

These figures have been challenged by the Educational Policies Commission of the National Education Association,[7] which quotes data gathered by the United States Office of Education to the effect that in 1956–1957, 65 per cent of all ninth grade pupils studied algebra; 41.6 per cent of all tenth grade pupils, geometry; 70 per cent of the upper half of eleventh grade pupils, chemistry; and 50 per cent of the entire upper half of twelfth grade enrollment, physics.[8]

There is little disposition on the part of educators to be satisfied with the status of science and mathematics in American schools. Even when made available to students, these subjects are all too frequently assigned to teachers who are inadequately prepared to teach them. "According to data from the Research Division of the

---

[6] For a description of the offerings in Russian schools, see *Soviet Commitment to Education*, Report of the First Official U.S. Education Mission to the U.S.S.R. (Washington, D.C.: United States Office of Education, Bulletin, 1959, No. 16).

[7] "The Contemporary Challenge to American Education," *N.E.A. Journal*, March, 1958, pp. 188–200.

[8] *Ibid.*, p. 198.

National Education Association," writes the Educational Policies Commission,

American high schools employed about 5,000 new teachers of mathematics in 1956–1957. For these positions, the institutions in which teachers are educated had graduated some 2,500 persons qualified to teach mathematics, of whom only about 1,700 entered teaching. In 1956–1957, 5,500 new teachers of science were employed by American high schools, altho the higher institutions had graduated only 4,320 qualified to teach science. On the whole, the best prepared gravitated to the schools which offered the best salaries and best working conditions. The under-prepared will doubtless be found in schools which already suffer from other educational deficiencies.[9]

It would be a mistake to appraise the importance of science and mathematics exclusively from the standpoint of defense or competition between the United States and other nations for positions of influence abroad. For some time economists have been calling attention to the phenomenal increase in middle-class occupations in this country which owe their origin to what Sumner Slichter terms the "new industry of discovery"—occupations related to the emergence of ever new processes and new products. These new occupations require of their participants not only vocational skill, narrowly conceived, but a level of educated intelligence, or general education, more exacting than that possessed by the run-of-the-mine individual in the past. Closely related to these new trends is the rapid elimination of unskilled labor.

All this suggests new demands upon the school curriculum and better provision in the future than in the past for the education of all American youth—the able, the mediocre, and the dull. Consequently, any suggestions made out of a sincere desire to render the curriculum more relevant to the needs of the times merits careful consideration. Obviously, too, failure on the part of the schools to stimulate the gifted to make full use of their talents in ways beneficial to themselves and their society can be serious.

Unfortunately, as we saw in Chapter 7, there is substance to these criticisms. It will be recalled, for example, that Havighurst and Rodgers conclude, after thorough investigation, that 60 per cent of superior youth fail to continue with their education after

---

[9] *Ibid.*, p. 195.

graduation from high school. Twenty per cent of this group do so for lack of financial resources and 40 per cent for lack of motivation. In February, 1958, a committee of the American Association of School Administrators submitted a report to its parent body entitled, *"The High School in a Changing World."* In submitting this report, the committee pointed out that between June and September, 1957, more than 200,000 high school seniors in the top 30 per cent of their classes failed to go on to college.

Critics Claim the Curriculum Is Out of Joint

Plainly, then, the times suggest a re-evaluation of the curriculum of the schools so that shortcomings may be identified and corrected. Since education is both a first line of defense from enemies abroad and an indispensable condition of well-being at home, everything hinges upon the manner in which schools measure up to the tasks assigned to them. But this suggests, as well, the critical importance of accurately identifying mistakes and proposing appropriate remedies. Criticism, if relevant, should be responsible. Superficiality in analysis and hasty conclusions in the way of recommendations for change might well be fatal.

Unfortunately, it is superficial analysis and hasty prescription that most easily catch public attention. Nor is criticism limited to irresponsible voices. Laymen, as well as scholars, who would not venture to pass judgment on matters in the field of their speciality without adequate supporting data, do not hesitate to speak with authority on the work of the public schools. What follows is a sampling of criticisms made within a few short months of the spectacular launching of Sputnik I and II.

As with one voice, "responsible" critics condemn the curriculum of school and college as this has developed over the past fifty years. Both in subject matter and in method, it is said, the energies of our young people have been misdirected, with the result that our schools are fiddling while Rome burns.

Nor do these critics find it difficult to identify the basic cause for this tragic misdirection of emphasis. It is the educational philosophy of John Dewey, with its false emphasis upon "life adjustment" education, which has brought about "the crisis in public education today." This from no less an authority than the

former Attorney General of the United States, James P. Mc-
Granery, in an address at Mount St. Mary's College, marking the
150th Anniversary of that institution.[10] It is this philosophy, our
prosecuting attorney contends, which has produced "shallow
citizens with flabby minds, tragically ill-fitted to meet the stern
challenges of leadership." It is this philosophy, too, which we
should hold responsible for the fact that during the past forty
years, substandard curricula have been directed by educators
whose methodology has far out-distanced their knowledge of subjects taught. Nor can we hope to better the situation with higher
salaries. The "erroneous philosophy" must first be cast out.

The indictment of John Dewey is, of course, not original with
Mr. McGranery. John Dewey has long been a whipping horse in
educational discussions. But if one is honestly attempting to
appraise trends in contemporary education and John Dewey's
relation to them, should we not expect him to read what Dewey
has written? In so doing, he might discover that mastering Dewey's
thought is in itself a fairly effective cure for flabby-mindedness!
Certainly he would learn that no one has condemned a superficial
emphasis upon life adjustment more vigorously than John Dewey.
Perhaps he would conclude as well that those who accuse Dewey
of indifference to intellectual discipline are not unlike the critics
of Spinoza who charged that philosopher with atheism at one and
the same time that many, who knew him better, described him as
a god-intoxicated man. So it is with Dewey and education for
intelligence!

But let us continue with our critics.

Some Say Our Youth Have Become "Soft"

A second cause for misdirection in education results from a deplorable "softness" in our young people and a general tendency to
avoid the hard. Not only have we rendered too easy the curriculum of the schools, but, complains Claude Feuss, former headmaster of Philips Academy at Andover, we have been voting ourselves and our children longer and longer holidays "at precisely
the moment when we need to utilize more profitably all the time
available." So enervated have we become by prosperity, continues

---

[10] Reported in *The Washington Post and Times Herald,* April 13, 1958.

Feuss, that even in the field of sports, according to an authority whom he quotes approvingly, "athletic clubs are vanishing because the average boy 'won't stick to anything tough.' " [11]

American Schools Are Viewed As Inferior to Their European Counterparts

Under these conditions, in the eyes of our critics, American schools afford a sorry comparison with their European counterparts. In the European school, serious intellectual work goes on, uncorrupted by pupil choice or an adaptation of the curriculum to individual differences. In Europe, also, subjects are studied in their logical and natural sequence, whereas the curriculum in this country is unplanned and illogical, according to Professor Marc Raeff, Associate Professor at Clark University.

Our high schools are like cafeteria, offering discrete fragments of modern knowledge, not related to each other, not grounded in any serious common foundation, and changing their "bill of fare" at every twist and turn of popular fad and fashion. From a disparate array ranging from accounting to zoology, the student is asked to make his selection. . . . [He] can take most courses in any order he wants. So it may happen that he takes chemistry before physics, or physics without grounding in mathematics, or makes a chronological jumble of history courses. Taking up an ill-assorted, disconnected set of subjects every year, the student's attention is never called to the common foundations and the essential problems of each; his mental energy is dispersed as he switches rapidly from one field to the other, without stopping long enough to master any thoroughly.[12]

Professor Raeff does not inform his readers how many secondary schools he visited in the United States as a basis for this indictment of their curricula.

What one misses in comparisons of American with European schools, particularly with those of England and France, is any serious attempt to weigh the comparative merits of a system of education based upon a rigid selection of students and of cur-

---

[11] "Money Is Not Enough," *Saturday Review*, February 1, 1958, pp. 8–12.
[12] "We Do Not Teach Them How to Think," *New York Times Magazine*, January 26, 1958, p. 58.

ricula keyed to the education of an elite group and the American effort to serve all youth in a democratically constituted student body. Do we wish, for example, to adopt a plan of selection, now under severe attack in England, which virtually determines for young people at the age of eleven or twelve what careers shall be open or closed to them? [13] Again, should we not ask ourselves how wise it is to concentrate upon the education of an elite to such an extent that no more than 10 per cent of all young people above the age of sixteen continue with their education in contrast with approximately 70 per cent in the United States? May not this failure to provide more generously for the 90 per cent in England and France constitute a road block to progress, in the light of changes in economic society to which we have called attention above?

Byron S. Hollinshead remarks in this connection that the training of an echelon of workers and citizens below the level of the elite is "desperately important in all fields of endeavor if a civilization is to advance." Indeed, he goes on to say, it is this lack of training of the masses which retards the social, economic, and political development in what are called the undeveloped countries. "The leaders are there. It is the trained followers who are lacking." [14]

Before Americans decide to scrap their educational system and adopt a European model, it might be well for them to ask the question, "How valid is the assumption that the exclusively academic and highly pressurized education we are asked to admire, yields in the end a type of mind and personality superior to the American product? Are the able students of European schools actually superior as adults in originality and flexibility of thought, in adaptability to changing conditions, and in the fruits of their research?" [15]

---

[13] See in this connection, George Z. Bereday, "Equal Opportunity and Comprehensive Schools in England," *Educational Forum*, January, 1958, pp. 133–138.

[14] Byron S. Hollinshead, "Is European Education Better?" (Washington, D.C.: American Council on Education), p. 2. Reprinted from the *Educational Record* of April, 1958.

[15] Hollinshead writes: "What the more exact critics say is that the European schoolboy is further advanced in mathematics, physics, and chemistry at a certain age than his American counterpart. Let us grant the truth of this, although it is equally true that the American youngster is more advanced in certain other respects. To be fair, the question of comparison should be as follows: In a certain

A negative reply to the above is not the equivalent of saying that all is well in our own garden. A curriculum designed to serve different interests and abilities requires, by its very nature, experts in guidance who will help young people to choose their courses wisely and encourage them to work up to the full level of their ability. In this respect, as in many others, we are sadly wanting in personnel. No doubt, too, the full potentialities of subjects taught remain unexploited in American schools; although we might do well to ascertain whether this follows from an inability to man classrooms with adequately trained teachers or from the design of the curriculum.

It is also possible to grant that young people in this country should be spurred on to greater effort without accepting the attendant assumption that this can best be done by adopting wholly the point of view of a recent French report on education: *"L'œuvre d'éducation consiste essentiellement à transmettre aux générations l'héritage des civilisations passées."* Or one need not agree that the picture "of the French youngster hurrying home from school each day to sit over his homework long into the night, learning under his mother's tutelage the same things she learned a generation before—Latin, Greek, the history of the French kings, German and English, mathematics and science" is the most healthy of educational pictures. To quote once again from Hollinshead, "One can be lost in admiration for the hard work and high standards involved in this program, without believing that rote learning and a heavy emphasis on past civilizations constitute the best preparation for solving modern problems." [16] There is some basis, moreover, for questioning whether working under intense strain in adolescence, in a highly charged academic atmosphere, is better for the academically gifted than an opportunity to browse widely, with some ease and freedom, and to sample numerous fields, including the nonacademic. The truth is that we have altogether too little data on these matters, although we are not

---

subject, say mining engineering, at the end of the course, say at age twenty-two, are European students of a given native ability better prepared in their field than American students of the same native ability? This would be a very hard question to answer because the European might be ahead in some respects, the American in others, but the question does, at least, indicate how difficult such comparisons are" (*ibid.*, p. 4).

[16] *Ibid.*, p. 3.

without evidence of the sad effects upon precocious youths in late adolescence of early excessive pressure. Perhaps a wise course lies somewhere between European and American practice in dealing with gifted youth. But, once more, let us not identify the determination to employ the talents of gifted youth more wisely than at present with the overly simplified dictum of "more hard work in education." The latter, as a motive, easily becomes a cloak with which to hide poor teaching. Competent teachers encounter little difficulty in enlisting the active cooperation of young people in their education. What is more characteristic, indeed, of youth than continuous, even passionate concentration upon projects which hypnotize them with their interest?

We Have Strayed Away from the Valid Education of Yesterday It is Claimed

Closely allied with groups who paint the virtues of European education are those who would have schools revert to a curriculum similar to that which prevailed some two hundred years ago. One of the chief spokesmen for this group is Mortimer Adler. Adler and his colleagues are less frank today in their criticisms of an overemphasis on science than were they some years ago, but they still insist that science is merely an instrument and only those who are disciplined in the liberal arts are competent to use this instrument wisely. Similarly, they oppose education for life-adjustment. "With all of this talk about 'life adjustment' and 'preparation for life,' " writes Adler, "that is precisely what our schools are not doing. We have not adjusted their programs to the demands of life in an industrial society in which it is possible for all men to live as only the few could live in the past." [17]

Adler would evidently have our schools reverse the trend of recent years in the direction of diversified curricula and provide for all youth what he terms a "liberal schooling." By a "liberal schooling," Adler means "precisely what was understood by it in our colonial schools and colleges, which produced such men as Alexander Hamilton, James Madison, John Jay, Jefferson, John

---

[17] Mortimer Adler, "Pre-Sputnik Ills Now Come to Light: We Fail to Honor Learning and Leisure," *The Washington Post and Times Herald*, April 6, 1958. Reprinted from *The Chicago Sun-Times*.

Adams and all the others who were the founders and statesmen and first citizens of our Republic."

The suggestion that our schools and colleges return to the curriculum of the past is interesting in that one of its professed objectives is to better the scholarship standing of American schools. Nevertheless, it rests upon two false assumptions, both of which offend against scholarship. One is that the schools and colleges of the colonial period did in fact afford students a liberal education superior to the present. The truth is that their offerings were most meager. The only subjects required for admission to American colleges, for example, prior to 1800, were Latin, Greek, and arithmetic.[18]

This is not to disparage the education of Jefferson, John Adams, and others, but, rather, to call attention to the fact that their intellectual interests were aroused and sustained more by what the schools and colleges of their day failed to include in the curriculum (especially science and mathematics) than what they offered to their students.

Incidentally, too, it is well to observe that the phrases, "liberal arts" and "liberal schooling" are far from clear in what they denote. As employed in contemporary discussion, one is led to believe they apply to a specific content and to a specific discipline which derives from this specific subject matter. On the contrary, if anything, it is the name only which is constant. The actual content of the trivium and the quadrivium, which, we are told, constitute "the sole valid content of an education today as yesterday," has undergone significant change in the course of the centuries.

Secondly, Adler's contention that a sound education is one identical for all runs counter to contemporary findings in psychology. What he proposes is, in fact, to substitute one serious error for another. Today's schools commonly offend by subjecting the able, the mediocre, and the dull to a diet appropriate to the two latter groups. Adler would remedy this situation by requiring all students to accept what best suits the able on the theory that what is appropriate or fitting for the academically minded is most worth while for all others!

---

[18] Elmer Ellsworth Brown, *The Making Of Our Middle Schools* (New York: Longmans, Green & Co., Inc., 1914), p. 231.

A pertinent refutation of this position comes from Rear Admiral Hyman G. Rickover, although the words quoted were directed not at Adler and his thesis but at the comprehensive high school, which the Admiral mistakenly assumes provides an identical education for all levels of ability: "A school system which insists on the same instruction for the talented, the average, and the below-average child prevents as many children from growing intellectually as does a system that excludes children because of the social, political, or economic status of their parents. Neither system is democratic." [19]

Some Basic Considerations

It is not sufficient, however, to point out the inadequacies of contemporary criticisms of the schools or the limitations in remedies proposed. The times require a clarification, if possible, of the purposes of education in a democracy. This a number of organizations have attempted to do in the course of the past two decades, as, for example, the Educational Policies Commission of the National Education Association, the American Association of School Administrators, the Association for Supervision and Curriculum Development of the National Education Association, and numerous other groups which speak from both a sense of responsibility and intimate acquaintance with the ongoing work of the schools.[20] An interesting illustration of a contribution from sources not fully exploited is a report prepared by twenty-three members of the faculty of Cornell University in Ithaca, New York, for the public schools of Ithaca. This committee originated out of local concern for an accelerated course in science, in the light of the assumed superiority of Russian education in science. In answering

---

[19] An address delivered at the inauguration of Dr. Ernest Weber as President of Brooklyn Polytechnic Institute and reported in *The New York Times*, April 20, 1958. See also, *Education and Freedom* (New York: E. P. Dutton and Company, 1959), p. 155. For a better informed appraisal of the American comprehensive high school, see James Conant's *The American High School Today* (New York: McGraw-Hill Book Company, 1959), Section II.

[20] See, for example, *Policies for Education in American Democracy* (1945) and the more recent statement on "The Contemporary Challenge to American Education" (1958) by the Educational Policies Commission of the National Education Association. See also *The High School in the Changing World*, Thirty-sixth Yearbook of the American Association of School Administrators, 1958, and the yearbooks of the Association for Supervision and Curriculum Development.

the specific inquiry directed to it, the committee stated, "our greatest need is not a special program which will put a few exceptional students in college a year earlier but one which will substantially increase the quality and extent of preparation for college work of all college candidates and particularly of those of outstanding ability." [21] By this, however, the committee does not mean one curriculum for all students. Instead, it suggests for junior and senior high schools a basic course, a course for prospective science majors, and a course for prospective majors in the humanities.

A Differentiated Curriculum Is Essential

The precise nature of differentiation in the curriculum of the secondary school will differ appropriately with localities and the composition of student bodies, but the conviction that equality of opportunity spells differentiation rather than uniformity in education would appear to be an established principle in American education, a principle that applies both to content and to method. Take, for example, the acknowledged necessity that our schools provide more adequately than at present for the gifted student. Were the schools to identify giftedness with academic ability alone, serious results might follow. Modern society is highly diversified and requires for its continued progress the contributions of many types of ability. Consequently, to key instruction of the gifted exclusively to the admitted needs of the academically and verbally proficient or to gather in the academically gifted alone, on the assumption that we have thus identified the gifted, would fall short of what is essential in order to serve better the pathfinders of tomorrow.

What we have said of giftedness in general is equally true within a specific field. Take, for example, the contemporary concern for more adequate provision for science and mathematics. Obviously, these subjects should be taught so as to attract and to stimulate students who are to man our research laboratories in both pure and applied science. But the science which beckons the future research worker is by no means identical with that required

---

[21] This report is summarized by Gene Currivan in his column "Education in Review," *The New York Times*, February 23, 1958.

for the more practical-minded farmer or engineer. Nor is it identical with the science which all students need to understand and to direct their lives in ways relevant to a world permeated with the applications of science.

Science Has a Unique Contribution to Make

It is unfortunate that in discussions of the place of science and mathematics in the schools, little, if any, mention is made of the potential contributions of science to an intellectual and moral discipline appropriate to today's world. Rather is science thought of as a "mere instrument" or a form of magic which enables the initiated to create gadgets and to bring forth rare inventions. This is to neglect the one contribution of science in which young people on all levels of ability and all types of mind should share in common, namely, a disciplined way of thinking which serves not only as an effective tool in the solution of problems but as a way of thinking and a way of living that have profound implications for democracy.

It is often said that a democratic society is an open society—that progress in all significant areas of living depends upon the assured right to freedom of thought and expression. Now, for both the formulation and the application of the principle of free inquiry we are heavily indebted to the example of the scientific community. In this community, dissent from established truth or the projection of a new idea is viewed as a stimulus to progress, not as heresy to be suppressed or repelled. In the scientific community, also, the principle that conflicts are best resolved through the use of rational methods of discussion and investigation has long been an axiom. That is to say, for the scientist, it is not authority, tradition, or superior force that determines the truth or the validity of an idea but its relevance to the circumstances or the context in which it arises, its implications and consequences in the deepest and fullest sense of that word. In short, in science, there is no better test than "By their fruits, ye shall know them."

Similarly, other characteristics of science as a method of thinking have relevant implications for relations between people. Over and above its applications in a specific field (characteristics which John Dewey has described in his *How We Think*) science, as a method, has developed methods of procedure which go far to implement the democratic ideal.

Traditionally, both the subject matter and methods of instruction in our schools have been keyed to the imparting of facts and principles already salted down. More and more, however, we find ourselves today in the position of the college student serving as a guide to an "old grad," who, in a sentimental mood, had decided upon a visit to his alma mater. After visiting one after another of his favorite haunts, he bethought himself to inquire of his former teachers and, in particular, of a professor of economics. "Oh," replied the student, "he is still teaching, and he continues to ask the same ten questions in his final examinations."

"That should make it easy for you," commented the older person. "All you have to do, is to remember the questions and 'bone up' on the answers."

"Well, it is not quite so simple as that," replied the student ruefully. "You see, the old boy studies the trends and changes the answers!"

To study the trends and to change the answers, including some of the major premises that have come down to us, is one of the imperatives of modern life. Moreover, for our schools to fail to impart this discipline to the young is more serious today than yesterday, in view of the trends in economic and social life to which we called attention in Chapter 6. There, it will be recalled, we pointed out that for a steadily increasing proportion of our youth, schooling has come to replace responsible participation in life outside the school.

In the past, participation in economic and social activities of home and community provided an intellectual discipline which tended to offset and correct a one-sided emphasis within the school. In a homogeneous and relatively unchanging society, one generation can reap and sow in accordance with precepts and principles derived from past experience. This is also true of the conduct of a business or a profession and the practical affairs of life. In each of these areas the major premises and the valid ways of procedure are known and can be conveyed to the young with a sense of assurance.

But neither time nor place of residence remain unchanged for Americans. They have been and still are a mobile people. As they moved west and encountered new conditions of soil and climate and ways of life, success turned ever upon the ability and the willingness to seek out, to test, and to live by new principles and to modify and revise old established truths. Progress, in short, has been due not only to the fortunate circumstance of ever new resources to exploit but, in large measure as well, to the willingness of the American people to employ the methods of experimental thinking. Methods, however, which life outside the school rather than the discipline from within imparted to young people.

Today, the opportunities for young people to acquire this discipline outside the school are less common than yesterday. Consequently, the school, as a supplementary institution, is called upon to key its instruction, not only in science but in other relevant areas as well, to the facts of change.

Criticism As a Questioning of Basic Assumptions

From this survey of public education under fire, it would appear that the critics of the schools are concerned less with the inhibiting conditions under which public schools are operating today (inadequate building facilities, unattractive salaries for teachers, the lack of esteem in which the profession of teaching is held, large classes, limited financial resources, etc.) and more with the validity of certain basic assumptions which have given character to education in the United States. As an introduction to chapters to follow, it may be helpful to review these assumptions.

First is the assumption that both private and public education realize their unique functions best when private schools receive their support solely from private sources and public funds are used exclusively for public education.

This principle dates from the beginnings of public education in this country. Although it is true that in the eyes of many today this principle derives its strength from the interpretation which the United States Supreme Court has given to the First Amendment to the federal Constitution, its origin and general adoption resulted from painful experience of the states with public support of nonpublic schools. As Justice Frankfurter remarked in *Mc-Collum* v. *Board of Education* (Champaign, Illinois), "Separation in the field of education . . . was not imposed upon unwilling states by superior law. In this respect the Fourteenth Amendment merely reflected a principle then dominant in our national life. To the extent that the Constitution thus made it binding upon the States, the basis of the restriction is the whole experience of our people."

Today, however, this basic assumption is questioned on the theory that insofar as Congress and state legislature are enjoined to "pass no law respecting an establishment of religion," this prohibition was intended to do no more than to forbid government from assisting one religion to the exclusion of others and was in no sense designed to prohibit the extension of aid to all religions on an "equal and fair" basis. Finally, it is also questioned as a matter of public policy by religious organizations which are finding it increasingly difficult to finance church schools out of their own resources, as well as by what seems to be an increasing number of individuals and groups who no longer share the conviction of the founders of public education that a free education is an indispensable condition of perpetuating a free society.

A second assumption defines the task of the school in areas of controversy and doubt and on matters in which a community is not of one mind. No one has formulated this principle of procedure more clearly than Charles W. Eliot in his inaugural address as President of Harvard College in 1869. In the course of a review of the educational values implicit within the main branches of learning, he comes to the "philosophical subjects." These, he insists, should never be taught with authority. "They are not the established sciences; they are full of disputed matters, open questions, and bottomless speculations. It is not the function of the teacher to settle philosophical and political controversies for the pupil, or even to recommend to him any one set of opinions as better than another. Exposition, not imposition of opinions is the professor's part. The student should be made acquainted with all sides of these controversies, with the salient points of each system. . . . The very word education is a standing protest against dogmatic teaching." [22]

---

[22] Charles W. Eliot, *Educational Reform: Essays and Addresses* (New York: The Century Co., 1898), pp. 7-8.

Few would contend that this principle has found consistent application in dealing with problems upon which the public is as a house divided against itself, but despite distortion and open violation, it has nonetheless remained a fixed star by reference to which good teachers have sought to direct their course. It is also an ideal that elicits the support of American communities once the issues become clear and they are asked to decide between education and indoctrination. But it is precisely in times of crisis, when waves of fear and hysteria seep through the country, that it easily becomes blurred.

Still a third principle of public education is designed to insure equality of education opportunity to the children of all the people, despite differences in economic circumstance, race, nationality, creed, or, indeed, any characteristic other than those which call for general attention in order to insure an open door to talent and ability.

General realization of the implications for democracy of equality in education has led to the substitution of the multiple-track and enriched curriculum for the narrow, single-track curriculum of an earlier day. It has also led to efforts on both state and national levels to offset the disadvantages that weigh upon children in states of low income through the creation of equalization funds and grants of federal aid. Repudiation of the principle of equality, in turn, explains the contrast that may be found all too frequently between the educational opportunities available to residents in a wealthy neighborhood and those afforded poorer districts of the same community or state, or between white schools and Negro schools, where segregation is a persistent pattern.

Attacks upon this principle are seldom made openly, a fact which testifies to its potential and inherent vitality. For example, it is easier for those who oppose increasing school budgets designed to provide for greater equality in education to contend that "progressive education costs too much" than to face squarely the question, "Shall this community guarantee to its minorities educational facilities equal to those possessed by the majority?" It is easier to assert that the curriculum of the school is robbing the home of its legitimate functions than to discuss frankly and openly the wisdom of providing courses in home economics, child care, or ample facilities for creative opportunities in art, crafts, music, and recreational activities. Or, again, it is easier to proclaim that the schools of today are "keeping young people in school too long for their own good" than to face realistically what fruitful alternatives are open to young people other than prolonged schooling in view of the steady exclusion of these same young people from healthy responsibilities of an economic and social character in home and community.

Here as elsewhere, however, the choice is not always one between pure white and pitch black. Nor are the dictates of equality at all times easy to interpret. How, for example, in constructing the school budget, shall we balance the necessity of providing an open road for talent and ability through adequate provision for the gifted against the equally important objective of prolonging the education of all in order to close the vicious gap between the age at which universal education commonly ends and employment opportunities of a promising character begin? Differences of judgment between people who are equally devoted to the principle of equality seem to be inevitable.

Conflicting interpretations of equality likewise emerge from differences of philosophy. Does equality in education imply an identical curriculum for all, as Mortimer Adler, Robert M. Hutchins, and others insist, or does it suggest adapting the curriculum to the child from the first to the last day of his schooling?

Questions of this character are involved in our last assumption. This relates to the supplementary function of the school, to which we gave attention in Chapter 3. Schools are the institutional expressions of attempts on the part of a community to provide for the young through cooperative and associated action experiences which parents and guardians cannot provide individually.

As we observed earlier, what constitutes an essential supplementation to education in home and community varies with time and circumstance. In a homogeneous society there is little disagreement on what and how to teach. Tradition and unchallenged practice tend to confirm both subject matter and the conceptions of learning which find expression in methods employed. But when rural life gives way to urban life and urban influences and cultural uniformity yields to plurality of cultural patterns, the functions of the school both lose their onetime clarity and become bones of contention between the partisans of the old and those who would use education to ring in the new.

Here, then, are a few basic principles of American education that are undergoing review, a review rendered both pertinent and imperative by questions such as the following: How shall we interpret the principle of separation of church and state in relation to education? Should we continue to deny public support to nonpublic schools or do new times suggest a return to an earlier policy of "cooperation" between government and religious organizations? Should the public school continue as a secular institution or should religion be made once again to permeate the curriculum? Shall we insist that public education remain true to the principles of freedom of inquiry in dealing with problems on the cutting edge of the future or shall the customer as represented by community sentiment determine what is to be taught? Finally, shall our schools continue to organize the subject matter of instruction in harmony with long-established principles of traditional education or do new times generate both new needs and new ways of meeting these needs?

The chapters that follow will deal with these and related questions in more detail.

Suggested Reading

Bereday, George Z. "Equal Opportunity and Comprehensive Schools in England." *Educational Forum,* January, 1958, pp. 133–138.

Conant, James B. *The American High School Today* (New York: McGraw-Hill Book Co., Inc., 1959).

Educational Policies Commission. "The Contemporary Challenge To American Education." *N.E.A. Journal,* March, 1958, pp. 188 ff.

Feuss, Claude. "Money Is Not Enough." *Saturday Review,* February 1, 1958, pp. 8–12.

Hechinger, Fred M. *The Big Red Schoolhouse* (Garden City, New York: Doubleday Company, Inc., 1959), chaps. 3, 6, 9.

Hollinshead, Byron S. "Is European Education Better?" American Council on Education, 1958. Reprinted from *Educational Record,* April, 1958.

Keats, John. *Schools Without Scholars* (Boston: Houghton Mifflin Co., 1958).

Latimer, John F. *What's Happened To Our High Schools?* (Washington: Public Affairs Press, 1958), chap. 7.

Rickover, H. G. *Education and Freedom* (New York: E. P. Dutton & Co., Inc., 1959), chaps. 1, 7–11.

Thayer, V. T. *Public Education and Its Critics* (New York: The Macmillan Co., 1954).

United States Office of Education. *Soviet Commitment to Education.* Report of the First Official U.S. Education Mission to the U.S.S.R. (Washington, D.C.: United States Office of Education, Bulletin, 1959, No. 16).

Woodring, Paul. *One Fourth of a Nation* (New York: McGraw-Hill Book Co., Inc., 1957).

ᛝᛝᛝ

CHAPTER

18

Church, State, and Public Education

Separation of Church and State As Official Doctrine

In a discourse on religious liberty delivered over a hundred years ago, the distinguished jurist, Jeremiah S. Black stated: "The manifest object of the men who framed the institutions of this country, was to have a state *without religion* and a *Church without politics* —that is to say, they meant that one should never be used as an engine for any purpose of the other. . . . Our fathers seemed to have been perfectly sincere in their belief that the members of the Church would be more patriotic, and the citizens of the State more religious by keeping their respective functions separate. For that reason they built up a wall of complete and perfect partition between the two." [1]

This interpretation of the American principle of separation of church and state was emphatically affirmed by the United States Supreme Court in 1947 and again in 1948. Speaking for the Court in each instance, Justice Hugo Black declared,

Neither a state nor the Federal Government can set up a church. Neither can pass laws which aid one religion, aid all religions, or

---

[1] Quoted by Justice Frankfurter in his concurring opinion in *McCollum* v. *Board of Education,* 333 U.S. 203 (1948). Frankfurter describes Black as "one of the most distinguished of American judges."

prefer one religion over another. Neither can force nor influence a person to go to or to remain away from church against his will or force him to profess a belief or disbelief in any religion. No person can be punished for entertaining or professing religious beliefs or dis- beliefs, for church attendance or non-attendance. No tax in any amount, large or small, can be levied to support any religious activi- ties or institutions, whatever they may be called, or whatever form they may adopt to teach or practice religion. Neither a state nor the Federal Government can, openly or secretly, participate in the affairs of any religious organizations or groups and vice versa. In the words of Jefferson, the clause against establishment of religion by law was intended to erect "a wall of separation between Church and State." [2]

This concept of complete separation of church and state was considerably weakened in its applications to released time pro- grams in religion in a subsequent decision of the Court in *Zorach* v. *Clauson*. In the latter decision the Court sanctioned "adjusting the schedule of public school events to sectarian needs" so as to permit religious organizations to conduct classes in religion on school time but off the school grounds. Contrast, for example, the words quoted above from Judge Jeremiah S. Black with this equally crucial statement of Justice William O. Douglas, who spoke for the Court in the *Zorach* v. *Clauson* case:

When the state encourages religious instruction or cooperates with religious authorities by adjusting the schedule of public events to sec- tarian needs, it follows the best of our traditions. For it then respects the religious nature of our people and accommodates the public serv- ice to their spiritual needs. To hold that it may not would be to find in the Constitution a requirement that the government show a callous indifference to religious groups. That would be preferring those who believe in no religion over those who do believe. Government may not finance religious groups nor undertake religious instruction nor blend secular and sectarian education nor use secular institutions to force one or some religion on any person. But we find no constitutional requirement which makes it necessary for government to be hostile to religion and to throw its weight against efforts to widen the effec- tive scope of religious influence. The government must be neutral when it comes to competition between sects. It may not thrust any

---

[2] In *Everson* v. *Board of Education*, 330 U.S. 1 (1947) and the McCollum case. Attorneys for the state of Illinois in the latter case had requested the Court to declare the statement quoted an *obiter dicta*. It was to deny this request specifically that Justice Black repeated the words quoted.

sect on any person. It may not make a religious observance compulsory. It may not coerce anyone to attend church, to observe a religious holiday, or to take religious instruction. But it can close its doors or suspend its operations as to those who want to repair to their religious sanctuary for worship or instruction. No more than that is undertaken here.[3]

These declarations of principle by the United States Supreme Court have established as national policy (one binding alike upon the states and the federal government) essentially what the states, acting individually and on their own initiative, had previously made as their own policy. As is well known, when the First Amendment to the federal Constitution was adopted, this was in no way binding upon the states. Each member of the Union was left free to determine for itself what should be its relation to religious corporations and, since education was clearly recognized as a state and not a federal function, the definition of the relation of government to public education became a matter of state rather than federal determination.

One of the first states to blaze the trail in definition was Connecticut. In revising its constitution in 1818, Connecticut faced the problem of utilizing funds received from the sale of public lands. Should these be devoted exclusively to the development of public education or should they be used to promote the interests of both public and private schools? The answer given was in harmony with the conviction that both state and church would profit from an absence of dependence upon each other. Accordingly, the constitution provided, first, that the support and maintenance of church buildings and ministers should be "by a tax of the members of any such society only, to be laid by a major vote of the legal voters assembled at any society meeting" and, second, that "the fund, called the School Fund, shall remain a perpetual fund, the interest of which shall be *inviolably appropriated* to the support and encouragement of the public, or common schools, throughout the State . . . and no law shall be made, authorizing said fund to be diverted to any other use than the encouragement and support of public or common schools. . . ."[4]

---

[3] 334 U.S. 306 (1952).
[4] Quoted in Conrad H. Moehlman, *About the Church As Educator* (New York: Hind, Haydon and Eldridge, 1946), p. 7.

Connecticut's example was followed by states in the East as well as by western applicants for admission to the Union, with the result that by the end of the century, all but two states had prohibited by constitutional provision or through legislative act either the teaching of sectarian doctrines in the public schools or the use of public funds for religious schools, or both.[5]

Since these developments antedated the applications of the First Amendment to the states through the Fourteenth Amendment, Justice Frankfurter was moved to remark in *McCollum* v. *Board of Education* that "Separation in the field of education . . . was not imposed upon unwilling States by force of superior law. In this respect the Fourteenth Amendment merely reflected a principle then dominant in our national life. To the extent that the Constitution thus made it binding upon the States, the basis of the restriction is the whole experience of our people."

The First Amendment Is Made Applicable to the States

Although education under the Constitution still remains primarily a state rather than a federal responsibility, the Congress of the United States has on numerous occasions both assisted education in the states and provided for educational projects under the auspices of the federal government. General assistance to education began, in principle at least, under the Continental Congress with a provision in the Ordinance of 1785 that "there shall be reserved the Lot 16 of every township for the maintenance of public schools within said township." Federal assistance has, on the whole, been in accordance with the twofold principle that public funds made available to education shall be used exclusively for public education and that public education shall remain free of sectarian instruction. In line with this policy, Congress in 1896, when appropriating funds for education in the District of Columbia, specifically stated: "And it is hereby declared to be the policy of the Government of the United States to make no appropriation of money or property for the purpose of the founding, maintaining, or aiding by payment for services,

---

[5] See James O'Neill, *Religion and Education Under the Constitution* (New York: Harper & Brothers, 1949), pp. 143–144.

expenses, or otherwise, any church or religious denomination, or any institution of society which is under sectarian or ecclesiastical control. . . ." [6]

Inasmuch as both state and federal governments are directly responsible to the people, it is not surprising to find the two keeping step in matters of supreme concern to the people. Not until well into the present century, however, was it clearly established that an essential agreement on policy in the relation of religion to education was rendered obligatory by the Fourteenth Amendment to the federal Constitution.[7] In 1922, the state of Oregon undertook to require all children to attend public schools. The obvious intention of this legislation was to abolish private schools. The constitutionality of this act was challenged by the Society of the Sisters of the Holy Names of Jesus and Mary, and the case found its way, eventually, into the United States Supreme Court. In rendering its decision, the Court declared that the Oregon statute "unreasonably interferes with the liberty of parents and guardians to direct the upbringing and education of children under their control" and violates the provisions of the Fourteenth Amendment that no state shall "deprive any person of life, liberty, or property, without due process of law. . . ." [8]

After this decision a more specific application of the Bill of Rights in the federal Constitution to the states was inevitable, and in 1925, in the case of *Gitlow* v. *New York,* the Court ruled that the rights of freedom of speech and press "which are protected by the First Amendment from abridgement by Congress—are among the fundamental personal rights and liberties protected by the due process clause of the Fourteenth Amendment from impairment by the States." [9] Subsequent decisions of the Supreme Court have confirmed the principle that the restrictions

---

[6] U.S. Statutes at Large, 29:411 (June 11, 1896). Still again, when passing the Smith-Hughes Act, Congress stipulated: "No portion of any monies appropriated under this act for the benefit of the States shall be applied, directly or indirectly . . . for the support of any religious or privately owned or conducted school or college" [*ibid.,* 39:936 (February 23, 1917)].

[7] For a helpful discussion of the applications of the Fourteenth Amendment to the states in matters of religion, see Alvin W. Johnson and Frank H. Yost, *Separation of Church and State in the United States* (Minneapolis, Minn.: University of Minnesota Press, 1948), chap. I.

[8] *Pierce et al.* v. *Society of Sisters,* 268 U.S. 510 (1925).

[9] 268 U.S. 652 (1925).

placed upon Congress in the First Amendment are now applicable to the states through the Fourteenth.[10] Consequently, when the Court in *Everson* v. *Board of Education* and *McCollum* v. *Board of Education* rendered this fact explicit, it should have caused no surprise.

By way of summary, then, we may say that the principle of separation of church and state in the United States has come to mean the following:

1. Religious convictions and religious organizations are, as James Madison expressed it, "wholly exempt" from "the cognizance of civil society." By this is not meant that government is either indifferent to or hostile to religion, but, rather, that the maintenance and the promotion of religious institutions and the regulation and control over religious ideas are denied to all governmental authority. The religious conscience is thus protected from infringement upon its free exercise, and religious corporations are assured complete freedom to further their doctrines. But the price of freedom is a constitutional ban upon the public support of sectarian interests.

2. As applied to education, the principle of separation of church and state requires (a) that all funds appropriated by state and federal governments alike are to be used exclusively for public education and (b) that no public funds may properly be granted to any institution in which sectarian doctrines are taught.

"Neither So High Nor So Impregnable Today" Is the Wall of Separation

This interpretation of the principle of separation of church and state is no longer as favorably received as it was fifty years ago; nor is it as consistently adhered to as was once the case. As the late Justice Rutledge was moved to observe in the case of *Everson* v. *Board of Education,* "Neither so high nor so impregnable today as yesterday is the wall raised between Church and State by Virginia's great statute of religious freedom and the First Amendment, now made applicable to all States by the Fourteenth. New Jersey's statute sustained is the first, if indeed it is not the second

---

[10] For a list of these, see Johnson and Yost, *op. cit.,* p. 14.

breach to be made by the Court's action. That a third and a fourth, and still others may be attempted we may be sure." [11]

Judge Rutledge had in mind, as the second breach of principle, a decision of the Supreme Court in 1930 which sanctioned the furnishing of free textbooks to children in attendance upon parochial as well as public schools. Here, as later in the Everson case, the Court saw no direct aid as such to a church school, holding rather that the child and not the institution was being assisted, and "the taxing power of the State is exerted for a public purpose" when the books distributed are identical with those used in the public schools and are nonreligious and nonsectarian in character.[12]

The decisions of the Supreme Court in *Cochran* v. *Louisiana State Board of Education* and in *Everson* v. *Board of Education* (the one approving the distribution of free textbooks to parochial school children and the other the refunding of bus fares to the parents of children in attendance upon parochial schools) seemed to foreshadow a lowering of the "wall of separation" between church and state. Indeed, the words of Justice Hugo L. Black on behalf of the Court in the latter instance prompted Justice Jackson in his dissenting opinion to observe that the majority opinion seemed "utterly discordant" with the grounds upon which it had based its conclusions and reminded him of "Julia who, according to Byron's reports, 'whispering "I will ne'er consent"—consented.' "

Encouraged by the Court's evident intention to find ways of affording aid to children in attendance at church-related schools, if not to the institutions themselves, friends of the latter have insisted that all federal legislation designed to aid education within the states should include provision for "auxiliary services" to nonpublic schools. As Cardinal Spellman is reported to have said, "We must oppose any bill that fails to guarantee at least non-religious textbooks, bus rides, and health services for all

[11] The Supreme Court had ruled favorably on the right of the state to reimburse parents for the expense of transporting children to parochial school in public conveyances and on public routes. The Court interpreted this provision as a public health measure. At the same time it laid down the general principle that the state cannot "aid one religion, aid all religions, or prefer one religion over another."

[12] *Cochran* v. *Louisiana State Board of Education*, 281 U.S. 370.

children." [13] To realize this minimum objective, the Cardinal and others would follow the precedent established by Congress in 1946 in passing the National School Lunch Act. This act provided that in those states which forbid the use of public funds for nonpublic schools, machinery should be set up to distribute monies to nonpublic schools through channels independent of the state.

Insistence that federal legislation on behalf of education within the states should include a subsidy for auxiliary services to non-public schools has generated widespread controversy and bitterness. It has also been a major factor in blocking successfully all bills designed to provide direct general aid to public schools. Principle has clashed with principle and the score thus far is zero. Partisans of a "strict and lofty neutrality" on the part of the state toward religious interests have seen in efforts to secure at least a token recognition of church-related schools a determination to reverse the traditional principle that public funds are to be used exclusively for public education; whereas the friends of nonpublic schools have seized upon the manifest need of federal aid to education in the states as an opportunity to revise or to modify the principle of separation so as to permit government assistance to religious organizations on a "nonpreferential" basis.

Conflicting Interpretations of the Intentions of the Fathers

Opposition to a "wall of separation" between church and state involves both theoretical and practical considerations. The validity of the Supreme Court's interpretation of the First Amendment, as reviewed above, is now challenged (1) on historical and legal grounds and (2) as a policy appropriate to conditions as they exist today, however appropriate it may have been in 1791.

We turn first to the interpretation which James Madison and his associates had in mind when phrasing the religious clause of the First Amendment: "Congress shall make no law respecting an establishment of religion, or prohibiting the free exercise thereof. . . ."

---

[13] Quoted in *The Nation's Schools*, September, 1949, p. 27.

Contradictory interpretations turn upon the emphasis we give to the word "respecting" and to the phrase "an establishment of religion." What did the framers of the First Amendment and the people of the states who approved it have in mind? Does the Amendment prohibit Congress, and now the states through the Fourteenth Amendment, from lending support to "any and all" religious establishments or does it merely ban assistance to a preferred establishment? Are we to believe with Leo Pfeffer that ". . . the word 'establishment' had a broad meaning comprehending almost every tangible manifestation of religion or at least organized or institutional religion. An incorporated church was a 'religious establishment' in Madison's veto message. A place where persons worshiped was a 'religious establishment.' Jefferson considered even a non-sectarian Presidential proclamation of religion interdicted by the First Amendment. Madison considered the institutions of Congressional chaplains and military chaplains as religious establishments." [14]

Or shall we agree with James O'Neill, who also quotes from the record to sustain the position that the Amendment was "designed to meet the wishes of the people of the various states who had adopted resolutions, memorials, and petitions, recommending that the Federal Constitution should make clear that 'no particular sect or society ought to be favored or established by law in preference to others. . . .' The words 'an establishment of religion' interpreted in the light of their history cannot properly be held to mean 'any, even non-preferential assistance to religion.' " [15]

To resolve this problem is no easy task. Competent historians and learned jurists have assumed opposite positions with respect to it. The best we can do, within the limits of this chapter, is to summarize briefly the arguments on behalf of each position and refer the reader to more detailed discussions elsewhere.[16]

---

[14] From a debate on "The Meaning of the Establishment Clause" by Leo Pfeffer and James M. O'Neill in *The Buffalo Law Review*, Spring, 1953, pp. 225–278. Quotations from these individuals, the sources of which are not otherwise indicated in the following material, are taken from their arguments on this occasion.

[15] *Ibid.*, pp. 243, 247.

[16] Since the decisions of the Supreme Court in the Everson and McCollum cases, there has been renewed interest in the First Amendment and its implications for education. The resulting number of books published is too large for inclusion here. However, the following are representative of conflicting points of view:

The State Shall Play No Favorites

A forceful presentation of the contention that nonpreferential aid to religion is not interdicted by the Amendment is found in the writings of James M. O'Neill. O'Neill argues that the authors of the amendment had nothing more in mind than (1) preventing the federal government from assisting one religion in preference to all others and (2) safeguarding the religious conscience from interference by the state. To support this interpretation, O'Neill attempts to demonstrate that the amendment merely reflects a position with respect to relations between church and state which the states of Virginia, North Carolina, Rhode Island, and New York had arrived at by 1788. In the language of Virginia, this provided that "no particular religious sect or society ought to be favored or established by law in preference to others."

O'Neill further insists that we distinguish between the concept of free exercise of religion and that of an establishment of religion. The Amendment relates to both but the realization of the one, he holds, is not conditioned upon the denial of the other. Freedom of religion, for example, can be protected, as in England, when one establishment of religion receives favored consideration. It can also be safeguarded under either single or multiple establishment. Consequently, he argues, in banning "an establishment of religion" and putting all religious organizations on an equal footing before the law, the authors of the Amendment had no intention of prohibiting legislation of a nonpreferential character; nor was it necessary so to do in order to insure the free exercise of religion.

In further support of his position, O'Neill draws upon the writings of Jefferson and Madison. For example, he sees in Jef-

---

R. Freeman Butts, *The American Tradition in Religion and Education* (Boston: Beacon Press, Inc., 1950).

Conrad Moehlman, *The Wall of Separation Between Church and State* (Boston: Beacon Press, Inc., 1951).

James O'Neill, *Religion and Education Under the Constitution* (New York: Harper & Brothers, 1949).

Wilfrid Parsons, *The First Freedom, Considerations on Church and State in the United States* (New York: D. X. McMullen Co., 1948).

Leo Pfeffer, *Church, State and Freedom* (Boston: Beacon Press, Inc., 1953).

V. T. Thayer, *The Attack Upon the American Secular School* (Boston: Beacon Press, Inc., 1951).

ferson's Bill for Religious Freedom in Virginia (1786) nothing to sustain the notion that government should be prohibited from "the use of public funds in impartial support of religion." This bill, according to O'Neill, provided that

In Virginia no man shall (1) be compelled by government to attend or support any religious worship, place, or ministry whatsoever, nor (2) be punished or interfered with by the government on account of his religious opinions or beliefs, but (on the contrary) every man shall be free (so far as government is concerned) (3) to profess and argue for his religious opinions and beliefs, and, (4) such activities shall in no way affect his civil capacities. . . . The Virginia statute has no clear reference of any kind to public money, sectarian schools, religion in education, or the complete separation of church and state.

O'Neill insists further that both as a citizen in Virginia and as President of the United States, Jefferson was well aware of the many ways in which government funds were being used to assist religion on a nonpreferential basis.

Similarly, from an examination of the writings of James Madison, O'Neill finds no support for the view that Madison opposed nonpreferential assistance to religion. For a time, Madison, in common with Alexander Hamilton and others, saw no necessity for an amendment to the Constitution relating to freedom of religion, the press, speech, or of assembly. The federal government was a government of enumerated powers, and since the Constitution in its original form conferred upon Congress no authority to legislate on these matters, it was concluded that there was no occasion to include in the Constitution specific prohibitions against their exercise. Eventually, however, Madison yielded to both popular demand and the express injunctions of states which had adopted the Constitution with the understanding that it would be amended to include a Bill of Rights. As chairman of the committee in the House of Representatives charged with the formulation of these amendments Madison had much, if not most, to do with the final wording of the First Amendment. Consequently his original phrasing of the religious clause, "Nor shall any national religion be established," assumes importance. Further evidence of Madison's position, as O'Neill sees it, is found in the *Detached Memoranda*, written after Madison's retirement from the presidency. In this Madison is quoted as saying, "They [the people of the United States] have the noble merit of unshackling the conscience from persecuting laws and of establishing among religious sects a legal equality."

Since Madison's *Memorial and Remonstrance* is frequently referred to and was specifically used by Justice Rutledge in the McCollum case as evidence of Madison's opposition to all forms of establishment of religion, plural as well as singular, O'Neill gives special attention to it. The *Memorial and Remonstrance* was written in opposition to a bill before the Virginia Assembly which would have brought public support for "Teachers of the Christian Religion." Although providing for the payment of taxes in support of the ministers of the various denominations, it excluded from this assistance others than the teachers of the Christian religion.[17]

Madison voiced his opposition to this bill in part as follows: "Who does not see that the same authority which can *establish Christianity, in exclusion of all other religions, may establish with the same ease any particular sect of Christians, in exclusion of all other Sects?* That the same authority which can force a citizen to contribute three pence only of his property for the support of *any one establishment, may force him to conform to any other establishment in all cases whatsoever?*" (italics supplied by O'Neill).

To O'Neill these words indicate nothing more than Madison's objection to the establishment of Christianity as a state religion in Virginia and the consequent preferring of one establishment over others. It should not be interpreted as voicing opposition to state assistance to any and all religions.

O'Neill turns next to the records of Congress, the Presidents of the United States, and the states since the adoption of the federal Constitution. "Under every Congress," he writes, "we have had chaplains in the House and Senate; chaplains in the army and navy, and, of course, we have chaplains in such federal institutions as hospitals and asylums. The federal government spent large sums of money appropriated by Congress in support

---

[17] It did, however, permit nonreligionists to designate that their tax should be used for "the encouragement of seminaries of learning . . . and to no other purpose whatsoever."

of Christian missionaries to the Indians. The United States government is still using federal funds for impartial support of religious activities."

Similarly, "Every President of the United States from George Washington to Harry Truman, including both, have throughout their administrations used federal funds in aid of religion in "various guises, forms and degrees. . . . Every President since Washington has continued to use government funds impartially in support of religious activities without recommending any change in the Constitution, or any change in Congressional legislation, or issuing any countermanding order as Commander-in-chief of the army and navy. I am confident that President Eisenhower will continue to use federal funds in impartial aid of religion in various ways."

Finally, O'Neill challenges the validity of the reasoning by which the United States has used the Fourteenth Amendment as a means of rendering compulsory upon the states the provisions of the First Amendment and thus nullifying state autonomy in matters religious and educational. "The Supreme Court," he writes, "did not recognize that the Fourteenth Amendment placed on the several states the restrictions of the First in regard to freedom of religion, speech and the press until a half-century after it became part of the Constitution.

"In the light of these facts, no one has a right to believe that Congress in adopting the Fourteenth Amendment *intended* to forbid state support of religion or religious education." [18]

Governmental assistance to all religions on a nonpreferential basis, and, accordingly, to church-related schools of all denominations without distinction, is hardly consistent with the basic tenets of religious groups which hold that "Only the life of Christian faith can guarantee man in his present state the moral life; and the Christian life is lived entirely through the one true church of Christ." [19] Nevertheless, we find representatives of religious groups who so believe lending support to O'Neill's thesis.

An able presentation of this position appears in a series of

[18] "Church, State and the Constitution," *Commentary*, June, 1947, pp. 564–565.
[19] From *Statement by Catholic Bishops of America on Secularism and Schools*, *The New York Times*, November 16, 1952.

articles contributed to *America* by John Courtney Murray, S. J.[20]

Murray suggests that confusion in contemporary discussions of the First Amendment and its implications for the relation of government to education follows from the tendency to conceive of the First Amendment as a theological as well as a political document. As a political document the Amendment rejects the medieval theory "that religious unity was essentially constitutive of social unity and that community of faith was integral to the common good" and substitutes the principle "that the rights of conscience will be most securely protected and the political ends of the American state most effectively furthered by guaranteeing the equality of all religious consciences (and, by implication, of all religious bodies) before the law." Experience, continues Murray, had shown that governmental insistence upon religious conformity defeated its own end—unity. Consequently, the Amendment prohibited "the use of governmental authority to create an official American faith and enforce adherence to it as the bond of national unity. . . . The political community was to remain separate from the religious community with all of its inner divisions and the religious community was to be free to be divided."

Now, continues Murray, this is all that the First Amendment means. "Every person is a civic person, a member of organized society, subject to the authority of its government" and he is also "a religious person, a creature of God, subject to the religious conscience, and ordained to an end transcending time. This dualism is inherent in the very nature of man." As citizens, then, all men whatever their religion have a right to be equal in their civil liberties and in their access to the benefits of organized society, and as religious men, they possess the right, as against the state, "to follow in every rational way the will of God as it is known to them through conscience."

This distinction between an individual as a citizen and as a religious person, according to Murray, does not commit the state to the doctrine "that all churches are simply voluntary societies, of equally human origin and of equal value in the sight of God, each of them offering to man an equally good way to eternal salvation." This would be to believe "that the First Amendment

---

[20] See particularly *America*, December 7, 1946, pp. 261–263, and February 15, 1947, pp. 541–545.

canonizes Liberal Protestant ecclesiology in an extreme form, and anathematizes as un-American all dissenters." Neither does it identify "religious freedom" with the total absence of public support for religious organizations on a nonpreferential basis. Nor, finally, in the field of education does it either dictate or sanction the exclusive use of public funds for public education, since this would do violence to the general welfare and constitute an unreasonable limitation upon religious and parental rights.

Our government had recognized "the co-existence and free functioning of two types of schools—the non-profit, tax-exempt church-related schools (the original unit of American education) and the public school (later growth)." [21] Now, argues Murray, the state, under the Constitution, is not interested in whether or not a child attends a public or a private school. This is a parental decision. But it is interested in its children. The state also requires school attendance, although it leaves the parent free to determine the type of school attended. Therefore, if parents of parochial school children are to be put on a parity with those of public school children, they cannot rightfully be cut off from aid. To argue that a parent who for private reasons decides to send his child to a private school thereby cuts his child off from state assistance to his education is to frustrate both state and parent. "By his 'freedom' under separation of Church and State, the parent frustrates the State as *parens patriae;* and by its obligations under separation of Church and State, the state frustrates the parental right by making its exercise the reason for penalty." [22]

There Shall Be No Public Assistance to "Any or All" Religious Establishments

A second interpretation of the First Amendment conceives its adoption as a culminating stage in the evolution of religious freedom in America. Union of church and state characterized a majority of the colonies during the colonial period. Only in Rhode Island and the Middle Colonies—Pennsylvania, Delaware, New Jersey—was there anything analogous to toleration of reli-

---

[21] "Separation of Church and State: True and False Concepts," *America,* February 15, 1947, p. 543.
[22] *Ibid.,* p. 544.

gious differences. Elsewhere to challenge the assumption that "the Christian life is lived entirely through the one true church," as each colony conceived the church was hazardous indeed. Convinced as each community was that religious orthodoxy was essential not only for the salvation of the individual's soul but for the well-being of the community as well, deviation from the straight and narrow path of conformity brought severe penalties. When Nathaniel Ward declared in early Massachusetts that "all Familists, Antinomians, Anabaptists, and other Enthusiasts shall have free liberty to keep away from us," he voiced sentiments by no means peculiar to his own colony or his own day. As late as the Revolution, in one Massachusetts town alone "eighteen dissenters were in jail for refusing to pay ministerial rates in support of the established worship, and in all but one colony (Pennsylvania) it was illegal to celebrate the mass in public.[23]

The evolution of religious liberty in America has been one of gradual emancipation of the individual from the consequences of this union of church and state. In general, it has involved the following steps: (1) the right of dissenters in religion to reside in a colony without molestation; (2) the right of an individual to refrain from attending the established church and to maintain the church of his choice, while, of course, continuing to pay taxes in support of the established church; (3) the prohibition of one established church; and (4) legalizing the principle, as Jefferson phrased it, that it is "sinful and tyrannical" for the state to force contributions from an individual in support of *any religious belief,* be this his own or that of another.[24]

The question at issue with respect to an interpretation of the religious clause in the First Amendment turns upon whether or

---

[23] Pfeffer, *op. cit.,* p. 225. Even in the Virginia of Jefferson and Madison, a Christian who ventured to deny the Trinity was subject to three years' imprisonment, and if a parent, he might be denied the custody of his own children.

[24] Jefferson's own words were: "Whereas Almighty God hath created the mind free . . . to compel a man to furnish contributions of money for the propagation of opinions which he disbelieves, is sinful and tyrannical; that even the forcing him to support this or that teacher of his own religious persuasion, is depriving him of the comfortable liberty of giving his contributions to the particular pastor, whose morals he would make his pattern, and whose powers he feels most persuasive to righteousness." Section II of this Bill also reads in part, "Be It Enacted By the General Assembly, That no man shall be compelled to frequent or support any religious worship, place, or ministry whatsoever . . ." [quoted in R. Freeman Butts, *The American Tradition in Religion and Education* (Boston: Beacon Press, Inc., 1950), pp. 52–53].

not in its adoption the people of the United States were giving expression to convictions representative of step three or step four.

Supporters of the latter position contend that the Amendment gives constitutional expression to both a political and religious conviction which large numbers of people in the colonies had come to hold, namely, that religious convictions and religious organizations should be removed from the concern of government. Attempts in the past to enforce conformity in religious belief and to assist religious organizations in the plural as well as the singular had not only proved unsatisfactory but had given rise to the conclusion by many conventionally minded men as well as the rationalists, Deists, Unitarians, and others of an unorthodox point of view that religious organizations and the state would thrive best when the interests of the one were completely divorced from the interests of the other.

For example, in 1785, the Virginia Baptists opposed the "Bill Establishing a Provision for Teachers of the Christian Religion" on the grounds that "no human laws ought to be established for this purpose; but that every person ought to be left entirely free in respect to matters of religion; that the holy Author of our religion needs no such compulsive measures for the promotion of his cause; that the Gospel wants not the feeble arm of man for its support; that it has made, and will again through divine power make its way against all opposition; and that should the Legislature assume the right of taxing the people for the support of the Gospel, it will be destructive to religious liberty." [25]

And John Leland, a Baptist leader in Virginia, wrote in 1791 that "government has no more to do with religious opinions of men than it has with the principles of mathematics." [26]

Liberals in matters religious assumed an identical position but for different reasons. The exercise of religion, as they saw it, was a "natural right" and was thus excluded from the legitimate area of governmental concern. Religious organizations were viewed as private corporations, free to operate within the state but dependent for their support upon the voluntary contributions of their members and friends.

Leo Pfeffer writes in this connection:

---

[25] Moehlman, *The Wall of Separation Between Church and State*, p. 80.
[26] Pfeffer, *op. cit.*, p. 229.

Many of the political leaders of the Revolutionary and post-Revolutionary period had come under the influence of Deism and not a few were apathetic if not antagonistic to formal religious worship and institutionalized religion. It is significant that the first four presidents of the United States were either Deists or Unitarians. But liberalism in religion was not limited to the leaders; rationalism and skepticism had made substantial progress among the urban masses. Paine's *Age Of Reason* was one of the most widely read books of the period, and not more than one out of eight Americans and probably as few as one out of every twenty-five was affiliated with any church.[27]

To men of this frame of mind, Thomas Paine's statement in *Common Sense* seemed most sensible. "As to religion, I hold it to be the indispensable duty of government to protect all conscientious professions thereof; and I know of no other business which government hath to do therewith."

The determination of religionists and nonreligionists alike to separate religion from government is evidenced by attempts to abolish both single and multiple establishment. The traditional requirement that all men, irrespective of their religious affiliations, should be taxed in support of an established church led dissidents to identify religious liberty not only with the freedom to worship according to one's own conscience but also with exemption from taxation in support of another man's religion. The significance of this identification of religious freedom with freedom from taxation in support of an alien faith, it is argued, is overlooked today by the advocates of nonpreferential assistance to religion. That Madison and Jefferson so conceived religious liberty seems amply demonstrated by their writings,[28] as well as their actions when serving as presidents of the United States.[29]

---

[27] *Ibid.*, p. 231.

[28] In 1783 Jefferson proposed the following article for incorporation in the Constitution of Virginia: "The General Assembly shall not have the power to infringe this constitution; to abridge the civil rights of any person on account of his religious beliefs; to restrain him from professing and supporting that belief, or to compel contributions, other than those he shall have personally stipulated for the support of that or any other . . ." [Saul K. Padover, *The Complete Madison* (New York: Duell, Sloan & Pearce, Inc., 1943), p. 113].

[29] Both Madison and Jefferson (and, for that matter, Jackson as well) considered even the issuing of a Thanksgiving proclamation unconstitutional. To ease his conscience, after yielding to political considerations in this matter, Madison was careful to employ nonsectarian terms. Madison likewise considered the payment of chaplains for Congress a violation of the Constitution and suggested that their salaries be paid out of the voluntary contributions of the members of Congress.

In a letter to Edward Livingston, dated July 10, 1822, Madison wrote of the American experiment with religious liberty:

Notwithstanding the general progress made within the last two centuries in favor of this branch of liberty, and the full establishment of it, in some parts of our country, there remains in others a strong bias toward the old error, that without some sort of alliance or coalition between Government and Religion neither can be duly supported. Such indeed is the tendency to such a coalition, and such its corrupting influence upon both parties, that the danger cannot be too carefully guarded against. . . . It was the belief of all sects at one time that the establishment of Religion by law, was right and necessary; that the true religion ought to be established in exclusion of every other; and that the only question to be decided was which was the true religion. The example of Holland proved that a toleration of sects, dissenting from the established sect, was safe and even useful. The example of the Colonies, now States, which rejected religious establishments altogether, proved that all Sects might be safely and advantageously put on a footing of equal and entire freedom. . . . We are teaching the world the great truth that Governments do better without Kings and Nobles than with them. The merit will be doubled by the other lesson that Religion flourishes in greater purity, without than with the aid of government.[30]

To perpetuate the beneficial results of a strict neutrality on the part of government in matters relating to religion, the framers of the First Amendment sought to establish as a constitutional principle the proposition that all authority over religion is prohibited to government. Credance is given to this interpretation by the obvious failure of the friends of multiple establishment to phrase the Amendment specifically so as to premit nonpreferential assistance to religion.

Two efforts of this character were made in the Senate after the amendment had passed the House. One suggested wording ran as follows: "Congress shall make no law establishing one Religious Sect or Society in preference to others, or prohibiting the free exercise thereof, nor shall the rights of conscience be infringed."[31] The second read: "Congress shall make no law establishing any

---

[30] Quoted in Saul K. Padover, *The Complete Madison*, p. 309.
[31] *Journal of the First Session of the Senate of the United States of America* (New York: John Greenleaf, 1789), p. 116.

particular denomination of religion in preference to another, or prohibiting the free exercise thereof, nor shall the rights of conscience be infringed." [32]

Both of these suggested revisions failed of passage. The wording as we have it today was arrived at in conference between the Senate and the House. In the light of the abortive attempts to legalize nonpreferential assistance to religious sects, it would seem that the wording finally arrived at was intended to ban public aid to establishments in the plural as well as in the singular.

This conclusion is further confirmed by trends within the states in the period immediately preceding and following the approval of the First Amendment by the people of the states.

Following their break with England, the original thirteen states faced the necessity of adopting constitutions to replace their colonial charters. In this process their attitudes toward the establishment of religion and freedom of conscience became clear. Between the years 1776 and 1791, nine of the thirteen states (including Rhode Island, which retained its original charter) wrote into their constitutions unmistakable prohibitions against establishments of religion, plural as well as singular. Evidently experience with multiple support of religious establishments (or, to use the contemporary phrase, "cooperation between government and religious bodies") had been no more satisfactory than that with single establishment. Consequently they had come to agree upon one and only one method of safeguarding both the integrity of religious organizations and the religious conscience: to deprive government of all authority to promote or to regulate religion or to impose taxes in its support.

Are we to suppose, it is asked, that these same states, when faced with the necessity of passing upon the First Amendment, would have endorsed a policy on the federal level which they had just denied to government on the state level?

Moreover, subsequent developments within the four lagging states were in harmony with the trend in opposition to government support of any and all religions. Maryland in 1810, Connecticut in 1818, New Hampshire in 1819, and Massachusetts in 1833 joined with their sister states in prohibiting all public support of religious establishments. Reference has been made to

---

[32] *Ibid.*, p. 117.

the Connecticut constitution of 1818. A comparison between the relevant clauses of the Maryland constitution of 1776 and that of 1810 is likewise pertinent. For example, the version of 1776 stated that the Legislature is authorized "in their discretion . . . to lay a general and equal tax, for the support of any particular place of worship or minister. . . ." In 1810, however, the wording was changed to read, "That it shall not be lawful for the general assembly to lay an equal and general tax on the people of this state for the support of any religion."

Finally, the advocates of complete separation of church and state contend that the obvious deviations in practice from a strictly neutral position (such as the support of chaplains in the armed forces, chaplains in the Congress, tax exemption of religious organizations, and grants to hospitals operated under religious auspices etc.) are to be looked upon in part as atavistic reminders of an early identification of government and religion and, in part, as outright violations of the Constitution to which attention has been called. On the whole, as Leo Pfeffer observes, when we compare the attention paid to religious matters in the Continental Congress with the total absence of any positive provision for religious interests in the federal Constitution, what is significant is "how few and comparatively minor these vestiges are." [33]

Reversal in Popular Attitude

The discussion thus far has centered pretty much upon what our fathers had in mind in adopting the religious clause of the First Amendment to the federal Constitution. Were we to agree upon its meaning and purpose in 1791, we might still disagree upon the appropriateness of this interpretation in the light of conditions today.

Indeed, what seems to be a gradual transformation in popular attitude toward the concept of separation of church and state, as this evolved in the nineteenth century, accounts in large measure for the nature of the problem as we encounter it today. Until comparatively recently, it was commonly agreed that religious organizations derived health and vigor from their independence of government. Witness the comments of James Bryce in his

[33] Pfeffer, *op. cit.*, p. 271.

chapter on "The Church and the Clergy," in his *The American Commonwealth:* "Half the wars of Europe, half the internal troubles that have vexed European states . . . have arisen from theological differences or from rival claims of church and state. This whole vast chapter of debate and strife has remained virtually unopened in the United States. There is no Established Church. All religious bodies are absolutely equal before the law, and un-recognized by the law, except as voluntary associations of private citizens." [34]

A change in the relation of religion to education became visible around 1913. As we have seen, our first schools were established by religious communities and were designed to mold the minds of the young in orthodox patterns. Only gradually did the sectarian school give way to the nonsectarian school, a school in which the emphasis in religious instruction tended to shift from points of sectarian difference to items upon which all Protestants were agreed. Eventually, however, the nonsectarian school satisfied neither the Catholic nor the non-Christian. Consequently, the principle of respect for the integrity of religious conviction was further extended, and the Protestant-oriented nonsectarian school came gradually to exclude religious practices and religious mate-rials which offended the sensibilities of nonconformists. Since the Protestant Bible was unacceptable to Catholics, many of the states ceased to require Bible reading in the schools. By 1913, two states only retained mandatory provisions for its use. Devo-tional exercises of a sectarian character likewise seemed to be on their way out, particularly in communities of diverse religious background. Indeed, by the turn of the century, a distinctively American institution seemed in process of evolution—a secular public school. By this is meant a school which strives to minister to needs common to all young people who live in communities that are heterogeneous in matters religious but which carefully avoids indoctrination in a realm where, as Justice Frankfurter has said, "conflicts are most easily and most bitterly engendered."

Pennsylvania was one of the first states to reverse this trend with the passage of a law in 1913 which made the reading of the Bible compulsory in all public schools. By 1946, thirteen states

---

[34] *The American Commonwealth*, 2nd ed., rev. (New York: Commonwealth Pub-lishing Co., 1908), vol. II, p. 643.

had taken similar action, and in twenty-four states Bible reading was specifically permitted. In eight states only was the Bible evidently not in use.[35] Religious instruction on a "released time" basis likewise dates from 1913, but although this practice spread rapidly, the full strength of it has been difficult to measure because of the frequency with which communities not only have adopted the plan but also abandoned it.[36] Moreover, there has been a growing demand, in recent years, for the inclusion of some form of religious instruction within the curriculum of the school.

These changes in public attitude and their relation to education in moral and spiritual values will receive consideration in a later chapter. We will turn first, however, to a parallel development: increasing dissatisfaction with a policy that restricts the use of public funds exclusively to the support of public education.

Suggested Reading

Butts, R. Freeman, *The American Tradition in Religion and Education* (Boston: Beacon Press, Inc., 1950).

Catholic Bishops of America, *Statement on Secularism and the Schools, The New York Times,* November 16, 1952.

Howe, Mark de Wolfe, "The Constitutional Question," *Religion and the Free Society* (New York: The Fund of the Republic, 1958).

Kempner, Maximilian, "The Supreme Court and the Establishment and Free Exercise of Religion," *Religion and the Free Society* (New York: The Fund for the Republic, 1958).

Konvitz, Milton R., *Fundamental Liberties of a Free People: Religion, Speech, Press, Assembly* (Ithaca, N.Y.: Cornell University Press, 1957).

Moehlman, Conrad, *The Wall of Separation Between Church and State* (Boston: Beacon Press, Inc., 1951).

O'Neill, James, *Religion and Education Under the Constitution* (New York: Harper & Brothers, 1949).

---

[35] *The State and Sectarian Education* (Washington, D.C.: National Education Association Research Bulletin, February, 1946), p. 34.

[36] In 1948, the year of the McCollum decision, it was estimated that approximately 2,500 communities were providing religious instruction in cooperation with public schools for nearly 2,000,000 pupils. Despite the declarations of the Supreme Court in *McCollum* v. *Board of Education* and *Zorach* v. *Clauson* that the use of school buildings for religious instruction on released time is unconstitutional, the practice continues in a number of states.

Pfeffer, Leo, *Church, State and Freedom* (Boston: Beacon Press, Inc., 1953).

Thayer, V. T., *The Attack Upon the American Secular School* (Boston: Beacon Press, Inc., 1951).

/\.\/\.\/\

19

Public Assistance to Nonpublic Schools

Factors Which Weaken the Policy of No Public Assistance to Nonpublic Schools

The prevailing attitude of the American people toward public education at the turn of the century was well expressed in the words of Theodore Roosevelt.

We could suffer no national calamity more far reaching in its effects than would be implied in the abandonment of our system of non-sectarian schools; and it is a very unfortunate thing for any man, or any body of men, to be identified with opposition thereto—it is not really a question of sects at all; it is merely an illustration of survival or importation here on the utterly un-American and thoroughly Old World idea of the subordination of the layman to the priest; it is an issue between intelligent American laymen of every faith on the one hand, and ambitious, foolish or misguided supporters of a worn out system of clerical government on the other. Our public schools are here to stay.[1]

Nevertheless, as was suggested in the last chapter, by 1913 there were clear indications of a drift away from the commonly accepted principle that public funds are to be used exclusively for public education and that sectarian instruction should find no place

---

[1] Quoted by Agnes Meyer in an address delivered before the National Education Association, July 3, 1952. *Addresses and Proceedings,* vol. 90, p. 70.

in the classrooms of the public school. Multiple factors have doubtless contributed to this change of mind.

Not least in importance is the fact that with the common acceptance of separation of church and state, the principle received but slight emphasis in the curriculum of school and college. What one generation of Americans had struggled to attain and succeeding generations took for granted, many who came after knew only vaguely.

Heavy immigration from countries in which separation of church and state is unknown constituted a second factor not unrelated to the first. Thus, there is little in the conscious tradition of large segments of the population today to create an acute awareness of the significance of the principle of separation in American experience.

Still a third factor is the expanded influence of the Catholic Church, with its commitment to the doctrine that the church is to provide instruction, both secular and sectarian, and the state is to subsidize when it does not entirely support these activities. For example, in 1800, Catholics comprised no more than 1 per cent of the population of the United States. By 1900 this figure had risen to 16 per cent, and by 1948 Catholics comprised approximately 18 per cent of the total population and one-third of the entire church membership of the country.[2] As Irwin Widen has pointed out, "Catholicism does not approach majority status; but because of the fragmentation of Protestantism the Catholic Church is by far the largest single denomination in this country, with more than three times the membership of the second-ranking Methodist Church." [3]

Not only has the Catholic Church increased in numbers, but as its members have come to participate in the manifold activities of the American community, it is but natural that they should grow in influence. Moreover, in recent years, the discipline of the church has hardened with respect to education. Increasing emphasis has been placed upon the importance of parochial schools, and, in consequence, pressure is exerted upon the faithful both to send their children to these schools and to con-

---

[2] Irwin Widen, "Public Support for Parochial Schools: Why the Issue Has Reemerged," *History of Education Journal*, Winter, 1953, pp. 58–72.
[3] *Ibid.*, p. 60.

tribute toward their maintenance. Coming as this does at a time when the cost of education has increased manyfold, it is not surprising that Catholic laymen as well as the clergy should look to the state for relief. This relief, it is felt, might well take the form, first, of granting to the parochial school a fair share of tax funds devoted to schools and, second, "Federal aid minus Federal control" on the national level.[4]

Fourth, Catholics are not alone in their desire to maintain church schools or in their determination to persuade the state to relieve their patrons of the financial burden of so doing. As indicated earlier, members of the Protestant clergy in recent years are insisting with increasing vigor that public schools must either find ways of including religion in the curriculum or, as Henry P. Van Dusen, President of Union Theological Seminary puts it, they "will be driven to the expedient of the church-sponsored school." [5] Nor is this an empty threat, as evidenced by an increase of 61 per cent in the number of Protestant dayschools in 1951–1952 as compared with the number in 1937.[6]

Has Public Policy Weakened the Churches?

For a period in our history, states Charles Clayton Morrison, editor emeritus of *The Christian Century*, "Protestants welcomed with relief the shifting of the burden of general education from

---

[4] A recent suggestion is that parents of children in attendance at nonpublic schools receive either "certificates of money value for their children's education in the school of their choice" or credit upon their income tax returns for tuition paid to nonpublic schools.

See also the statement of Jesuit educators meeting at Georgetown University with respect to grants from the federal government in support of mathematics and science. The educators urge that these be "on an across-the-board basis for all students and all institutions" (reported in *The Washington Post and Times Herald*, January 5, 1958). For a discussion of the problem of Catholic education as Catholics view it, see Urban H. Fleege, "Issues and Problems Facing Catholic Secondary Education," *Catholic Education Review*, November, 1952, pp. 272–273. Also see the statement of the Catholic Bishops of America on *The Place of the Private and Church-Related Schools in American Education*, *The New York Times*, November 20, 1955.

[5] Quoted by Will Herberg, "The Sectarian Conflict Over Church and State," *Commentary*, November, 1952, p. 452.

[6] *Ibid.*, p. 452. Herberg points out that the over-all figures, some "2,094 schools, almost entirely elementary, with about 190,000 pupils" is not as yet impressive. Nevertheless, the determination of Protestant leaders to sever relations with public education can well be serious for the future of public education.

the church to the secular community or the state. They believed that they could supplement the work of the public school with effective religious instruction in the church and the home." This confidence they have now lost: "The modern home is notoriously incompetent in this field. The Sunday school with its one hour a week of religious instruction, by volunteer teachers, under conditions of slack discipline is barely a gesture toward education. It cannot command the respect of pupils accustomed to the vastly superior methods, discipline, and prestige of the public school." Consequently, Morrison is forced to conclude, "Protestantism cannot long maintain its position in American life while it allows its children to grow up in religious illiteracy. Its devotion to the public gives it the right to demand that the ban on religion in the curriculum be removed." [7]

Faced, as they fear they are, with the prospect of losing their dominant position in American religious life, Protestants view with increasing concern the evolution of the nonsectarian public school (often of Protestant orientation) into a genuinely secular school. For this reason, many of their leaders have joined with Catholics in charging public schools with promoting the "deadly menace of secularism."

Oddly enough, this increased anxiety on the part of Protestant and Catholic leaders seems to have gone hand in hand with a corresponding increase in church membership! For example, at the time of the adoption of the Constitution, probably no more than one out of twenty-five people in the population was affiliated with any church; [8] whereas, today, the ratio is approximately one out of every two. Moreover, between 1926 and 1950, church membership increased by 59.8 per cent as against a 28.6 per cent increase in the population.[9]

---

[7] "Can Protestantism Win America?" *The Christian Century*, vol. 63, pp. 425–427. It should be pointed out, however, that Morrison parts company with all who would have the state subsidize nonpublic schools.

[8] Anson Phelps Stokes, *Church and State in the United States* (New York: Harper & Brothers, 1950), vol. I, pp. 229–230.

[9] Herberg, *op. cit.,* p. 454. Herberg further states that the Catholic Church grew by 53.9 per cent and Protestantism by 63.7 per cent. "Most of this increase, however, was accounted for by the expansion of the Baptists, especially the Southern Baptists. The churches affiliated with the National Council, the authoritative national Federation of Protestant (and some Eastern Orthodox) Churches, grew only 47.7 per cent, falling short of the total increase as well as of the comparable Roman Catholic growth."

It is interesting to observe that this was also a period of phenomenal growth in our public school population. For example, between 1900 and 1950, the proportion of all children and youth enrolled in school between the ages of five and seventeen increased from 72.4 per cent to about 80 per cent. Nor was this confined to the elementary school and the age of compulsory school attendance. High school enrollments increased from 5 per cent of the total school enrollments at the beginning of the century to 20 per cent of the total in 1950, and the college population in this same period increased from 4 per cent to 21 to 30 per cent of the population between the ages of 18 and 21.

This expansion of the school population horizontally as well as vertically has, of course, been reflected in attendance at private as well as public schools. But the most conspicuous developments have been in public education. For example, in 1900 private schools enrolled 17.59 per cent of all secondary school pupils. In 1950 this percentage stood at approximately 10 per cent.[10]

In the light of these data, it is difficult to conclude that the growth of the secular public school has brought disastrous effects upon church membership! On the contrary, might we not infer, with some basis in fact, that just as religious organizations in the United States, under conditions of nongovernmental assistance, have manifested a vitality superior to that evidenced in Europe under state support, so a system of public education which refrains from indoctrinating in religion gives evidence of at least no deleterious effects upon membership in religious organizations?

Despite these facts, church leaders have concluded that more than an attitude of benevolent neutrality in matters religious is required of public education.

Finally, some analysts see in the mounting demand for religious instruction in public schools and the disposition to replace the secular school with private schools of a religious orientation evidence of a distressed state of public mind, widespread and

---

[10] It should be pointed out, however, that nonpublic school enrollments on both the elementary and secondary levels have increased in recent years. Nonpublic schools (elementary) increased from 9.5 per cent of the total enrollments in 1937–1938 to slightly less than 12 per cent in 1950, and the proportion of nonpublic school enrollments on the secondary level increased from 6.3 per cent in 1933–1934 to 10 per cent in 1949–1950. (See Rose Marie Smith, "Rising Enrollments in Non-Public Schools," *School Life*, May, 1950.)

varied in character. This, they hold, results from many causes: profound changes in ways of living, economic disturbances, the aftereffects of war, depression and dislocation of populations, together with continued threats of war.[11] According to this interpretation, dissatisfaction with the work of the schools in the realm of values, as in other areas, is but one manifestation of a wider trend which finds expression in a "loss of nerve," or a disposition to seek refuge in religion from the storms that beset the contemporary world.

Be this as it may, there is no doubt of the determination of numerous groups and individuals "to turn back the hands of the clock" and to insist upon "distributive justice" in the allotment of funds for education to public and private schools. This determination manifests itself on the federal level in attempts to incorporate assistance to nonpublic schools in all legislation designed to aid education in the states; on the state level parochial groups have made an effort to obtain aid from the states through the merging of public and parochial interests. What seems to the partisans of separation nothing less than an improper as well as illegal violation of public trust on the part of boards of education assumes quite a different appearance in the eyes of laymen who are consistently exposed to the arguments of religious leaders, whose infallibility they do not question, that right and justice require public support of both public and nonpublic schools.

We will turn now to a brief summary of the arguments employed to justify public support of nonpublic schools.

The Argument in Support of Public Assistance to Church-Related Schools

1. First is the argument that since nonpublic schools render a public service, they are entitled to compensation or some form of support. For example, Cardinal Spellman has stated that Catholic schools "save others of the nation's taxpayers half a billion dollars yearly through the voluntary support of parochial schools, in

---

[11] For a more adequate discussion of factors which have stimulated concern for religion in education, see the chapter entitled "Education Between Two Wars" in V. T. Thayer, *Religion and Public Education* (New York: The Viking Press, 1947).

addition to the capital expense of the buildings." [12]

This contention has been made with considerable force in connection with proposed federal legislation on behalf of education. Since the parochial school carries a sizable burden of education, it is argued that it is entitled to receive at least token assistance in the way of auxiliary activities—health, transportation, free textbooks and instructional materials. "Public and non-public schools," insists Father William E. McManus of the National Catholic Welfare Council, "are both eligible claimants to Federal aid. Why? Both types serve the public interest; their graduates are full-fledged American citizens, entitled to vote, qualified for public office and subject to call for military service. Consequently, non-public school pupils are entitled at least to those essential health and welfare services that are commonly furnished to public school children." [13]

It is obvious that the principle at issue is of greater importance than the amount of money involved in the support of auxiliary activities. Were we to subtract from the relatively small sums it is proposed Congress should appropriate to the states that proportion which would be diverted to nonpublic schools, the amount thus made available for auxiliary services would be small indeed. This fact is frankly recognized by the advocates of aid to nonpublic schools. Nevertheless, they insist that failure to include specific provision for such aid justifies opposition to all measures designed to assist education in the states. In the words of Father McManus,

During the next few years we shall see a great increase of local, State and Federal government activity in education, health and welfare. If government takes an impartial attitude toward both public and volun-

---

[12] Quoted in the New York newspaper, *The Daily Compass*, June 30, 1949. See also statement of the Catholic Bishops of America on *The Place of Private and Church-Related Schools in American Education* in which the Bishops state: "The private and church-related schools are part of the American system. Manifestly, they exist; they exist by right; and they are unquestionably carrying a large share of the educational burden. Their teachers, religious and lay, have dedicated themselves to a high purpose, have labored hard to acquit themselves worthily, and the entire nation is their debtor. . . . The students of these schools have the right to benefit from those measures, grants, or aids, which are manifestly designed for the health, safety and welfare of American youth, irrespective of the school attended" (*The New York Times*, November 20, 1955).
[13] "Show Down on Federal Aid," *America*, June 29, 1949, p. 456.

tary agencies, i.e., shows a readiness to assist any agency that serves the public interest, this development is good. If, however, government on any level adopts a doctrinaire policy that only public agencies in all three fields shall be eligible for tax funds, the development is bad. . . . If the policy is carried to its ultimate, e.g., denial of tax exemption, then private schools, hospitals and welfare agencies may be forced out of business.

Opposition to an unjust Federal-aid bill may be the first step toward a right decision in other fields.[14]

If insistence upon aid for auxiliary services is but the first step in the validation of the principle of public assistance to non-public schools, it is relevant to inquire, "What is the goal ultimately envisaged"?

One answer is found in the practice now followed in Canada (where taxpayers indicate the school, Protestant, Catholic, or public, which they wish their funds to assist) and in those European countries where dual systems of education receive sustenance and support from the state. To finance this dual system of education (better, multiple system, since under this arrangement numerous denominations are involved) it is suggested that the state assume direct responsibility for financing education without reference to taxes paid, or, as John E. Wise, S.J., has suggested, it might follow a policy of using Catholic taxes for Catholic schools, Methodist taxes for Methodist schools, Baptist taxes for Baptist schools, and so on down the line of religious denominations represented in the body politic.[15] At the moment, the precise formula is less important than winning general recognition and acceptance of the principle of "distributive justice."

2. A second argument in support of public assistance to non-public schools turns upon "implementing" the legal right of a child to attend a private school in lieu of a public school. As we have seen, this right was specifically affirmed by the United States Supreme Court in the case of *Pierce* v. *Society of Sisters,* in which the Court declared unconstitutional a statute of the state of Oregon designed to require all children to attend public schools. "The child is not the mere creature of the state," declared the

[14] *Ibid.*, pp. 456, 457.
[15] See John E. Wise, S.J., "Federal Aid for Religious Schools," *School and Society,* December 8, 1945, p. 364.

Court; "those who nurture him and direct his destiny have the right coupled with the high duty, to recognize and to prepare him for additional obligations." Among these rights and obligations is that of parental determination of the school, public or private, in which he shall receive his education.

But of what value is this right unless parents are genuinely free to exercise it? "If parents have the right to send their children to any adequate school, public or independent," one prominent member of the clergy has argued, "then obviously all these schools must be allowed to exist without unfair discrimination or undue favoritism." At present, however, the parent who chooses to send his child to a nonpublic school suffers from two handicaps: (1) he is disadvantaged when auxiliary services are provided for public school children and denied to children of nonpublic schools and (2) he is subjected to "double taxation," by which is meant he pays a tax in support of public education as well as tuition to the nonpublic school in which he enrolls his child.

3. Closely allied to this second argument is the contention that to restrict public funds to the use of public schools is to create an undesirable monopoly of public education. This charge takes on special significance in a period of reaction to all measures suggestive of "creeping socialism" and constitutes an indictment today that is in no way limited to individuals and groups identified with religious schools. Private schools are now envisaged as exemplars of the spirit of free enterprise and public schools condemned as representing a trend in the direction of totalitarianism.[16]

Support is given to this position, as we have seen, by the arguments of Robert C. Hartnett and John Courtney Murray to the effect that "the state should always aim to assist social institutions to perform their appointed tasks, rather than to replace them with public (i.e., political) agencies." [17]

4. A note of urgency is given to the arguments reviewed by the hard fact that nonpublic schools of all types are finding it increasingly difficult to maintain their existence in the face of rapidly rising costs of operation.

---

[16] See the discussion of Robert Cyrus Hoiles, pp. 321–322, Chapter 16. Also see the statement of Catholic Bishops of America of November 20, 1955, on *The Place of the Private and Church-Related Schools in American Education, op. cit.*

[17] See Robert C. Hartnett in *America*, April 9, 1952, pp. 65–68.

This burden falls especially heavily upon Catholics since they face a religious injunction far more imperative than that imposed upon the members of other church groups. For example,

Catholic children may not attend non-Catholic neutral or mixed schools, that is those which are open also to non-Catholics and it pertains exclusively to the Ordinary of the place to decide, in accordance with the instructions of the Holy See, under what circumstances and with what precautions against the nature of perversion, attendance at such schools may be tolerated. Neutral schools are those which exclude religion by prescinding from it, such as the public schools in the United States. Mixed schools are those which admit pupils of any or no religion.[18]

The financial strain upon Catholics has become heavier with the years, not only as a result of increasing costs characteristic of the times but also because of increased efforts to expand the facilities of Catholic secondary and higher education. This is evidenced by the fact that while enrollments in Catholic elementary schools have not increased proportionately in the past three decades, Catholic secondary schools in 1947 enrolled three and one-half times the number enrolled in 1920.[19] If we bear in mind also that secondary education involves a higher per-pupil cost than does elementary education [20] and that the shortage of nuns as teachers necessitates supplementing the teaching staff with more costly lay teachers, the financial burden imposed upon the faithful becomes formidable indeed.

Protestant church schools are unable to draw upon religious orders for teachers to the same extent as Catholics, and, in consequence, faculty costs are higher for them. Neither do Protestant churches exercise a discipline over their members sufficient to provide the funds essential to establish and maintain schools which can compete with public schools. It is not surprising, therefore, to find Protestant advocates of church schools joining with Catholics in the demand that ways and means be found for the

---

[18] Canon Law 1347. T. Lincoln Boriscaren and Adam C. Ellis, *Canon Law: Text and Commentary* (Milwaukee, Wisc.: Bruce Publishing Co., 1946), p. 704.

[19] Widen, *op. cit.*, p. 67. See also "New Survey of Catholic High Schools Shows Striking Growth, Points to Needed Changes," *Catholic Educational Review*, June, 1949, p. 406.

[20] Frederick G. Hochwalt, "Financing Catholic Education," *Educational Record*, April, 1949, p. 203.

state to subsidize private schools. This demand, too, can be clothed in good American garb, as, for example, in the observation of Professor Van Zyl of Calvin College that "if we want to have a healthy social structure and preserve our democracy, and if private schools are among the best guarantees of liberty and freedom, then we ought to give private initiative more support." [21]

5. Finally comes the argument that to provide positive religious instruction to the children of our nation constitutes in itself a public service which the state cannot safely leave to the chance circumstance that private resources may be found to sustain it. Under an interpretation of the First Amendment which excludes the concerns of religion from the purview of the state, and extends this interpretation to state-conducted education, public schools are circumscribed in their efforts to provide a genuine moral education. Public schools thus become "godless institutions." But not only is education in morality severely handicapped, continues the argument, democracy is weakened since it too is dependent upon a religious underwriting of Judean-Christian origin. To perpetuate democracy we must make certain that religion be not excluded from education. Consequently, if the facts of religious diversity or rigid interpretation of the Constitution require the omission of religion from public education, it is a matter of public moment that private schools assure its continuance. Certainly we cannot afford "to identify freedom of religion with freedom from religion."

Here, briefly summarized, are arguments which induce many to advocate an interpretation of the principle of separation of church and state which does no more than to prohibit the state from favoring one religious orientation over others and which sanctions positive "cooperation" between the state and religious organizations.

The Argument in Support of a Policy of Nonassistance

We turn now to a rebuttal of the position just reviewed and to the positive considerations favoring a strict interpretation of separation of church and state in education.

---

[21] Reprinted in *Christian Science Monitor*, April 9, 1948.

1. Let us examine first the argument that since nonpublic schools render a public service they are entitled to receive public support.

This argument overlooks the very important consideration that insofar as nonpublic schools do in fact relieve public schools of a pupil load, this follows not from common planning, or mutual agreement, but rather from accident. Nor is there any effort to envisage the enrollment problem of the community as a whole as a preliminary to a decision as to how its pupil population can be most effectively housed and educated. Rather is it a case in which the private school, on its own initiative, decides to serve its own interests. Not infrequently, as a result, the housing of the pupil population is far from economically determined, and it is an open question whether a community richly supplied with both private and public schools is not actually wasting the resources potentially available for the education of its young. And what shall we say of a public policy which requires the state to reward the competitors of an institution established to serve the public to the extent that these competitors weaken and circumscribe its activities?

The fallacy in the public welfare argument also becomes evident when we inquire into the character of the education afforded by those nonpublic schools which are claimants for public assistance. The purpose of the church-related school is not, as is often implied, to provide young people with two types of education, the one secular and the other religious, each separately conceived and administered. Rather is it to organize instruction so that all subjects are permeated with a sectarian interpretation. Consequently, in asking the public to finance such a school we are suggesting that the state support not only a concept of religion and of life that is peculiar to but one segment of the public but to promote as well general education of a parochial character.

Indeed, it is the expressed purpose of insuring a parochial interpretation of all subjects in the curriculum that justifies in the eyes of their patrons the maintenance of church-related schools. Science, literature, history, even mathematics are not conceived solely as secular subjects to be taught in a manner more or less identical with that in a public school. On the contrary, they are designed to promote a uniquely religious interpretation of life. For example, the Commission on American Citizenship at the Catholic University of America has been engaged since 1939 in the preparation of curriculum materials specifically designed for Catholic schools.[22] These efforts have in mind not merely to provide a positive parochial interpretation of the general curriculum but, in some instances, to correct what is considered to be a wrong emphasis in public education. Thus George N. Shuster in discussing the problem of literature teaching with a group of Catholic teachers condemned the "domination of literature courses in Catholic schools by English Protestant classics" and posed the question, "Do we want to form a Catholic mind or not?" [23] and George Johnson, formerly Educational Director of the National Welfare Conference, contended that "To attempt to make children and youth conformable to the image of the Savior by means of some occasional religious instruction and then teach them the arts and sciences in conformity with the spirit of the world is to court failure. . . . In the Catholic school, religion is not regarded as just one branch in the curriculum. It is not confined to mere religious instruction. It is the foundation, the heart and soul of all other disciplines." [24]

For individuals or groups to organize and conduct private schools with a view to furthering a parochial conception of life is, of course, a right guaranteed under the Constitution. Are not the nonpublic schools precluded from a claim upon the public purse precisely because they are assured the right to utilize education for ends private and parochial rather than public? As Justice Jackson remarked in his dissenting opinion in the Everson case, "We cannot have it both ways. Religious teaching cannot be a private affair when the state seeks to impose regulations which infringe upon it indirectly, and a public affair when it comes to taxing citizens of one faith to aid another, or those of no faith to aid all. If these principles seem harsh in prohibiting aid to Catholic education, it must not be forgotten that it is the same constitution that alone assures Catholics the right to maintain these schools at all when predominant local sentiment would

---

[22] See, for example, a three-volume basic curriculum for elementary schools entitled *Guiding Growth in Christian Social Living* and a series of readers entitled *Faith and Freedom Readers.*

[23] Quoted in *Providence Evening Bulletin,* October 31, 1947.

[24] *Atlantic Monthly,* April, 1940, p. 500.

forbid them." Obviously, what Justice Jackson writes with reference to Catholic schools applies as well to schools of all denominations.

2. The contention that parents of children in parochial schools suffer from double taxation fails to distinguish between an assessment compelled by government in support of a public service (one from which society as a whole benefits and for want of which all are disadvantaged) and an assessment which one assumes voluntarily by virtue of his identification with a cause which he individually deems worthy and essential.

No one will deny that the development of a dual system of education in this country imposes a heavy burden upon the membership of religious organizations committed to this policy, a burden which promises to become heavier rather than lighter as parochial education expands from education on the elementary level into secondary and higher levels as well. It is understandable, too, that individuals whose devotion to nonpublic schools is drawn upon to the point of exhaustion should seek ways and means of relief from taxation on behalf of a system of education in which they have little faith. Nor is the disposition to submit to public taxation in support of public schools, under these circumstances, strengthened by the charge, so frequently encountered today, that public education, in being neutral towards religion, is, in fact, hostile to it.

Even so, the remedy is not to exempt from taxation all who prefer to substitute private services for public. To adopt this as a principle would be to paralyze the most vital activities of government. What, for example, would be the consequences of its application in areas other than education in which the state undertakes directly to meet common needs? Should we exempt individuals and corporations from taxation for the support of a police department, for example, in the event that they prefer to substitute the protection of a private security guard? Or consider the example of the government requiring each individual to be immunized in the face of a general epidemic of a contagious disease and providing vaccination free to all through the resources of a public health department to insure that this be done. Would we sanction the state's assumption of medical fees paid to private physicians by those who prefer to substitute the services of their family doctor?

The obvious reply is, "No," because the taxes so imposed have in mind the health, welfare, and safety of all, and it is to the interest of the public that no one be overlooked. Similarly, public schools are established because of general recognition of the fact that the community as a whole benefits from them and suffers from their neglect. Consequently, taxes in their support are imposed upon the childless as well as parents, upon nonpatrons as well as patrons.

3. A similar fallacy underlies the contention that the state must implement the legal right of a child to attend the school of the parent's choice. As we have seen, the United States Supreme Court, in *Pierce* v. *Society of Sisters,* clearly affirmed the parent's right to send his child either to a public or to a private school. From this, some infer that unless the parent is financially assisted in his decision to use the private school, and not disadvantaged by "double taxation," the right remains an empty right.

The error here consists in the assumption that the obligation to *recognize* a right carries with it an additional obligation *to create the conditions* of its realization. This, too, would be a hazardous principle to adopt. Does governmental protection of the right of free speech, for example, require the state to furnish a hall and to round up an audience for each individual who may feel impelled to exercise the right of free expression? Or, to resort to the absurd, does the guaranteed right to marry the individual of one's own choice obligate the state to provide a list of eligibles for each young man or woman eager to enter into the bonds of wedlock? So to argue would indeed commit us to the welfare state with a vengeance!

But if we say "No" to instances of this character, upon what grounds do we insist the state should finance the right to attend the school of one's choice? Is not the freedom of a parent to send his child to a private school one thing and the obligation of the state to finance this right altogether another?

Justice Rutledge, in *Everson* v. *Board of Education,* appropriately remarked in this connection:

Of course discrimination in the legal sense does not exist. The child attending the religious school has the same right as any other to attend the public school. But he foregoes exercising it because the same guaranty which assumes the freedom forbids the public school or any agency of the state to give or aid him in securing the religious instruction he seeks.

Were he to accept the common school, he would be the first to protest the teaching of any creed or faith not his own. And it is precisely for this reason that their atmosphere is wholly secular that the children are not sent to public schools under the Pierce doctrine. But that is a constitutional necessity, because we have staked the very existence of our country on the faith that complete separation between the state and religion is best for the state and best for religion.

4. Confusion of thought, equally serious, applies to the charge that unless the public assists both nonpublic and public schools in the discharge of their "appointed tasks," it is guilty of fostering a monopoly in education.

In what sense is the term "monopoly" used here? Surely not in the sense that in controversial matters, such as in politics, economics, and religion, the public school is free to impress one and only one point of view upon the minds of the young. On the contrary, is it not a basic principle in public education (in contrast with a principle often sanctioned and sometimes lauded in private education) that in matters upon which the public mind is as a house divided against itself, the school must refrain carefully from promoting but one point of view? And is not one criticism leveled at public education by the partisans of a parochial conception of life that it is guilty of "neutralism" in areas where the critics would substitute dogmatism?

Nor is the "deadly monopoly" of public education in any way similar to state education in a totalitarian country, despite the overly zealous indictment of individuals to this effect.[25] One unique feature of public education in the United States is its independence of the state, even local governments, as Europeans understand state control of education. Indeed, there is no uniform pattern of American education—unless it be in the existence of a high degree of local autonomy exercised by boards of education. In the United States 85 per cent of the school boards are elected by the people. This fact, together with the control such boards

---

[25] See article by Lewis C. Fay, "'Abolish Public Schools,' Says Owner of Newspaper Chain," *The Nation's Schools*, August, 1952.

exercise over the curriculum of the school, hardly resembles the highly centralized control over education which emanates from the ministry of education in European countries and should insure the protection of the American people against the educational evils of the "slave state."

What, then, is meant when the friends of church-related schools warn against the monopoly of public education? No more than the exclusive use of funds for public education and the obligations of self-financing that this imposes upon private education. Is it not misleading to characterize this as a monopoly of public education when the field is left open to private initiative? And what is the alternative? For the state to finance free enterprise in education? Surely, this is a strange and novel conception of private initiative!

A strange interpretation, yes. But also a suggestion which, if followed, might prove equally disastrous to private and public education inasmuch as the hand that controls the purse is seldom satisfied until it also controls policy.

5. This takes us to the dangers of state interference in private and parochial education which are implicit in governmental support. It is well to remind the advocates of state subsidies for nonpublic schools that this was once the practice in American education. But characteristic of this period also was government control of the education thus afforded. Americans are unaccustomed to the conception of relations between church and state in which the church functions as a self-determining agency in education and the state meekly assumes the burden of financing this education. Rather has it been one in which state subsidies have led to a determining voice in matters of policy. Howard Beale, in his *History of Freedom of Teaching in American Schools,* recites instances in which the states have presumed to dictate the internal structure of educational institutions to which articles of incorporation have been granted. Thus, in 1834, the legislature of Missouri, in approving a charter for an academy at Troy and Independence, stipulated that "no preference shall be given or any discrimination made (in the choice of trustees, professors, or teachers, or students) on account of religious sentiments; nor shall any trustees, professors or teachers at any time, make by-laws, ordinances or regulations that may, in any wise, interfere with

or in any manner control the conscience, or the free exercise of religious worship." [26]

To be sure, the Missouri legislature, in this instance, was animated by what some would consider an excessive spirit of nonsectarianism. But this does not alter the fact that a government which pays the piper may decide at any time to call the tune. And is there not ample evidence today of a growing disposition on the part of state legislatures as well as the Congress of the United States to dictate to educational institutions how they should order their houses sufficient to suggest to independent schools the folly of jeopardizing an autonomy which constitutes their *raison d'être?* Well might they ponder Justice Jackson's words in *Everson* v. *Board of Education:* "Nor should I think that those who have done so well without this aid would want to see this separation between Church and State broken down. If the State may aid these religious schools, it may therefore regulate them. Many groups have sought aid from tax funds only to find that it carried political controls with it. Indeed this Court has declared that 'It is hardly lack of due process for the Government to regulate that which it subsidizes.' " [27]

On the other hand, unless the state is privileged to regulate and supervise education within schools dependent upon it for support, it would be committed to a principle difficult to sanction. As the writer has elsewhere stated:

There is no suggestion on the part of groups now seeking public aid that they accept public control or supervision over the education they provide, in return for assistance received. On the contrary, their basic position, sincerely and honestly stated, is that separation of church and state in education implies that the state shall finance while the church defines and carries on this education. In so far as standards might be imposed by the state, they would be superficial and external, restricted to matters such as the physical conditions of buildings and, perhaps, the minimum and maximum salary to be paid to teachers, but unrelated in any vital sense to the content and quality of instruction. Certainly there would be no effective supervision of the nature, quality, and integrity of the thinking promoted by teachers, or a tender concern for methods of inquiry and reflective thinking which

---

[26] New York: Charles Scribner's Sons, 1941, p. 94.
[27] The statement within single quotation marks is from *Wickard* v. *Filburn*, 317 U.S. 111.

are indispensable in the education of free men. On the contrary, state support of non-public schools would permit public support of educational programs which might be formulated outside of this country, and contrary to democratic institutions and the democratic way of life. In short, a decision to subsidize non-public schools by means of public funds not only constitutes a revolutionary change in American public policy, but commits the democratic state in principle to the support of an education which it would not control—indeed, to what might be an *undemocratic* education.[28]

If it is felt that these dangers to private education are largely theoretical, there is no denying the disastrous consequences that would follow for public education by the diversion of public funds to nonpublic schools. It is difficult to exaggerate the serious situation which already confronts public education for want of adequate support. School enrollments are mounting steadily. Additional school buildings are called for, and existing structures are sadly in need either of repair or replacement. Classrooms are overcrowded and large numbers of children are in schools which operate on a double, often a triple, session basis. A critical shortage of teachers exists, and there is no immediate prospect of remedying this situation substantially in the light of existing salary schedules. Surely, this is no time in which to weaken public education further by diverting into other channels funds so desperately needed.

Nor is this merely a simple question of apportioning funds between two school systems. There are at present some 256 religious sects in this country. Once the principle of state assistance to nonpublic schools begins to operate, hungry mouths will appear in abundance, each demanding its fair share (or, shall we say a lion's share?) of the public purse. The inevitable result would be a steady expansion of appropriations on behalf of nonpublic schools and a contraction in those available to public schools.

Not only would subsidizing nonpublic schools sap the material resources of public education, but it would also result in a lowering of educational standards in both types of institutions. What reason is there to believe that the character of nonpublic education would improve as each denominational school became the

---

[28] V. T. Thayer, *The Attack Upon the American Secular School* (Boston: Beacon Press, Inc., 1951), pp. 134–135.

recipient of public aid? It is true that private schools have, on occasion, developed and tested out new methods of teaching and new organizations of subject matter, from which public schools, less free to use their pupils as guinea pigs, have profited. By and large, however, public education in this country has served as a stimulus for raising the standards and broadening the educational vision of nonpublic schools. Once the bleeding process is inaugurated, however, and the vitality of the public schools lowered, we may expect the work of nonpublic schools to sag as well.

Should the State Assist Auxiliary Activities?

It may be objected that the discussion has centered thus far upon the issue of direct assistance to nonpublic schools, which is largely hypothetical, except, possibly, in a few states in which overly jealous officials of a religious persuasion have violated the law and have sought to merge parochial and public schools. Since the partisans of parochial interests at the moment ask for no more than public assistance for auxiliary activities, it is with this that we should concern ourselves. Moreover, it may be added that there is no legal barrier to aid of this character, since the Supreme Court has ruled that these services benefit the child rather than the institution.

For example, in the matter of free textbooks, Chief Justice Hughes, in speaking for the Supreme Court in 1930, held that the constitution is not violated when the state supplies textbooks free to children in private as well as public schools, provided the books are identical with those used in the public schools and are nonreligious and nonsectarian in character. In these instances, said the Court, "Individual interests are aided only as the common interest is safeguarded." [29] Transportation of children attending nonpublic schools, health services, free lunches for needy children, and the like are likewise viewed by the courts as of direct benefit to the child and only incidentally as aids to the school. Consequently, one may ask, "Why confuse these services with the larger question of direct aid to nonpublic schools?"

The answer is supplied by representatives of the interests which have struggled so vigorously to persuade state and federal govern-

---

[29] *Cochran* v. *Louisiana State Board of Education,* 281 U.S. 370 (1930).

ment to assume the obligation of financing auxiliary services. On the federal level, for example, those who advocate specific provision for auxiliary services in all federal legislation designed to aid education in the states have frankly admitted that their concern is with the principle this would establish rather than with the amount of assistance that might be forthcoming. As Robert C. Hartnett states in his pamphlet on *Federal Aid to Education,* "It is surely not the amount of money involved in Federal aid for bus transportation which arouses our interest . . . we are fighting to have our schools recognized as part of the American system of education." [30]

Since both principle and practical considerations are involved, let us examine more closely this question of public support of auxiliary services in nonpublic schools.

In the first place, it is important to observe that they are not all of the same order. They differ significantly both in nature and importance. Since, however, the term is a blanket one it can be used to blur the line that legitimately separates aid to the individual (in this instance the child) from aid to an institution with which he may be associated.

Take, for example, the public transportation of children to nonpublic schools. This has been sanctioned by the United States Supreme Court (*Everson* v. *Board of Education*) as a public health or safety measure. Said the Court, in justifying its decision, "The State contributes no money to the schools. It does not support them. Its legislation, as applied, does no more than provide a general program to help parents get their children, regardless of their religion, safely and expeditiously to and from accredited schools."

In dissenting from the majority decision, however, both Justice Jackson and Justice Rutledge point to inaccuracies of fact and interpretation in the majority opinion and the danger that the Court was engaged in broadening the concept of public welfare

---

[30] New York: American Press, 1950. It is doubtless this concern for principle that leads the advocates of federal aid in support of auxiliary activities to insist that all proposed legislation be so worded that this assistance would be assured nonpublic schools in all states, irrespective of state constitutions. Thus, in those states which forbid state authorities at present to distribute public funds to sectarian institutions, special agencies would be set up to insure that children in nonpublic schools receive the benefit of federal grants.

to such an extent that the purposes of the First Amendment might eventually be annulled. Justice Jackson, for example, emphasized that the New Jersey statute did not, in fact, provide for the free transportation of all children. Children in attendance upon private schools "operated for profit in whole or in part" were excluded under the terms of the act. The test of eligibility for assistance thus turned upon whether or not a child chanced to attend a school of a given type. Accordingly, the Justice concluded,

It seems to me that the basic fallacy in the Court's reasoning which accounts for its failure to apply the principle it avows, is in ignoring the essentially religious test by which beneficiaries of this expenditure are selected. A policeman protects a Catholic, of course—but not because he is a Catholic; it is because he is a man and a member of our society. The fireman protects the Church school—but not because it is a Church school; it is because it is property, part of the assets of our society. Neither the fireman nor the policeman has to ask before he renders aid "Is this man or building identified with the Catholic Church?" But before these school authorities draw a check to reimburse for a student's fare they must ask just that question, and if the school is a Catholic one they may render aid because it is such, while if it is of any other faith or is run for profit, the help must be withheld.

Of the dangers involved in employing loosely the concept of public welfare, Justice Rutledge warned that it might well lead to an undermining of the First Amendment. This approach, he states,

if valid, supplies a ready method for nullifying the Amendment's guarantee, not only in this case and others involving small grants in aid for religious education, but equally for larger ones. The only thing needed will be the Court again to transplant the public welfare —public function view from its proper nonreligious due process bearing to First Amendment application, holding that religious education is not "supported" though it may be aided by the appropriation, and that the cause of education generally is furthered by helping the pupil to secure that type of training.

That Justice Rutledge's reservations were not entirely imaginary seems obvious in the light of the actual operation of bus service for children in the two types of schools. Normally, transportation of public school children is furnished only within a defined area (that is, to children attending the school nearest to their homes). This is not true of children in nonpublic schools. Court approval of the New Jersey statute is widely used to sanction not merely free transportation on public highways, where traffic hazards are to be expected and the principle of public health and safety may be applicable, but to maintain bus routes without reference to place of residence and thus to render it convenient for children to attend the nonpublic school. Surely this goes beyond the necessities of public welfare and contributes directly to the advantage of the church school.

Free textbooks constitute a second category of auxiliary services and a problem unique in itself. As indicated earlier, the furnishing of textbooks by the state to children in public and nonpublic schools was approved by the Supreme Court on the theory that the child rather than the school is aided thereby. In the words of the Louisiana court,

One may scan in vain to ascertain where any money is appropriated for the purchase of schoolbooks for the use of any church, private, sectarian or even public schools. The appropriations were made for the specific purpose of purchasing schoolbooks for the use of the children of the state, free of cost to them. It was for their benefit and the resulting benefit to the State that appropriations were made. True, these children attend some school, public or private, the latter sectarian or non-sectarian, and that the books are to be furnished them for their use, free of cost, whichever they attend. The schools, however, are not the beneficiaries of these appropriations. They obtain nothing from them, nor are they relieved of a single obligation because of them.[31]

With this position Chief Justice Hughes was apparently in agreement. In upholding the decision of the lower court he also stated that the Fourteenth Amendment was not violated when the state supplies textbooks free to children in private as well as public schools, provided, however, that the books thus distributed are identical with those used in public schools and are nonreligious and nonsectarian in character.

The proviso that the textbooks be nonsectarian in character runs counter to a major purpose of the religious school, namely,

---

[31] *Cochran* v. *Louisiana State Board of Education, op. cit.*

to permeate all instruction with a religious point of view. Consequently there is a very real temptation for religious groups to exercise pressure upon those charged with responsibility for the selection of books to choose those which meet religious criteria. A conspicuous example of this occurred in New Mexico, where textbooks in the form of readers and books in the fields of history, geography, and the like, published specifically for the use of schools of one religious persuasion, were included in the official list of books adopted by the Department of Education and were used in public as well as nonpublic schools.

Needless to say, pressure upon public authorities to select textbooks favorable to a parochial point of view might well endanger freedom of teaching. The determination of pressure groups to control teaching in controversial areas already constitutes a serious problem. Let the few states which now provide textbooks free to children of all types of schools increase in number to fifty, and the practice of impartial and objective teaching will encounter still graver obstacles. Perhaps a quotation from what the writer has elsewhere stated is pertinent here:

The privilege which parents enjoy of educating their children in private schools has a two-fold benefit. It insures freedom of private schools to deviate from what is generally accepted; even to experiment in methods and ideas, without severely injuring the public, and, on occasion, with benefit to the public. On the other hand, it leaves the public school relatively free to draw upon an objective and impartial scholarship in the selection of its teaching materials and in determining what it shall stress. True, a good school avoids indoctrination in controversial areas and is careful to call the attention of students to principles that are of doubtful validity or are in dispute. But it is one thing to be free to present all points of view and it is another thing to teach adequately when the weight and momentum of the institution is to prior commitment. Let the public adopt the practice of furnishing textbooks free to non-public as well as to public schools and education will cease to be free. Special interests and parochial conceptions under the guise of religious convictions or absolutes, which no one may question, will soon operate to destroy the integrity of textbook selection, corrupt the atmosphere in which textbooks are written, and render impossible the education of the free mind.

These results will satisfy no one. To the extent that the state remains neutral and independent in its choice of the materials of education, it will be accused of unfair treatment of sectarian groups or of introducing "disturbing" materials of learning to the students. To the degree that parochial interests intervene and seek to control this selection they will exercise an unwarranted, even dangerous control over the education of children outside their legitimate spheres of influence. Inevitably, then, the furnishing of free textbooks to children in parochial schools will result in that intermingling of secular and religious concerns which Madison, Jefferson, and others sought to prevent by the adoption of the First Amendment to the Constitution.[32]

The question of health services, in contrast with the problems of transportation and free textbooks, is relatively simple. In these days when the necessities of an adequate national defense and the draft confront the people of the United States in an acute form, few would deny the public importance of insuring the minimum essentials of health care for each and every child. Nor is there objection to state intervention in order to protect a child from neglect or the mistaken notions of parents and guardians. With respect to health needs the welfare of the child and the well-being of the community take precedence over all other interests.

These considerations should also control the organization and administration of health services. Several years ago the Federal Council of Churches of Christ in America put forth suggestions designed to meet the health needs of children and at the same time to prevent these being used for narrow interests. These suggestions involved the divorcing of welfare services from the question of aid to education. "By thus drawing a clear distinction between aid to schools and welfare services for children," stated the Council, "we believe that necessary assistance can be given to education without making it the object of sectarian controversy or compromising the principle of separation of Church and State for which the Council has always stood."

In line with this policy, the Council suggested that all health services which are publicly supported be placed under the supervision and administration of a public agency. By centralizing administration it was hoped overlapping and duplication of machinery would be avoided.

---

[32] *Ibid., op. cit.,* pp. 121–122.

This may prove to be a happy solution with respect to health services and constitute a wise precedent to follow not only with health projects but in the administration of other services to children of a public character. Certainly every effort should be made to prevent the duplication of facilities and personnel which would follow inevitably upon the division of administration of services between public and private agencies.

The Problem of Desegregation Introduces a New Factor

Thus far we have discussed almost exclusively the efforts of religious groups to secure public assistance for nonpublic schools. Only incidentally have we referred to the attempts of individuals who oppose public education outright and thus seek to bring about a return to privately supported education. The reason for this is that advocates of this policy constitute an insignificant minority of the population.

Since the decision of the United States Supreme Court in 1954 which declared unlawful the exclusion of children from public schools on grounds of race, a new factor has been introduced into the situation and a new danger confronts public education. In a number of the southern states, state constitutions have been revised and laws passed which will permit the abolition of public schools and the subsidizing of private schools in the event that a federal court orders the admission of Negroes into a white school. Private schools, however, cannot spring into being fully equipped at a moment's notice. Furthermore, private schools now operating in the South are chiefly of sectarian affiliation and are thus not eligible to receive public assistance. Consequently, the constitutional prohibition of public aid to nonpublic schools constitutes one of the most formidable obstacles to the southern program of "massive resistance" to desegregation. Under these circumstances, we may well expect (indeed, we may now witness) the southern politican, who, in the past, has been one of the most vigorous supporters of public education in Congress and out, to undergo a change of heart and to ally himself with the forces already described in order to modify, if not to rescind, the constitutional principle of separation of church and state.

So much for the problem of public assistance, direct and indirect, to nonpublic schools. There remains the concern, to which we referred at the conclusion of the last chapter, that in adopting an attitude of neutrality toward religion, public schools are neglecting an essential education in moral and spiritual values and are contributing to the weakening of the moral fibre of our democracy, that religion is neglected in the secular school and, in consequence, ways and means must be found for its inclusion in the curriculum.

To this problem we now turn.

Suggested Reading

American Jewish Committee, *Religion in Public Education: A Statement of Views* (New York: American Jewish Committee, 1957).

American Jewish Committee, *Summaries of Rulings of State Attorneys General with Respect to Church-State Questions as They Affect Public and Parochial Schools* (New York: American Jewish Committee, 1958).

Catholic Bishops of America, *Statement on the Place of the Private and Church-Related Schools in American Education, The New York Times,* 1955.

Farrell, A. P., "The Relation of Government, Religion and Education," *National Catholic Educational Association Proceedings,* 1949, pp. 164–168.

Fuller, E. E., "Public Schools and Separation of Church and State," *School Executive,* February, 1949, pp. 11–18.

Hartnett, Robert C., S.J., "The School in the American Community," *America,* April 9, 1952, pp. 65–68.

Herberg, Will, "The Sectarian Conflict Over Church and State," *Commentary,* November, 1957, pp. 450–462.

National Education Association, *The State and Sectarian Education, Research Bulletin,* Vol. XXXIV, No. 4, December, 1958.

Progressive Education, "The Issue of Sectarianism," February, 1949, pp. 97–128. This entire issue is devoted to the problem of sectarianism in education.

Religion and the Schools (pamphlet) by Robert Gordis, William Gorman, F. Ernest Johnson, and Robert LeKachman (New York: Fund for the Republic, 1959).

Thayer, V. T., *The Attack Upon the American Secular School* (Boston: Beacon Press, Inc., 1951).

.\/.\/.\/.\

20

Religion and Morality in Public Education

Religious Freedom As Originally Conceived

In his oration commemorating the two hundredth anniversary of the landing of the Pilgrims at Plymouth, Daniel Webster pictured these sturdy individuals as pledging, "If God prosper us, we shall here begin a work which shall last for ages; we shall plant here a new society, in the principles of the fullest liberty and the purest religion. . . ."

The debt which Americans owe to the founders of New England is in no way lessened by a more realistic appraisal of the motives which animated them. They were indeed determined, as were many others, to establish a new society in the new world; but they scarcely envisaged its realization through the application of the "principles of fullest liberty." On the contrary, to insure the practice of the "purest religion," as they conceived it, required the enforcement of the most rigid conformity of thought and conduct. The religious conscience which prompted them to establish communities in the new world, where they might worship without restraint, demanded that this worship be not defiled by the presence of individuals of a contrary conscience.

The original American settlements were thus religiously homogeneous and the purpose of the schools established was to transmit to the young the faith of the fathers without deviation. Nevertheless, the free air of America eventually fostered an identification of religious freedom with the freedom of individual conscience both in thought and in modes of worship. This carries with it the right to deviate as well as to conform, to travel at one's own risk as well as to follow the majority. That is to say, under the law, no human being is now authorized to decide for another what is valid or invalid in religion. Truth and error in religious matters are exclusively determined, if at all, by an authority higher than man.[1]

Contributions of the Nonsectarian School

The establishment of the nonsectarian school marked the first significant application of the concept of religious freedom to education. Unlike New England and the South, the Middle Colonies were heterogeneous in nationality and creed from the beginning. Here Quaker and Mennonite, Lutheran and Reformed German, Baptist and Methodist, Presbyterian and Anglican, even an occasional Catholic and Jew rubbed shoulders with each other. Proximity and the financial difficulty each sect encountered in supporting its own school created conditions favorable to cooperation. Eventually the Quakers and, later, other denominations conceived the plan of enrolling in their schools the children of the unorthodox as well as the orthodox. The presence in the same school of pupils of varied religious origins under conditions favorable to mutual respect and understanding tended to shift the emphasis in religious instruction from points of sectarian difference to items upon which all denominations might agree. Thus nonsectarian religious instruction came into being.

Nonsectarian instruction was admirably adapted to the needs of education on the western frontier where the population was varied in background, but it was also well received in the original colonies as these, too, increased in numbers and diversity of composition. During the nineteenth century it gave impetus to the states to extend the principle of separation of church and state to

---

[1] One expression of this freedom occurs in the eloquent words of the United States Supreme Court in *West Virginia* v. *Board of Education*. Said the Court: "If there is any fixed star in our constitutional constellation it is that no official, high or petty, can prescribe what shall be orthodox in politics, nationalism, religion or other matters of opinion or force its citizens to confess by word or act of faith therein" (319 U.S. 141).

the field of education. Thus, as old and new states came to establish public school systems, they tended to erect a "wall of separation" between the public treasury and nonpublic schools through the adoption of constitutional provisions which restricted the use of public funds to public education and forbade the appropriation of any funds to any institution in which sectarian doctrines were taught.

In the beginning, however, nonsectarian instruction meant little more than the elimination of doctrines which divided Protestant from Protestant. Later, in a more complex situation, it became evident that the identical principle forbade instruction in matters that set Catholic apart from Protestant and both from Jew. Consequently, materials of instruction and practices that were once taken for granted came under review and were gradually eliminated. Most conspicuous of these was the reading from the King James version of the Bible, the reciting of Protestant prayers, and the singing of songs of an obviously parochial tinge, to which Catholics and Jews and other non-Protestants objected.

To be sure, these developments did not occur without dissent and dissension. Repeated appeals to the courts to interdict sectarian practices in the schools were instituted in state after state with contradictory results; one state court, for example, would rule that the Bible is a sectarian document to be banned from the school, whereas another would hold that it is basically nonsectarian, in the sense that it is the "mother of sects" which overarches sectarian doctrines, and its use, accordingly, is not only appropriate but desirable.[2]

These conflicting decisions are explained by the obvious fact that what constitutes sectarian or nonsectarian content of instruction varies with communities, implying one thing, let us say, in a southern community that is 100 per cent Protestant in composition and quite a different thing in a northern commercial or industrial area inhabited not only by Protestants but by Catholics and Jews and those of no religious affiliation at all.

Were we to generalize from the practices followed in schools throughout the country in the course of the nineteenth century,

---

[2] For a more detailed review of the status of Bible reading, prayers, and other religious exercises, see V. T. Thayer, *The Attack Upon the American Secular School* (Boston: Beacon Press, Inc., 1951), chap. VII.

we should doubtless conclude that few institutions were genuinely nonsectarian or secular in character. But this is to confuse the outward and visible expression of principle with its inward and motivating spirit.[3] What was accepted by the public and the courts alike was the *principle* of nonsectarian instruction. This principle, in turn, testified to a mounting spirit of religious toleration, a practical application of the Golden Rule to religious doctrine, since it dictated, in substance, the exclusion from the public school of positive instruction in tenets of religion to which any group might object. Otherwise stated, an institution that represented the public as a whole was legally obliged to refrain from grinding the ax of any one segment of the community in controversial matters. In line with this principle, public schools in state after state gradually abandoned compulsory reading of the Bible, singing denominational songs, using parochial prayers and other exercises of a sectarian character as objection to them became manifest.

Pressure Mounts in Support of Religious Instruction

As stated earlier, the decision of the state of Pennsylvania in 1913 to require the reading of the Bible in public schools marked the turning of the tide with respect to the developments thus hurriedly reviewed. By 1946, thirteen states had adopted similar legislation of a compulsory character. In twenty-four states Bible reading was permitted, and in only eight states was the Bible evidently not being used in the public school.[4] Demands for compulsory Bible reading and a return to the daily use of the Lord's Prayer were followed by the introduction of programs of religious instruction on "released time," a device by which children are given instruction in religion on school time by teachers of the denomination of the parents' choice. By 1948, the year of the adverse decision of the United States Supreme Court with respect to this practice

---

[3] A pamphlet, *The State and Sectarian Education* (Washington, D.C.: National Education Association, 1946), gives an excellent picture of practices in the various states in this area prior to the McCollum decision. Also see *Summaries of Rulings of State Attorneys General with Respect to State-Church Questions As they Affect Public and Parochial Schools* (New York: American Jewish Committee, 1958).

[4] *The State and Sectarian Education, op. cit.*, p. 34.

(*McCollum* v. *Board of Education,* 333 U.S. 203), it was estimated that from one and one-half to two million pupils in some two thousand to twenty-five hundred communities were involved in these programs. Nor did the practice stop with the decision of the Court. Subsequent interpretations of the ruling by state officials and a second decision of the Supreme Court in 1952, in *Zorach* v. *Clauson* (343 U.S. 306), to the effect that public schools may adjust their schedules to permit pupils to attend classes in religion which meet off the school grounds have continued the practice. Indeed, a survey of the actual situation today would indicate a not inconsiderable use of public school classrooms during the school day for instruction on released time, despite the clear implications of the McCollum and the Zorach decisions.[5]

The results of religious instruction on released time have not been altogether satisfactory, however, viewed either from the standpoint of religious groups or from that of school administrators. The obvious disruption of the school schedule, the segregation of children into sectarian groups, the not infrequent isolation of the nonconformist child, and the frequent use of unskilled personnel for instruction trouble conscientious laymen as well as educators and have frequently induced boards of education to abolish programs once initiated. To this must be added, in all sincerity, the uneasiness with which many have viewed the willingness, if not insistence, of ardent advocates of released-time instruction to ignore both the spirit and the letter of the law, at the same time that they argue the indispensability of religious instruction as one means of fostering a healthy obedience to law in the hearts of the young!

On the other hand, these programs fall short of what many religious leaders would have the school assume as a sacred obligation, namely, to bridge the gulf between secular and religious education. This can only be done, they believe, when religion finds its way into the heart of the curriculum. They propose, accordingly, that the public schools introduce a "common core" of

---

[5] For example, Erwin L. Shaver, executive director of week-day religious education of the Division of Christian Education of the National Council of Churches stated (*Religious Education,* January-February, 1953, p. 42) that 15 per cent of the communities participating in the released-time programs were conducting classes in the public schools. Shaver also estimated in February, 1952, that some 1,890,000 Protestant school children were enrolled in released-time programs in some 3000 communities. (See *Religious News Service,* February 13, 1952.)

religious instruction into the curriculum. This common core, to quote Henry P. Van Dusen, involves "not merely the institution of courses in one department in the curriculum or required attendance in such courses," but, as well, "a fundamental reorientation of every subject in the curriculum and its presentation in every course." [6] The content which Van Dusen and others of similar purpose have in mind is supposedly common to the major faiths of Protestantism, Catholicism, and Judaism.

The demand that public schools incorporate in the curriculum a common core of religious instruction has enlisted the active interest of a considerable group of Protestant leaders, some of whom, indeed, have threatened to withdraw Protestant support from public education unless means be found to introduce religious instruction into the curriculum.

Several years ago the Committee on Religion and Education of the American Council on Education put forth a compromise proposal. This committee found that public schools are engaged at present in "three over-lapping and confused policies and practices." These are avoidance of religion, planned religious activities, and a factual study of religion. Of the three, the committee prefers the third, the factual study of religion. "This approach," the committee states, "has distinctive merits. It is thoroughly consistent with modern educational theory and practice. It is applicable to any school, college or university, in addition to, or in substitution for, other practices. Its justification lies principally in the requirements of a fundamental general education. Such practice need not supplement planned religious activities, but it will tend to fill a vacuum caused by avoidance of religion." [7]

The committee recognizes that genuine difficulties must be overcome if its recommendations are not to be used, on the one hand, as a Trojan horse for the introduction of sectarian teaching and, on the other hand, to sanction an objectivity which concentrates so exclusively upon bare facts that it fails to stimulate young people to come to terms with the issues of life. Consequently, it urges an experimental program "in a few carefully selected situations to discover what is involved, and, insofar as possible, to

---

[6] *God in Education* (New York: Charles Scribner's Sons, 1951), p. 78.

[7] *The Function of the Public Schools in Dealing with Religion: A Report of the Exploratory Study Made by the Committee on Religion and Education* (Washington, D.C.: American Council of Education, 1953), p. 83.

obtain answers to certain important questions" before communities generally attempt its adoption. The problem, as the committee envisages it, "is one which makes peculiarly imperative a scrupulous observance of the constitutional principle of religious liberty," and it is mindful that "One of the most important aims of such studies and experiments should be how this principle can be applied to all—minorities and majorities alike." [8]

Not all advocates of the study of religion and the "erasing of religious illiteracy" are as scrupulously concerned to respect the sensibilities of minorities or to realize the obligations of a teacher to his students in an area where honest men differ fundamentally. Indeed, they are convinced that "objectivity" is undermining both religion and the democracy which they believe derives its life blood from religion. The spirit of nonsectarianism, they contend, has overshot its mark and has led to a "religious vacuum" in public education which militates against religion. This vacuum they propose to fill by a "factual study of religion" which differs little, if at all, from that proposed by the advocates of a "common core" of religious instruction. Certainly, the "facts" presented constitute a none too critical description of the orthodox faiths and their organizational expressions in contemporary life and exclude an equally sympathetic presentation of the views of numerous groups which have abandoned orthodoxy together with the grounds for this deviation. In short, the purpose is less the pursuit of truth in a highly confused and complex area of living and more the "saving of souls" as one segment of the community conceives salvation. [9]

What Is Meant By "Religion and Morality"?

How shall we resolve this question of the place of religion in public education?

The answer would seem to turn upon the meaning which the ordinary citizen, as well as the teacher and administrator, ascribes to the terms "religion and morality" in the unique context of public education. Nor can this meaning be arrived at lightly, since it goes to the heart of the concept of democracy in a pluralistic

---

[8] *Ibid.*, p. 86.
[9] For a helpful bibliography in this area, see *ibid.*, pp. 127–145.

society. For a time it was assumed that separation of church and state constituted a happy formula for achieving unity within diversity. Is this equally true in a period in which education has become well-nigh universal and a substantial proportion of the children of the country attend public rather than church-related schools? Can these schools maintain "a strict and lofty neutrality" with respect to religion and at the same time educate for character?

To answer these questions we shall have to examine both the nature of religion and morality under the unique conditions of public education.

Let us begin with religion.

How shall we interpret this term as applied to education? When is religion sectarian and, therefore, if we are to follow the injunctions of the courts, to be banned, and when is it unobjectionable?

Unfortunately, the advocates of religion in the schools tend to by-pass this question, often deliberately, since, as one report frankly admits, the difficulties of "trying to secure a definition mutually acceptable to all is obvious." [10] Nevertheless, failure to define specifically what is meant by religion can be disastrous in a country in which tolerance and respect for religious conscience is a condition of harmonious relationships and common action. Moreover, lack of clarity is certain to create confusion and contradiction, even futility of effort, in situations where the distinction between religious instruction and education in moral and spiritual values is all important.

In seeking our definition, we should bear in mind that definitions, in order to be helpful, are relevant to a purpose, and the purpose in the case under discussion is to erect a fence between the legitimate functions of the family and parochial organizations, on the one hand, and the functions of the school as a representative of the community as a whole, on the other. To borrow Robert Frost's phrase used so appropriately by Justice Frankfurter in *McCollum* v. *Board of Education,* "good fences make good neighbors."

An acceptable definition of religion, from the standpoint of the writer, is one employed by the courts in considering the relation

---

[10] *Conversations on Higher Education and Religion* (Haddam, Connecticut: Edward W. Hazen Foundation, 1942), p. 6. This deals with the proceedings and conclusions of a conference which had as its objective furthering both the introduction of courses in religion in the curriculum of public and private colleges and the "fullest opportunity for participation on the part of students in religious activities."

of religion to public education. This conceives of religion as being a concept of the Deity, or a God-theory, that is, the view one holds of the nature of an Ultimate Reality which shapes our ends and the implications for living which men derive from these concepts. It was this definition of religion that Justice Field propounded in *Reynolds* v. *United States* (98 U.S. 145) when he stated, "The term religion has reference to one's views of his relation to his Creator, and to the obligations they impose of reverence for His being and character, and of obedience to His word."

That this concept of religion is in substantial harmony with that of the leading advocates of positive religious instruction in the schools seems evident from the writings of responsible leaders such as Henry P. Van Dusen, President of Union Theological Seminary, Luther Allan Weigle, formerly Dean of the Yale Divinity School, and James A. Pike, formerly Dean of the Cathedral of St. John the Divine in New York City, as well as the pronouncements of a representative group of educators and religious leaders in the 1947 Report of the Committee on Religion and Education of the American Council on Education.[11] In stating what is meant by religion, the committee wrote as follows: "In simple terms religion implies an ultimate reality to which supreme allegiance must be given. To this ultimate reality men have from time immemorial given a name—God. The religious man finds warrant for all his conceptions of worth, of right, of duty, and of human destiny in his relation to this ultimate reality. . . . Religion affirms overwhelmingly a reality that transcends the flux of events and constrains men toward the true and the good."[12]

Likewise, Luther A. Weigle, in criticizing the decision of the United States Supreme Court in *McCollum* v. *Board of Education,* asserts that it encourages an "Uneasy working partnership between atheists and positivists on the one hand and religious individualists and ultra-fundamentalists on the other," who favor an interpretation of separation of church and state "which confines God to the church and outlaws Him in the state." This neutrality, he further asserts, has the practical effect of foisting an

---

[11] American Council on Education Studies: *Reports of Committees and Conferences,* April, 1947. This report should not be confused with the more recent report, *The Function of Public Schools in Dealing with Religion* referred to above.
[12] *Ibid.*, p. 11.

atheism—"or a non-theistic humanism" upon the schools which is inconceivable since "They may be neutral as to the strife of sects; but they cannot be neutral as to God." [13]

This concept of religion runs counter to the convictions not only of naturalists but also of many religious liberals who hold to a concept of Ultimate Reality and of human nature significantly different from that of Weigle and his associates. Doubtless the same is true of many teachers who can hardly be characterized as religiously illiterate. Neutrality in religion would seemingly require these instructors to refrain from efforts to persuade their pupils to adopt the conception of an Ultimate Reality which appeals to them and the parochial morality which derives from this partisan view. But in suppressing the evangelical impulse to promote the faith to which they are committed, are we to insist that they inculcate doctrines which they themselves cannot accept? In discussing this dilemma, I. N. Thut remarks,

The constitutional provisions for religious freedom clearly recognize the limitations in man's ability to know God fully and completely. . . . It is a deep-rooted American tradition that a man's God-theory is his own personal business and that he has a right to keep it as private as his breakfast or his bath. . . . In this atmosphere of freedom, it is small wonder that a multiplicity of God-theories has appeared. There is, for example, the Quaker theory, which looks upon God as a kind, loving father, who walks so closely with each of his children that no man or institution should be permitted to come between them. Then there are the well-known Congregationalist and Unitarian theories which disagree so sharply on the question of whether God has three forms or one. Similarly, the Mormon theory and the Shaker theory lead to decidedly opposite views on the matter of procreation. Some sects picture God as a fearful Being likely to punish violently anyone who dares approach Him without proper credentials. Others look upon Him as a somewhat vague, formless spirit that may be felt in one's heart but may not be known otherwise directly.[14]

From these facts Thut draws the conclusion that public schools must choose between one of two courses open to them.

---

[13] These quotations are from an article entitled "Freedom of Religion and Education," *Christianity and Crisis*, July 24, 1950, pp. 97–103.

[14] "Shall the Public Schools Teach Religion?" *Teacher Education Quarterly* (Connecticut State Department of Education), Winter, 1951, pp. 75–79.

Either they must teach all the pupils about all the current God-theories, including atheism and agnosticism, with a view to giving each child an opportunity to choose his own faith regardless of the wishes of his parents; or they may indoctrinate all pupils in a particular God-theory, again without reference to the preferences of minority group parents. The first alternative is not popular because it obviously defeats the primary purpose of those who most vociferously advocate religious instruction in the public schools; namely, the opportunity to propagandize in favor of a particular God-theory. The second course would do unpardonable violence to one of the first principles of democracy; namely, freedom of conscience.[15]

Are we to conclude that inasmuch as there is in fact no nonsectarian religion, religious concepts are to go unmentioned in the school?

Religion As Structure Versus Religion As Function

Some have sought a middle ground by drawing a distinction between religion as a "structure" and religion as a "function." By religion as a structure is meant what Thut has characterized as a God-theory. Essentially, it is a theology together with its implications for conduct (specific doctrines with their rituals and symbolism and approved practices, which distinguish one faith from another) whereas religion as a function refers to a "quality of behavior" or to the ideals and standards which, presumably, all religious structures in a given culture approve and which, it is believed, can be distilled and promoted independently of any one specific faith or creed.

As we shall see later, this distinction between common ideals and the parochial systems of belief which are thought to underwrite them has its value. But we may question whether the use of the term religion to designate both content and function may not confuse rather than clarify when applied to the practical problems of whether or not public school classrooms should be used as a media of instruction in religion.

One source of confusion derives from the fact that advocates of the distinction between structure and function are by no means in

[15] *Ibid.*, pp. 78–79.

agreement as to where the one leaves off and the other begins. Some draw the line in such a manner as to differ little, if at all, from the advocates of a common core of religious content. Others, as for example, Ward Madden,[16] conceive of function as analogous to, if not identical with, the process of education. As such, it is none other than the weighing of one proposed line of conduct against another, the resolving of conflicts among ideals through the reconstruction of old or the creation of a new ideal which will guide men as a cloud by day and a pillar of fire by night. Activities of this character are common to all men. They involve the thoughtful process of matching the assumptions or major premises common to one's family, local community, or national culture against the context of ever changing circumstance, with a resulting clarification or reinterpretation and, on occasion, even revision of these basic assumptions and principles. If this is what we are to mean by religion as a function, it embraces, as Ward Madden admits, atheists as well as religionists and, indeed, all men who live, move, and have their being in one and the same culture. Moreover, if the term religion is to be applied to this process, obviously religious education becomes an essential ingredient of all good education.

The concept of religion as a function furthers a spirit more democratic than that which insists upon incorporating a specific content of religion in the curriculum of the school. It is more democratic in the sense that its advocates would not have the school display favoritism toward any particular religious faiths. It also runs counter to the assumption which has so frequently pitted brother against brother, namely, that adherence to one arbitrary faith is an indispensable condition of morality. Rather is it more in harmony with a favorite phrase of John Adams, "There was virtue in the world before there was orthodoxy in it."

This tolerance is a decided asset to education in a society in which the religious atmosphere resembles the ancient tower of Babel.

Nevertheless, many will prefer a more neutral term to designate the objectives of the functionalists. They see little value and a potential danger in maintaining a distinction that is essentially fictitious: one of thought rather than actuality. They fear that

---

[16] *Religious Values in Education* (New York: Harper & Brothers, 1951).

when a teacher in a classroom attempts to develop the "religious attitude" he will be tempted to ground this attitude in a religious premise, one which he may believe inoffensive or nonsectarian but which others will immediately identify as sectarian.

As we shall see later, it is possible to avoid this difficulty by recognizing that the sources of morality are plural and more fundamental than any one religious faith, as conventionally understood, a fact that makes it advisable to avoid the confusion which goes with the distinction between structure and function.

What Place, If Any, Has Religion in Public Education?

We return, then, to our original query. Is there no place for religion in public education? Must we insist upon its total elimination from the school?

The answer is "No." Certainly there is a place for religion so long as the school sincerely attempts to avoid indoctrination. Theoretically, at least, the educational task in matters relating to religion is no different from that confronting the classroom in other areas where the community (not merely the local community but the wider community as well) is as a house divided against itself. Under these circumstances, and insofar as it is possible to deal with the topic educationally (that is, in the absence of emotional tensions which render impossible a sympathetic and generous understanding of rival points of view), it is the obligation of the school to inform, enlighten, and further appreciation and understanding of religious institutions. Ideally, a consideration of religion and its expressions, institutional and personal, in the school should result in the members of one denominational group viewing the adherents of another more sympathetically and generously than was true prior to study. This should hold true for the orthodox and the unorthodox, the believer and the nonbeliever. It would also be desirable for each individual to clarify his own position, which may or may not be that of the instructor or a fellow student.

What this implies specifically will vary with the age level of young people and with circumstance; but the principle is identical on all levels. It draws a clean-cut distinction between the "factual study of religion," as occasion arises in history, literature, science, music and art, the social studies, and the like, and all efforts on the part of the school to determine for a student his religious faith. As different and contrasting points of view become evident, young people will doubtless appreciate and respect the position of a teacher who makes clear that religion is no exception to the general rule that in matters controversial the public school is the representative of society as a whole and the partisan of no one segment.

Were classroom instruction in religion to deal justly with all faiths, the "study of religion" would include not merely the views of the orthodox faiths but the religious convictions of minority groups as well, including the "liberals," the agnostics, the humanists, and others who may have abandoned orthodoxy. It would not emphasize exclusively factors which impel some men toward religion but would investigate as well the grounds that have persuaded people equally sincere to seek the solutions to life's problems in nonconventional formulas.

It is obvious that few communities will venture to introduce religion into the curriculum of the public school under these broad and generous conditions, despite the fact that in a democracy which aspires to raise free men, responsible and seasoned in their thinking, it is a goal toward which to strive. In the meantime, and until a community has reached the point where it will permit a genuinely objective consideration of religion and not merely use a "factual study" as a device with which to promote the theological convictions of dominant groups, we must view "the study of religion" with extreme caution. Certainly, to authorize the use of school time for instruction in religion by its partisans is to sanction an educational procedure we should roundly condemn, were it applied to other areas of disagreement and controversy.

Does Moral Education Require a Religious Underpinning?

Some will object to these conclusions on the ground that they represent an all too grudging concession to the claims of religion. "How," they may exclaim, "is it possible to educate in moral and spiritual values, if religion is permitted only when sicklied over with the pale cast of thought?"

This takes us to the heart of our problem. How can the school educate for character without positive instruction in religion?

In dealing with this problem we must repeat that by religion is meant a specific content of belief, a "God-theory," as Thut has well described it, or a theological concept upon which men are by no means agreed; whereas by qualities of character and moral ideals is meant those common and accepted ways of thinking and feeling and acting in our relations with others which all men recognize will raise the standard of our living together.

Despite its importance for public education, this distinction is none too clear in the popular mind. Many still cling to a oneness in thought between doctrine and conduct characteristic of an homogeneous rather than a heterogeneous culture.

In a discussion of the nature of religion in various societies, John Herman Randall, Jr., tells us that there are some societies in which the social materials of religion are "moral, or imaginative or artistic rather than intellectual." In these societies religion is as much a way of life to be pursued as it is a set of beliefs to be accepted as true. But, as he points out, these societies are characteristically homogeneous in their religion. In the western world which has lacked this homogeneity for centuries, and in which Protestantism has long been an important influence, the theoretical aspects of religion have consistently loomed large.[17]

It was the theological aspect of religion which concerned our fathers when they instituted the policy of separation of church and state. They had come to realize from painful experience that the traditional assumption of a one-to-one relation between religious belief and individual and social morality was no longer sound and that, however essential it may have been in the past to insure social cohesion, in a land of many faiths it had become destructive of unity.

This was, of course, a revolutionary insight and led to an equally radical change in public policy. For ages men had assumed that conformity in thought was the *sine qua non* of social morality.

---

[17] William Ernest Hocking, Brand Blanchard, Charles William Hendel, and John Herman Randall, Jr., *Preface to Philosophy* (New York: The Macmillan Co., 1946), p. 314.

It was this assumption which seemingly justified religious wars and pitted brother against brother and child against parent. It was this conviction, too, that prevailed in all but two or three of the American colonies, causing the Puritan to ban from Massachusetts all but Congregationalists and even the more tolerant Virginian to deny residence to any but Episcopalians. In the Middle Colonies alone were the seeds of a more tolerant attitude sown. Here the adherents of many faiths had at long last devised practical ways of living in relative peace with each other and, on occasion, cooperative programs for action which overarched and counteracted the divisive influences of competing theologies.

We cannot review here the many factors in American life which led our people to abandon the one-religion, one-society theory. Were we to do so, however, the nonsectarian school would loom large both as a cause and an effect, since one logical outcome of religious instruction in this institution was the obvious conclusion that the virtues common to the members of diverse religious denominations are rooted in something more basic than the creedal differences which divide them religiously.

This basic unity seemed, for a time, to reside in a common core of Protestant theology, but with further diversity and the sharing of common experiences on the part of Catholic and Protestant, an extension of the theological basis of morality became necessary, and Christianity, as distinct from its denominational expressions, was accepted as a foundation of sound morality. Then came the Jew and other non-Christians to participate in American life, and the more liberal-minded individuals were impelled to modify still further their conceptions of an indispensable religious basis for morality. Thus what was once exclusively Christian has become the "Judeo-Christian metaphysics." It is this basic content of religious belief that we are now told must be imparted to all children in the public school if they are to acquire and practice virtue.[18]

But the end is not yet! Modern means of communication and the emergence of the United States as a world power, with interests and responsibilities penetrating into all corners of the earth, render imperative further insight into and a further extension of the foundations of a morality common to all peoples, irrespective

---

[18] American Council on Education Studies: *Reports of Committees and Conferences,* February, 1945, p. 33.

of differences in religion. A condition of realizing a "One World" is the emergence of a one-world morality, by which is meant ways of thinking, feeling, and acting together common to all men which harmonize interests, channel differences, and foster rich and creative relations between individuals and groups.

One step in this direction is to recognize the limitations in the common view of a *necessary* relation between religion and morality.

John Stuart Mill was one of the first to question this necessary relationship when, in his *Three Essays on Religion,* he pointed out that the Greeks serve as an illustration of a people whose morals were independent of religious sanction. Indeed, for them, the problem was to instruct their gods, since the morality of mortals was obviously superior to that of the immortals! The religion of Buddha likewise refutes the common western notion that morality is dependent exclusively upon a power outside of ourselves that makes for righteousness. Buddhism is primarily a system of ethics, one of conduct, without the inducements of reward and punishment characteristic of Western religions. A follower of Buddha strives for self-control, wise moderation in the indulgence of passion, and brotherly love and living sympathy with others but denies a creation or a creator and spurns the notion of a personal immortality.

It is important to observe what has been said up to this point and what has not been said. We have said that the building of a morality which overarches parochialism and renders possible mutually fruitful ways in which people can live together in a heterogeneous society and a world of plural cultures requires a recognition of no *necessary* connection between religious dogma and moral conduct. But we have not said that this holds true of all men and in all places. Perhaps we should recognize different stages in the evolution of morality and religion as well as differences between individuals and groups in this regard. William James once designated differences between individuals as differences between the tender-minded and the tough-minded individual. For some, the tender-minded, there seems to exist an indispensable relation between a cosmic underwriting of their moral convictions and practices. Others, the tough-minded, can keep their moral pots boiling with purely human fuel. Moreover, just as there are abundant instances of faith without works, so there are numerous instances of men of good works who profess no faith in the conventional sense.

The Sanctions of Morality Are Plural

These facts define the responsibility of the public school in matters of religion and morality. They suggest that psychologically, at least, both the sources and the sanctions of morality are plural—parochial and general, sectarian and secular. From this it follows that the public school should avoid indoctrinating for the parochial and encourage intelligent identification with ideals and standards common to the culture.

May we illustrate.

Religious denominations vary widely in what they condemn or sanction in the lives of their members. One sect, for example, condemns as sin the practice of birth control. Another will justify it on religious and moral grounds in order that parents may discharge better their obligation to raise children under optimum conditions. One religious sect condemns the drinking of tea and coffee for reasons that others cannot understand. Some evangelical groups frown upon smoking, card playing, and dancing. Others of equal sincerity would provide a social hall in connection with the church where these activities might be indulged in by adolescents as one means of preventing delinquency.

Contradictory and conflicting as these standards are, they have in common the injunctions or the sanctions of religious authority as the faithful conceive and interpret this authority. But this authority is parochial and the public school cannot with justice indoctrinate its pupils in either a parochial religion or a parochial morality. Insofar as it deals with the parochial at all—and to avoid it completely is impossible—it should do so exclusively on an informational level and in a manner designed not to convert but to further that mutual understanding, appreciation, and toleration which people must possess if they are to dwell together in peace and friendship in the same world.

So much for one category of moral codes and principles. A second consists of standards and ideals, directions for living, common to a wider culture, as, for example, the constituents of the "American way of life," which, despite some local differences embrace southerner and northerner, New Yorker and Californian, in a community of ideals and attitudes and dispositions of sufficient potency to set them apart as a unified group (Americans) from the members of other national and cultural groups.

Broader still are the ideals of the "free peoples" as these find expression in the day-by-day relations within family and community life in contrast with those of peoples long denied direct and effective participation in determining their own destinies. Although the average citizen in a democracy is often unable consciously to formulate these ideals, honoring them all too frequently in the breach, they nevertheless give form and substance to his daily activities. High on the list of these ideals are an essential respect for the worth of the individual and the uniqueness of his personality; the concept of a reciprocal relation between society and the individual of such an order that, on the one hand, the validity of institutions and laws is measured by the degree to which they meet the needs and enrich the lives of people and, on the other hand, the appropriateness of individual action and expression is judged by their effects upon others; and, finally, the principle that conflicts between interests are resolved best through the mediating operations of intelligence, a process in which all contestants are accorded a fair hearing and the solution arrived at consists of the most reasonable adjustment and the most adequate and happy harmonizing of these interests.

Broad and general as these ideals, concepts, and principles are, they lead to a thousand and one practices and accepted ways of living which distinguish a democratic culture from one autocratic and totalitarian.

Now, this democratic morality, if we may so characterize it, has evolved in the modern world out of diversity and the practical effort to encourage creative and mutually fruitful relations between individuals and whole peoples within a pluralistic culture. Although it is possible, and, indeed, it has often happened, that the principles and precepts of parochial religions have contributed to the development of democratic morality, it is also true that they have functioned at times as obstructive agents, particularly when dogma dominated other considerations.

This suggests a difference in the methods of thinking characteristic of the two types of morality, a difference of significance for the school. Parochial morality commonly starts with an accepted major premise in the form of a precept or principle derived from tradition and authority. Consequently, the solution of a moral problem consists, in the main, in identifying the appropriate moral injunction applicable to the situation in doubt. Once this is identified, the answer to the problem follows as the conclusion from the premises of a syllogism. A morality that is designed to ease and free and enrich relations among people who share some principles in common but differ fundamentally in others involves a procedure more flexible and more complicated.

Insofar as the problem at issue relates to premises upon which there is no agreement among the participants, there comes into operation what might be termed a Golden Rule as applied to absolutes. That is, the devotees of each sacred principle are expected to respect the convictions of their neighbors and to act on the assumption that what one man accepts as of ultimate validity for himself shall be of no more than relative or suggestive value in the thinking or the conduct of the other.

In many situations this will be as far as the participants can go, a willingness to abide by the principle of live and let live. But the process contains the seeds of a more embracing morality, one sensitive to considerations to which the prior absolutes were blind, i.e., the changing circumstances of life.

A sensitive response to changing circumstance in moral matters leads to conclusions different from those characteristic of parochial morality; the difference, shall we say, which marks off the Pharisee from the Good Samaritan. It recognizes an organic connection between the individual personality and his surroundings and, in consequence, a degree of relativity in moral matters to which dogmatic morality closes its eyes.

We may illustrate with family relationships. In the homogeneous community, to which we have referred constantly, there grows up a generally accepted and rigidly enforced pattern of relationships between man and wife, child and parent. Woman in this type of society "knows her place" and tends to keep it! So with other members of the family. As we move from one cultural group to another, however, the definition of what constitutes the right and proper behavior varies significantly. In one family the patriarchal relationship between father and child persists. In another this has given way to a democratic familiarity between parents and children in which all are known by their first name and the family council is used by child as well as adult to determine the solution of common problems. In other families still other patterns obtain. If representatives of these contrasting family groupings are brought together in one and the same community, under conditions in which the children play together, attend the same school, form friendships, and eventually intermarry, problems of differing values that are of unique importance for education emerge. The problems posed by contrasting values are particularly acute during adolescence when an individual begins to be concerned about the respective roles of boy and girl, young man and woman, husband and wife. Nor are these young people helped in their progress toward healthy, responsible, and mature personalities by the efforts of adults to impose upon them one arbitrary concept of a child's duty to his parents or the ideal marriage relationship. Rather will the most satisfying and creative patterns vary from individual to individual, reflecting in each instance experiences peculiar to that person (family background and his or her reaction to his past) and the influence of contrasting patterns which, in their effects upon each other, tend to generate new and distinctive ways of life.

Parochial morality and the morality of a wider culture in a dynamic and changing society thus differ significantly in their attitudes toward principles and their applications. The first commonly derives its directives from sources outside the lives of the individuals immediately employing them. These directives not only constitute the "eternal verities" which change not, but in their applications to practice they are detailed and specific. Since they fall within the category of "right for right's sake though the heavens fall," they allow for little adaptation to circumstance. Morality of the wider culture and interacting relationships, on the other hand, consists of principles which permit greater flexibility of application. Consequently, the goal of education with respect to them is less that consistency which Emerson considered the hobgoblin of small minds and more a moral thoughtfulness which weighs principle against principle and novel data against both principle and familiar circumstance. Toward this end, all subjects of the curriculum, the daily life of the classroom, extracurricular activities, and school-community relations have their contributions to make. Moral education in school, in other words, is not so much a special subject to be taught as it is a central concern permeating all school experience.

Finally, in our classification of moral values, are the universals of still wider application, universal in the sense that they overarch and penetrate all civilized communities. To these all good men are true, irrespective of race, nationality, creed, or class. They constitute the social cement of all civilized societies and range from principles such as the Golden Rule to the common virtues of honesty, reliability, temperance, self-control, and the like.

These values and virtues, as those in our second grouping, are formal and abstract in statement. It is only when applied to specific situations by individuals under conditions that are at once novel and familiar that they come to life. This accounts in part for the ineffectiveness of purely verbal instruction in moral principles. Only in individual action, in the day-by-day associations with people under circumstances that are never quite identical, can precept and practice give vitality and meaning to each other.

Their formal and abstract character in no way weakens their importance, however. They lack specificity merely because they are the essence of wisdom gleaned by untold numbers of generations of men under all manner of conditions. They are the tested and validated formulas for promoting the interpenetration of interests, harmonizing and channeling relations between person and person, person and group, group and group and for carving out ever-widening and more profitable spheres of community action in a world where basic differences and disagreements stubbornly persist. Moreover, the universals, in common with the second order of values, are more solidly grounded when recognized as independent of and superior to the claims of any one parochial or sectarian religion. Indeed, as the anthropologists have pretty well established, religion is less the source and validator of this morality than is moral experience both the matrix and the ultimate testing ground of what is durable and valuable in religion.

Legitimate Areas of School Concern

We conclude, then, that for the practical purposes of public education moral and spiritual values may be grouped under three headings. First are the parochial values, intimately associated with a parochial religion. In American society these values are the cherished ways of living peculiar to one or more of the subgroupings within a larger all-embracing culture. Occasionally they dominate one community or one region and give to the inhabitants of that area the false appearance of a moral universality. Second are the nonsectarian and secular values common to the members of a diversified culture (as, for example, the people of the United States as a whole) despite other differences in race, nationality, and creed. Last, but of supreme importance for the evolution of morality in the future, are the universal values which enlist the loyalties of all men in all cultures.

This classification should help us to determine what is legitimate and what is illegitimate with respect to religion and morals within the field of public education. Neither parochial religion nor parochial morality are properly to be "taught" in the public school, if by "taught" we mean manipulating the school situation with an eye to molding the lives of young people in conformity with them. Positive instruction here should be clearly and exclusively the responsibility of family and church and sectarian agency. Values in the second and third categories, on the other hand, are of a different order. They are the values common to all members of a culture and are acknowledged by all to be the primary conditions of fruitful communication and mutually beneficial relationships of living. They are the tested general formulas for promoting the interpenetration of interests and resolving conflicts between people as these conflicts arise. To help young people recognize, acquire, and wisely apply these values calls for more than indoctrination in specifics. It involves rather the acquisition through practice of disciplined but flexible ways of thinking, feeling, and acting that have as their objective "raising the standard of men's living together."

As we have seen, one significant contribution of the nonsectarian school was the discovery that common values are grounded in something more fundamental than the creeds which divide men into warring schools. Their primary source is the imperative need of people to communicate with one another in mutually fruitful ways and to engage in transactions of mutual benefit and concern. The public school, like the secular school, is uniquely qualified to promote these common values precisely because of its public and secular character. Consequently, were the American people to yield to the temptation to ground the common principles of morality in one or more religious orientation, be this narrowly denominational or as vague and general as the "Judeo-Christian affirmation," they would succeed only in warping their character and limiting the range of their application. On the other hand, once the American public school interprets its function as being concerned with the development of disciplined ways of thinking, feeling, and acting which ease and free communication and further profitable interrelationships among men of all faiths and many cultures, it will contribute toward the eventual realization of a long-desired era of peace on earth and good will toward men.

Suggested Reading

Bower, W. C., *Moral and Spiritual Values in Education* (Lexington, Kentucky: University of Kentucky Press, 1952).

Committee on Religion and Education, *The Function of the Public Schools in Dealing with Religion* (Washington, D.C.: American Council on Education, 1953).

Educational Policies Commission, *Moral and Spiritual Values in the Public School* (Washington, D.C.: National Education Association, 1952).

Johnson, F. Ernest (ed.), *American Education and Religion* (New York: Harper & Brothers, 1952).

Madden, Ward, *Religious Values in Education* (New York: Harper & Brothers, 1951).

"Religion in the Public Schools: A Symposium," *Religious Education,* July–August, 1955, pp. 211–246.

Thayer, V. T., *The Attack Upon the American Secular School* (Boston: Beacon Press, Inc., 1951).

⋀⋀⋀⋀

CHAPTER

21

How Free Is Freedom to Learn?

"Ye Shall Know the Truth, and the Truth Shall Make You Free"

In Chapter 17, we drew attention to a number of assumptions which have given form and character to American education. One of these, the assumption that in areas of controversy and doubt the function of the school is to develop in students an understanding and sympathetic insight into relevant points of view, together with their implications, but not to indoctrinate, served to guide the discussion of the last chapter. Its application, however, is by no means restricted to the disputed role of religion in public education. It defines as well the function of instruction in other areas where ideas and suggested programs of ac*t*.on compete for the loyalties of men. Here, too, its validity has been openly challenged in recent years by individuals and groups determined to purge textbook and library of subversive influences and to control education in harmony with parochial and partisan interpretations of the orthodox.

To these developments we now turn.

It is sometimes said that once the public grasps the full implications of education in a free and changing society, problems of censorship will take care of themselves and pressure groups will find it difficult, if not impossible, to control teaching. There is much to be said in support of this view since, in the last analysis, it is public opinion that both erects and sustains the safeguards of an untrammeled education. But to win and to retain public sup-

· 428 ·

port is no easy accomplishment.

One difficulty derives from the very nature of a free society, that is, a society in which the loyalty of its members is not constrained. Under normal circumstances this gives both an inner stability and a durability wanting in an autocratic and totalitarian society. But it also fathers a delay in organizing resistance to impending dangers and enables the enemies of democracy, often, to gain their ends through piece-meal tactics. All too frequently a school board or the governing body of an educational institution under attack delays forthright action on behalf of freedom to teach, on the theory that the storm may blow over, only to discover, too late, that issues which should have been clear are blurred. Or representatives of an institution free from assault hesitate to speak out in defense of a sister institution on the principle of "Why stick out our necks when our ox is not being gored?" Or "Why call 'Wolf! Wolf!' when there is no wolf at our door?" Or, still again, "These criticisms are not new. They have been made frequently before and the situation has righted itself. We may be certain that history will repeat itself." In the meantime, the public is ill-prepared to cope understandingly with the issues involved.

The guest editorial for the *American School Board Journal* in September, 1953, illustrates this siren voice. The author, Edward A. Fitzpatrick, writes consolingly:

To the school board members who are readers of this magazine, there is no need to tell you that whatever is meant by "book burning" or "freedom of knowledge," *there is no issue because there is no problem.* . . . We can readily give assurance to "intelligent foreigners" and to the naive American readers who accept the "cardboard" world of the Washington reports that, in the local communities—East, West, North and South—large and small, early American or later American —there is no book burning in the United States, nor is there any real danger to intellectual freedom.

Less reassuring have been the attempts of state legislatures to ban textbooks and teaching materials that border on or are associated with "subversive ideas" or the recommendations of a committee of the California Legislature in 1948 to the effect that books be excluded from the public schools quite apart from their

content but solely because they contain references to the writings
of individuals such as Charles A. Beard, Zechariah Chafee, Jr.,
Stuart Chase, Dorothy Canfield Fisher, Robert and Helen Lynd,
Lewis Mumford, Lincoln Steffens, and the well-known English
authors, Beatrice and Sidney Webb and others, all of whom the
committee believed have been bent upon undermining the foundations of our democratic society. Disturbing, too, are the findings
of the Committee on Tenure and Academic Freedom of the National Education Association, as published in the *N.E.A. Journal*
for May, 1951. This committee reported that

Presence in the school curriculum of items to which a particular
group is sensitive is causing a greater degree of voluntary censorship
today than ever before.

The committee has evidence to indicate that voluntary censorship
by administrators and teachers—to avoid conflicts with groups—is a
far more insidious force than the overt acts of boards or legislatures.

Organized minority groups representing fraternal, patriotic, religious, business, labor, and racial organizations often are unwilling to
recognize that points of view other than their own have a right to be
presented by teachers in any study of current controversial issues. Such
groups need help in understanding that the schools must guarantee
the right of the learner to have access to all relevant information in
studying society's unsolved problems.

These problems deal with management and labor; local, state, national and foreign governments; communism, fascism, isolationism,
socialism; public housing; ownership of public utilities; socialized
medicine; universal military training; federal aid to education; sex
education; consumer education; race and religion.

On the other hand, instances are not wanting to demonstrate
that once the issues of a free education are clearly envisaged by
the public, many communities will give loyal support to the principle that "Ye shall know the truth, and the truth shall make you
free."

Typical of this attitude was the manner in which citizen groups
in Arlington, Virginia, faced an attack upon textbooks used in
their schools. Immediately following a widely publicized charge
that six textbooks in history and economics were "slanted toward
collectivism and socialism," a committee of citizens representing

civic organizations subjected this indictment to detailed examination. One subcommittee reported as follows upon one book:

Of the eighteen direct quotations offered . . . as "proof" of this alien slant, only five were found to be accurate in the sense that the actual words were actually found in the textbook, and that the meaning of the sentence was not changed by the surrounding material. In the opinion of the sub-committee, none of these five quotations prove much of anything unless it is that the world has changed in the past twenty-five years.

The other quotations which we managed to locate were falsifications and distortions. Either qualifying material given with the sentence was omitted in order to present a false impression, or the sentence itself was perverted, twisted and mutilated to give a meaning never intended by the author.

Community action of this character constitutes a healthy contrast to the often hasty decision of boards of education to remove books from classroom and library with little or no investigation of the accuracy of charges leveled against them or summarily to dismiss teachers who have been indiscreet enough to bring controversial materials into the classroom and to encourage their students to think critically about them.[1]

Two Conflicting Traditions in American Education

We commonly speak of the "right" to free inquiry as an American tradition, and in evidence, we are prone to point to the First Amendment of the federal Constitution with its guarantee of freedom of thought and expression. But is this strictly accurate?

---

[1] An encouraging symptom indicating that the situation is healthier today than several years ago, in this respect, was the action of the school board of Hanover, New Jersey, in the spring of 1958. An English teacher had asked her pupils to read John Hersey's *Hiroshima* and to write essays based upon the book. Several of the papers were published in the school paper, some of which were critical of the use of the atomic bomb. Veteran groups in the community responded angrily and demanded that the teacher be dismissed. The teacher, in turn, submitted her resignation to the Board of Education, admitting to "an error of judgment." Whereupon, the Board refused to accept the resignation and emphasized the importance of teaching "students to think by presenting all the facets of a problem and challenging their minds into making free decisions . . ." (*The Washington Post and Times Herald,* June 20, 1958).

To understand better the problems of freedom in American education we should remind ourselves that, in strict accuracy, there are two traditions operating within our schools—one is a tradition of conformity and education for indoctrination and the second is education for the free mind. Nor is it established as yet which of these two trends is to prevail.

We will consider briefly these two traditions.

Education for conformity is consistent with the original purpose and character of our early schools. These, as we have observed, were established by religious communities for the purpose, among other things, of raising up the young in the one true faith and to fortify them against the wiles of that "Old Deluder Satan," who was known even to use the Scriptures for his ends. Under these conditions, it was highly important that methods and materials of instruction meet standards of orthodoxy. Accordingly, the Bible, together with approved commentaries, constituted the chief objects of study and the criteria with which to appraise other materials. Rigid censorship operated on all levels of education, from infant school through college. "Let the master take special Care," enjoined the Charter and the Statutes of the College of William and Mary, "that if the author is never so well approved on other accounts, he teach no such Part of him to his Scholars, as insinuates anything against Religion and Morals." [2]

Secondly, the rapid development of our country with its spectacular increase in population has led in each generation to a phenomenal growth in numbers of schools. At all times, as a people, we have been driven by an insatiable appetite for education. But at no time (and this is pathetically and critically true of the present) has the supply of adequately equipped teachers matched the needs of school and college. A considerable proportion of the instructors has consistently lacked preparation and training, and at no time have the rewards of teaching either in salary or status attracted permanently to the profession a quality of personnel equal to that drawn to the law, to medicine, or to the higher echelons of business and industry. Moreover, throughout our history teaching has suffered from the lure of rival occupations, with the result that it has been, to a considerable extent,

---

[2] Quoted in Elmer Ellsworth Brown, *The Making of Our Middle Schools* (New York: Longmans, Green & Co., 1914), p. 130.

an occupation of transients, individuals who use teaching as a steppingstone to a more attractive career. This, too, has influenced the nature of teaching and the methods of thinking and learning common to our schools. The textbook, for the ill-prepared teacher as well as for the pupil, has been an authoritative source of information, a body of material to accept with little question rather than to weigh and ponder and appraise. What the Bible has been to the orthodox clergyman or the faithful layman, the textbook has been to large numbers of teachers and pupils. In each instance, reading is conceived of as a skill one acquires in order to identify what to believe and seldom, if at all, as an operation essential and preliminary to the sifting and winnowing process of critical thought.

To these considerations we should add the evangelical purpose with which Americans have commonly endowed their schools. Beginning with the extensions of manhood suffrage in the period following the Revolutionary War and continuing throughout the nineteenth century with each successive wave of new immigrants, the school has constituted a melting pot of conformity for new entrants into the advantages and responsibilities of American life, political and civic as well as economic. For the children of the newly enfranchised as well as for the children of immigrants the school has exercised a molding influence essentially conservative in character. Its functions, as conceived by the dominant forces within the community, have been more to transmit a culture than to welcome new ingredients, to assimilate the children of immigrants (often creating out of them strangers to their parents) rather than to encourage the evolution of new patterns of living out of the ever changing contributions of the newcomers to the American scene. Richard D. Mosier, in his suggestive study of the McGuffey readers, reveals the motives which long gave character to the content of these books. Both manhood suffrage and immigration quite naturally disturbed the conservative mind, but this mind also recognized that if one generation were introduced to the solid middle-class virtues of American society, all might be well. Moreover, with an open frontier and a rapidly expanding economy, there seemed for a time to exist a pre-established harmony between the Puritan virtues and those which make for individual success. Accordingly, we find the authors of the readers accepting "the premise that the Christian virtues of thrift, labor, honesty, punctuality and good-will carried men to the successes which daily would be witnessed by the humblest citizen." [3] At the same time the use of the text for this evangelical purpose tended to confirm a concept of teaching and learning friendly to conformity and relatively indifferent to the empirical use of firsthand experience in resolving the issues of life.

Finally, the psychology of learning should be mentioned since for a long period in our educational history it conceived of the mind as a receptacle to be filled with the appropriate information, ideas, and principles. "What is the business of the teacher?" asks the author of *American Education,* a volume published in 1851. He replies, "His position is strictly that of a conveyor of knowledge—moral and intellectual—to a yet unoccupied and growing mind. To do this successfully, requires that his instruction should carry to that waiting mind a conviction of its *truth,* and that he should also connect that truth with the duties of life." [4]

This conception of the relation between teacher and pupil is in agreement with the popular notion, long dominant in American life and education, that schooling serves the practical purpose of disposing youth to accept a culture essentially foreign to native interest or to acquire a trade, a vocation, or a profession with which they can better their stations in life. Nor need one deprecate the phenomenal achievements of American education in technological advancement and in raising the cultural level of our people in order to realize its limitations in fostering a discipline keyed to novelty and the solution of problems the answers to which are neither known in advance nor derived from the application of the rules of a syllogism.

Here, then, are a number of influences which have affected generation after generation of Americans in school and college, with the result that large numbers of students have left these institutions with the conviction that a major purpose of education is to mold men's minds rather than to impart a discipline which will enable young people to become in fact the architects of their own fortunes. Nor should we be surprised when earnest

---

[3] Richard D. Mosier, *Making the American Mind* (New York: Kings Crown Press, 1947). See Chapter IV particularly on "The Morality of the Middle Classes."
[4] Quoted in William Heard Kilpatrick, *Source Book in the Philosophy of Education* (New York: The Macmillan Co., 1923), p. 270.

citizens and conscientious parents, concerned with the shape of things to come, consider it a sacred obligation to keep a watchful eye upon the contents of the textbooks which properly are to constitute the warp and the woof of the growing mind. Or, again, when communities, once homogeneous in character, become heterogeneous and include individuals who advocate a variety of conflicting and "questionable" points of view, we should not be surprised to find that some individuals and groups turn to censorship. Are not, indeed, the waves of hysteria and conformity which so often threaten to submerge the spirit of free inquiry in the classroom the logical outcome of the school's own activity?

The Tradition of Freedom

There is a tradition of conformity in American education. But there is also a second tradition, one born of diversity, which thrives on differences, creating solid bonds of unity within these differences on both local and national levels. This tradition has profound implications for the emerging role of the United States in world affairs.

As indicated earlier, this tradition of freedom found expression first in sectarian and later in secular education, both logical developments of religious toleration and freedom of conscience. But the growth of religious liberty was no isolated phenomenon. It, in turn, was derived from multiple factors: the continuous immigration of people of diverse religious faiths and national backgrounds; the westward movement with its continuous creation of new communities out of mixed origins and traditions; the leavening influence of wars which did much to wear down parochialism and to promote the idea of a common allegiance to common principles—political, economic, moral; and the intellectual contribution of European thinkers, particularly the English forerunners of freedom. Consequently, when the authors of the Declaration of Independence asserted on behalf of the American colonies, "We hold these truths to be self-evident, that all men are created free and equal, that they are endowed by their Creator with certain unalienable rights . . ." and "That to secure these rights governments are instituted among men, deriving their just powers from the consent of the governed," they were giving utterance to a way of thinking which had become firmly grounded in the daily experience of ordinary men and women, as well as in the philosophical speculations of the distinguished members of the Continental Congress. Indeed, it was doubtless the firsthand contact with democratic communities in evolution on the frontier, direct observation of the actual creation and the maintenance of law and order through the efforts of the people themselves, that enabled the intellectual leaders—Thomas Jefferson, John Adams, Benjamin Franklin, and others—to envisage an application of John Locke's words more radical by far than contemplated by that philosopher:

Men being by nature all free, equal and independent, no one can be out of this estate and subjected to the political power of another without his own consent, which is done by agreeing with other men, to join and unite in a community for their comfortable, safe and peaceable living, one amongst another, in a secure enjoyment of their properties, and a greater security against any that are not of it. . . . When any number of men have so consented to make one community or government, they are thereby presently incorporated, and make one body politic, wherein they the majority have a right to act and include the rest.[5]

On the other hand, when Jefferson was moved to swear "upon the altar of God eternal hostility against every form of tyranny over the mind of man," he was but applying to his own day, and in a unique manner, a principle which John Milton a century and one-half earlier had urged upon Oliver Cromwell in the latter's hour of victory: "Again, it is my earnest wish," wrote the blind poet to the Protector,

that you would give permission to those who are inclined to freedom of inquiry, to publish what they have to communicate at their own peril, without the private inquisition of any magisterial censor: for nothing could contribute so much to the growth of truth; nor would all science be forever measured out to us in a bushel, and be bestowed at the pleasure of the half-learned. . . . Lastly, it is my fervant wish, that you should not be afraid to listen either to truth or falsehood, of whatever description that may be: but that you should listen the least of all to those, who never fancy that they themselves

[5] John Locke, *Treatise on Civil Government*, chap. VIII.

are free, unless they deprive others of their freedom; who labor at nothing with so much zeal and earnestness, as to enchain not the bodies only, but the consciences of their brethren; and to introduce into the church and state the worst of all tyrannies, the tyranny of their own misshapen customs and opinions. May you ever take part with those who think it just that not their own sect or faction alone, but all the citizens alike should have an equal right to be free.[6]

We are saying that English political thought found in America fruitful soil for further growth and development. Consequently, a concept that under European conditions and in the daily presence of ancient institutions and confirmed habits and customs of an authoritarian background was necessarily of slow growth easily acquired under American conditions the status of an axiom. Of these axioms, the principle of freedom of thought and expression loomed large as the indispensable conditions for the discovery of truth and the maintenance of a healthy society. But since the colonies had to fight a War of Independence to secure these blessings of liberty and freedom, our fathers deemed it wise to include a Bill of Rights in their new constitutions. That they were prudent in so doing is evidenced by the numerous occasions in which the courts have since found it necessary to reaffirm the sacred status of freedom of inquiry and expression in the face of repeated attempts to undermine them.

Implicit in the concepts of freedom of inquiry and expression is the ideal of an open society. An open society, writes Herbert J. Muller, in his *Uses of the Past,* "is an adventurous society that has broken with universal prehistoric custom of regarding ancient customs as magical or sacred, that views its institutions as man-made for human purposes, that welcomes variety and change instead of enforcing rigid conformity, and that accordingly provides its members with personal opportunities beyond mere obedience. It is Athens as opposed to Sparta." [7]

An open society neither comes into being through spontaneous generation nor perpetuates itself without effort. It requires of its members a discipline of mind and spirit which its schools cannot

[6] Quoted in Irwin Edman and Herbert W. Schneider, *Fountainheads of Freedom* (New York: Reynal and Hitchcock, 1941), p. 334. (This title is now published by Harcourt, Brace & Co.)

[7] New York: Oxford University Press, 1952, p. 71.

safely neglect to develop in the young, disciplined ways of thinking and living that give reality to Abraham Lincoln's concept of
a government of the people, by the people, and for the people.

This second tradition, the tradition of free inquiry, is now
embodied in the constitutions of both state and national governments and finds classical expression in the Bill of Rights. Nevertheless, its applications in education are far from commonplace.
All too few are the schools and colleges which appraise their work
in terms of their success or failure in equipping students with the
habits of mind and character requisite for effective living in an
open society.

Implications for Subject Matter and Method

Obviously these two traditions dictate quite different procedures
in school, whether viewed from the standpoint of method or the
choice of subject matter.

First a word with respect to method.

It must be emphasized that education for the free intelligence
as against education for conformity in no way precludes instruction in the specific and definite. There are bodies of knowledge,
for example, as well as techniques and skills in human relations
and in practical affairs that have met not only the tests of time
but all known criteria of validation. These must be imparted to
the young, if the latter are to carry on from where their elders
have left off. For example, no educator worth his salt would object to a mastery of the three R's or to the conscious acquisition
by his pupils of an abiding loyalty to the common virtues and
the ethical principles of a democratic culture. On the contrary,
these must be transmitted to our youth if modern civilization is
to survive, let alone progress.

But the *methods* of imparting the definite and the specific need
not be, nor can they safely be, distinguished sharply from instruction in the uncertain. They should be keyed to an open rather
than a closed society. The student of an ancient civilization should
be trained in the habit of forming tentative judgments on many
items since further research may require their revision. In this
respect he is not unlike his fellow student who specializes in constitutional law, which can be fully understood only when past

decisions of the courts are weighed against both present and probable future trends, or the medical student who is planning to devote himself to medical research, or still another who is entering upon a trade or a vocation in which a skill of today may be replaced by a new process tomorrow. In short, there are few if any areas of learning today in which either facts or processes can wisely be taught as unchangeable. Even in the operations of simple arithmetic, the pupil who has learned to question the accuracy of his work until verified has an advantage over his comrades who follow only a rule of the thumb. And when we consider how persistently time undermines knowledge presumably pegged down, education for conformity and passive acceptance in any area should be recognized as a slender reed upon which to lean.

Now, methods which perhaps are no more than questionable when dealing with the certain and the noncontroversial become positive handicaps in areas where uncertainty and doubt or irreconcilable differences in values are persistent characteristics. But these are precisely the aspects of life with which the contemporary mind is called upon to deal increasingly. To employ methods of indoctrination here or to fail to develop the discipline of mind essential in order to live resourcefully with tentative conclusions is to do a disservice both to the student and to the society in which he is preparing to play a responsible role.

Viewed in this perspective, classroom consideration of questions for which there are no immediate or conclusive answers constitute an indispensable grist for the educational mill.

Not all problems of a controversial nature, however, lend themselves to classroom consideration, since what is desired is growth in the ability to enter with understanding into points of view which run counter to one's own convictions and habits. When community sentiment or divisions within a class group reach a degree of partisanship and emotional excitement which precludes objective discussion and investigation, the most valuable lesson the instructor can convey is to announce, "We shall have to postpone further deliberation on this problem until we are sufficiently mature to cope with it."

It is this necessity of reducing factional excitement and the educational value of seeing the world through the eyes of another that renders debate a questionable tool. In comparison with a sincere effort to gather together and to envisage all the data relating to an issue, debating encourages the high lighting of data favorable to but one point of view and the playing down or elimination of facts equally relevant which may be unfavorable to a partisan conclusion. To be sure there are occasions in life when one is called upon to assume the position of a debater; but debate as an educational tool, designed to foster a genuine search for truth and nothing but the truth, is severely limited. Indeed, it is more appropriate in the professional training of an attorney, a salesman, or a lobbyist—one whose occupation requires the skills of an advocate and a special pleader—than in the education of a responsible citizen striving to find his way in a world in which objectivity and suspended judgment and an ever watchful eye for the neglected aspect are of critical importance.

Controversial problems thus constitute a valuable means for education in the democratic and cooperative methods of thinking discussed in Chapter 9. To exclude them from the curriculum or to educate for certainty where there is no certainty is to ask our schools to commit intellectual suicide.

Functions of the Textbook

The contrast between instruction in an authoritarian and totalitarian society, on the one hand, and a free society, on the other, applies as much to content as to method, a fact not fully realized by those earnest individuals who would safeguard our institutions from "subversion" by means of a rigid censorship of textbooks and other materials of instruction. Well might the latter ponder these words of David K. Benninghauser:

The enemy of free public education can frequently be spotted by his attitude towards materials of instruction. He cannot escape the consciousness that if he were in complete control of education he would see to it that only *approved* literature could be found in classrooms and libraries. To his mind, a textbook is equated with the official, orthodox doctrines to be taught to the young people; a magazine by its very presence in the school library, must be considered approved, authoritative information. Therefore, any teaching material allowed in the school is "correct" and not to be questioned by pupil or teacher. Because teaching and indoctrination are one and the same, he distrusts free inquiry, he becomes a censor and demands the banning of any materials he finds objectionable.[8]

But what positively should we expect of a textbook, apart from the technical requirements of size of type, appropriateness to age level, ample illustrative material, appropriate level of vocabulary, and the like?

Certainly, in a text which purports to deal with contemporary society and its developments, including its "growing pains," we should expect a clear and unbiased account of the factors and conditions that have given rise to the present. This calls for an objective presentation that lays a solid foundation in fact sufficient for the student to appreciate "all points of view," as well as a fair and unbiased description of the schools of thought which divide men with respect to proposed lines of action.

By objectivity we have in mind something more than a coldly intellectual attitude, or the mere listing of the pros and cons of a question at issue analogous to a balancing of the credits and debits in an account book. What is required is a mature understanding of the problems of change at points where change has disturbed living relationships that have long been cemented. This can be conveyed at times by representative accounts in the text of an intimate and personal character, by supplementary reading, or by the moving picture, a novel, a play, or other dramatic material designed to convey to the student a full and rich understanding of why individuals think, feel, and act as they do with respect to the issues of life. To the extent a textbook or other classroom material imparts this "round-about" knowledge of issues in dispute, it fulfills a major mission.

Finally, in a good text, we should look for suggestions and references which stimulate and assist an instructor and his students to engage in further investigation and inquiry.

Objectivity, then, looms large in the appraisal of any textbook which presumes to deal with areas of doubt in any field. Its major function, within this context, is to supplement the work of the teacher in helping the young to realize how few are the fields of knowledge in which the frontiers are closed and to acquire not so much the answers to life's problems as the courage and the

---

[8] *Harvard Educational Review*, Summer, 1951, pp. 138–154.

will and, above all, the "know-how" with which "to follow knowledge like a sinking star, beyond the utmost bound of human thought."

Richard M. Pearson, the late Director of the Educational Division of The Macmillan Company, has described the purpose of the textbook in common sense terms in answer to the question, "Can Textbooks Be Subversive?" "Textbooks," he suggests,

are neither purveyors of opinion nor molders of young peoples' minds. They are instruments of learning, selected locally in most cases nowadays, to meet local needs and to suit local preferences. . . . The main job of education, in which textbooks assist, is not to fill children full of facts. It is rather to help them and keep them, as their mothers and fathers were before them, alert, self-reliant, intellectually inquisitive human beings, capable of thinking for themselves, making their own choices, forming their own opinions and responding to the challenges that life offers. Textbooks can help in that process, not only by telling young people what their fathers long since knew but by encouraging them to be on the lookout for things that their fathers have never known.[9]

Once a textbook meets the criteria of objectivity, there is no reason why its author should not share with his readers his conclusions on mooted questions discussed. Not to do so in areas in which he may have done original research or in which he has special competence might result only in depriving his readers of valuable raw material for their own thinking. In other words, the test of the value of a text is not a matter of whether or not the author expresses views in agreement with the instructor or confirms the opinions and prejudices of groups dominant in the community. Rather is it a question of the degree to which a book, or other instructional material, functions as an adequate educational tool; whether, in short, it both introduces students to significant areas of the field under study and stimulates them to engage in original thought with respect to problems discussed, with the full knowledge that they have come to grips with issues upon which honest men do not see eye to eye.

To appraise a textbook in these terms is a professional responsibility, a task for experts rather than for the man on the street

---

[9] *Phi Delta Kappan,* January, 1952, pp. 248–250.

or the layman with his own ax to grind. Nor is it altogether identical with a procedure keyed primarily to "good public relations," a procedure in which a committee of representative laymen is asked to pass judgment upon books under attack or to serve as an "advisory committee" in the winnowing and sifting of books to be used in library and school. The solution of the textbook problem, in the present atmosphere, is less one of calming troubled waters or of freeing specific texts from criticism than it is that of educating the public to a full understanding of the educational functions classroom and library are to serve.

Some years ago the board of education of one of our large eastern cities established a committee on human relations consisting of representatives from civic organizations to suggest ways and means of using the schools as one means of improving intercultural relations within the city. The committee recognized the strategic importance of textbooks and classroom instruction in furthering mutual understanding of the many religious and racial groups represented in the schools. This moved one earnest member of the committee to suggest that the group undertake to read all textbooks in use in the schools for the purpose of identifying passages to which anyone might object! These passages were to be called to the attention of publishers and their elimination insisted upon as a condition of retention and use. It required long and strenuous argument to convince this individual and others that a procedure of this character might well result in texts barren of any point of view and with all the juices of life extracted from them, and, in addition, it would deprive teachers and pupils of the educational opportunity of identifying these passages on their own initiative and weighing and appraising their worth from the standpoint of accuracy, objectivity, bias, and prejudice.

This is not to suggest that expressions of bias and prejudice are to be searched out for inclusion in the curriculum (although on occasion this might very well be a valuable exercise). Unfortunately, not all teachers are sufficiently competent to assist their students to cope constructively with open expressions of prejudice or gross inaccuracy, and fewer still are competent to detect more subtle deviations from truth. For this reason care must indeed be exercised in the choice of material used in the school. But this does not sanction substituting lay for professional judgment in the selection of educational materials or appraising these materials apart from the context in which they are to be used. There is a very real danger that lay committees, composed of representatives of special interest groups—labor unions, chambers of commerce, racial and religious organizations, and the like—who lack expertness in the fields covered by the text, will arrive at conclusions regarding its use that will deprive the classroom of the opportunity and the responsibility of engaging pupils in critical thinking or restrict attention to the least common denominator of common agreement on moot issues. Such laymen may even plead on behalf of a special point of view that may be dominant in the community.

Conflicting Views As to the Role of the Public

Does this mean that we should exclude the public altogether from participation in the selection of educational materials?

Some educators answer in the affirmative. They believe with Professor Preston H. Epps of the University of North Carolina that "so far in our history, no group has been able to view our society and setup as objectively and intelligently as a group of professional scholars. So far, we have wisely looked to such scholars to write the textbooks through which we want our youth to be introduced to the various fields of knowledge." [10] And they fear with Edward N. Saveth that to involve the public,

is not without its own perils: by inviting the community to participate in the defense of textbooks, is there not some risk of further inflaming tempers and ideologies, of further widening the gap between objective criticism and partisan denunciation? Is there not real danger of further involving teachers and teaching materials with sections of the community that may be ignorant, irresponsible, and all too willing themselves to flex the muscle of censorship? Might it not end with an ugly spectacle of stereotype pitted against stereotype, smear against smear? [11]

---

[10] Quoted in an article on "What To Do About Dangerous Textbooks" by Edward N. Saveth. Reprinted from *Commentary*, February, 1952, pp. 99–106, and distributed by the American Jewish Committee.

[11] *Ibid.*, p. 10.

Other educators go so far as to employ the analogy between physician or surgeon and teacher. What parent, it is asked, would presume to advise the medical expert on the comparative merits of different prescriptions for an illness or suggest to a surgeon the instruments he should use in performing an operation? Is it not equally rash for the layman to invade the territory of the expert in promoting the health of mind or warding off illness?

This analogy overlooks a significant difference between the status of the medical profession and that of teaching. In the eyes of the layman the licensed teacher and the licensed physician are by no means comparable. He knows full well that the average physician possesses a competency the layman cannot match, whereas all too frequently teachers are encountered who are sadly wanting in background and training. On both the elementary and secondary school levels the classroom teacher is called upon to deal with subject matter in areas where his knowledge is frequently less accurate or extensive than that of many parents of students in his class, and the occasions are all too common in which professional incompetence has been sufficiently obvious to lower the status of the profession in the eyes of the public. Add to this the common knowledge that low salaries together with an indifferent social status have attracted the mediocre and discouraged the able from entering the profession of teaching, and we can readily understand why the average citizen or parent accords less weight to the professional judgment of his child's teacher than to that of the family physician.

But were the public to accord respect where respect is due, there are other significant differences between the relations of the medical and the teaching professions to their clients. What surgeon, for example, would insist that the success of an operation turns upon the active participation of a child's parents? Many educators, on the other hand, argue with sound reason that the education of a child is incomplete without the active cooperation of his parents. With what consistency, then, can the school demand the exclusion of the latter from areas in which they are most vitally concerned?

It would seem that the solution of the problem of community participation in professional activity turns upon the avoidance of two extremes, a professional insulation which deprives the young person of significant interrelationships with his social as well as his natural environment, on the one hand, and the erasing of all distinctions between lay and professional responsibility in determining the content and method of instruction, on the other. It is one thing to recognize the need for a functional participation of both layman and professional in the work of the school. It is another to assume that these functions are identical.

This suggests a concluding word with respect to ways and means of vitalizing instruction and generating confidence in the professional work of the school.

A Constructive Role for Parents

The advantages of utilizing the specialized knowledge and experience of lay experts in the community in the construction of courses of study and resource units, in the selection of equipment, and, occasionally, in the work of the classroom have long been recognized. Particularly is this applicable to vocational education where it is most essential that the skills and techniques imparted should keep in step with developments outside the school. But equally valuable results follow in general education when the work of the classroom is recognized by pupils as of living concern to men and women of talent and ability outside the school. In some institutions advisory committees of parents, whose special interests and abilities parallel the work of the school, have been organized to serve as resource groups to which departments, such as art, science, language, and literature, as well as vocational subjects, might turn for advice and counsel and, on occasion, for classroom participation. From these groups teacher and student may derive the stimulus that comes from direct contact with adult practitioners. On the other hand, in these instances of cooperation it remains the responsibility of the teacher, with his special knowledge of child development and psychology, to keep clear the distinction between adult standards and criteria, or the expectations of the specialist, and those relevant and appropriate to the age levels of the learners.

As the school receives from the adult community, so should it contribute. Parents are appreciative when the school shares with them and interprets for them modern methods of teaching and learning in the traditional subjects and the principles of healthy emotional and social development which give character to child rearing in home and school. As the writer has elsewhere stated,

There is an intimate connection between the psychology of child rearing we employ and the kind of society in which we hope our young people are to live, move, and have their being. To help children make their own the discipline that marks the difference between democratic and autocratic ways of living is no easy task. What it demands of parent and teacher varies with age level and stage of development of children. Theoretically, at least, the school is the professional agent of the community in child rearing. To discharge its function wisely and effectively involves an understanding relationship with the parent community. Let this be achieved, and, again, ill-informed attacks upon the schools to the effect that "progressive education increases delinquency" will gain little headway.[12]

Relations of intimacy and mutual understanding between home and school which give substance and vitality to education under normal circumstances constitute a first line of defense when textbooks or instructional materials are subject to attack. Once mutual understanding between school and home has become as a two-way street, charges of subversion are less easily generated than is possible where school and home and community lack intimacy of contact. But in either case, criticism should be met, if possible, in an *educational* manner. On the principle that "Ye shall know the truth and the truth shall make thee free," the first step should be to welcome an investigation. Boards of education do well, under these circumstances, to appoint a committee of representative and competent citizens to examine into the validity of criticisms made and to render a report to the board and the community. These reports, should, if possible, do more than answer the specific question of whether or not criticisms are accurate or false. They should attempt as well to clarify for the public the basic principles that are to guide teacher and student and community in a democracy when dealing with problems upon which not even experts are agreed or the answers to which are of necessity in doubt.

Nor should the students—particularly on the secondary and college levels—be excluded from participation in determining the truth or falsity of charges made. What is more vital in arousing

---

[12] V. T. Thayer, *Public Education and Its Critics* (New York: The Macmillan Co., 1954), p. 159.

the interests of students both in the topic under study and in the appropriateness of its treatment by the text or the instructor than to set the young people themselves upon the task of determining the accuracy of indictments made? What better way, in fact, might students gain insight into methods of sound evaluation and techniques of valid criticism?

We conclude that there are very important respects in which laymen of specialized ability as well as the average citizen of intelligence and understanding, even the students themselves, may be involved in evaluating materials of instruction without infringing upon the unique function, nay, the obligation of the teaching staff to exercise an essential freedom in the selection and use of the tools of its trade.

Thus far our discussion has centered upon freedom to learn. What shall we say of the freedom of the instructor, his rights and his obligations as a citizen and a teacher?

The problem merits a special chapter.

Suggested Reading

Alberty, Harold, *Reorganizing the High School Curriculum,* rev. ed. (New York: The Macmillan Co., 1953), chap. XII.

Anderson, Archibald, "Protecting the Right to Teach Social Issues," *Progressive Education,* October, 1948, pp. 23 ff.

Association for Supervision and Curriculum Development, *Forces Affecting American Education* (Washington, D.C.: National Education Association, 1953).

Commager, Henry Steele, "Is Freedom Really Necessary?" *Saturday Review,* February 21, 1953, pp. 11 ff.

Griffin, Alan, "The Teacher As Citizen," *Educational Leadership,* October 15, 1952, pp. 4 ff.

Phi Delta Kappan, issue devoted to the topic, "Textbooks and the Schools," January, 1953.

Saveth, Edward N., "What to Do About Dangerous Textbooks," *Commentary,* February, 1952, pp. 99–106.

Thayer, V. T., *American Education Under Fire* (New York: Harper & Brothers, 1944), chap. VIII.

Van Til, William, "The Making of Their Modern Minds," *Social Education,* October, 1939, pp. 467–472.

Wilhelms, Fred T., "Letter to a Teacher on Handling Controversial Questions," *Progressive Education,* October, 1948, pp. 8–12.

.M.M.M.

CHAPTER

22

How Free Is Freedom to Teach?

The Rights of a Teacher and His Rights As a Citizen

"The kind of virtue that can be produced by guarded ignorance," writes Bertrand Russell in his *Unpopular Essays*, "is frail and fails at the first touch of reality."

If this observation be valid, it would seem that a school or a college, dedicated to the interests of the public as a whole, should assure its teachers every freedom to teach without the limitations of outside dictation. Nevertheless, freedom to teach as freedom in other areas must be a responsible freedom and in no way implies the freedom of an adult to decide at will the pattern he would give to a growing mind.

What does responsible freedom to teach imply in a world of conflicting and confused ideologies?

As a general proposition, it implies the right of a teacher to function as a citizen as well as to speak his mind on public issues and not to lose his professional status thereby; to read without fear that other citizens are looking over his shoulder to determine the fitness of what he reads or scrutinizing his mail with a view to ascertaining what magazines and books come into his home; to attend meetings addressed by all manner of speakers without being judged guilty of subversive leanings. Indeed, the freedom to read and the freedom to hear should be recognized as a professional obligation in areas of controversy as well as a privilege of citizenship, since it is one means of enriching class instruction.

All this needs to be recognized more clearly in view of the impending danger that governing boards of schools and colleges —influenced by the loyalty and security programs of state and federal governments, which are fast transforming civil servants into a class apart, safely insulated from normal contacts with reality—will adopt similar criteria of reliability and thus reinforce the traditionally ivory tower existence of the teaching profession.

This is not to say that the line of distinction between the rights and obligations of the teacher as citizen and those of teacher as teacher is clearly marked at all points. An instructor's tender concern for the quality of his influence upon the young (particularly in the elementary and secondary school) often renders impossible a consistent and clean-out distinction between his functions as citizen and his functions as teacher. It is one thing, for example, for a teacher, imbued with the spirit of reform, to participate actively in political and civic movements in a large metropolitan area, where he often lives in one place and practices his profession in another, and quite a different matter to undertake to remake the out-of-school environment of his pupils in a small and intimate community. In the latter instance the effects of his actions upon relations with his pupils as well as his "rights" as a citizen will have to determine both the extent and the manner of his participation in out-of-school activities. Again, it is impossible for the teacher of small children, let us say of kindergarten and primary age (where the teacher functions as a parent substitute, and success depends upon the teacher's ability to share his professional knowledge with parents, helping them to guide constructively the emotional and social as well as the intellectual development of their young), to live two lives—one, the confidante of old and young alike, the other, an active reconstructionist of the social order. Nor is the role of an instructor of boys and girls at the hero worship stage identical with that of a college professor. In the first instance, the teacher must be mindful of the tendency of young people to idealize his behavior and to use what they believe they see in the structure of his personality (qualities often read into his person by the admiring pupil rather than actually present there) in the building of their own personalities. This suggests a circumspection with respect to ideas expressed, a deliberate effort to high light the details of democratic methods of thinking and of living, and perhaps a more conscious practicing of what one preaches than is demanded of a teacher on the college and graduate levels. In the latter case, the views of the instructor can be viewed objectively, somewhat on a par with those of a reference book in the library, whereas with the teacher of the young, views easily become living ingredients in the teacher's personalities. For these reasons, the activities and behavior of the teacher outside as well as within the classroom and school carry a different moral at different age levels and cannot be a matter of indifference either to the instructor or to those responsible for his selection and retention.

It would seem, then, that although the rights of a teacher as a citizen are to be respected and certainly teachers as a class are not to be disfranchised, the two are not as east and west which never meet. It is also clear that teaching involves a unique relationship between teacher and taught, a relationship which at some points and at some age levels involves the home and the community within the professional concerns of the teacher more intimately than at other points and other age levels. But at no time do the rights of the teacher as citizen sanction the corruption of his activities and responsibilities as a teacher. When these two areas overlap to the point of conflict, then the instructor must decide upon which to concentrate exclusively. "Teachers," to quote Bertrand Russell once again, "are more than any other class the guardians of civilization." This implies a respect for the personality of the growing individual and, on the teacher's part, the exercise as well as the transmission of a discipline keyed to a future essentially unknown. This discipline precludes molding others either in the image of a teacher's own ideas or his own personality. In this sense (not in the sense of caprice or lack of direction) the classroom should be child-centered, and neither the privileges of citizenship nor the obligations of teaching sanction the affiliation of a teacher with any organization or pressure group, be this religious, political, economic, or social, which presumes to dictate to him what and how he should teach. The moment an instructor subordinates himself to an external discipline of this character and attempts to mold the minds of his students according to predetermined patterns or seeks to transform them into passive instruments for the ends of others, he is guilty of conduct unbecoming of a teacher and should be dealt with accordingly.

A classic statement of policy emphasizing a respect for the integrity of the student as well as the obligation of a free society to keep open the channels of knowledge is found in the declaration of the First Committee on Academic Freedom of the American Association of University Professors in 1915. This runs, in part, as follows:

Members of the academic calling have as their function . . . to deal at first hand, after prolonged and specialized technical training, with the sources of knowledge; and, to impart the results of their own and of their fellow specialists investigation and reflection, both to students and to the general public, without fear or favor. . . . To the degree that professional scholars, in the formation and promulgation of their opinions, are, or by the character of their tenure appear to be, subject to any motive other than their own scientific conscience and a desire for the respect of their fellow experts, to that degree the university teaching profession is corrupted; a society at large fails to get from its scholars in an unadulterated form, the peculiar and necessary service which it is the office of the professional scholar to furnish. . . .

An inviolable refuge from tyranny should be found in the university. It should be an *intellectual experiment station,* where new ideas may germinate and where their fruit, though still distasteful to the community as a whole, may be allowed to ripen until finally, perchance, it may become a part of the accepted intellectual food of the nation or of the world.

Underlying this concept of academic freedom is the assumption stressed above, namely, that the right to inquire, to learn, and to teach is more than a personal privilege or an individual right. It is one of the conditions of a free society remaining free. As Justice Frankfurter remarked at the Anniversary Dinner in honor of John Dewey's ninetieth birthday, "Without open minds there can be no open society, and if there be no open society the spirit of man is mutilated and enslaved."

Has Academic Freedom Gone Too Far?

Convincing as this may be in the abstract, it is obviously unsatisfactory as a universal principle to many people who are fearful that alien and un-American ideas are undermining American institutions. They believe large numbers of teachers are utilizing academic freedom not to sustain and enrich democracy but with the deliberate purpose of destroying it. Consequently, they are convinced that the procedures which have become established in law and practice in order to assure the right of students to learn and of teachers to teach require review and modification. As Sidney Hook insists, it is one thing to father heresy and quite another to engage in a conspiracy against society.

Be this as it may, there is no question but that the existence of a Communist conspiracy and the methods of infiltration employed by Communists, on the one hand, and the means used by investigating committees of state legislatures and Congress in recent years to combat this conspiracy, together with the actions taken by the trustees of educational institutions with respect to faculty members under suspicion, on the other, have forced a review not only of the principles of academic freedom but of the relation of political authority to education.

In an essay entitled, "Academic Freedom Revisited," [1] T. V. Smith states that encroachments upon academic freedom have commonly had three sources: (1) First, "sacerdotalism," or the "bellicose orthodoxy of those who hold that in matters religious and spiritual all that is essential has already been discovered and is in fact owned by him and his group." Individuals and groups of this persuasion set themselves up as watchdogs to determine the limits and conditions of instruction in matters of religion. (2) Second, "big business," which has often exercised pressure upon faculty selection and retention, with an eye to safeguarding economic interests from heretical concepts or from criticisms hostile to the status quo. (3) A third source of criticism and attempts at coercion of academic freedom, according to Smith, is political and comes from the politicians. In each case, observes Smith, the attacks have come from outside the institution concerned and have been directed against specific individuals. Their object has been conservative, that is, to shield parochial and partisan groups from the dangers sensed by these interests as implicit in untrammeled inquiry. Moreover, their antagonists, or victims, have been individuals rash or bold enough to challenge

---

[1] T. V. Smith in *Essays in Honor of Horace Kallen: Vision and Action* (New Brunswick, N.J.: Rutgers University Press, 1953), chap. I.

conventional notions or the prevailing practices of firmly entrenched groups. On these occasions, friends of academic freedom have appealed to the principle of free enterprise in ideas so admirably expressed in the familiar words of Justice Holmes:

But when men have realized that time has upset many fighting faiths, they may come to believe even more than they believe the very foundations of their own conduct that the ultimate good desired is better reached by free trade in ideas—that the best test of truth is the power of the thought to get itself accepted in the competition of the market, and that truth is the only ground upon which their wishes safely can be carried out. That, at any rate, is the theory of our Constitution. It is an experiment as all life is an experiment. . . . While that experiment is part of our system I think we should be eternally vigilant against attempts to check the expression of opinions that we loath and believe to be fraught with death, unless they so imminently threaten immediate interference with the lawful and pressing purposes of the law that an immediate check is required to save the country.[2]

The necessity to defend innovation in ideas against attack from those congenitally committed to the principle that

> Come weal, come woe,
> My status is quo,

has generated certain habits of mind which characterize the liberal in education as elsewhere. One is the habit of looking for the truths of tomorrow within the nonconformities of today. This has given to nonconformity as such not only a respectability but an aspect of urgency. He who would be wise must be a nonconformist. Would you elicit the respect of future generations? Then honor the ideas of the minority rather than of the majority, of the radical, not the conservative of today!

Secondly, past attacks upon academic freedom have been commonly identified with onslaughts upon individuals who are sufficiently able and courageous to think creatively and with an originality denied the common run of men. Accordingly, they who anticipate a tomorrow different from today easily assume that the interests of the future require giving sympathy and support to educators under attack.

---

[2] *Abrams* v. *U.S.*, 250 U.S. 616, 624 (1919).

For these reasons, liberals, lay and professional alike, were ill-prepared to cope with an invasion of our educational institutions by well-organized and disciplined disciples of the left, pliant tools of outside groups who deliberately used academic freedom as a cloak for the indoctrination of the young in a dogmatic philosophy—a philosophy which requires of its followers not the encouragement but the extinction of originality of thought and independence of behavior.

This novel situation, the presence in our institutions of higher learning of teachers devoted not to freedom of inquiry but to its ultimate extinction has confused and divided liberals. Some continue to insist, with Thomas Jefferson, that there is no ultimate danger so long as reason is left free to cope with error, and, therefore, they insist that the traditional methods of procedure which the lovers of freedom have sought to incorporate into administrative procedure are equally applicable to the Communist and the non-Communist. Others insist upon distinguishing between the "heretic" and the "conspirator" and would modify the principles determining the selection and retention of faculty members in the light of this distinction. This difference in fundamental point of view among the friends of academic freedom is serious and is reflected in the pronouncements of members of the profession both as individuals and as professional organizations and in attitudes assumed with respect to the activities of investigating committees of Congress and state legislatures with respect to "subversion" in American education.

The Issue of Membership in the Communist Party

In March, 1952, the Committee on Academic Freedom and Tenure of the American Association of University Professors submitted to the annual meeting of the Association its conclusions regarding university policy bearing upon faculty membership in the Communist Party and Communist front organizations. Declared the committee, with the approval of the delegates,

The tests of the fitness of a member of the academic profession should be his professional competence, his integrity and character, and his ability and willingness to engage in vigorous, objective instruction and research; these to be measured by the accepted principles and standards of the profession. A teacher who is guilty of misusing his classes or his other relationships with his students for biased partisan propaganda, or is guilty of a legally defined subversive act, is responsible as an individual for the violation of professional principles or the law of the land, as the case may be, and should be dismissed, provided his guilt is established by evidence adduced in a proceeding in which he is given a full measure of due process. . . .

In discussing the intent of this resolution, Ralph Himstead, formerly General Secretary of the Association, has said,

It is clear from this excerpt that the American Association of University Professors does not accept the formula of guilt by association. The views it has stated on this subject are, we believe, realistic, and what is more important, consonant with the principles of the Academic Profession, of Anglo-American Law and of our Constitutional System. We believe that our colleges and universities can be protected, and are being protected against subversive individuals without doing violence to these basic principles. Pursuant to the affirmative tests of professional fitness, set forth in the resolution cited, higher education is protected not only against subversive acts of teachers who may be members of the Communist Party, but also against subversive acts of teachers who are "fellow travelers" or crypto Communists.[3]

Himstead and the American Association of University Professors evidently ground their position on the theory that the principles of both academic and constitutional freedom are designed to protect the individual as teacher and as citizen. Basic to these guarantees is the fact that *actual conduct* rather than mere association constitutes guilt or innocence. Consequently, membership in the Communist Party (as long as it remains a legal organization) should not imply conduct "unbecoming a teacher." The test of a teacher's fitness turns rather upon activities within the classroom and/or actual behavior outside the classroom.

This position has received support from quarters other than

---

[3] *Academic Freedom in the United States*. Papers contributed to the Fifteenth Annual Spring Conference of the Division of the Social Sciences of Howard University (Washington, D.C.: The Howard University Press, 1953), p. 13.

those exclusively professional. For example, the late Senator Taft, one-time trustee of Yale University, was bold enough to assert during the McCarthy era that the grounds for action against Communist teachers should be based upon conduct only, and the American Civil Liberties Union in *A Statement of Principles Concerning Civil Liberties and Obligations of Students and Teachers in Public and Private Schools and Colleges,* issued in April, 1952, declared that "The central issue, in considering a teacher's fitness, is his own performance in his subject and his relationship with his students. The A.C.L.U. opposes as contrary to democratic liberties any ban or regulation which would prohibit the employment as a teacher of any person solely because of his views or associations as Communist or Fascist." As this group sees it, "Even though a teacher may be linked with religious dogmatists or political authoritarians, the A.C.L.U. believes that he must nevertheless be appraised as an individual." [4]

The argument in support of this general position has been well stated by Professor George E. Axtelle of New York University. Speaking out of a rich experience on all levels of education, Axtelle puts forth three basic considerations: [5]

1. To exclude a teacher from the profession on grounds other than professional performance is to ignore the fact "that communist party members understand and interpret communism and party discipline and the party oath variously. Not only is there variety of understanding and interpretation, there is great variety of character. Not all communists are liars and traitors. Many honestly confuse communism and liberal democracy, and actually observe the canons of liberalism."

This argument is obviously more pertinent when applied to membership in the Communist Party of some years ago than it is today and to "cells" in academic institutions in nonmetropolitan areas of the country than in large cities such as New York and Chicago, where, even fifteen or twenty years ago, the activities of the party were more openly in harmony with the doctrine that the ends justifies the means than in less populous regions. In few

---

[4] Published by the American Civil Liberties Union, 170 Fifth Ave., New York City.

[5] "Communism and Academic Freedom," *The Standard,* December, 1949, pp. 99–107. Statements attributed to Axtelle in this chapter are taken from this article.

institutions, indeed, has membership on the part of the teaching profession involved more than an open and active expression of intellectual dissent with the status quo. Seldom has party discipline required members of the profession to engage in specific activities of a conspiratorial character designed "to undermine American institutions." This fact doubtless prompts Axtelle to refer, by way of illustration, to the dismissal of a member of the philosophy department of the University of Washington, "because he acknowledged party membership. Yet there was no evidence that he was other than an honest scholar." A second member of this faculty "was put on probation because he confessed he had been a party member, but was one no longer. There was no evidence in his case that he had been other than an honest and competent teacher while a party member."

2. Secondly, Axtelle contends that adoption of a policy which entails the automatic discharge or the automatic exclusion of teachers from an educational institution once they are known to be Communists, "would make for a psychology of orthodoxy which would be devastating intellectually." He believes that "much of the attack upon communists and communism springs from a fear of ideas which depart from the conventional pattern. Nothing could so seriously undermine our democracy and the whole future of our kind of civilization as a national psychology hostile to critical intelligence. This is much too great a price to pay."

Here again the situation is somewhat changed since Axtelle wrote these words. Not only has present membership in the Communist Party been used as a cause for the discharge of teachers, but the fact of past membership has also been cause for dismissal.[6]

---

[6] In Arlington, Virginia, to take but one example, a teacher who was found to have joined the Communist Party in the mid-1930's and became disillusioned and resigned from the party in the mid-1940's was "persuaded" to resign from her position in the course of the school year 1958, when these facts became known, despite the fact that in all known respects her work had been above reproach and it was clear that her original motives for joining the party had been idealistic rather than "subversive."

It should be said that action of this character is, however, of doubtful legal validity, despite decisions of some state courts sanctioning the dismissal of a teacher on grounds of active membership. For example, the Supreme Court of Pennsylvania upheld the discharge of a public school teacher merely because of active membership in the Communist Party and without any evidence of the "advocacy" condemned by the Smith Act decision. [See *Report on Civil Liberties—January, 1951-June, 1953* (New York: Civil Liberties Union), p. 59.] On the other hand, in

Unfortunately, the trend of events has given substance to the warning issued by John Dewey in a letter to *The New York Times* of June 21, 1949. Dewey pointed out that the indirect consequences of automatic dismissal might well be more harmful in the end than the evils this policy is designed to prevent. "Such a movement," he wrote, "gets taken up into a larger movement where it goes beyond that intended by the scholarly leaders who proposed something which in abstract logic was justified." [7]

declaring unconstitutional an Oklahoma statute which required a loyalty oath of all state and local employees, the United States Supreme Court, with Justice Clark speaking for the Court, declared:

"Due process does not permit the dismissal of folks solely on the basis of organizational membership regardless of their knowledge concerning the organization to which they may belong. A state servant may have joined a proscribed organization unawares of its proclivities and purposes. In recent years many completely loyal persons have severed organizational ties after learning for the first time the character of the groups with which they have belonged. At the time of affiliation the group itself may not be known to be subversive. Under the Oklahoma Act the fact of association alone determines disloyalty and disqualification. It matters not whether the association existed innocently or knowingly.

"To thus inhibit individual freedom of movement is to stifle the flow of democratic expression and controversy at one of its chief sources.

"We hold that the distinction observed here is a basic distinction. Indiscriminate classification of the innocent with knowing activities must fall as an assertion of arbitrary power. This oath offends due process." (Quoted by Ralph Himstead in paper read at the Fifteenth Annual Spring Conference of the Division of the Social Sciences held at Howard University on March 11, 1953. *Academic Freedom in the United States, op. cit.,* p. 23.)

[7] That Dewey's fears were well grounded is evidenced by the tendency of governing boards to dismiss teachers called before legislative committees who may have refused to answer questions on the ground that they "constituted an improper inquiry into their personal beliefs and political associations." In Philadelphia (according to a special report issued by the Greater Philadelphia Branch of the American Civil Liberties Union) some twenty-seven teachers were discharged for "incompetence," who for various reasons had refused to answer questions put by the Velde Committee or the Superintendent or both. "At the hearings, the teachers were not allowed to present testimony as to their professional competence, their reputations among students and parents, or as to their loyalty. Each teacher had long since subscribed to the oath required by the Pennsylvania Loyalty Act (the Pechan Act), affirming that he was not a member of a subversive organization. No charge of disloyalty (or of perjury) was involved in the proceedings. Failure to answer questions of the Superintendent of Schools or of the Velde Committee was accepted by a majority of the School Board as conclusive evidence of 'incompetence,' despite the fact that the Pennsylvania Tenure Act for the protection of school teachers from arbitrary dismissal contains no such concept of incompetence" (p. 2). . . . In one case, "the Superintendent admitted that it was the mere fact of being" in a position to be called before the Committee "that constituted bad judgment amounting to incompetency, and counsel for the School Board stated the 'only charge here is her appearance before the Velde Committee.' This is an amazing doctrine—that any one called as a witness, however innocent, is guilty of bad judgment" (p. 32). [See *Academic Freedom: Some Recent Philadelphia Episodes* (Philadelphia: American Civil Liberties Union, Greater Philadelphia Branch, 1955).]

3. Finally, Axtelle draws attention to the danger that the exclusion of party members as such from teaching positions will put a premium upon deceit and duplicity and perhaps will even encourage some to take their professional communism more seriously than they otherwise might do. "We must beware lest we adopt a policy which closes the doors leading out of the party without closing those leading into it. Members draw together more closely around the party for self-protection. Yet unless the conditions and appeals which lead into the party are changed we may close the exits from the party and increase its strength."

When Is Membership in Out-of-School Organizations "Conduct Unbecoming of a Teacher"

It is not necessary to deny the weight of these arguments in order to appreciate their shortcoming in the light of the unique character of Communist activity in recent years. The question at issue is not the right of an individual instructor or a group of instructors, engaged in cooperative research, to conduct this research without hindrance or to impart the conclusions of genuine inquiry to students free from internal or external interference. Nor is it a question of whether an instructor is privileged to share with his students the results of his own deliberations on problems of the day insofar as these are relevant to subjects under study or investigation, be these conservative, liberal, or radical or consistent with or destructive of the status quo. Rather the problem is how best to cope with "conduct unbecoming of a teacher" when this conduct involves (1) acceptance of outside dictation with respect to what and how one shall teach in areas controversial and (2) the deliberate effort to select and interpret the subject matter of instruction with a view to molding student judgment in conformity with this outside dictation.

This is no simple problem, as witness the fact that educators are divided not so much on the diagnosis of the disease as on the remedy. The arguments reviewed are not designed to safeguard either subversives or subversion. Rather are they the considered and sincere views of individuals who cannot accept as cure what, in their judgment, may work greater havoc than the disease. As so frequently happens, the choice is not one between an obvious right and an obvious wrong, or what is clearly wise or demonstrably foolish. It is between a lesser and a greater evil as honest men, deprived of scientifically validated scales, attempt to appraise this evil.

To a considerable extent, the contentions of Axtelle and those who go with him turn upon the dangers implicit in the application of an automatic rule, a mandate which ignores the uniqueness and the peculiarities as well as the exceptions that commonly distinguish a specific from a general situation. And what living situation does not involve other than general characteristics? On the other hand, those who think differently are convinced that these consequences are less serious than the failure to exercise a professional discipline in situations where professional misconduct seems obvious. Moreover, the advocates of sterner methods point to the radical difference between conditions today and some years back. In the 1930's and the early 1940's it was possible for an earnest individual to confuse the aims and objectives of the Communist Party with those of a liberal and democratic socialism, or with a party of dissent and reform operating squarely within the American tradition. But he is an innocent, indeed, one totally out of touch with reality, who, today, remains so confused. Nor is it necessary to lean upon the findings of legislative committees, such as those of the Congress or the California Senate Committee on Un-American Activities to correct this misunderstanding. The exhaustive investigations and reports of commissions, such as that appointed by President Truman to determine whether the Communist Party should register as an agent of a foreign power, as well as testimony gathered in judicial proceedings under the Smith Act (evidence which one must accept quite apart from one's judgment as to the wisdom of the act itself), together with the sad experience of numerous educational institutions with Communist activity in classroom and on the campus, should remove any doubts on this matter. Nor in the light of this data can educators afford to ignore the difference between protecting a teacher in the exercise of his privileges and obligations as a citizen outside the classroom and the corruption of the teaching function which follows when, with a "captive audience," an instructor identifies his functions as a teacher with those of a citizen engaged in propaganda.

Admitting the very real dangers to intellectual freedom implicit in a policy of excluding members of the Communist Party by virtue of this membership from the classroom of educational institutions under public control, these dangers are less serious than the practical effects of the alternative policy suggested by the opponents of this procedure. How, as a matter of fact, would an institution of higher learning administer the test of fitness to teach as suggested in the following declaration of policy adopted by the Columbia chapter of the American Association of University Professors on April 14, 1953?

The basic test of the fitness of a teacher should be his professional competence and personal integrity as demonstrated in his teaching and research . . . failure to satisfy standards of professional competence and propriety must be proved by evidence based on a man's actual conduct. Present active or long continued membership in a totalitarian party creates a certain presumption against the member's ability and desire to exercise full use of academic freedom, and evidence of such association should be considered in determining his fitness to be a member of the academic community. Membership in any lawful organization does not, however, in and of itself, constitute sufficient ground for disqualifying a person from continued membership in an academic community.[8]

One of the virtues of instruction on the college and university level has been the mature relationship which it is assumed exists between student and teacher. Both the methods employed and the selection of subject matter taught are commonly left entirely in the hands of the instructor. There is no classroom supervision by one's superiors similar to that which ordinarily prevails in the elementary and the secondary school. And although some may regret this fact on the ground that it enables inefficient and even immature instructors to engage in educational malpractice, it is questionable that higher education, on the whole, would benefit from the introduction of the meticulous type of supervision widely followed in institutions of lower grade.

How, then, is an instructor appraised? Often by his writings rather than his teachings, a cynic might reply. More seriously, we

---

[8] Reprinted in *School and Society*, July 11, 1953, p. 11.

should say, by his professional colleagues on the basis of his research and his publications. To this must be added student judgment based upon the experience of successive generations of students. Seldom, and certainly not exclusively, is he judged on the basis of one or more specific occurrences in the classroom.

On the whole, this is sound and healthy; but it hardly serves the purpose of detecting the subtle manipulation of data by one skilled in the art or the deliberate efforts of a teacher to use the tools of his craft to convert his students to a point of view dictated for him by an outside organization committed to the undermining of democratic institutions. Consequently, unless our educational institutions are prepared to introduce a method of student reporting or the continuous visitation of an instructor by his colleagues which does violence to the freedom now enjoyed by college professors, the proposal to test fitness by actual conduct in the classroom is virtually a proposal to do little or nothing at all.

Nor are the methods of supervision through classroom visitation now used in elementary and secondary schools of a character designed to detect subversion. As James Marshall has pointed out, subversive teaching

. . . does not occur in the presence of a supervisor. The evidence, therefore, must in the main be obtained from pupils. Their testimony is not to be ignored; but anyone who has to decide the guilt of teachers on the testimony of children knows how unreliable this can be. Furthermore, to encourage children to report on their teacher's loyalty is in itself damaging to the social structure of the nation. Teachers stand *in loco parentis,* and the encouragement of spying on them is a symbol of if not a lesson in spying on parents. This has been the pattern of Nazism and Communism, a mechanism of the Gestapo and NKVD. It is disruptive of the personality development of the young and might well interfere with the wholesome growth of conscience.[9]

As was mentioned earlier, we face a choice between evils. What is required is a policy that will prevent public education from subversion within, at a time of national danger, without subverting the processes of free education. The lovers of freedom are evidently agreed on the general proposition "that a member of any

---

[9] "The Defense of Public Education from Subversion," *Columbia Law Review,* May, 1951, pp. 587–604.

political party or group which asserts the right to dictate in matters of science or scientific opinion is not free to teach the truth and thereby is disqualified." [10] They are not of one mind, however, as to whether actual membership in the Communist Party carries with it a discipline contrary to honest teaching. The view presented here assumes that the subjection of the Communist Party to foreign dictation and the nature of the discipline which this party exercises over its members have been sufficiently demonstrated to justify a policy of identifying membership in the party with conduct unbecoming a teacher in an educational institution supported and maintained by the public. It is also contended that a decision of this character is less destructive of academic freedom than is reliance upon a policy of spying upon teachers. Not only are the methods of the latter likely to be detestable in themselves, but there is danger that what originates as an attempt to identify "misconduct" will end as an unwise interference with the free play of ideas in the classroom.

This leads to a further consideration. What is sought is a policy which distinguishes between an heretical ideology, on the one hand, and reprehensible conduct, on the other. Despite recent improvements in general attitude of the public over that of a few years ago, the atmosphere is more hostile than friendly to the survival of free institutions. Instances are still common in which an individual's interest in nonconventional ideas or a minority cause are equated with communism, or "thinking like a Communist." Moreover, the names of individuals so branded have a way of finding a place in the unevaluated files of legislative committees investigating un-American activities and of being used uncritically by "patriotic" organizations to harry and embarrass and even to blacklist an otherwise innocent individual.[11]

Under these circumstances every effort should be made to enable educational institutions under public control (and private institutions as a condition of professional self-respect) freely to exercise the right and the obligation to judge a teacher on the basis of professional conduct, as distinct from intellectual orthodoxy as defined by the self-appointed guardians of orthodoxy.

---

[10] From a statement of policy adopted by the Graduate Faculty of Political and Social Science of the New School for Social Research in 1944.

[11] See Ralph S. O'Leary, "Minute Women, Daughters of Vigilantism," *The Nation,* January 9, 1954, pp. 26–28.

Who will contend, for example, that the colleges of California would long retain their professional integrity if the testimony of Richard M. Combs, Chief Counsel of the California State Senate Committee on Un-American Activities, before the "Jenner Committee" of the United States Senate accurately describes a permanent policy? Mr. Combs outlined an arrangement which he states existed between the State Senate Committee and the college presidents of the major California colleges. According to this arrangement, the colleges undertook to employ as full-time members of the staff, ex-F.B.I. agents and ex-navy and military intelligence people. These people

. . . maintain a liaison with our committee. We in turn make available to them the accumulated documentation, the material that we have accumulated during the 14 years. But we soon found that it was even more necessary to prevent people from getting on faculties and obtaining positions in the educational institutions than it was to get rid of them once their positions became solidified.

So the committee developed a procedure whereby applicants for positions are referred to us, their names are, and if we do have any documentation concerning their Communist activity over a long period of time we make that available to the university as a guide to indicate whether or not the individual should be employed.[12]

According to the testimony of Mr. Combs, some one hundred faculty members were severed from their positions during the period June 4, 1952, and the date of his testimony on March 24, 1953.

Observe that nothing is said by Mr. Combs or in the report of the Jenner Committee to indicate the manner in which "people who are either Communists or about whom there is evidence of Communist activity" are so identified. Since, however, the California Senate Committee is one and the same as that which recommended the banning of textbooks from public schools which offend by listing in their bibliographies the writings of individuals such as Charles A. Beard, Stuart Chase, Dorothy Canfield Fisher, Lewis Mumford, and others similarly distinguished, we may

---

[12] *Report of the Subcommittee to Investigate the Administration of the Internal Security Act and Other Internal Security Laws to the Committee on the Judiciary,* United States Senate, July 17, 1953, p. 12.

question the scrupulous care with which this committee determined the fitness or unfitness of the one hundred undesirable
faculty members!

To draw a clear line between conduct unbecoming a teacher
and the appropriate area of private conviction is not always easy.
Nevertheless, the attempt of governing boards to hew to this line
is practical insurance against situations that are all too common,
if subversion is identified with what officials consider anathema
in ideas.

Some, however, reject the attempt to maintain this distinction
as the equivalent of appeasement. To appease the enemies of freedom in the academic world, they contend, is as fatal as it is to
appease the enemies of democracy in the political arena. Nor will
they agree that we have drawn the line accurately between conduct and freedom of thought. "Surely," they argue, "membership in a lawful organization should not, in and by itself, disqualify a person from functioning within the academic community."

To this we reply that the distinction between membership in a
lawful as against an unlawful organization is not of necessity
relevant to the point we are making. Today, the Communist
Party is an outlawed party. Consequently, membership in it may
properly disqualify an individual from employment in a school
or a college which is conducted under public auspices and supported by public funds. But this does not render moot the question of membership in *any* organization outside an educational
institution which presumes to dictate the functions and responsibilities of a teacher as teacher. No one will contend, for example, that membership in a religious organization, such as a
church, should disqualify an individual from teaching in a school
or college. Far from it! Indeed, in a church-related school and in
many a public school church membership is considered an asset
to be added to a teacher's professional qualifications. But in a
number of states the question of whether members of a religious
order that requires submission to a discipline superior to all
other disciplines as well as a commitment to spread the doctrines
of the parent church shall be privileged to teach in public schools
has become an acute issue. Nor is this issue disposed of by the suggestion that conventional clothes be substituted for the distinctive

religious garb when members are engaged in the act of teaching. It is not the outward and visible insignia that is in question but the inner commitment which lends itself to the possibility of partisan and parochial instruction.

Similarly with membership in any organization, be it religious, political, economic, or social. The moral is clear, although, admittedly, its administration is difficult: The obligation of governing boards and teachers alike is to serve the public by insuring the rights of students in a public institution to receive a public, or a secular, education rather than one partisan and parochial.

Criteria for Determining the Retention or Dismissal of Teachers

The position outlined above differs little from that suggested by the writer as early as 1943, when the friends of academic freedom were more divided than they are today on the problem of Communists as teachers or of membership in well-disciplined organizations outside educational institutions which presumed to control the performance of teachers.[13] It was necessary then as it is imperative now to stress safeguards for teachers whose academic fitness has been challenged.

1. Both the criteria and the procedures to be followed in the selection of a staff member are different from those which might be used appropriately when considering his dismissal. Too often this difference is ignored. On the elementary and secondary levels particularly, and to a lesser degree in colleges and universities, factors other than competence in classroom instruction enter prominently. Since the concerns of the school have been enlarged to include objectives other than exclusive emphasis upon intellectual development—guidance in emotional and social growth, education for character as well as of the "mind"—the qualifications for teaching have likewise increased in number and quality. The selection of a prospective teacher is thus influenced of necessity by factors such as the complexion of the community, the

---

[13] We can do little more at this point than to state the general principles of procedure. For a more detailed consideration of methods to follow in determining fitness to teach, see A.A.U.P. Bulletin on *Academic Freedom and Tenure*, March, 1958. American Association of University Professors, 1785 Massachusetts Avenue, N.W., Washington 6, D.C.

character of the parent as well as the student body, and the kinds of relationships which obtain or are desired between school and society. These more varied and intimate concerns are receiving ever greater attention in the selection of members of the staff of the modern school and college and are relevant factors as well in determining retention. Nevertheless, the two—factors of selection and retention—are not identical. Nor need the evidence required to refuse employment be as conclusive as that justifying retention.

2. Precisely because Communist Party discipline has varied in different sections of the country, involving no more than an intellectual commitment to economic reforms in some instances and insistence upon the subordination of act and thought to external discipline in others, regulations regarding membership in the party should carry no *ex post facto* penalties. Unfortunately, Congressional committees, bent upon collecting and exhibiting the scalps of victims with a none too tender regard for the personalities concerned, have violated the standards of due process in a manner which no institution can safely imitate. Moreover, since it is well known that many a young person has joined the Communist Party, particularly in the 1930's, with the noblest of intentions, the factor of time cannot be ignored. Little will be lost and much may be gained if an institution or a school system establishes a regulation respecting membership in the Communist Party which enables all members of the staff freely to decide where *in the future* their loyalties are to lie and to abide by the consequences.

3. Again, every precaution should be taken to insure competent and professional judgment on the conduct of any teacher who may be charged with the abuse of his functions. The American conception of justice has been sorely tried, if not corrupted, in recent years. As against the traditional axiom that a man is innocent until proven guilty, the reverse has all too often been the case. How many people today hold to the principle that it is better for ten guilty men to go free than for one innocent man to be declared guilty? Surely an educational institution should set an example of equal and exact justice. Specifically, this entails judgment by one's peers and meticulous reliance upon due process. In deciding the fate of a teacher as a teacher there is no

place for the use of anonymous witnesses, the refusal of the right to confront and to cross examine one's accusers, or the practice of keeping secret from the accused the nature of the charges against him.

In recent years, the obvious abuse of the protections afforded by the Fifth Amendment of the federal Constitution by witnesses appearing before committees of Congress has led a number of educational institutions to dismiss without further consideration members of their staffs who have used the amendment to justify their refusal to answer questions put to them. As experience has shown, this is a highly arbitrary procedure and runs counter to the principles of due process as well as recent decisions of the United States Supreme Court [14] in *Slochower* v. *Board of Education* (350 U.S. 551, 1956) and *Watkins* v. *United States* (354 U.S. 178, 1957).

The Case of the Fellow Traveler

There remains the case of the "fellow traveler," the individual who "follows the Communist line," but who lacks membership in an unlawful or a conspiratorial organization. One who is identified more by his thoughts as expressed and his occasional behavior than by demonstrated membership in the Communist Party or other subversive organization.

Insofar as the conduct of the "fellow traveler" outside the classroom or his instruction inside the classroom violates the standards of professional integrity, the case is clear. However, in the absence of clear evidence to this effect, there are no adequate grounds for his dismissal. Moreover, when and if he is thus charged with misconduct, the decision as to his guilt or innocence should follow only upon due process of academic law. Unless our educational institutions observe scrupulously procedures designed to protect the innocent as well as to identify the guilty, we shall move rapidly into a situation in which the American people will have transformed their way of life in the image of the totalitarians. Repeated experience should have taught us that the most effective way to deal with heretical ideas is to subject them to open criticism, not to suppress them, to refute heresy and dangerous

---

[14] *Ibid.*, pp. 5–10.

ideas with intelligence, not to do violence to their advocates. As Henry Steele Commager has wisely observed,

There is no real choice between freedom and security. Only those societies that actively encourage freedom—that encourage, for example, scientific and scholarly research, the questioning of scientific and social orthodoxies and the discovery of new truths—only such societies can hope to solve the problems that assail them and preserve their security. . . . A nation that silences or intimidates original minds is left only with unoriginal minds and cannot hope to hold its own in the competition of peace or of war. As John Stuart Mill said in that essay on Liberty to which we cannot too often repair, "A state which dwarfs its men in order that they may be more docile instruments in its hands . . . will find that with small men no great thing can really be accomplished." [15]

As indicated above, the principle upon which we may justify the exclusion of members of the Communist Party from the faculty of an educational institution applies equally to affiliations with other groups which exercise control over the teaching process. The attempt of Communists to infiltrate into educational institutions has thus resulted in a clarification of the nature of academic freedom. As I. B. Berkson has well stated, "academic freedom is an obligation rather than a right." It is a discipline. "It is a corollary of the belief in the value of scholarship and scientific inquiry for the extension of knowledge and the service of human welfare. In substance, it makes the ethics of the profession of scholars and scientists supreme over the arbitrary control of outside forces—of the state, the church, the political party, and, not least, of public opinion." [16]

The nature of academic freedom is thus clearer in the minds of laymen as well as members of the profession than before the "Communist conspiracy" threatened the integrity of academic performance. But we should recognize also that the manner in which governing boards have dealt with teachers under suspicion has probably injured the cause of free inquiry as much if not more than have offending members of the profession, for the latter have

---

[15] "Is Freedom Really Necessary?" *The Saturday Review*, February 21, 1953, pp. 11 ff.

[16] *The Ideal and the Community* (New York: Harper & Brothers, 1958), p. 258.

been relatively few in numbers. Seldom have the protections which institutions of higher learning extend to members of their faculties under attack from without been afforded to teachers of elementary and secondary schools. Here summary dismissal without appeal has all too often been the rule rather than the exception. Indeed one may question whether the principles of academic freedom as defined by the American Association of University Professors have any genuine application to public education below the college level. On these lower levels both the definition and the applications of the principles of freedom are as virgin soil awaiting cultivation. How open, for example, is the opportunity for an unbiased consideration of the problem of desegregation in education in a southern classroom today? Or how genuine are the rights of the teacher either as teacher or as citizen in a southern state which writes into law the provision that any institution which employs a teacher who is known to have contributed to the National Association for the Advancement of Colored People thereby sacrifices its right to receive public funds? Nor is the South alone in this frame of mind. Let an issue equally acute arise in a northern community and similar pressures will play upon the schools.

Despite these discouraging facts, it is doubtless true, speaking generally, that both the lay public and members of the teaching profession are more keenly aware of the nature and the value of academic freedom today than prior to the "Communist menace." If the attempt to resolve the problem of communism in American education has in fact contributed to this end, perhaps the sacrifice of many an innocent victim will not have been altogether in vain.

Suggested Reading

Academic Freedom Committee of the American Civil Liberties Union, *On the 1953 Statement of the Association of American Universities, "The Rights and Responsibilities of Universities and Their Faculties"* (New York: American Civil Liberties Union, 1958).

American Association of University Professors, *Academic Freedom and Tenure*, A.A.U.P. Bulletin, March, 1958.

Berkson, I. B., *The Ideal and the Community* (New York: Harper & Brothers, 1958), chap. XV.

Hook, Sidney, *Heresy, Yes. Conspiracy, No* (New York: John Day Company, 1953), chaps. VI, VIII, IX, XII.

Hullfish, H. Gordon, *Keeping Our Schools Free*. Public Affairs Pamphlet No. 199. Public Affairs Committee, 22 East 38 Street, New York 16, New York.

Taylor, Harold, *On Education and Freedom* (New York: Abelard Schuman, 1954), chap. VII.

Thayer, V. T., *American Education Under Fire* (New York: Harper & Brothers, 1944), chap. IX.

ΛΛΛΛ

CHAPTER

23

Segregation in American Education

Class and Caste in American Society

Distinctions of class are present in all communities, although the degree of their visibility varies widely. Of the visibility of caste, however, there is no question. Nor is there reason to doubt that caste distinctions foster inequalities in education.

Even so, the implications of caste are by no means everywhere the same. They differ as between groups affected, a fact which renders it easier for the members of some groups to emancipate themselves than for members of others, as witness the comparative ease with which an educated Mexican or an Oriental, even an Indian, can break through caste barriers in contrast with the difficulties confronting a Negro. These implications likewise differ with geographical location. In Hawaii, for example, caste distinctions based on race and nationality are of low visibility, despite the fact that some thirteen or more racial groups live side by side in a relatively small area.

In contrast with the hospitable attitude in Hawaii, we find states of the Union, primarily in the North and the West, in which discrimination exists but is publicly frowned upon and people are highly sensitive to the rights of minorities, but for reasons quite different from those in Hawaii. The population is heterogeneous in its composition and most, if not all, races and creeds represented have suffered at one time or another a minority status. In seeking equality for its members each group realizes that consistency and expediency dictate that what one claims for oneself should be accorded to another. Consequently, organized efforts are made to insure this general equality through law and education. In New York, for example, both "fair employment" and "fair educational" practices have the sanction of law, but the machinery of enforcement relies as much upon the use of persuasion as upon penalties for violation. It seeks to erase false apprehensions from the minds of employers and employees regarding the consequences of nonsegregated working conditions or from the minds of parents who fear violence if their children attend mixed schools; it furnishes expert advice on ways and means of introducing new practices and of avoiding, if not eliminating, difficulties that have their roots in racial and religious prejudice.

Despite these attempts to prevent segregation and to insure equality of treatment for all races, evidences of the reverse abound in the North and West. As William R. Ming, Jr., pointed out in 1952, "there are public schools and local school systems with racial patterns and practices hardly distinguishable from the segregated school patterns of the Deep South. Among these states are New York, Pennsylvania, Illinois, Ohio, Arizona and New Mexico." [1] These pockets of resistance result often from restrictions of residence, either accidental or by design. Again, they follow upon the invasion of a community, long homogeneous in its racial complexion, by groups different both in race and cultural level. This holds true of the immigration of Mexican laborers into the West and Southwest and of the heavy migration of Negroes from the Deep South into northern and western communities. Even in communities where concepts of equality were thought to have been firmly rooted in tradition and law, devices of one sort or another have been resorted to in order to bring about segregation in schools, residential districts, housing developments, and employment.

In some instances, as in the states of New Mexico, Arizona, Kansas, and Wyoming, this sentiment found expression, prior to the Supreme Court decision of 1954, in the passage of laws which rendered segregation optional in education.

Finally, there is the South in which distinctions of caste have

---

[1] "The Elimination of Segregation in the Public Schools of the North and West," *Journal of Negro Education*, Summer, 1952, p. 265.

become deeply rooted in both custom and law, and segregation accurately expresses long accepted ways of feeling, acting, and thinking. People have passed from childhood into adolescence and on into adulthood without either experiencing or contemplating a relationship other than one of segregation between the races. What seems axiomatic to the liberal in the North is viewed by the southerner as a threat to the foundation of his society, and the attempts of the former to change the ways of the latter seem an unwarranted invasion by an external meddler.

Rigid as caste distinctions are, there is little consistency either in definition or practice when it comes to identifying the status of individuals of mixed blood. Lord Bryce, in his *American Commonwealth,* observed that "In Latin America whoever is not black is white." [2] Not so in the United States. Interestingly enough, but tragic in its implications, the decision of the United States Supreme Court in the case of *Plessy* v. *Ferguson,*[3] which gave legal sanction to the "separate but equal" doctrine, grew out of an incident in Louisiana in which the great-grandchild of a Negro parent had ventured into a passenger car reserved for whites. M. R. Konvitz states that the definitions of a Negro "are all made from the standpoint of the white person who seeks to avoid contact with a person who *he* considers to be a Negro, without regard to what the latter may have to say about the matter." [4] In some states "everybody having a known trace of Negro blood in his veins, no matter how far back it was acquired—is classified as a Negro." [5]

Enforced segregation of the races likewise varies among the states. Prior to the 1954 decision of the United States Supreme Court on segregation in education twenty-nine states forbade the marriage of a white person and a Negro, five the marriage of a white and an Indian, and fourteen that of a white and a Mongolian or an Oriental. In 1951 segregation on buses and on street cars was mandatory in eleven states. Similarly, the states of Arkansas, Georgia, Louisiana, Missouri, Oklahoma, South Carolina, Tennessee, and Virginia had enacted statutes requiring segregation

---

[2] 1910, vol. II, p. 555.

[3] 163 U.S. 537 (1896).

[4] M. R. Konvitz, "The Extent and Character of Legally Enforced Segregation," *Journal of Negro Education,* Summer, 1951, p. 526.

[5] G. Myrdal, *An American Dilemma* (New York: Harper & Brothers, 1944), p. 113.

in the use of parks, playgrounds, bathing and fishing facilities, boating facilities, amusement parks, race tracks, billiard and pool rooms, circuses, theaters and public halls.[6] Segregation in hospitals and penal institutions is likewise common. Oklahoma required that separate telephone booths be installed when "there is a demand for such separate booths." Separate washrooms are, of course, common in factories, in business houses, and in public and semi-public institutions. South Carolina forbids Negroes and whites, in the cotton textile factories, to work in the same room, to use the entrances and exits at the same time, or to "use the same stairway and windows at the same time."[7]

Mandatory segregation has assumed many forms. Most frequent is that forbidding the marriage of whites with individuals of another color. Mandatory segregation in education ranks second. In 1950, sixteen states insisted upon segregation in their colleges and universities and twenty states either required or rendered permissive segregation in public schools.[8]

It should be observed that the seventeen states which, prior to 1954, had rendered mandatory a dual system of education (Alabama, Arkansas, Delaware, Florida, Georgia, South Carolina, Louisiana, North Carolina, Tennessee, Kentucky, Texas, West Virginia, Missouri, Maryland, Oklahoma, Mississippi, and Virginia) fall within the low per capita income belt. That is to say, those states which have found it most difficult to provide adequate educational facilities for their children, irrespective of color, have been most insistent upon maintaining dual systems of education. The inevitable result is to lower the level of education for both white and Negro children and to render deplorable, in many instances, the educational status of the latter.

Efforts to Realize Separate But Equal Education in the South

Immediately prior to the decision of the Supreme Court in 1954, prompted in no small measure by the fear that the Courts would

---

[6] Konvitz, *op. cit.*, p. 431.

[7] *Ibid.*, p. 432.

[8] *Ibid.*, pp. 427–428. Since the decision of the United States Supreme Court on segregation in education the United States courts have rendered a series of decisions declaring laws of the character described above unconstitutional.

eventually declare segregation in education unconstitutional, southern states undertook to bring about a greater semblance of equality between Negro and white schools. Heavy bond issues were launched for this purpose, and ambitious building programs were undertaken. In some instances this has resulted in larger per capita expenditures for the Negro than for the white pupil and, temporarily at least, superior physical facilities. Thus it was possible for the Virginia court to state, in *Dorothy E. Davis et al. v. County School Board of Prince Edward Co.,* that "in 29 of the even hundred counties in Virginia, the school facilities for the colored are equal to the white schools, in 17 more they are now superior, and upon completion of work authorized or in progress, another 5 will be superior. Of the twenty-seven cities, 5 have Negro schools and facilities equal to the white and 8 more have better schools than the white."

Similarly in Missouri the per capita expenditures for the education of colored pupils in 1948–1949 was $175.32 as against $166.31 for white pupils.[9]

Both Virginia and Missouri are richer in financial resources than most southern states. When we consider the problem which confronted the South as a whole in order to equalize building facilities, teachers' salaries, pupil-teacher ratio, instructional materials, and other essentials, the task would have been Herculean. For example, in 1946, states with a dual system spent on the average $104.66 per white pupil and $57.57 per Negro pupil. To equalize expenditures would have required either doubling, practically, the cost per pupil for Negro children or reducing severely the amounts now available for white pupils. In view of the fact that twelve of the sixteen southern states are already taxing themselves more heavily than the national average of effort,[10] it is questionable whether equalization would have been brought about without lowering the standards below an acceptable level.

It is too late to do more than speculate on what might have evolved out of a sincere effort to apply the doctrine of "separate but equal facilities" in education in the South. Many who cannot justify segregation on principle nevertheless believe that equal

[9] Federal Security Agency, Office of Education, *Statistical Circular,* No. 286, January, 1951.

[10] *Facts on Federal Aid* (Washington, D.C.: National Education Association, September, 1950).

though separate schools for the two races would have prepared the ground for a more peaceful transition from segregation to integration than now seems possible.

There is much to be said for this assumption. But it is also pertinent to ask whether an emphasis upon equal but separate facilities might not have resulted in confirming or perpetuating the custom of separate schools, unless used deliberately as a transition program (which, of course, was quite the opposite of the intentions of southern leaders). In each instance, much would depend upon the nature of the education provided. How realistic is it to suppose that those who are opposed to integration would administer a separate education so as to lead to its eventual elimination?

Moreover, can equality in education be in fact realized in an atmosphere of compulsory segregation in other areas of living? Are not conditions outside the school, as well as inside, essential in order to insure equality of instruction in any genuine sense? Surely it is futile to suppose that schools will provide differentiated opportunities for children in education on a segregated basis unless, upon the conclusion of that education, there exists something akin to an open door to business, the professions, and other positions of dignity and respect in the community.

Steps Leading Up to the Decision of the Supreme Court of May, 1954

Before considering the implications of the momentous decision of the United States Supreme Court in May, 1954, on the question of segregation in education, it might be well for us to review briefly the steps which led more or less inevitably to the ultimate rejection of the "separate but equal" doctrine.

The history of the doctrine reveals a steady transformation in its meaning, beginning with the period in which the eyes of the courts were exclusively upon separation with little concern for the facts of equality or inequality to the final period in which it was recognized that genuine equality and separation are irreconcilable.

Prior to the Civil War, civil rights and the conduct of education were the exclusive prerogatives of the states. Upon the defeat of the seceding states, and as a condition of their readmission to the Union, Congress undertook to insure the equality of the Negro with the white. These efforts assumed the form of specific acts of Congress relating to civil rights, the adoption of the Thirteenth, Fourteenth, and Fifteenth Amendments to the federal Constitution and a requirement that all applicants for statehood would have to include in their constitutions provision for the establishment and the maintenance of free public schools. The most notable of these acts of Congress was that of 1875, which stated as its purpose "to Protect all Citizens in Their Civil and Legal Rights." This act provided that "All persons within the jurisdiction of the United States shall be entitled to the full and equal enjoyment of the accommodations, advantages, facilities and privileges of inns, public conveyances on land and water, theaters, and other places of public amusement; subject only to the conditions and limitations established by law, and applicable to citizens of every race and color, regardless of any previous condition of servitude." [11] By 1883, when the Supreme Court of the United States declared the Civil Rights Acts unconstitutional, the people of the North had become sufficiently weary or disgusted and ashamed of the excesses of the Reconstruction period to leave the fate of the Negro in the hands of the South, and white supremacy under state autonomy was quickly re-established. Disfranchisement under one guise or another and segregation in education as in other areas followed.

It was during this period that state courts developed the doctrine of "separate but equal" facilities as applied to education, which later received approval on a national basis at the hands of the United States Supreme Court. The occasion for this was a statute enacted by the state of Louisiana which required segregation on railroad trains. This act was violated by a passenger, one of whose grandparents had been a Negro. With Justice Harlan dissenting, the Supreme Court in *Plessy* v. *Ferguson* confirmed prior decisions of state courts to the effect that segregation is not discrimination when equal but separate facilities are provided.[12] In arriving at this decision the Court, as we have said, drew upon

---

[11] Konvitz, *op. cit.*, pp. 425–435.

[12] For an excellent review of these decisions, see Harry E. Groves, "A Reexamination of the 'Separate but Equal Doctrine,'" *Journal of Negro Education,* Fall, 1951, pp. 520–534.

prior rulings of state courts, which, in turn, oddly enough, derived from a decision of a Massachusetts court in 1849.[13]

The Massachusetts constitution contained a clause to the effect
that all persons are equal before the law "without distinction of
age or sex, birth or color, origin or condition." A Negro child
claimed the right under this clause to attend the school nearest
to her home rather than the one to which she was assigned because of her race. In denying this right, the Court stated in part:
"But when the great principle [of equality] comes to be applied
to the actual and various conditions of persons in society, it will
not warrant the assertion, that men are legally clothed with the
same civil and political powers, and that children and adults are
legally to have the same functions and be subject to the same
treatment; but only that the rights of all, as they are settled and
regulated by law, are equally entitled to the paternal consideration and protection of the law, for their maintenance."

That is, according to the Court, equality is a philosophical
rather than a practical principle!

The decision of the Court in *Plessy* v. *Ferguson* was quickly
extended to education. In *Gong Lum* v. *Rice* (277 U.S. 78 [1927])
the principle received explicit recognition by the United States
Supreme Court. A Chinese girl in Mississippi had objected to
compulsory attendance at a Negro school and sought to compel
her admission to a white school. Speaking for the majority of the
Court, Chief Justice Taft stated that "it is the same question
which has been many times decided to be within the constitutional power of the state legislature to settle without intervention
of the Federal courts under the Federal Constitution."

The decision in *Gong Lum* v. *Rice* gave little consideration to
the actual facts of "equality" of facilities. Nor did earlier decisions. So intent had they been upon approving the provision for
separate facilities that the courts overlooked the other side of the
equation. Not until late in the 1930's did the term "equal" as well
as "separate" receive critical appraisal.

In 1938, the United States Supreme Court refused to sanction
the mere existence of separated facilities in education, and in the
absence of equal facilities for Negroes, the Court ordered the
University of Missouri to admit a qualified Negro applicant to

---

[13] *Roberts* v. *The City of Boston* (5 Cush. 198, 206, Mass., 1849).

its law school. This decision seemed to establish the principle that where equal facilities were not provided, Negroes were entitled to be admitted to the corresponding white institutions. It was this more detailed attention to the facts of equality which led the Supreme Court in *Sweatt* v. *Painter* [14] to insist upon the admission of Herman Sweatt to the University of Texas Law School, despite the existence of a law school established exclusively for Negroes, which was, however, inferior to the white school. In making its ruling the court called attention to the fact that the Negro law school could not possibly provide equal preparation for legal practice because of differences in student body, faculty, library, and other intangibles "incapable of objective measurement." It also pointed out that the prospective lawyer would be at a disadvantage to prepare for practice in an academic vacuum, apart from the association with the body of classmates with whom he must deal when admitted to the Texas Bar.

Keener appreciation of what constitutes genuine equality in education received further emphasis in *McLaurin* v. *Oklahoma State Regents* [15] with Chief Justice Vinson again speaking for the Court. In response to a decision of the District Court to the effect that the state of Oklahoma was obligated under its constitution to afford McLaurin "the education he sought as soon as it provided that education for applicants of any other group" and that the Oklahoma statutes under which McLaurin had been denied admission to the university were unconstitutional, the Oklahoma legislature amended its statutes so as to permit the admission of Negroes to institutions of higher learning along with white students when identical courses were not available in Negro schools. But the legislature also stipulated that instruction under these circumstances "shall be given at such colleges or institutions of higher education upon a segregated basis." In conformity with this legislation, McLaurin was admitted to the graduate school of the University of Oklahoma, but under regulations which required him, as the Court emphasized, "to sit apart at a designated desk in an anteroom adjoining the classroom, to sit at a designated desk in the mezzanine floor of the library, but not to use the desks in the regular reading room; and to sit at a designated table and

---

[14] 339 U.S. 629 (1950).
[15] 339 U.S. 636 (1950).

to eat at a different time from the other students in the school cafeteria."

Justice Vinson pointed out that these regulations set "McLaurin apart from the other students. The result is that the appellant is handicapped in his pursuit of effective instruction. Such restrictions impair and inhibit his ability to study, to engage in discussions, and exchange views with other students, and, in general to learn his profession."

The Sweatt and McLaurin cases bore upon the admission and the treatment accorded Negro students in higher education. It was inevitable that cases involving the "separate but equal facilities" for education on the elementary and secondary levels should eventually find their way to the Supreme Court. Kansas, South Carolina, Virginia, and Delaware, together with the District of Columbia, soon fulfilled this expectation.

In the Kansas case the state court had ruled that under the Plessy doctrine segregation constitutes no violation of the Fourteenth Amendment, but it had also held that education under segregation is not and cannot be equal. On the other hand, the courts of South Carolina and Virginia had refused to grant that segregation of necessity spells inequality. On the contrary, the Virginia court boldly proclaimed that "Maintenance of the separate school system has not been social despotism" but has even "begotten greater opportunities for the Negro." In each instance, however, the courts recognized existing inequalities in facilities and ordered the school board concerned, in the words of the Virginia court, "to proceed with all reasonable diligence and dispatch to remove the inequality existing."

It is obvious that in order to remedy conditions of inequality even "with all reasonable diligence and dispatch" takes time. In the Sweatt and McLaurin cases the Court took this fact into account and ordered immediate relief for the victims of injustice. Similarly, a Delaware court drew attention to the fact that to grant an extension of time in which to remedy general conditions of inequality is, in effect, to ignore the rights of the individuals who are presently appealing for a redress of grievances.

In the Delaware case, Negroes resident in one school district were denied admission to the elementary and secondary schools reserved exclusively for whites and were required to attend schools for Negroes which were both remote from their homes and inferior in quality. The defendants denied that segregation in education violates the federal Constitution and produced evidence to demonstrate that building programs were, in part, on their way and, in part, in a planning stage to offset whatever inequalities might exist.

Chancellor Seitz, who rendered the opinion for the Court, concluded "that the separate facilities and opportunities offered these plaintiffs, and those similarly situated, are not equal to those afforded white children . . . and that, in consequence, the State by refusing these plaintiffs admission to Claymont solely because of their color, is violating the plaintiffs' rights protected by the Equal Protection Clause of the Fourteenth Amendment."

These cases, together with one from the District of Columbia, quickly found their way to the United States Supreme Court. Since the cases from Kansas, South Carolina, Delaware, and Virginia, although premised on somewhat different facts and different locations, nevertheless involved a common legal question, they were considered together and were consolidated in one opinion. The Court's decision, delivered by Chief Justice Warren, was rendered on May 17, 1954. With it, compulsory segregation in education in the United States ceased to be legal. In the language of the Court: "We conclude that in the field of public education the doctrine of 'separate but equal' has no place. Separate educational facilities are inherently unequal. Therefore, we hold that the plaintiffs and others similarly situated for whom the actions have been brought are, by reason of the segregation complained of, deprived of the equal protection of the laws guaranteed by the Fourteenth Amendment."

At the same time, "because of the great variety of local conditions," continued the Court, "the formulation of decrees in these cases presents problems of considerable complexity," and it requested the parties involved to present further argument on questions propounded by the Court. These questions were discussed before the Court in the fall of 1954 by representatives of the states involved, the District of Columbia, and the Attorney General of the United States. On May 31, 1955, the Court rendered a final decree regarding methods of implementing its original decision. This decree left the way open for the localities affected to bring about a gradual transition from segregated to nonsegregated schools. Under the supervision of the district courts, consideration was to be given to problems peculiar to each locality, provided "the defendants make a prompt and reasonable start toward full compliance with our May 17, 1954 ruling." The Court made it clear, however, that flexibility is not to be confused with any retreat from its original decision that segregation is unconstitutional. It goes without saying, emphasized the Court, "that the vitality of these constitutional principles cannot be allowed to yield simply because of disagreement with them."

It is thus obvious that although the rate at which communities are to conform to the Court's decision may vary, the direction all must follow is clear. Compulsory segregation in education, as an established and acceptable institution, belongs to the past.

Recent Changes in the Status of the Negro

It is sometimes said that the Supreme Court is not insensitive to public opinion and that it, no less than Congress—although less rapidly to be sure—follows "election returns." This may or may not be true. It is nevertheless relevant to observe significant changes that have taken place in the status of the Negro in American life since the *Plessy* v. *Ferguson* and the *Gong Lum* v. *Rice* decisions, changes of which the Court must have been aware in outlawing compulsory segregation.

First is the emergence of what Harry S. Ashmore terms an indigenous leadership. This leadership, "still heavily reliant upon intellectuals for the most part," [16] unlike the earlier leadership of Booker T. Washington, demands more than the opportunity to secure an economic toehold in American society. It demands full recognition of the Negro's right to the privileges of first-class citizenship and, quite specifically, in recent years, an end to segregation in public education. The members of the Court, as well as the general public, must have been impressed by the fact that the case for the plaintiffs was most ably presented by a group of Negro lawyers.

Although Negroes are still far from attaining the goals which

---

[16] Harry S. Ashmore, *The Negro and the Schools* (Chapel Hill, N. C.: The University of North Carolina Press, 1954), p. 132.

their leaders have set for them, significant progress has nonetheless been made. Slowly, they have gained entrance into a number of the professions—law, medicine, education, and the like—and have succeeded also in securing membership in a considerable number of professional organizations in the South as well as in the North. For example, in 1948, the Missouri State Teachers Association admitted Negroes to its fold, and since 1947, twenty-seven state and county medical societies including the southern states have either admitted Negro physicians or amended their rules so as to make this possible.

Professional recognition prior to May 17, 1954, reflected an attitude shared by an increasing number of southerners. Speaking of the great mass of southerners in the early 1940's, Professor Howard W. Odum stated they identified the Negro "as a Negro and nothing more." They "did not appraise the Negro as the same sort of human being as they themselves are." [17] Once this attitude is changed, however, and the Negro is recognized as a *person,* the groundwork is laid for a new attitude toward the restrictions that have kept him as a thing apart. This change, in turn, follows upon the improved educational, economic, and cultural status of an increasing number of Negroes which is also characteristic of recent years. Deplorable as conditions of Negro education still are in most of the southern states, the progress of recent years has bordered upon the miraculous. For example, in 1916 there were 69 Negro high schools in the South with less than 20,000 pupils in attendance.[18] By 1950, taking the country as a whole, Negroes aged twenty-five and over had completed an average of seven years of school, and about 15 per cent of all Negroes aged eighteen to twenty-four were enrolled in school.[19] Considering the South alone, Negro school attendance in the period of 1940 to 1950 increased twice as fast as the total population. Moreover, on the higher levels of education in the South as well as in the North, a steadily increasing number of white people, through their association with Negroes in institutions of

[17] *Ibid.,* p. 130.

[18] *Ibid.,* p. 19.

[19] *Employment and Economic Status of Negroes in the United States,* Staff Report to the Subcommittee on Labor and Labor-Management Relations of the Committee on Labor and Public Welfare, United States Senate, Eighty-second Congress, pp. 8–9.

higher learning, have come to appreciate qualities of intellect and character strikingly different from the conventional stereotype. Indeed, there are communities in the South as well as in the North in which there is no longer a wide gap separating the cultural status of the Negro from that of the white.

Despite the educational and cultural progress of Negroes, economic advance, in the sense of an open road for Negroes to positions of responsibility and trust in the higher echelons of business and industry, lag far behind opportunities for whites. In the South, particularly, supervisory and white collar positions in business and industry are difficult to secure. In this respect the racial pattern has not changed conspicuously in the last decade.[20] Nevertheless, the situation is not altogether static. The Negro is finding a place in the professions. Here and there the policy of total exclusion from labor unions, or recognition only on condition of lower status and pay, is being modified. Furthermore, the exodus of Negroes from agriculture and the enlarged proportion who are working in manufacturing foreshadows a change in economic and cultural status. Thus the proportion of Negroes employed in agriculture, taking the country as a whole, declined from 41.7 per cent in 1940 to 25.2 per cent in 1950, whereas the number of employed Negro men working in manufacturing increased from 22 per cent to 26 per cent between 1950 and 1952.[21]

The improved economic status of the Negro is related to the shift in the center of Negro population from the rural areas in the South to urban localities and from the South as a whole to the North. The consequences of this migration are revolutionary in their possibilities and may well transform the problem of segregation and integration in education.

For example, one area of intense resistance to integration in education is the rural community with its fixed prejudicies and its caste prescriptions firmly rooted in custom and tradition. But it is precisely from the rural South that the Negroes are leaving in the greatest numbers. One consequence of the transfer of Negroes from agriculture to industry is to leave some counties in the South without any Negroes in the population "and others where

---

[20] From report of a survey conducted by the National Planning Commission and reported in *The Washington Post* of November 2, 1953.

[21] *Employment and Economic Status of Negroes in the United States, op. cit.,* p. 12.

Negroes have become so few that segregation in the schools is already coming to be looked upon as a nuisance." [22] Again, in moving from the country to the city the Negro family tends to secure for its children an education superior in quality to that afforded by the rural community, a factor which is reflected in the superior holding power of the school.[23]

Most significant is the migration in recent decades of the Negro from the South to the North. Between 1940 and 1950 more than one million Negroes left the South. During this period the Negro population in the South increased only 1.5 per cent whereas the Negro population in the rest of the United States increased 56.6 per cent. In six of the southern states the Negro population between 1940 and 1950 declined in the following proportions: Alabama, —.4; Georgia, —2.0; Kentucky, —5.7; Mississippi, —8.2; Arkansas, —11.6; Oklahoma, —13.8.

In the remaining southern states the percentage of gain in Negro population was as follows: Florida, 17.3; Louisiana, 3.9; North Carolina, 10.7; South Carolina, 1.0; Tennessee, 4.3; Texas, 5.7; Virginia, 11.0.[24]

It is impressive to compare the growth of white and Negro population in the southern states. As indicated above, the Negro population in the South increased by 1.5 per cent, or 138,375 in the period 1940–1950. During this same period the white population "increased more than the white population of the United States as a whole, and more than the white population of the non-South." [25] Indeed, the total white population of the United States declined in this period from 76.6 per cent to 76.1 per cent, whereas the white population of the South increased from 23.4 per cent to 23.9 per cent. Between 1900 and 1950 the white

---

[22] Ashmore, *op. cit.,* p. 128.

[23] "During the 1940–1950 decade, average daily attendance in southern schools increased 218,000. There was virtually no net gain in the rest of the nation, the rising school population on the west coast being offset by decline elsewhere. Thus the South's increasing school burden was nearly equal to the net increase for the United States as a whole. This took place in the face of an overall population gain in the South that was less rapid than that of other regions. Although total white population in the region rose 16.5 per cent between 1940 and 1950, white school attendance went up about 3 per cent. On the other hand, Negro school attendance also rose 3 per cent in the face of only 1.5 per cent increase in the total Negro population" (*ibid.,* pp. 57–60).

[24] From the U.S. Census of 1950, Series P-B.

[25] Ashmore, *op. cit.,* p. 163.

population of the South gained 18 million or ten times that of the Negro, and between 1940 and 1950 the white increase of 4.5 million was thirty-three times as great as that of the Negro. Below is a state-by-state comparison of the per cent of change in the white and Negro populations in the South during the decade 1940–1950.

TABLE 4

*Per Cent of 1940–1950 Change
in White and Negro Populations in the South*

White Population	Per Cent Gain or Loss	Negro Population	Per Cent Gain or Loss
Alabama	12.5	Alabama	−.4
Arkansas	1.1	Arkansas	−11.6
Florida	56.7	Florida	17.3
Georgia	16.8	Georgia	−2.0
Kentucky	4.2	Kentucky	−5.7
Louisiana	18.8	Louisiana	3.9
Mississippi	7.4	Mississippi	−8.2
North Carolina	16.2	North Carolina	10.7
Oklahoma	−3.4	Oklahoma	−13.8
South Carolina	19.3	South Carolina	1.0
Tennessee	22.6	Tennessee	4.3
Virginia	28.1	Virginia	5.7

SOURCE: Harry S. Ashmore, *The Negro and the Schools* (Chapel Hill, N. C.: The University of North Carolina Press, 1954), pp. 163–164.

The proportion of Negroes to whites in the South is rapidly falling. In the North, by contrast, it is rapidly gaining. Thus, as against the numerical increase in the South between 1940 and 1950 of slightly more than 138,000 Negroes, the non-South recorded an increase of 2,000,000. Of this increase in the Negro population of the non-South, seven states stand out most conspicuously: Illinois, Ohio, and Michigan in the midwest; New York, New Jersey, and Pennsylvania in the northeast; California on the west coast; and the District of Columbia. According to the 1950 census, the percentage of increase in these states was as follows: Pennsylvania, 35.8; New Jersey, 40.4; District of Columbia, 49.9; Ohio, 51.1; New York, 60.7; Illinois, 66.7; Michigan,

112.3; California, 271.8.[26]

Nor has this phenomenal movement of population distributed itself evenly throughout the states most intimately affected. The Negro is in search of economic and cultural opportunities superior to those available to him in the South. These he tends to find in the large cities rather than in the rural communities. The result has been an extremely rapid increase in the Negro population of northern cities within the past decade and a half. For example, Cincinnati, Ohio, had a 40.7 per cent increase in its Negro population between the years of 1940–1950, as compared with a 6 per cent increase in the number of whites. Other cities of the non-South with a high percentage of increase in their Negro population between 1940 and 1950 might be mentioned by way of illustration: South Bend with an increase of 128.8 per cent; Gary, with 92.4 per cent; Tucson, Arizona, with 65.9 per cent; Hobbs, New Mexico, with 122.4 per cent; and Elkhart, with 100.8 per cent.[27]

Finally, the integration of the armed forces should be mentioned in this enumeration of factors leading to a new status for the Negro. This policy is both cause and effect in that it could not have been brought about without a change in public mind, and it is operating to undermine traditional attitudes. Intimate association on the battlefield as well as in the training camp, together with the demonstrated efficiency of integrated units in the Korean conflict, has transformed the sentiments of many in the armed forces with respect to the Negro and has challenged the validity of discriminatory practices in civil life. Taken together with the pressing need to counteract Communist propaganda abroad, which pictures the Negroes as a submerged and oppressed people and uses this picture as evidence of the American's attitude toward all colored people, integration within the services clearly foreshadows desegregation in other areas of living.

Desegregation in the North and the Border States

An early reaction to the concentration of a Negro population in northern communities was educational segregation. In some

---

[26] *Ibid.*, p. 53.

[27] Robin M. Williams and Margaret W. Ryan, *Schools in Transition* (Chapel Hill, N. C.: University of North Carolina Press, 1954), p. 10.

instances this resulted more or less naturally from residential patterns, but it was not uncommon for school administrators and boards of education through gerrymandering of school districts and other administrative devices to bring about a segregation neither authorized nor required by law. But paralleling the more recent invasion of the non-South by the Negro there has developed a dominant sentiment in opposition to segregation. Prior to the Supreme Court decision in May of 1954, only four states of the non-South—Arizona, Kansas, New Mexico, and Wyoming —had authorized local communities to segregate children in school on the basis of race. Eleven states lacked legal provision regarding segregation, and sixteen had adopted laws expressly prohibiting it.[28] In large measure the trend away from segregation testifies to the influence of a

. . . general redefinition of minority rights which has occupied the nation since it took up arms against a racist enemy in World War II. This has been reflected in persistent pressure from Negroes now organized as never before, and from human relations agencies, church and civic groups, and school administrators themselves. The threat of legal action has played a part, too, as has the economic fact that it is often cheaper to integrate than to provide new or improved facilities for a small group of Negro pupils. The press of the non-South has been a positive force in the process, for even the most conservative newspapers are now generally sympathetic to the Negro's demand for equal treatment.[29]

The change in public attitude in the non-South with reference to segregation plus differences in state law and methods of its enforcement have contributed to considerable variation in methods employed in transition from segregated to integrated pattern in education. For example, in 1949, Indiana adopted an act forbidding segregation in the schools of the state but incorporated in the law no provision for its enforcement.[30] In Illinois, legislation in opposition to segregation dating from 1874 was strengthened in 1945 to assure desegregation, but the means of enforcement were largely financial. That is to say, an amendment

---

[28] Ashmore, *op. cit.*, pp. 67–68.
[29] *Ibid.*, p. 68.
[30] For the text of this law, see Williams and Ryan, *op. cit.*, pp. 252–256.

to an appropriation bill in the 1949 Legislature provided that "No part of the money appropriated by this act shall be distributed to any school district in which any student is excluded from or segregated in any public school, within the meaning of 'The School Code,' because of race, color, ancestry or national origin." [31] On the other hand, New Jersey, in revising its constitution in 1947, incorporated a clause which expressly forbids segregation in the public schools "because of religious scruples, race, color, ancestry or national origin." [32] Not content with this, the state set up an agency which has endeavored to prepare communities for the transition from segregation to integration by means of expert guidance.[33]

In 1953 a study of desegregation in some twenty-four communities of the non-South was undertaken under the general direction of Harry S. Ashmore and financed by the Fund for the Advancement of Education. The results of the investigation are embodied in a volume by Robin M. Williams and Margaret W. Ryan entitled, *Schools in Transition*. This study makes it clear that problems of desegregation in education are in no way confined to the South. The communities reported upon are in the non-South although, as the authors state, in some instances, "they have enough similarities in customary behavior patterns to be suggestive." In the light of developments in the border states since May, 1954, it is perhaps accurate to state that the picture and the suggestions which emerge correspond pretty much with the situation as it exists outside the "hard core" states of Alabama, Florida, Georgia, Louisiana, Mississippi, South Carolina, and Virginia.[34]

Suggestions for Effecting Transition from Segregation to Desegregation

What suggestions emerge from events in the states which have undertaken compliance with the rulings of the Supreme Court?

---

[31] Illinois Statutes, 1949, H.B. 1066, p. 53.

[32] Article I, Section 5.

[33] See Joseph L. Bustard, "The New Jersey Story: The Development of Racially Integrated Public Schools," *Journal of Negro Education*, Summer, 1952, pp. 275–285.

[34] Virginia was included in this list at the time of writing these words. Events since then have altered the picture in a state where the widest differences exist among counties.

1. In the vast majority of instances, desegregation has progressed with less stress and strain than anticipated. Of the twenty-four communities studied by Williams and Ryan, integration took place "with a smoothness and lack of open friction which typically surprised officials and teachers." Where violence was encountered, as in Cairo, Illinois, "there was some evidence that the violence in this case resulted from a configuration of other community tensions which were focused temporarily on an unpopular move." [35]

Violence in the South resulted from efforts of Arthurine Lucy to gain admission into the University of Alabama and President Eisenhower's decision to send troops into Little Rock, Arkansas, to enforce compliance with the decree of a federal court. These instances of violent objection to the admission of one or more Negro students into what were previously all-white institutions have received wide publicity, as did the attempts to change the pattern of segregation in Clinton, Tennessee, and Sturgis, Kentucky. But these incidents should not blur the essential fact that, by and large, in the North and the border states, where segregation has long prevailed, the transition to integration, even in opposition to local sentiment, has proceeded with less resistance than might have been anticipated.[36] It should also be said that when violence has occurred, this has frequently resulted from the efforts of individuals and groups outside the school community which have made resistance a cause to be furthered.

2. A direct relationship has been found to exist between advanced planning on the part of boards of education, the administrative staff of the schools, and teachers and success with integration. Louisville, Kentucky, is a striking illustration of a city in which foresight and careful preparation designed to bring about the cooperation between school and community organizations

---

[35] Williams and Ryan, *op. cit.*, p. 238.

[36] *Ibid.*, p. 241. Writing in *The Washington Post and Times Herald* for June 29, 1958, a former member of the Arkansas Law School faculty draws attention to the following facts: ". . . that the University of Arkansas Law School voluntarily integrated as early as 1946–47 and that for at least ten years integration has been an accomplished fact in the State University." Similarly, "the coeducational high school in Fayetteville has been integrated for some eight years and the student body voted almost unanimously to drop any scheduled football games if the opponents objected to playing against Negro members of the squad. (None did.)" Moreover, in "the delta community of Hoxie, integration has proceeded without mishap since outsiders were enjoined from interference two years ago."

has rendered possible rapid transition from segregation to integration. On the other hand, a do-nothing policy, or evidence of irresolution, uncertainty, and confusion of purpose, particularly indifference on the part of police power, serve to encourage resistance and to provide a fertile opportunity for the invasion of forces from without bent upon maintaining segregation.

3. Closely related to the above is the importance of channels of communication between racial and cultural groups within the community. Where committees or organizations concerned with bettering human relations are active, the transition proceeds with relative ease. Or if difficulty threatens, resources are at hand with which to meet it. In a number of instances, these groups have conducted forums and discussion meetings designed to prepare parents of the schools, as well as citizens at large for impending change, to clarify problems and to anticipate their constructive solution. Similarly, within the school system, prior preparation on the part of the administration, including the careful selection of principals and faculty for areas in which difficulties are expected, has marked the difference between success and failure.

4. Both on the higher and the lower levels of education, little resistance has been found in student bodies. Moreover, where tension and outright disorder have occurred, the sources of difficulty have frequently been from outside rather than inside the institution. A remark frequently made by students is, "we would get along all right if our parents and outsiders would only leave us alone."

5. There is evidence to suggest that a policy of gradual integration is less successful than more ambitious attempts to bring about transition. Gradual integration, often, not only prolongs the agony of change but inhibits organized efforts to effect desegregation. When but one grade in an elementary school, for example, undertakes integration, the parents of the school as a whole are less concerned about cooperating actively with the administration. Divisions and contrasts within the school itself are easily used to keep the pots of opposition boiling. On the other hand, advocates of a gradual approach contend that piecemeal integration provides an opportunity to prepare Negroes more effectively to hold their own educationally in mixed schools and eases the difficulties involved in merging Negro and white

teaching staffs. At present writing it is doubtful that the final answer is clear as to the most effective methods of bringing about integration. Doubtless this will vary with communities.

6. Finally, experience thus far indicates no more than a loose correlation between the initial attitude of the community toward segregation and success with desegregation.

The Problem of the Deep South

What we have said thus far applies to communities outside the area of hard core resistance to desegregation. In the May, 1958, issue of *Southern Educational News*,[37] a publication which adheres strictly to a factual and objective reporting of progress toward desegregation, there occurs a survey of progress in the seventeen southern and border states. This reveals that 764 school districts had begun or completed desegregation and 2125 biracial districts remained segregated. The survey indicates further that all of West Virginia's districts, either in policy or in practice, and approximately 80 per cent of Kentucky's Negro pupils were desegregated. Moreover, desegregation had either begun or been completed in 29 per cent of Delaware's districts, 70 per cent of Kentucky's, 91 per cent of Maryland's, 80 per cent of Oklahoma's, and 17 per cent of Texas'. However, only 15 of the 1354 biracial school districts outside the border states had either begun or completed desegregation. The number of Negroes who were in these mixed classes in these 15 districts was 270. The states involved are Arkansas, North Carolina, and Tennessee.

Within what we have characterized as the "hard core" states, programs of "massive resistance" have been adopted with the hope of blocking, or, at least, retarding steps toward desegregation. Laws have been passed designed to impose interminable delay upon attempts of Negroes to gain admission to white schools by forcing applicants to resort to a series of administrative steps (such as applications to pupil placement boards armed with multiple criteria, "other than race," to employ) and, ultimately, complicated appeals to courts. In six states, the legislatures have provided by law for the abolition of public schools, in the event the courts should order their schools to desegregate.

---

[37] Vol. IV, no. 11.

So successful has massive resistance been that progress toward desegregation has slowed down noticeably. Since, moreover, the attempt to block desegregation has led in most instances to a transfer of control over the schools from the locality to the state, the future of public education in these states is fraught with uncertainty. The number of pupils affected in the six states to which we refer "constitute 59 per cent of the white pupils and 69 per cent of the Negro pupils in the ten-state area of the Middle and Deep South."

Some Significant Aspects of the Problem

One difficulty in dealing with a problem as complex as that of desegregation in education is the temptation to oversimplify. This tendency is accentuated in this instance because the problem is, in fact, both simple and complex. As a legal problem, it is relatively simple insofar as the law insists that all people be viewed as individuals and not as members of a group, be this racial, religious, economic, or social. Accordingly, in its decision of May 17, 1954, the Supreme Court said no more than that Negroes are persons and that no person can be denied the services of an institution established and maintained by the public by virtue of his racial background. That is to say, public services cannot be discriminatory. The Court did not say that all schools must be integrated or that some schools may not be segregated. This will depend upon circumstances. It did say, however, that no qualified pupil may be denied admission to a school because he is black rather than white, yellow rather than brown, etc.

As a social problem, however, the transition from a segregated society to an open society is extremely complicated. Nor is it rendered simpler by the disposition of both those who would continue segregation and those who would eliminate it to center upon but one or two factors in the situation and to ignore others. For example, the segregationalist tends to ignore the effects of segregation upon the personalities of white and Negro children alike, but particularly the Negro. Moreover, he insists upon grouping all Negroes under one stereotype and refuses to consider the scientific conclusions of anthropologists with respect to race. Indeed, he frequently goes farther and excludes from library and classroom materials bearing upon racial distinctions, lest they influence the minds of the young in ways opposed to his own convictions. On the other hand, the northern opponent of segregation is equally prone to ground his position on an abstract principle, one that ignores the stubborn influence of long-established folkways and patterns of living upon the mind and the disposition of the southerner. For this reason, the northerner needs to be reminded that not all opposition to integration in the South is racial or solely racial. Many a southerner—mistakenly or not—objects to the education of his child with Negroes upon cultural grounds. Faced with the necessity of sending his children to school with children of an obviously lower cultural level, a school in which the majority of the children may possess habits of speech and conduct altogether different from what he wishes his child to acquire, he vigorously opposes this intermingling. If he is unsuccessful, he is disposed to follow the example of many a northerner and send his child, if possible, to a private school.

This is understandable. It is less understandable, however, that he fails to recognize similar feelings on the part of the educated and cultured Negro, whom he would force to keep his children in a segregated school of deplorable status. The latter, too, may wish his child to receive the best possible education and can view only with frustration and indignation a situation in which the principle of nondiscrimination permits white children of cultural backgrounds high and low to intermingle in one and the same school from which his children are excluded solely on the basis of race.[38]

Two basic principles are operating in the South with respect to segregation. One is the traditional assumption of the equality of all individuals before the law. As applied to public institutions and their services, this means that each person, irrespective of

---

[38] It may be appropriate to point out in this connection that what constitutes race in the segregation picture is also sadly oversimplified. Writing in this connection, Max Lerner states, "But, even when you single out pigmentation from all other genetic traits, there are still a bewilderingly large number of color gradations and combinations in America that would defy a corps of skilled ethnologists: the varieties of black, white, yellow, red, mulatto, quadroon, octaroon, almost white, 'passing,' Creole, Indian-white, Indian-Negro, Caribbean-Latin, Hawaiian-Filipino-Chinese mixtures. Where the culture is, like the American, made up of human material from many ethnic groups that were crossbred to start with, and where it has carried the biological and cultural cross-breeding so far, the stalking of ethnic purity has an ironic irrelevance, and to base caste on it becomes a cruel fantasy." [*America As a Civilization* (New York: Simon and Schuster, 1957), p. 515.]

birth, has an equal claim upon these institutions and services. It also means that each individual is to be judged in terms of what he is and can demonstrate himself to be, not in terms of the accidents of race, creed, or economic circumstance. Each child is thus assured an inherent right to reach for the stars. Nor is it for the state to cripple his arms!

The second principle is one of practical procedure, born of repeated experience in creating and maintaining ever-widening opportunities for individuals with the help of government. It holds that the opening of new roads to opportunity, as reform through governmental action, is better achieved through education than compulsion. Progress thus turns more upon transforming confirmed and habitual ways of thinking, feeling, and acting than upon using the big stick—although there are occasions when the latter in the form of the law seems to influence mind and disposition.

The passage of compulsory school attendance laws illustrates this second principle. Not until a goodly proportion of our people came to realize the importance of school attendance was it possible for the state to enforce compliance with laws which made mandatory the attendance at school of all children within a given age range. But once compulsion reflected public sentiment, the enforcement of compulsory attendance laws was not difficult. It remains to be seen whether the decision of the United States Supreme Court with reference to segregation is at all analogous to the passage of compulsory school attendance laws.

In concluding, a word should be said about the problem of education once segregation disappears. Where cultural differences among the members of racial groups are extreme, the problem will gradually merge into one analogous to that of differences among classes. In meeting these difficulties the experience of a school system such as that in Hawaii may be suggestive. The public schools of Hawaii have faced the necessity of Americanizing wave after wave of different racial and cultural groups. Under these conditions it was impossible to educate the children of all groups in the same classroom or to keep all classes, even schools, of identical grades abreast. But no rigid segregation on racial or cultural lines has followed. Although the children of one class or school have been identified as of superior academic accomplishment, the door admitting the child from the lower group to the upper has been open without distinction as to race or social status. In short, the method employed has been a special adaptation of homogeneous sectioning. For communities in the South, where the cultural differences are extreme, the experience of Hawaii may prove suggestive as an alternative to the present policy which condemns the child of an educated and cultured Negro family to waste his abilities in a class with standards ill-adapted to his interests and capabilities. The city of Washington, for example, has met the problem of wide differences in educational and cultural levels on the part of young people in the newly integrated schools by the introduction of a "four-track" curriculum, which seems to have resulted in a general bettering of educational standards. These curricula, be it observed, serve students without racial distinction, only distinctions of ability.

One obvious benefit that seems to have resulted from desegregation has been the high lighting in the minds of the public as well as of the educational staff the inferior education previously afforded Negro children. For example, Walter N. Tobiner, President of the Board of Education in Washington, D.C., states that one of the major problems revealed by desegregation has been "a very disheartening and almost appalling disparity between Negro achievement level and white achievement level." He adds, however, that this follows more from the previous opportunities afforded in each instance rather than from known facts of potentiality. Indeed, under integration, he adds, "a greater number of children are getting a better education than before." [39]

Educators who look forward to the eventual elimination of segregation in education should give serious attention to the problems which arise outside the classroom as well as within. Here, too, the experience of integrated systems has provided a fuller understanding than in the past of the cultural handicaps which afflict Negro children under segregation. We have in mind items such as the essentials of health education, standards of social behavior, and an identification with moral and ethical values which free one from the limitations and the handicaps of a parochial

---

[39] *The Washington Post and Times Herald,* April 7, 1958. In this connection, see also Agnes E. Meyer, "Race and the Schools," *Atlantic Monthly,* January, 1958, pp. 29–34.

grouping and insure for him the opportunity of wholesome participation in American society.

One of the valid arguments in opposition to segregation has to do with the effects of enforced separation upon a child's personality. A dual system of education, under the most favorable conditions, cannot prevent serious injury to the personalities of many who are thus set apart as inferior. Numerous investigations have established this fact. Convincing evidence of the judgment of experts in this field comes from an investigation conducted by Max Deutscher and Isidor Chein and published under the title of "The Psychological Effects of Segregation." [40] These writers undertook to determine the judgments of anthropologists, psychologists, and sociologists concerning the effects of segregation when equal provision of physical facilities exist. Out of 517 replies to the questionnaires sent to 849 social scientists, 90 per cent indicated their conviction that enforced segregation yields detrimental effects on the segregated groups, 2 per cent that it has no harmful effects, and 4 per cent refrained from expressing an opinion. Among the injuries reported were: the stresses created in the minds of children by the conflict between democratic schooling and its implications of equality and the practices of segregation with its implications of inferiority; the development of submissiveness, martyrdom, feelings of persecution, withdrawal tendencies, self-ambivalence in the personality of the "inferior group"; distortions in the sense of reality as a consequence of enforced segregation; the higher price paid for adjustment by members of the segregated groups who are necessarily maladjusted.

Impressive as this list is of the effects upon personality which result from segregation, we must not conclude that all evils will end with its abolition. The experience of a colored child in an integrated school in which his white brother enjoys the advantages of superior class status can be as harmful as segregation. Indeed, when a colored child is in the minority and can find no healthy outlet for his ability or is banned from equal participation in the normal activities of the school because of the mere fact of his color, it is questionable whether the effects are not as serious, if not more so, than normal relations with his fellows in a segre-

---

[40] *Journal of Psychology*, October, 1948, pp. 259–267.

gated school. This poses a problem which must be faced in the nonsegregated school if all children are to be permitted to enter into their birthright.

Thus the problem continues. Once segregation ends the problem of integration begins!

But will it end? Or will the stubborn resistance in hard core states and communities perpetuate segregation by one device or another? Already we hear suggestions for "voluntary segregation" or for the abandonment of public schools and the subsidizing of private schools on a segregated basis.

Of these and other efforts one southern editor remarks editorially:

What the various state legislatures are doing, as they busy themselves with plans to carry on school segregation without legal compulsion, is admitting segregation by law is finished . . . either this year, next or within the next few to come. . . .

As a matter of fact, segregation has been on its way out for a good long time and has been breaking down at the edges for more than a generation. . . . Two great forces have been at work on segregation and the problem of race. One is secular, the other religious. The Christian of today cannot help but wince at the full implications, and the jarring clash of his creed, with discrimination against any person because of color. . . . Christianity cannot well afford to be on the wrong side of a moral force, as it was in some areas when it defended slavery.

The other influence is secular. Segregation implies inferiority. There are those who argue it does not. But those segregated believe it does. . . . Across two great wars now we, along with other free peoples, have preached the rights of men everywhere to be free and equal—we have encouraged long-oppressed peoples to rise. . . .

An end to segregation—when it comes—will not, of course, force people to associate socially. That will remain, as now, personal choice. But it will bring on change—and this is what state legislatures in South Carolina, Georgia, Mississippi, Virginia and Alabama are, or will be, considering. They consider not how to retain legal segregation—which they see soon ending—but how to effect it without legal compulsion. . . . Segregation is on the way out and he who tries to tell the people otherwise does them great disservice. The problem of the future is how to live with the change.[41]

---

[41] Ralph McGill in *The Atlanta Constitution*, quoted by Harry S. Ashmore, *op. cit.*, p. 133.

Suggested Reading

Allport, Gordon W., *The Nature of Prejudice* (Cambridge: Addison-Wesley Publishing Co., 1954), chap. XII.

Ashmore, Harry S., *The Negro and the Schools* (Chapel Hill, N.C.: University of North Carolina Press, 1954).

Bustard, Joseph L., "The Development of Racially Integrated Public Schools in the North," *Journal of Negro Education,* Summer, 1952, pp. 275–285.

Committee on Social Issues, *Psychiatric Aspects of School Desegregation* (New York: Group for the Advancement of Psychiatry, 1790 Broadway, May, 1957), Report No. 37.

Dykema, Wilma and James Stokely, "New Southerner: The Middle-Class Negro," *The New York Times Magazine,* August 9, 1959, pp. 11 ff.

Lerner, Max, *America As a Civilization* (New York: Simon and Schuster, Inc., 1957), pp. 501–525.

Meyer, Agnes E., "Race and the Schools," *Atlantic Monthly,* January, 1958, pp. 29–34.

Myrdal, G., *An American Dilemma* (New York: Harper & Brothers, 1944).

Peters, William, *The Southern Temper* (Garden City, New York: Doubleday & Co., Inc., 1959).

Shoemaker, Don (ed.), *With All Deliberate Speed* (New York: Harper & Brothers, 1958).

Southern School News, Nashville, Tenn. (This is an invaluable monthly publication for anyone to use who is seeking information on progress in desegregation. It is an objective, fact-finding agency established by southern editors and educators in order to provide information on developments in education with respect to desegregation.)

Williams, Robin M., and M. W. Ryan, *Schools in Transition* (Chapel Hill, N.C.: University of North Carolina Press, 1954).

.A.A.A.

Federal Aid to Education

in the States

Traditional Federal-State Relations in Education

In Chapter 4 we observed that the ideal of local autonomy in education has given character to the organization and conduct of our schools since early in the seventeenth century. Only after local communities had first set the example, did state authorities undertake to require of all communities a responsibility which the pioneering few had already assumed. We also saw that education, in the course of time, has become a state function, and insofar as the subdivisions of the state do, in fact, exercise local control and self-determination, it is by virtue of authority delegated to them by the Constitution and the legislature of the states. An illustration of the manner in which the right of local autonomy once granted may be rescinded is found in the pupil placements acts of a number of southern states, acts which remove from local boards of education all authority to determine what schools individual pupils may attend.

Earlier chapters have also described the relation of the federal government to education. Immediately following the independence from England, Benjamin Rush and his associates in the American Philosophical Society undertook to devise plans for a national system of education. As late as 1795, indeed, the Society offered an award for the most effective plan of this character.

With the adoption of the Constitution, however, together with the Tenth Amendment, it became increasingly clear that responsibility for education was to become primarily a state rather than a federal responsibility.

The decision to lodge primary responsibility for education in the states did not preclude, however, all federal participation. Precedents set by the Continental Congress in 1785 and 1787 in connection with the sale of public lands in the Northwest Territory inaugurated a policy which the federal government has followed throughout the years. Beginning with the admission of Ohio to the Union in 1803, the central government adopted the practice of stipulating that the sixteenth section of public lands granted to the states be devoted to the support of public schools and two townships to the establishment of a university. To these provisions have been added, from time to time, grants of land and generous sums of money from government surplus funds.[1] Contributions from the federal government in support of special types of education, some permanent, some temporary, began with the passage of the Morrill Act in 1862 and have continued with little interruption since.

With few exceptions (such as aid to vocational education, the establishment of the National Youth Administration, and the Civilian Conservation Corps) federal grants have been free of attempts to exercise federal control and supervision over the educational activities thus fostered. That is to say, the principle that education, even when assisted by the federal government, is a state and local function has been carefully observed. The hand which has controlled the purse has scrupulously refrained from calling the tune.

Most educators and laymen who favor federal aid to education are agreed that this is as it should be. It was this conviction which prompted the Educational Policies Commission in 1941 to oppose the continuance of the National Youth Administration and

---

[1] For example, a significant portion of the surplus revenue was allocated to the states by the federal government in 1837 for purposes of public education. Other grants include the Direct War Tax Refund to three states in 1891: the Forest Reserve Income Act of 1908 (which assigned 25 per cent of the funds received from each forest reserve to schools or roads in states containing these reserves); and the Mineral Royalty Act of 1920. For a summary of federal grants to education, see Chris A. De Young, *Introduction to American Public Education* (New York: McGraw-Hill Book Co., 1942), pp. 9–22.

the Civilian Conservation Corps as federal agencies, despite the invaluable services they had rendered American youth in the 1930's, and to urge the transfer of their functions to the states, but with continued financial assistance from federal appropriations.[2] Similarly, in all legislation suggested or supported by organizations such as the National Education Association, the Council of Chief State School Officers, and the like, it has been carefully provided that funds so appropriated are to be turned over to the educational officials of the states for administration and distribution.

Within recent years the federal government has been asked for more than just grants-in-aid for specific activities such as vocational education, adult education, school lunch programs, nursery education, etc. Many have felt that both the national welfare and the ideal of equality of educational opportunity require that the federal government supplement state efforts in the support of general education.

What has led to these new demands upon the central government and what are the arguments employed both in support and in opposition to programs of federal aid?

Factors Which Suggest Increased Federal Participation in Financing Education

Educators are fond of quoting the founding fathers on the close correlation between education and free government. It was this early recognition which prompted Washington to stress in his Farewell Address that "it is essential that public opinion should be enlightened" and to urge his successors to "Promote, then, as an object of primary importance, institutions for the general diffusion of knowledge." Nor were those who followed him in the presidency indifferent to this injunction. From Jefferson to John Quincy Adams, presidents continued to recommend to Congress that it devote the proceeds from the sale of public lands to the advancement of education as well as to roads, rivers, and other "objects of public improvement." "The great object of the institutions of civil government," wrote John Quincy Adams,

---

[2] See the report of the Educational Policies Commission, *The Civilian Conservation Corps, the National Youth Administration and the Public Schools* (Washington, D.C.: National Education Association, 1941).

is the improvement of the conditions of those who are parties to the social compact, and no government, in whatever form constitutional, can accomplish the lawful ends of its institution but in proportion as it improves the condition of those over whom it is established. . . . Among the first, perhaps the very first, instrument for the improvement of men is knowledge, and to the acquisition of much of the knowledge adapted to the wants, the comforts, and enjoyments of human life public institutions and seminaries of learning are essential.[3]

Unfortunately, these convictions were those of the enlightened few rather than of the majority. The economy of the period was predominantly rural and the population thinly scattered over wide areas. Means of communication and transportation were also limited. Only the rare person was competent to envisage an injury to the nation as a whole from the neglect of education in any one segment of the population.

No Community Lives Unto Itself Alone

But this is not true of today. Increasing mobility of population has become dramatically evident. The steady trend toward industrialization, together with improved means of transportation and communication, has fostered movement from place to place at an ever accelerating pace. As W. H. Whyte, Jr., has shown in *The Organization Man,* corporate development has multiplied middle-class occupations many times. With this has come a phenomenal increase in the number of individuals who, with their families, periodically change their place of residence. To be sure, Americans have always been a mobile people, but the extent to which this has become a normal characteristic on all levels of society is peculiar to contemporary life. According to the Census Bureau, some 29 million Americans changed their homes between April 1, 1953, and April 1, 1954. Five million of these moved from one state to another. There were significant differences, to be sure, among communities and sections of the country. Of moment to educational policy, however, is the movement of persons from states in which economic conditions and educational facilities are most inadequate into states more favored. For example, between April 1, 1953, and April 1, 1954, 1,083,000 persons

---

[3] Quoted in Educational Policies Commission, *Policies for Education in American Democracy* (Washington, D.C.: National Education Association, 1946), pp. 20–21.

moved out of the southern states as compared with 682,000 who moved in, leaving that section with a total loss of 401,000.

A shift of population of this magnitude from underprivileged areas into areas of better economic status creates a severe strain upon the educational systems of the latter, rendering it difficult to maintain former standards and necessitating often significant changes in curriculum and teaching procedures. Consider, in this connection, the problem which confronted the school systems of California in the decade 1940–1950, where the total increase of population amounted to 50 per cent and the Negro population, largely from southern states with inadequate provision for Negro education, increased by 271.8 per cent! [4]

Intimately related to facts of mobility are the consequences which follow upon the steady elimination of unskilled labor from the American picture. The localities which today attract the ill-educated are not the Meccas for the unskilled to the extent they once were. Rather is the reverse true. Take, for example, the phenomenal exodus of population from rural to urban centers, an exodus which decreased the farm population by 4,700,000 between 1950 and 1958. For those who remain upon the soil, the applications of science and technology to farming assume added importance if success is to attend their existence. For those who move from rural to urban areas, an education which insures an introduction to occupations requiring both a general and a technical education is most essential. If an educational preparation has not been provided to people in advance of migration, the social, correctional, and educational agencies of the communities to which they move must suffer the consequences.

Inability to Finance Education

Failure on the part of a number of states to educate their youth is not entirely the result of ignorance and indifference, although these factors are not altogether absent. In large measure, it follows from financial inability on the part of communities of low economic status. As we saw in chapter 4, it is often the lack of

---

[4] For a discussion of "People in Motion," together with the implications of mobility, see Max Lerner, _America As a Civilization_ (New York: Simon and Schuster, Inc., 1957), chap. III, sec. 3.

resources rather than want of will which explains inequality in educational opportunity. This applies to communities as well as to individuals. For example, of the twelve states which in 1948 had from 243 to 280 school-age children per 1000 of the population, nine had a per capita income of less than $1000 in contrast with five states with 180 or fewer children per 1000 and a per capita income of $1594 or more.[5]

In his testimony before the Subcommittee of the Committee on Labor and Education of the House of Representatives, on April 30, 1958, Dr. Edgar Fuller, Excutive Secretary of the Council of Chief State School Officers, pointed out that the real-property tax, upon which local public services commonly depend, "is so unevenly distributed in every State that thousands of school districts find adequate local public school financing impossible." To offset this lack, the states supply nearly 5 billion dollars annually to school districts from state resources. In 1958, according to Fuller, approximately 50 per cent of these state funds were distributed to local school districts, the amount varying in accordance with the need. Even so, this was not sufficient to finance adequate programs of education in all districts. To secure additional funds has become increasingly difficult "because the financial incentives offered by the Federal Government to State legislatures through matching grants for welfare, health, highways and other services give these services priorities over education in the competition for State appropriations." [6]

Projective studies conducted by the National Education Association likewise indicate the future necessity of federal support of education. These studies reveal, on the one hand, that the school population is growing much more rapidly than the total population. Between 1946 and 1957, for example, the school-age population increased by 40.8 per cent in contrast with an increase of 21.1 per cent in the total population. Nor is there any present indication that this trend will not continue. Projections to 1965 indicate a further increase of 12.9 per cent in the total population with a school-age population rising twice as fast. On the other

---

[5] *Facts on Federal Aid* (Washington, D.C.: National Education Association, September, 1950), p. 4.

[6] Committee on Education and Labor, House of Representatives, *Hearings on Federal Grants to States for Education,* Eighty-fifth Congress, Second Session (Washington, D.C.: Government Printing Office, 1958), p. 172.

hand, the National Education Association studies point to a growing inability on the part of the states to cope with needs still unmet (classroom shortage, inadequate salaries for teachers, limited instructional equipment etc.) solely out of state and local resources. "Exclusive reliance on state and local taxation to do the job," concludes the Association, "means that it will not be done." [7]

Wide differences in ability to finance education result in corresponding differences in per capita expenditures for education. In 1947–1948, for example, four states were spending less than $100 per pupil in comparison with thirteen states in which per capita expenditures were at least twice that amount. Meager expenditures result in low salaries for teachers, understaffed schools, inadequate facilities and instructional materials, etc., plus little encouragement for young people to continue with their education beyond the compulsory period. These glaring contrasts among the states give the phrase "equality of educational opportunity" a hollow sound. Since, however, the federal government has access to resources far in excess of the states, it seems both logical and necessary that it employ these to offset the handicaps described.

National Defense Requires High Level of Education

In addition to economic and cultural considerations which seem to point to the necessity of federal aid to education, there are the imperatives of national defense. Startling advances in Russian scientific achievements have drawn attention to Russian emphasis upon science and mathematics and their applications to areas in which Russia and the United States are in keen competition. In this competition, however, the United States is sadly deficient in numbers upon which to draw, both in the way of students to teach and in competent instructors. Consequently, for the United States to perpetuate conditions which involve wastage of personnel and inferior instruction becomes a matter of national concern, and the institution of a program to offset educational deficiencies is therefore an important aspect of national defense.

Statistics of rejection from the armed forces for reasons of

---

[7] See statement submitted by the National Education Association to the Committee on Education and Labor, *ibid.*, pp. 127 ff.

"educational deficiency" reveal not only a serious wastage of personnel but also the extent to which lack of education in one state or one section of the country imposes burdens upon another. In the Southeast, for example, 202 out of each 1000 Negroes examined in World War II were rejected on grounds of "educational deficiency" in contrast with 50 rejections in the Far West out of each 1000 Negroes examined. A similar comparison of the rejection rate for whites, although less striking, is nevertheless significant: 52 persons per 1000 examined in the Southeast were rejected as compared with 9 rejections per 1000 in the Far West.

The consequences of differences in educational opportunities afforded Negroes and whites become evident when we compare Negro and white rejections. In the Southeast, where, as we saw, rejections of Negroes numbered 202 per 1000 examined, rejections for whites stood at 52 per 1000; and in South Carolina, every county without exception had a Negro rejection rate of 175 or more per 1000 examined in comparison with a white rejection rate of 47 per 1000.[8]

From these data, it is evident that what one community within a state or one state sows in the way of educational neglect, another community or state often reaps. It is also evident that failure to educate all young people up to the level of their ability bears directly upon the reservoir of talent available for the varied purposes of national defense as well as for continued advancement in a technological civilization. For this reason, as many now see it, to oppose federal aid to education testifies to a parochial-mindedness that may result in tragic consequences for the nation as a whole.

The Case for the Opposition

A policy which seems imperative to one group appears in quite a different light to another. Opponents of federal aid to education insist that it would result inevitably in an extension of federal control over matters that should remain exclusively within the

---

[8] For a discussion of the drain upon our national resources of the uneducated, see Eli Ginzberg and Douglas W. Bray, *The Uneducated* (New York: Columbia University Press, 1953).

authority of the states and would impose an unfair burden upon one section of the country in order to offset neglect and indifference in other sections.

Fear of Federal Control

Fear of federal control is based upon the common experience of identifying sources of financial support with centers of control. This fear need not always be realized. As we have seen, within the states the enlargement of units of finance has not resulted necessarily in centralizing school administration.[9] Moreover, the vast majority of educators as well as laymen who are desirous of increasing the contributions of the federal government to education are determined to disassociate aid from control. "Nothing contained in this act shall be construed to authorize any department, agency, officer or employee to exercise any direction, supervision or control over . . . any state educational institution or agency" is a common insertion in all proposed federal aid legislation.

In spite of these precautions the fear of ultimate federal control persists. Nor have recent decisions of the Supreme Court in the areas of religion and segregation on grounds of race helped to dispel this fear. In *McCollum* v. *Board of Education* (Champaign, Illinois), the Court outlawed positive religious instruction in all public schools. Similarly, in its decisions of 1954 and 1955 on segregation in education, the Court forbade the barring of any child from admission to any public school solely on grounds of race. Here is control, direct and detailed, it is said. If the federal government can substitute its authority for that of state and locality in these areas, who can say it will not pre-empt other areas tomorrow? Indeed, it might be added, does not the passage of the Powell Amendment by the House of Representatives in the Eighty-fifth Congress testify to the willingness of the Congress to interfere with the administration of education in the states when it so chooses? This amendment, it will be recalled, was designed to deny the use of federal funds to any community eligible for

---

[9] See Paul Mort and Donald H. Ross, *Principles of School Administration* 2d ed. (New York: McGraw-Hill Book Co., 1957), pp. 281–283, for an elaboration of this point.

assistance in the event that the community maintained segregated schools.

Prominent among the opponents of federal aid to education is the United States Chamber of Commerce. This organization bases its opposition on these grounds: (1) Federal control over education is certain to follow federal appropriations and will thus discourage state and local initiative, self-determination, and experimentation. (2) Unless control does in fact accompany federal grants, there is little assurance that backward states and communities will better present conditions. On the contrary, they will be tempted to use federal funds in order to lessen the present tax burden. (3) The assumed inability of the states to finance education out of their own resources is not well grounded. It is want of will rather than the absence of resources that accounts for the sad state of education. Once these states are persuaded to reform their tax structures, ample support for education will be forthcoming.

State and Local Initiative Will Be Undermined

In support of points one and two, the Chamber of Commerce argues that local initiative would be weakened if communities are permitted to receive federal funds without federal guidance and supervision. What inducement would they have to review critically present practice and standards? Or, for that matter, is it wise or provident to provide funds for the improvement of education in localities long impoverished without either suggestions or directions for bettering existing practice? As Edgar Lee Dessen stated in his testimony before the House Education and Labor Committee on May 26, 1958, "when people approve the transfer of financial responsibility for institutions to the state or federal level, they expect a similar transfer of responsibility for directing the organization and operation of them. These two responsibilities go hand in hand and cannot be separated by the words of any statute or the wishful thinking of people who want aid without control." [10]

---

[10] *Hearings on Federal Grants to States for Education, op. cit.,* pp. 287 ff. The quotation is taken from Dr. Dessen's statement as distributed by the United States Chamber of Commerce.

It was stated above that a majority of educators who favor federal aid to education wish this granted in such a way as to eliminate all possibility of federal control. Not all educators, however, grant the wisdom of this insistence upon state and local autonomy in the use of federal funds. Prominent among these dissenters is Theodore Brameld. According to Brameld, the validity of an appeal to the federal government in support of education rests upon three important premises: (1) the desirability of providing equal opportunity in education for all citizens "regardless of race, creed or economic status"; (2) "the necessity of an educated citizenry for the nation as a whole"; and, (3) "the increasingly collective" and interrelated structure of modern society.

It is clear, states Brameld, that educational equality cannot be provided in a number of states without outside assistance. Nor is there any assurance that the process of simply handing over federal funds will bring about equality. "Vast amounts of money can be spent by ingenious but irresponsible public officials without any certainty whatever that the children and adults for whose benefit it is intended will enjoy plentiful and excellent textbooks, well-trained and well-paid teachers, or up-to-date equipment." Consequently, it is time for the American people to face reality and to provide federal aid to the states with an essential degree of federal supervision.[11]

Obviously, if the ideal of educational equality is to be realized, a serious dilemma confronts the advocates of federal aid. Brameld is unquestionably correct in his contention that genuine equality cannot be provided without federal assistance in excess of any sums thus far suggested. The best that can be said of bills proposed up to the present is that they establish the principle of federal obligation to assist in bringing about equality of education among the states. Is it reasonable to assume that sums many times as large should be appropriated without assurance that they will be wisely spent? Can we assume that states and communities long underprivileged and backward, often politically as well as culturally, can transform their educational systems without guidance? Have we a right to require wealthy states to tax themselves for

---

[11] "The Bugaboo of Federal Control" in Theodore Brameld, *Ends and Means in Education* (New York: Harper & Brothers, 1952), pp. 73–83.

the improvement of others without guarantees respecting the use to which these taxes will be put?

On the other hand, is it not too much to expect that a centralized authority in Washington will supervise expenditures with an eye sufficiently sensitive to differences in needs among communities and in a manner best calculated to stimulate local pride and initiative and self-determination?

Is there no alternative, on the one hand, to federal grants without federal control and, on the other, to overly centralized control in Washington?

Some years ago the writer suggested a plan for the administration of federal aid to general education which was designed to avoid both the dangers of centralized control and the limitations of an exclusively state and local self-determination in the use of federal grants.[12] He still believes it merits consideration. It involves the creation of regional boards which, acting under general directives, would undertake to establish regional standards and criteria to be met by the states and communities of each region. These regional boards should be composed of representatives from state departments of education, laymen of public vision from each region, and representatives of the federal government. From regional boards thus composed, a unique combination of federal and regional direction of education might emerge, involving control over expenditures of federal funds but equally, if not more important, the cooperative definition and realization of standards and criteria appropriate and relevant to the needs of the states and localities affected.

Federal Assistance to Localities Is Not Needed

We come now to the contention that there is in fact no necessity for the federal government to supplement state and local resources in support of education. To tax the more progressive states to assist the less progressive, it is argued, not only imposes an unfair burden upon the former but assumes that the backward states are in fact in genuine need of this assistance.

The testimony of Mrs. William S. Shary before the Senate

---

[12] V. T. Thayer, *American Education Under Fire* (New York: Harper & Brothers, 1944), pp. 133-136.

Committee on Labor and Public Welfare [13] is typical of the contention of "unfair taxation." Mrs. Shary, as president of the New York Federation of Women's Clubs, calls attention to a resolution adopted by this organization first in 1952 and reaffirmed in 1956. This points out first that federal aid programs for education would cost the people of New York more than they would receive back in aid for their schools. Secondly, it would enable states of low income to build their schools in part at the expense of New York and thus keep their taxes low. Low taxes, in turn, would make it possible for these states to use the lure of low taxes with which to induce business and industry "to move from New York State and to locate their plants and factories in those states instead of New York."

To illustrate what New York might be expected to contribute for these purposes, Mrs. Shary refers to the federal aid bill rejected by Congress in 1957. Had this bill passed, fourteen states and the District of Columbia would have been required, in the first year of its operation, to pay out a total of 28 million dollars more than they would have received under it. New York, "the largest loser," would have contributed $8,540,000 more in taxes than it would have received back for school aid.[14]

State Resources Require No Supplementation

The Chamber of Commerce contradicts the contention of the National Education Association that states and localities are approaching the limits of their taxing ability in support of education. For example, Dr. Edgar Lee Dessen, speaking for the Chamber, contrasted the per capita debt of the states ($82 on the average; median, $64) with that of the federal government ($1574 per capita, as of March, 1958) to demonstrate that the states are in as favorable, perhaps more favorable, a position financially as

[13] April 5, 1958. A summary of Mrs. Shary's testimony, together with statements from representatives of the American Legion, the American Farm Bureau, the Association of Physicians and Surgeons, Inc., and the National Merit Scholarship Corporation—all in opposition to federal aid—is included in a circular distributed by the United States Chamber of Commerce.

[14] The reader may question why states not "dependent" upon federal aid are included in proposed grants. To avoid the taint of charity and to insure benefits to all states most bills provide for the distribution of funds in accordance with a formula whereby each state receives a certain sum for each child of school age.

the federal government. Dessen also drew a comparison between the per capita tax as levied by the states (average, $112; median, $118) with that of the federal government ($410) to establish the point that the states possess a borrowing power which renders unnecessary dependence upon the central government. "To relieve local and state governments of financial responsibility for education," concludes Dessen, "to say that financial resources available to them are inadequate, . . . weakens their motivation to correct inefficiencies resulting from local inertia or indifference." [15]

It is thus local inertia and antiquated state tax structures, contends the Chamber of Commerce, which explain the seeming lack of financial support for education on the local and state levels. For example, Harry A. Stansbury, managing director of the West Virginia Chamber of Commerce, testified before the Subcommittee of the Committee on Education and Labor of the House of Representatives,[16] that in twenty of the fifty-five counties of West Virginia, not one dollar of school-building bonds had been issued for more than twenty-five years, despite the fact that these counties were possessed of "aggregate assessments of $1,243,567,000 and school-bonding authority of $37,306,000 under the 3 per cent constitutional provisions." In one county, according to Mr. Stansbury, the state provides 55 per cent of all money spent on public schools. Even though this county has an idle bond capacity of $4,180,000 without a dollar standing against it, it spent in 1957 only $16,239, or half of 1 per cent, for school construction. In still another county, fully able to tax itself generously, the state furnishes 85 per cent of all money spent on public schools. Were the federal government to provide additional funds, it is argued, a sense of responsibility to promote good schools would shrink still further.

Unfortunately West Virginia is not the only state in which communities have permitted their schools to deteriorate rather than to impose local taxes. There remain, however, other states and communities in which property values are insufficient to finance good schools. At issue in these instances is the obligation,

---

[15] *Hearings on Federal Grants to States for Education, op. cit.*, May 26, 1958. Statement distributed by the United States Chamber of Commerce.

[16] *Ibid.*, June 3, 1958, p. 403.

if any, of the federal government to supply funds with which to improve buildings, better teachers' salaries, and provide instructional materials in a manner designed to stimulate rather than to lessen a sense of local responsibility for education.

Federal Scholarships Are Likewise Uncalled For

The United States Chamber of Commerce, in conjunction with other groups, questions not only the need of federal aid to general education but as well recent proposals for a program of federally supported scholarships. John M. Stalnaker, president of the National Merit Scholarship Corporation, is quoted as telling a House Committee that of the top 7500 students drawn from each state in proportion to population, 97 per cent are in college and of the next 7500 about 95 per cent are already in college.[17] He concludes that well over 90 per cent of the young people who might be eligible for federal scholarships are already encountering no difficulty in attending college. It is argued further that lack of motivation rather than want of financial resources keeps many young people from continuing with their education beyond high school graduation. Therefore, he concludes that federal grants would have little effect other than to establish an unfortunate precedent.

Needless to say educational groups challenge the representative character of these statistics as well as the validity of the conclusions drawn from them. Granted that lack of motivation operates to keep too many able young people from attending college, it still remains true that a sizable number fail to go on for want of financial resources. Nor are educators in agreement with Stalnaker's data. Far more accurate, they would say, is the picture which emerges from the testimony of Lawrence G. Derthick, Commissioner of Education, on the proposed Federal Scholarship and Loan Program. According to the commissioner, one-half of the graduates of public and private schools in the fall of 1950 who stood in the upper half of their classes did not go on to college on a full-time basis, and one-third did not go on at all. He stated further that of the students ranking in the upper 30 per cent of

---

[17] Quoted in *Sizing Up Federal Scholarships* (Washington, D.C.: Education Department, Chamber of Commerce of the United States, 1958).

graduating classes, 40 per cent did not go on to college on a full-time basis, and one in five failed to enroll altogether.[18]

The Sum of the Whole Matter

Statistics are essential as a basis for policy decisions. It is on statistics, however, as well as principle that we find fundamental disagreement between the advocates and the opponents of federal aid to education. A way can doubtless be found to arrive at accurate data. It is more difficult to secure agreement upon principle. Before one can arrive at a satisfactory conclusion on the question of federal aid to education, he should attempt to answer for himself some such questions as the following: Do I believe in the principle of equality of educational opportunity? How relevant is it to our relations with peoples abroad and our economic, social, and political development at home? Has life in the United States become, in fact, so intimately interrelated that deprivation in one section of the country affects intimately the well-being of other sections? How should we conceive of the functions of government? Is government an agent of the people, created and designed to realize needs through associated and cooperative actions which individuals alone cannot attain for themselves or which units of one size are unable to achieve except through cooperation? Or is government essentially an external instrument, devised to achieve certain limited purposes only, the healthy performance of which is conditioned upon keeping its functions to the minimum?

Until questions of this nature are squarely faced and answered, it is feared that little progress will be made in determining the role of the federal government in the field of education.

Before concluding this chapter, brief reference should be made to the role played by certain religious organizations in connection with federal aid legislation.

It is recognized that the principle of separation of church and state prevents the direct appropriation of public funds in support of church-related schools. However, on the basis of a decision

---

[18] *Scholarship and Loan Programs,* Hearings before a Subcommittee of the Committee on Education and Labor, House of Representatives, Eighty-fifth Congress, First Session, 1958, part 2, p. 769.

of the United States Supreme Court in 1930 (*Cochran v. Louisiana State Board of Education*), which approved the furnishing of free textbooks to children in attendance upon nonpublic as well as public schools, it is contended that public funds can properly be used in support of "auxiliary services" (free textbooks, transportation, health services) since it is the child rather than the institution that would benefit. To be sure, the sums that would be available for these purposes would be small indeed, considering the size of appropriations proposed thus far and the amounts that would remain after meeting the needs of education proper. This, however, has not acted as a deterrent, since, in the minds of those concerned the all-important consideration is to establish the principle that nonpublic as well as public schools are entitled to public assistance on a "nondiscriminatory" basis. Until this principle receives recognition, these interests believe their record of opposition to all forms of federal aid to education (other than that designed to assist individuals) is amply justified.

Suggested Reading

Brameld, Theodore, *Ends and Means in Education* (New York: Harper & Brothers, 1952), chap. 8.

Brodinsky, B. P., "Better Schools, Yes. Federal Aid, No." *The Nation's Schools,* May, 1949, pp. 23–26.

Burkhart, J., "Dangers of Federal Aid to Education," *School and Society,* September, 1955, pp. 83–84.

Committee on Education and Labor, House of Representatives, *Hearings on Federal Grants to States for Education,* Eighty-fifth Congress, Second Session (Washington, D.C.: Government Printing Office, 1958).

Committee on Education and Labor, House of Representatives, *Hearings on Scholarship and Loan Program,* Eighty-fifth Congress, First Session (Washington, D.C.: Government Printing Office, 1958), parts 1, 2, 3.

Committee on Labor and Public Welfare, United States Senate, *Hearings on Science and Education for National Defense,* Eighty-fifth Congress, Second Session (Washington, D.C.: Government Printing Office, 1958).

Fuller, Edgar, "Criteria for Congressional Action," *The Nation's Schools,* November, 1955, pp. 53–57.

National Education Association, *Facts on Federal Aid* (Washington, D.C.: National Education Association, September, 1950).

Norton, J. K., "The Need for Federal Aid," *School and Society,* March 17, 1956, pp. 87–90.

Stanley, Charles J., Jr., "Organized Interests and Federal Aid to Education," *School and Society,* January, 1951, pp. 1–4.

INDEX

/\.\/\.\/\.\

Index

Index